THE WORLD IN VENICE

Print, the City, and Early Modern Identity

Positing a dynamic relationship between print culture and social experience, Bronwen Wilson's *The World in Venice* focuses on the printed image during a century of profound transformation. City views, costume illustrations, events, and portraits of locals and foreigners are brought together to show how printmakers responded to an expanding image of the world in Renaissance Venice, and how, in turn, prints influenced the ways in which individuals thought about themselves.

Woodcuts and engravings of cities and inhabitants of Europe and of distant lands initiated a sudden and pervasive experience with alterity that redefined the relations of Europeans to the world. By condensing the world into pictures, print enabled a radically novel and vicarious experience of others. Wilson explores the overlapping and evolving relations between space, vision, print, and identity, and engages with current scholarly debates concerning ethnicities, gender and geography, copies and originals, travel, nationhood, fashion, urban life, visuality, and the body.

Venice was one of the largest cities in Renaissance Europe, a trading crossroads, and a centre of print. *The World in Venice* shows how Venetian identity came to be envisioned within the growing global context that print constructed for it.

(Studies in Book and Print Culture)

BRONWEN WILSON is an assistant professor in the Department of Art History and Communication Studies at McGill University.

The World in Venice

Print, the City, and Early Modern Identity

Bronwen Wilson

UNIVERSITY OF TORONTO PRESS
Toronto Buffalo London

Reprinted in paperback 2020

ISBN 978-0-8020-8725-6 (cloth)   ISBN 978-1-4875-2583-5 (paper)

Studies in Book and Print Culture

Library and Archives Canada Cataloguing in Publication

Title: The world in Venice : print, the city and early modern identity /
Bronwen Wilson.

Names: Wilson, Bronwen, author.

Series: Studies in book and print culture.

Description: Series statement: Studies in book and print culture |
Paperback reprint. Originally published 2005. | Includes bibliographical
references and index.

Identifiers: Canadiana 2020031503X | ISBN 9781487525835 (softcover)

Subjects: LCSH: Venice (Italy) – Civilization – To 1797. | LCSH: Venice
(Italy) – In art. | LCSH: Prints – Italy – Venice – 6th century. | LCSH: Art
and society – Italy – Venice – History – 16th century.

Classification: LCC DG678.235 .W44 2020 | DDC 769/.499453107–dc23

This book has been published with the help of a grant from the Canadian
Federation for the Humanities and Social Sciences, through the Aid to
Scholarly Publications Program, using funds provided by the Social Sciences
and Humanities Research Council of Canada.

University of Toronto Press acknowledges the financial assistance to its publishing program of the Canada Council for the Arts and the Ontario Arts Council,
an agency of the Government of Ontario.

Contents

Acknowledgments

Over the many years I have been working on this project, I have benefited from the suggestions and ideas of numerous friends and colleagues through discussions, reading groups, and responses to conference papers, earlier chapters, and related articles. For their interest and insights I thank Stephen Campbell, Ting Chang, Stanley Chojnacki, George Gorse, Holly Hurlburt, Frederick Ilchman, Leila Kinney, Sylvia Musto, Alex Nagel, Leslie Nordtvedt, Denise Oleksijczuk, Steve Ortega, Adrian Randolph, Dennis Romano, Charles Rosenberg, Christine Ross, Nina Rowe, Johanne Sloan, Will Straw, Helena Szepe, Bart Thurber, Nancy Troy, Aron Vinegar, and Chris Wood. Angela Vanhaelen's contribution to this project has been ongoing and is much valued. Debra Pincus fuelled my interest in Venetian art history and she has continued to both inspire and encourage me. Iain Fenlon was kind enough to read the entire manuscript, and his useful comments have been much appreciated.

Patricia Fortini Brown and Rose Marie San Juan were readers of the manuscript, and their criticisms and suggestions have contributed to the organization and ideas in this book in crucial ways. Moreover, their own work – on Venice and on print culture respectively – was also formative for the project from the start. For my dissertation advisers – Whitney Davis, Ed Muir, and Larry Silver – I reserve profound gratitude and also great respect; their intellectual acuity, insights, probity, and support have contributed in decisive and far-reaching ways to this book.

Several of my students provided valuable assistance. Finally, I want to express my sincere appreciation of the heroic efforts of Jill McConkey, Barb Porter, the copy editor Jim Leahy, and staff at the University of Toronto Press.

This book was made possible by the financial and academic support that I have received from Northwestern University, the University of British Columbia, McGill University, the Social Sciences and Humanities Research Council of Canada, and the affiliated Aid to Scholarly Publishing Programme. My research has benefited from the resources and kindness of many who assisted me at the British Library and British Museum in London, the Newberry Library in Chicago, the Bertarelli collection in Milan, the Archivio di Stato and the Marciana, Correr, Querini Stampalia libraries in Venice, and especially at Villa I Tatti in Florence.

Earlier versions of three sections of this book were published in *Renaissance Quarterly*, *Word & Image*, and *Studies in Iconography*. For consistency, I have changed 'u's and 'v's to modern Italian. This holds true for the bibliography as well, a decision made on the basis of the same practice in some electronic library catalogues.

There is one last reader of this manuscript to whom I am especially indebted. For David Vance's enduring support, kindness, love, and friendship, I dedicate the book to him.

Illustrations

THE WORLD IN VENICE

Introduction

For as geography is the natural eye and true light of history: all accounts
would forever remain obscure if we did not first become familiar with the
places, the attitudes of the people, and the quality of the country of which
we believe we are speaking.[1]

Lancelot du Voisin

With the advent of printed maps at the end of the fifteenth century, the
world and the viewer's place within it could be seen in ways never imagined before. The novelty of this experience overlapped with the discovery of worlds unknown to Europeans, which precipitated a vast array of
projects by authors and illustrators; this generated widespread interest
in geography. Atlases, travel chronicles, cities, islands, clothing, bodily
style, language, and even alphabets were ordered by geography and
widely distributed in printed books.[2] Collected into one 'manual' as
Mercator had described the atlas to Ortelius, these books condensed
the world, making it legible and compact. Printed images of the geography and inhabitants of Europe, and those of distant lands, initiated a
sudden and pervasive experience with alterity that redefined the relation of Europeans to their place in the world and forcefully shaped their
perceptions of it.

One of the largest cities in Europe, a trading crossroads, and a centre
of print production, Venice is emblematic of cultural and social changes
that occurred across the continent during this pivotal century. The
Veneto was home to more than 450 printers, publishers, and booksellers
during the sixteenth century, and these producers looked beyond the
local market to an international one.[3] Printmakers capitalized on the

fascination Venice held for foreigners by producing woodcuts and engravings of the city's topography, costumes, events, and people. Compiled into books, framed with legends, and identified by captions, these new forms of print enabled viewers to compare their place in the world with those of others. This book explores how an expanding image of the world came to be projected in prints, and how these profoundly new visual experiences transformed the ways in which identities accrued to individuals.

Venetians were enthusiastic producers of civic imagery in what became a project of self-promotion and redefinition. At the end of the fifteenth century, Venice was the capital of a vast empire, a mercantile centre, and a departure point for travellers to the East. The city's economy and interests were linked to broad global considerations. By the seventeenth century, however, its dominant trading position was usurped as the centre of European economic gravity shifted toward markets outside of the Mediterranean. Despite waning power on the international political stage – indeed, in response to it – an array of printed representations emerged to refurbish the city's fading prominence by projecting an image of Venice in which the extraordinary could be seen everyday. The city was re-envisioned – from the outside in – as a centre in which all the world could be seen.

As a result, the forces compelling Venetians to identify with the city began to change. In contrast to the image of civic consensus that was orchestrated by the institutions of the late medieval state, and sustained by the repetition of symbolic narratives in rituals and artworks for a local audience, identities in early modern Venice were increasingly shaped through exchanges with outsiders, exchanges that were multiplied through the medium of print.

'Without any doubt,' exclaims the Venetian to the foreigner in Francesco Sansovino's guidebook *Delle cose notabili che sono in Venetia,* Venice 'can be called the theatre of the world, and the eye of Italy.'[4] The city as a theatre was an early modern topos, but one that resonated with widespread perceptions of Venice as a stage teeming with foreigners. Published in 1561, Sansovino's text takes the form of a dialogue in which a Venetian guides a visitor through the city informing him of its rituals and customs.[5] It is the presence of foreigners, in fact, that makes Venice a 'singular city,' as Sansovino would write later, 'because being useful for those nearby nations, as from afar, all people from the most distant parts of the earth come together here (where they see people of different and discordant faces, costumes, and languages, but all agree, however, to praise the city while admiring it) to deal and trade.'[6] On a political level, the theatre topos was brought forward as a defence of republican political life by Paolo Paruta, the official historian of Venice after 1579, in his dialogue *Della perfettione della vita politica*, published in 1573. Paruta's interlocutor, Michele Surian, the spokesperson for the values of *Venezianità* (being Venetian/Venetian-ness), defends the crowd who participates in civic life: 'Man is placed in this world as in a theatre in which God sits as spectator of his actions.'[7]

Venice was also 'the eye of Italy,' another analogy prompted by its appearance in geographical maps; seen from above, the coastline of Italy resembles a human profile, and the insular landscape of Venice its oculus. This was extended into a political metaphor, as Peter Heylyn explained early in the seventeenth century: '*Europe* is the head of the world, *Italy* the face of *Europe*, and *Venice* the eye of *Italy*: it is the fairest, strongest, and most active part of that powerfull body.'[8] Heylyn conflates the city's singular topography with the well-known construct of the body politic, in which the eyes, the most rational part of the body, are the nobles who govern the more unruly members, which indicates that foreigners had come to understand the physical appearance of Venice as both a reflection and a condition of its good government.[9]

This myth of Venice as a model republic is a familiar story, and Sansovino's guidebooks, particularly his famous *Venetia città nobilissima et singolare* (1581), were instrumental in its dissemination.[10] A polymath and prolific author, Sansovino was himself a foreigner who came to Venice from Rome, and his early guidebooks betray the misinterpretations that accompanied his own subjective reflections.[11] However, his detailed explanations of Venetian symbolism in *Venetia città nobilissima* reveal his insider knowledge, his own *Venezianità*. In contrast to his earlier criticism of elaborate visual display by religious institutions, the 1581 publication conveys his investment in the political reality of the sixteenth-century myth.[12] Instructing his readers in the party line rather than probing political analysis, he represents civic concordance and liberty as effects of the city's 'lofty government.'[13] To this end he describes the admiration of foreigners for Venetian costumes and ceremonies, its officials and *letterati*, its buildings and artworks, but he also explains how modesty and sumptuary laws sustained this culture by subordinating individual desires in the interests of civic harmony.

The role of the individual within Venetian collectivity figures prominently in printed imagery discussed in this book. But I also hope to convey how internal differences and conflicts were concealed through these representations of collective identity and also how new uses and forms of print opened up new possibilities for identification. Produced in multiples, widely disseminated, and portable, the new media of woodcuts and engravings prompted visual strategies and uses of images that came to mediate between the state and the community, public and private, and the collective and individual. Furthermore, print opened up possibilities for exchanges between the city and the world; local images were themselves often responses to how Venice and Venetians were imagined by foreigners.

Exchanges between Venetians and foreigners in the city overlapped with, and were intensified by, the circulation of new forms of print, and Sansovino's formulation of difference – expressed through costumes, faces, and language – can itself be understood as both a cause and effect of the kinds of civic imagery discussed in this book. Arguably, the growth of travel literature was less a reflection of the fascination with exploration than a result of the intense awareness and construction of cultural differences that emerged in relation to this expanding global geography.

There is an aspect of the 'outside' that is more distinctive than the rest: the relation between Venice and the Ottoman Empire. Indeed, the diversity of publications concerned with the Turk – the nomenclature for Muslim more than a specific ethnic identity – including Sansovino's own publications, attest to the crucial role notions of the Turk played in the formation of Venetian identity. The erosion of their maritime state following the Ottoman conquest of Constantinople in 1453 contributed to Venice's turn toward the West, but relations with the East were continually reinvented, not abandoned. Sometimes adversarial, but more often ambivalent, encounters with Turks – in the streets and through representations – reveal the complex ways in which identities were becoming formulated.

If Sansovino's 1581 publication was the *summa* of Venetian guidebooks, Bernardo Salvioni and Donato Rascicotti's 1597 engraving offered viewers an epitome in pictorial form (fig. 1).[14] The bird's-eye view of the cityscape is accompanied with details of Rialto Bridge and Piazza San Marco (the city's economic and political centres), a legend, a dedication, and two parades of costumed figures. The multiple registers brought together in Rascicotti's print serve as both the departure point and the result of changes traced in this study. For what contributed to this new configuration of the city in parts? On one side these representations point to the conjoining of physical, social, and mental spaces; as

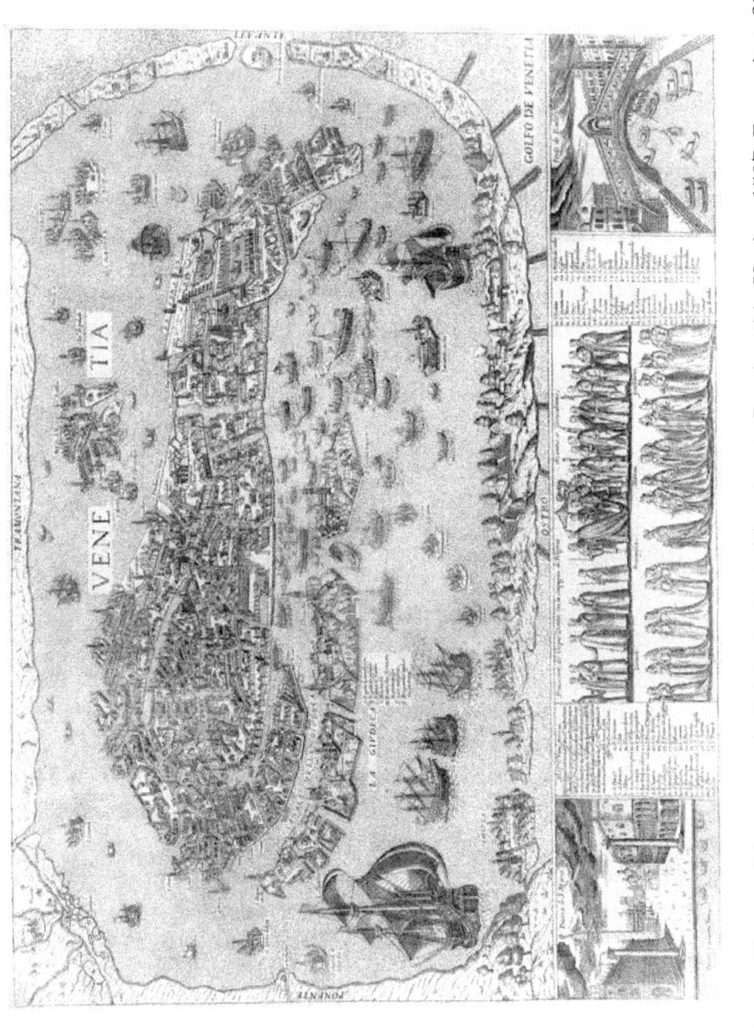

Figure 1 *Venetia*. Engraved by Bernardo Salvioni. Printed by Donato Rascicotti in Venice, 1597. Engraving, 382 × 507 mm [photo: Museo Correr, Venice]

Henri Lefebvre explains, 'the concepts or theories they imply – energy, space, time – can be neither conflated nor separated from one another.'[15] For Lefebvre, and as suggested by the linked pictorial registers in Rascicotti's engraving, space is something in motion; it is produced by, and consists of, modes of representation and social practices. Moreover, each register in the print engages the viewer in different ways. The combination of vantage points encourages the viewer to move between the legend and the map, between the architectural details and the cityscape, and between male and female processions. Finally, Rascicotti's engraving, with its highlights of Venetian life, targeted a foreign audience, to which copies by Roman and Sienese printmakers attest, underscoring once again the dialogue prints initiated between outsiders and insiders.[16]

In ways never experienced before, local identities came to be managed by the repeated circulation of images in print. Early modern viewers would have learned to negotiate their experiences through the very systems of ordering and conventions developed to represent the city and its inhabitants. This gradual process, the book posits, contributed to a growing split between sensate experiences of the world and visual, sometimes vicarious, ones. Potentially 'all one would have to do,' to use Louis Marin's apt words, 'is carefully examine representations in order to examine the world, to construct them in order to articulate being.'[17]

Perspective and the Subject

With its multiple points of view, the engraving also brings forward another theme of the book: the relation between the evolving concepts of place, space, vision, and identity. Perspective contributed to how these concepts changed, and here I introduce some aspects of this history in order to provide some context for the chapters that follow.

Medieval theories of space were based on metaphysics, physics, and theology.[18] The cosmos was understood as 'an ongoing event with man at its center,' a concept that bound space and time together.[19] During the Middle Ages space was identified with matter following Plato's *Timaeus*.[20] However, in the twelfth century this notion of space as something both material and empty was succeeded by Aristotle's identification of space with place, and his influential 'theory of positions in space.'[21]

Since the first century, the word 'place' not only was a metaphor for God but also denoted God,[22] and this idea is expressed in Nicolas of

Cusa's concept of God's gaze. For Cusa, a bishop writing in the middle of the fifteenth century, God's 'omnivoyant' vision, which sees 'roundabout and above and below,' has no fixed centre and thus could not be perceived.[23] Cusa explains this all-seeing gaze in the treatise he calls *The Image*, or *The Picture*, sent to a group of monks along with a painting of the face of Christ, 'the icon of God.'[24] In the preface he instructs his brothers to 'set it up somewhere, for example on the north wall,' and look at it together from different vantage points; 'from what ever side you may examine it (*inspicere*) each of you will have the experience (*experiri*) of being as it were the only one to be seen by it.' As evidence that the gaze 'turns it sight,' he recommends that one brother walk 'east to west,' and the other from 'west to east.' I cite this text at length since I return to Cusa later in the book.

> Owing to the revelation made by the witness (*revelatio relatoris*), he succeeds in realizing that the face abandons none of the walkers, even when their movements are contrary. He thus experiences the fact that this immovable face (*immobilis facies*) moves at the same time towards the east and towards the west, towards the north and towards the south; that it is directed simultaneously toward one place and towards all; and that its gaze follows an individual movement as well as all the movements at once. If he observes (*attendere*) that the gaze leaves none of the persons present, he will see (*videre*) that this gaze is concerned with each one with as much care as if he were the only one to have the experience of being followed, to the extent that the one who is being looked at cannot conceive that another might be the object of the same attention.

Thus the need of the second brother in the experiment, the witness who can confirm by voice that he too is seen by the gaze. Cusa's treatise and the painting were connected to his interest in demonstrating that 'theological matters are better seen with the mind's eye than they can be expressed in words.'[25] Moreover, 'seeing' could be advanced, even made true, by geometry: as Michel de Certeau has observed, the diagram with its coordinates – the monks walking east and west – resembles a map of the gaze.[26] God's field of vision is momentarily fixed as a point – the eyes in the painting on the north wall – as if the distant point of a perspectival construction.[27] Although still expressive of a cosmological view of the world in which man appeared to be at the centre of space which surrounded him on all sides, Cusa's efforts to illustrate God's gaze gesture toward a new abstract configuration of space in which the positions of individual bodies are defined in relation to each other.[28] For each of Cusa's walkers is constituted by the presence of the other, and those identities are ratified by the gaze.

Cusa's idea can be understood in relation to developments in fifteenth-century painting. Since early in the century, the use of artificial perspective had provided artists with the means to organize relations between figures on a flat surface in accordance with an Aristotelian concept of space. The illusion of space was not yet a modern one, since the space inside the representation was not conceived of as continuous, isotropic, and homogeneous.

As James Elkins observes, 'the phrase "perspective space" is a Janus figure,' for it conjoins a modern Cartesian theory of space as a priori and infinite, with the Renaissance practice of perspective, which was 'object oriented' instead.[29] Efforts to prove perspective through mathematics and geometry – to demonstrate, for example, that an elevation of an object is proportionally related to its dimensions in a perspective diagram – led to the representation of objects as diagrams. Already in Piero della Francesca's treatise, as Elkins explains, there is evidence of a shift away from the optical considerations of a viewer's 'eyes' and the 'rays' of sight, toward 'points' and 'lines.'[30] A century later, with the publication of Federico Commandino's treatise in 1558, the beginnings of a modern concept of isometric space emerged as measurable and abstracted from bodily experience.[31]

New techniques of surveying and geometry led to the ichnographic, or orthographic plan; instead of quantifying distances on the basis of the time taken to perceive them, distances could be measured *in* the representation.[32] The second chapter of Daniele Barbaro's 1568 treatise *Pratica della perspettiva* (1568) is devoted to the science of *ichnographia* in which he conceptualizes three-dimensional objects being '"raised" from their plans.'[33] Contributing to this new theory was a consideration of light and space in terms of accidents or properties. Hence the earlier understanding of place as surfaces, and space as the gaps between those surfaces, was replaced by a new understanding of space as something constructed from substances.[34] Space became redefined as homogeneous and a priori to the bodies situated within it, and bodies, as the other side of this equation, came to be understood as moving within space.[35]

An engraving of Piazza San Marco, *La meravigliosa Piazza de San Marco di Venetia,* printed in 1599 by Donato Rascicotti, and accompanied with a text by the architect Vincenzo Scamozzi dated 1599, illustrates this change (fig. 2).[36] Small figures move about the piazza in local and for-

Figure 2   *La meravigliosa Piazza de San Marco di Venetia*. Printed by Donato Rascicotti in Venice. Text signed and dated: V.S.A. [...] 1599 (Vincenzo
Scamozzi Architetto). Engraving, image: 375 × 500; text: 175 × 500
mm [photo: Museo Correr, Venice]

eign costumes, a common sight, explains the text, because the piazza is
regularly filled with people. Instead of depicting a procession – the par-
adigmatic view of the piazza in Venetian painting[37] – the text provides
the visitor with a list of processions that can be seen there. In the foreground, Venetia, the personification of the city as a woman, is flanked by
Minerva and Mercury, who embraces a globe. Their attributes attest to

the image of the city as a space of culture, peace, and wisdom; no mere
trading crossroads, the new maternal Venice engenders heroic action, as
the verse on her dais proclaims:

> You value me, virtue surrounds me
> Just and strong on land and in sea I reign,
> A fecund Mother of arms, arts, heroes.[38]

The print was also intended to promote Scamozzi's perspectival project
for the Procuratie Nove, the new residences seen on the right for the
nine Procurators, who like the doge were elected for life.[39] Although
begun in 1581, debates about the visual impact of the project inter-
rupted its completion; at the end of 1597, a year before the engraving
was made, construction recommenced during the reign of Doge Marin
Grimani, as Scamozzi notes in the text. The Procuratie were among
those projects given new impetus by Doge Nicolò da Ponte (1578–85)
that included completion of the library, the new prisons to the east of
the Palazzo Ducale, Rialto bridge, Fondamenta Nuove, and improvements to the arsenal. Significantly, these spaces and institutions found
throughout the city were being associated with each other, and the rhetorical effects of these designs became the focus of intense debates concerning the city's image. Scamozzi's design for the Procuratie, with its
triumphal perspectival Roman architecture, was at the centre of these
arguments, and the engraving demonstrates what was at stake.[40] For in
Scamozzi's new modern conception of the Piazza, the iconic status of
the buildings – the function of San Marco, for example, as a living symbol of the republic – has been subordinated to the visual effect of the
whole. The façade of the church has been brought into line with the
three-storey articulation of the structures that flank it. Moreover, below
the allegorical tableau, a text includes a legend that is keyed to the city's
architectural monuments. Reconceptualized as a container of space,
Piazza San Marco is an independent entity whose history, orientation,
and dimensions are described in the text and whose dimensions can be
gauged in Venetian feet with the use of the scale line seen on the bot-
tom left of the image. The reconfiguration of the Piazza in the print was
a response to a century of representational changes in which perspective, print, and architectural developments worked together to redefine
how the city was perceived.

Perspective was also used as a metaphor for sight, an idea strength-
ened with the integration of medieval theories of optics and Renaissance artificial perspective in the sixteenth century.[41] In his remarkably

popular catalogue of occupations, first published in Venice in 1585, Tomasso Garzoni defines optics – which he aligns with geometry – as the relation between perception and the visual field. Practitioners of the science of perspective – concerned with the straight and oblique lines of sight – translated viewers' perceptions of the world into images. In 'the act of seeing,' as philosophers explain it, objects are transformed from the invisible to the visible by the 'straight lines' that are emitted from, and return to, the centre of the eye. Vision is imagined as 'a powerful perspective ... [that] apprehends visible objects for its singular propriety.' The eye has become the locus of understanding and subjective judgment, and thus sight is 'the most certain of all senses.'[42] I use Garzoni's synopsis of what were complicated epistemological questions to highlight the ways in which vision, perspective, and the observer's identity were becoming correlated. And as prints came to mediate between 'visible objects' and the viewer, it was the representation that became a part of the observer's identity – that sense, as Garzoni suggests, of owning what one sees.[43]

Paolo Paruta's dialogue *Della perfettione della vita politica*, to which I referred above, addresses a more elite group of readers than Garzoni, but here, too, vision and images mediate between the material world of the body and understanding:

> Although our intellect may be divine from its birth ... nevertheless here below, it lives among these earthly members and cannot perform its operations without the help of bodily sensations. By their means, drawing into the mind the images of material things, it represents these things to itself and in this way forms its concepts of them. By the same token it customarily rises to spiritual contemplations not by itself but awakened by sensible objects.[44]

In the sixteenth century, this haptic experience of the city was becoming complicated by a world translated, to use Walter Ong's words, into 'a vast surface or assemblage of surfaces.'[45] For Ong, this process is analogous with the emergence of writing and the subordination of oral culture that he aligns with the development of modern subjectivity. In this book, it is the combination of new representational technologies, information about the world, and social exchanges that are seen to contribute to early modern identity.

Recent scholarship has pursued these lines of inquiry, drawing attention to uses of cartography and representations of space in early modern Europe, and to concomitant changes to the status of the subject.[46]

As John Hale has argued, making space legible through maps enabled 'Europeans to imagine, believably, the geographical space in which they lived,' an idea Tom Conley and Richard Helgerson have pursued in different ways for France and England respectively.[47] 'Not only does the emergence of the land parallel the emergence of the individual authorial self,' writes Helgerson, 'the one enforces and perhaps depends on the other.'[48] By representing the world and its place within it, according to Conley's formulation, the modern subject emerged in response to a split between 'an illusion of a geographic truth,' and its birthplace, mark, or signature inscribed within the representation.[49] While these authors consider visual imagery, their emphasis is on language – what Conley refers to as 'cartographic writing': the emergence of the self through the spatialization of language.

This book also explores intersections between geography and subjectivity, but my objects of analysis and emphasis on visual culture naturally raise different questions. First, as I argue, ideas that circulated in language reflected and constituted social exchanges in crucial ways, but visual imagery operates on a different register that implicates the body more insistently than texts. Both images and texts overlapped with the phenomenal experience of moving through the city, and with each other, but pictures draw on perceptual mechanisms that conjoin vision and identity through that 'belong to me' experience of visual experience. Second, instead of national identity, the printed imagery considered here focuses on the city or the region as the locus of cultural distinctiveness. Although to some extent this reflects the Italian context, this was a broader European interest connected to concerns with birthplace and citizenship. Moreover, the very process of forging civic categories of identity and reframing the individual in relation to the world outside seems to have facilitated identifications with national boundaries that are more clearly drawn in the early seventeenth century. In short, print enabled people to put the name with the city, the costume, the face. National distinctiveness was thereby a result, in part, of the systematic ordering of space, vision, bodies, and history seen in the series of prints examined throughout this book. The authorial 'self' who emerges as an effect of his or her production also figures in this study. The focus of the book, however, is on the didactic impact of visual conventions, on the effects of prints, and on the ways in which the medium was itself implicated in the etiology of the self.

Any study concerned with the historicity of the 'subject' reflects upon Jacob Burckhardt's 1860 thesis about the Renaissance 'discovery of the individual,' which remains a focus of scholarly debates.[50] Burckhardt's description of the veil of 'faith, illusion and childish prepossession' of medieval consciousness 'which melted into air' during the Renaissance, has been justly criticized.[51] Richard Trexler, Natalie Zemon Davis, and Stephen Greenblatt, among others, have rejected Burckhardt's autonomous individual in favour of a concept of identity formation as a process of exchange with others.[52] If, on one side, there was a new social mobility, so too were there new 'control mechanisms,' according to Greenblatt's influential concept of Renaissance self-fashioning.[53] In contrast to Burckhardt's autonomous individual, self-fashioning was a dialectical concept in which selves were formed in relation to others and through external representations and language.

For Alasdair Macintyre, the new figure of 'the individual' was introduced into moral theory in the texts of Machiavelli and Luther, which signalled a break with hierarchical authority. Luther transformed the community from 'the area in which the moral life is lived out' into 'merely the setting of an eternal drama of salvation.'[54] With moral authority severed from the church and transferred to the 'autonomy of the economic,' the subject became an individual in relation to God and subordinated to the secular world. The emergence of the individual was thereby tied to the separation of society from the state to which he or she became subjected. No easy process, this separation from a network of hierarchical social relations would have required a new set of terms with which to define oneself in relation to others. No longer constituted only by a familial and communal network, the identity of this modern subject would have been defined by the facts of a social vocabulary that was no longer prescriptive. Profession, name, and status no longer determined an individual's actions; instead, he or she had to choose, for when 'all desires are corrupt ... choice remains open.'[55]

If Luther transformed the theological context, Machiavelli was the author of the secular order, the first theorist of realpolitik. In view of people acting on behalf of their interests, moral rules had no validity except as 'means to the ends of power'; unconstrained by any social bonds, explains Macintyre, society was 'a potential raw material, to be reshaped for the individual's own ends.'[56] For Machiavelli ethics and politics were intertwined; the emergence of the individual and state were bound together by the effect of people on the institutions of the state and the extent to which the growth of the state pressed on individuals.

External impingements are also central to Stephen Greenblatt's notion of Renaissance subjectivity. However, instead of these social pressures forging an individual, with a body and ego of its own, he calls attention to ways in which sixteenth-century people moved between identities. Greenblatt cites the lack of concern among writers 'for the integrity or propriety of the first-person pronoun,' noting that medieval authors could easily 'assume the "I" of another.'[57] The emergence of the 'I' in texts reflected the use of the pronoun as a persona or mask. Following Thomas Hobbes's description of a 'person,' Greenblatt maintains that sixteenth-century selves were defined by the ownership of their words and actions and not their individual bodies. Discussing the well-known trial of Arnaud de Tihl, the ingenious imposter of Martin Guerre, Greenblatt explains that the latter was represented as a product 'of ... relations, material objects, and judgments,' rather than as a producer of them.[58] Instead of a subject or agent of his actions, the accused was defined as an object: by his visual characteristics and contours, his 'scars, features, clothing, shoe size.'[59] For Greenblatt the case points to 'a disconcerting recognition: that our identity may not originate in (or be guaranteed by) the fixity, the certainty, of our own body.'[60] Yet the crux of the case was the *return* of Martin Guerre to his village in the Pyrenees after twelve years of absence. For it was the face and body of the 'real' Martin Guerre that provided the unmistakable evidence; it was the two men, standing side by side, that enabled his uncle and sisters to recognize the differences between them. It was the gap between the performance of identity – the claims to ownership of words and actions achieved with remarkable success by Arnaud – *and* the body's unshakable corporeality, when confronted with another, that resulted in the failure of the imposter.[61] It is this unusual experience – comparing bodies and faces – that sixteenth-century printed visual imagery made habitual, thereby drawing attention to differences between individuals in profoundly new ways.

More recently, John Martin has asked if Burckhardt's thesis should be discarded in its entirety. For Martin, the increasing importance of sincerity at the end of the Renaissance was expressive of the subject's new sense of its interior self.[62] By the beginning of the seventeenth century, moreover, there was a distinction made between a subject's sense of its interior and exterior, between the 'heart' and the body's external appearance. These are conclusions supported by the present study, for printed imagery called attention to the contours of one's costume, the representational weight of the body, and the distinctiveness of one's own face. However if late sixteenth-century Venetians began to see themselves as others saw them, this impression of interiority was, in part, paradoxically, the result of finding one's identity in images. The incipient mirage of the 'individuated self,' moreover, was coextensive with coming into conformity; it was constituted from the outside in, by the repetition of similar images in prints, by the construction of categories of identity, by exchanges with others, and through an increase in the use of mirrors. More than ever before, there could be no isolated body, as subjectivity was increasingly constituted by the same images that bound individual bodies to the social.[63]

The Chapters

Chapter 1 traces the evolving image of Venice in printed maps. Beginning with Jacopo de'Barbari's 1500 woodcut, the chapter progresses to the early seventeenth century, and Giacomo Franco's miniature view on the frontispiece of his series of engravings of Venetian costumes and ceremonies. In contrast to de'Barbari's utopian image of the city as the centre of the world, Franco's transforms Venice into the world. Central here is the reciprocity between the stunning cityscape and its institutions and how printed images of the city came to mediate between the viewer's experiences of both. Maps altered the ways in which the city was perceived, and these changes reflect the broad historical turn away from mimesis toward abstraction as printmakers developed new pictorial strategies to reproduce the republic's social and physical organization on paper. These changes required that viewers learn to move between the legends, perspective views, processions, histories, and portraits that began to surround the image of the city. Throughout the century, the maps demonstrate the persistent efforts of printmakers to negotiate between the atemporal and abstract view of the city's topography seen from a bird's-eye view and the contingent experiences of the person in the street. Increasingly print translated sensate experiences of Venice into shared visual ones, and consequently these two once-overlapping understandings of the city were disengaged into representations of mental and physical experiences of space.

Costume books, the focus of chapter 2, were another response to interest in geography and travel literature, and printmakers in the Veneto were particularly enthusiastic, publishing about one-third of those books seen in Europe between 1540 and 1610. Following discoveries of lands unknown to Europeans, and in striking contrast with the regional variations seen in flora or fauna, the contours of the human body, unexpectedly, and perhaps surprisingly, appeared to be universal.

Thus it was dress – what was worn over the skin – that served as the locus of alterity, and printed costume books became a means to order an expanding image of the world. As I argue, sources and conventions used by illustrators to classify people would have prompted viewers to compare the silhouettes of their own costumes with those of the depicted foreigners.

In contrast to the vicarious travel offered by printed costume books, friendship albums accompanied students and merchants visiting Italy from north of the Alps. Signatures of friends and colleagues were collected alongside hand-painted coats of arms and imagery including costumes. The migration of Venetian types into what were essentially moral guidebooks brings to the fore those concepts that were important to foreigners about Venetians.

The chapter also addresses the social function of dress as signs of faith and status. Judicial proceedings illustrate how the state attempted to ensure that identities were clearly defined and also how those definitions could be undermined. Finally, I suggest that official concern with attire, together with printed costume imagery, may have called attention to the materiality of viewers' own clothes and to the representational weight of their bodies. Drawing on the visual conventions used in the prints, and the new forms of identification they may have elicited, I propose that these mechanisms may have contributed to the sense of one's own distinctiveness.

Identity and costume are also themes in chapter 3, but here the focus turns to some of the ways in which printed imagery overlapped with specific historical events. The first example is the confrontation with the Ottoman fleet at Cyprus and the ensuing battle of Lepanto in 1571. For Venetians, whose maritime power had been eroded by the Ottoman Empire since 1453, the confrontation threatened the very foundations of Venetian republican identity: noble status and masculine virtue. Of particular interest here are printed maps of the battle and how these may have intersected with other forms of visual imagery to reassert values of patrician rule over collective action.

In 1597, during the coronation of Dogaressa Morosina Morosini Grimani, it was patrician women who became a focus of Venetian cosmography. The extraordinary event provides insights into festivities in the late sixteenth century, when the civic function of rituals was becoming subordinated to their function as performances, often staged for the eyes of outsiders. Increasingly characterized by commentators as displays of splendour and pomp never seen before, processions became choreographed events, framed by architectural backdrops and publicized through printed pamphlets and engravings that extended their visual effects. Printed maps are also a focus here in relation to costume and female comportment.

Where the integration of the city's spaces and civic ceremonial in the early part of the century constituted forms of collective republican identity, the surge in printed visual imagery produced for festivities in the last three decades indicates that print became one form of countering the city's declining prestige on the world stage. In contrast to the continual ceremonies that characterized Venetian civic life, the battle at Lepanto and dogaressa's procession were unusual events that precipitated a new kind of historical reportage in which time is arrested in space.

If a map was like a portrait, so too did a portrait resemble a map. By the end of the sixteenth century, printed maps of Venice were framed with images of the doges, portraits accompanied maps of the world in the entrances to Venetian homes, and authors explained how the human face could be read like a map for signs of identity. Printed portraits and portrait books, the subject of chapter 4, were transforming the ways in which likenesses were viewed and used. Portrait books, with their distinctive serial format and combination of image and history, prompted viewers to contrast the faces of sitters, and these were cognitive skills also being cultivated by physiognomists. An analysis of this new attention to facial features begins the chapter.

If, as I argue in chapter 2, costume was the means to identifiy foreigners, then what about physiognomy? To address this question, I turn first to the Japanese embassy. Until 1585, with the visit of four young ambassadors, the Japanese had never been seen in Europe. Since these youths were converts of the Jesuit mission, travelled in Western clothes, and had the manners of courtiers, they appeared to be Europeans. Indeed, it seems to be this lack of difference that prompted chroniclers to look more closely at their faces. The struggle to describe their physiognomy, in the absence of a vocabulary to do so, provides an intriguing example of how Europeans looked at unfamiliar facial features before these had been codified as characteristics of race.

The extent to which, and how, ideas about race were developing in Europe in the sixteenth century is a complicated issue.[64] Terms like race and nation resonated differently from today; they were often used interchangeably. Stereotypes concerning the character and colour of groups on the basis of distance from, or proximity to, the equator had been circulating in language since before Ptolemy. Sixteenth-century Europeans, however, were accustomed to recognizing nuances in costume, habits, and language, rather than facial features as signs of differences. Even in the case of deeply entrenched prejudices concerning the Ottoman Turks, the focus of the third part of the chapter, these stereotypes circulated in language, and it was the costume that identified the type. However, by bringing the history of individuals together with their likenesses, portrait books urged readers to make connections between physiognomy and actions. By instructing viewers to look more closely at faces, portrait books drew attention to the differences between faces. The conventions of portrait books, aided by interest in physiognomy, thereby laid the groundwork for the modern alignment between facial distinctiveness and collective actions that has become characteristic of racism. The last three chapters, then, contribute to a prehistory for racism by showing how printed imagery constructed categories of identity before a repertory of visual characteristics had been assigned to the bodies and faces of some ethnic groups. By the end of the sixteenth century, as facial features became ascribed to specific modes of behaviour, faces came to define personality, and this became a framework for the modern alignment of identity with individuality.

In the Conclusion I consider the signatures of printmakers and inscriptions made by users of printed images and albums. At the end of the book I return to perspective to suggest ways in which some modern theorists of perspective have been reflecting, in part, on the split between the subject and the image that was materialized through print. Cognitive change is a slow process; nevertheless I hope to show how print participated in the changing status of the early modern Venetian subject. The novelty and the repeated experience of images and conventions instructed sixteenth-century viewers how to identify the text in the legend with the location in the map, to recognize places by the contours of local costumes, and to discern the differences between faces compiled in portrait books. In so doing, print both engendered identification with the familiar and revealed what was distinctive about the individual.

Unlike art historical monographs devoted to a single artist or monument, this book considers a vast array of visual representations produced by dozens of different artists. The study explores monuments in the history of art, personal manuscript albums, inexpensive prints, and also printed series that circulated to an international audience. Printmaking in the sixteenth century was itself a complicated business consisting of editing, illustrating, engraving, printing, publishing, and selling. Some printers, such as Giacomo Franco (1550–1620), a prominent figure in the book, practised all of these tasks himself.[65] Despite the ubiquitous appearance of popular prints in modern histories of Venice, the work of Franco, like that of many artisans, has been overlooked on account, in part, of the failure of these artists to fit into established categories of study, particularly art history and the history of the book. Often balancing the aspirations of artists who sought to elevate themselves above the manual efforts of artisans, and the exigencies of business in Venice, printmakers produced single sheets, pamphlets, and books on diverse subjects. The objects of analysis considered in this book were in fact prompted by contemporary practices, for many printmakers produced several of the forms of imagery considered here, and a few, such as Franco and Pietro Bertelli, made all of them: maps, costume books, prints of events, and portrait books.

Printed imagery, especially when considered in relation to social life, challenges conventional art historical approaches. Although archival research has brought forward information on the business of print, facts about who purchased the artifacts or how many sheets were pulled from presses or editions are rare. Writing this book has required new ways of assessing artifacts that cannot easily be accommodated within existing categories, such as those of iconography or style. The format, content, visual vocabularies, and sources used by printmakers were not local phenomena, but pan-European, making patronage, artistic intentions, and sometimes social history less useful modes of analysis. Content and pictorial conventions also crossed historical and geographical boundaries usually associated with stylistic differences. The subject matter itself led many printmakers to suppress their individual style as a means to underpin claims to objectivity.

Many often productive approaches can reduce the meanings of radically different visual representations to familiar historical narratives. In the Venetian context in particular, this situation is magnified by the conservative institutions of the republic. Its longevity was attributed to the maintenance of its traditions and their perpetual reinforcement. In Venetian painting, for example, styles changed throughout the sixteenth century, while the content of artworks was largely prescribed by convention. Considered within the terms of social art history, art production emerges, inevitability, from its historical context as both constituting and reflecting the myth of Venice, its republican ideology, and the confluence of patriarchal and oligarchic social relations. Given the civic focus of the imagery explored here, these symbolic and historical concerns remain important. My goal, however, is to show how these meanings were conveyed and embedded in diverse forms and conventions of print and to suggest how these representations intersected with each other and with social life.

In the past three decades scholars have witnessed a wealth of essays dealing with the problems of interpreting the past.[66] Contemporary sources, even official ones, can themselves be fictions. Chroniclers copy each other's accounts; local historians rehearse the official line; foreign visitors often repeat hearsay; and printmakers copy each other. This representational character of the sources is central to the history explored here. Indeed I hope to suggest a broader system of representations in which print participated.

In addition to a range of archival and printed sources, of particular interest here is the materiality of the objects themselves: what their format, scale, conventions, novelty, predictability, vocabularies, sources, texts, historicity, and order indicate about their function and how these encouraged new viewing practices. The meanings of prints can be as open-ended as their uses and readers, as the work of Roger Chartier, among others, has shown.[67] The printed images and texts studied here circulated widely, but some were also ephemeral. They were sometimes crude but also lavish, produced for a market, for a patron, and often for both. Prints could be shared among readers, posted on walls, seen in private, purchased as souvenirs, and pasted into albums. Print fostered new forms of production, new practices (business and creative), and new audiences (geographical and social). Indeed, at the end of the fifteenth century, print and perspective were developing technologies; but by the end of the sixteenth, the content and formats considered here were ubiquitous, impinging upon the world.

Some readers will question the relevance of modern theories for an analysis of the early modern context. However it seems to me that any project that seeks to understand how images caused effects is not only a historical problem but also a theoretical one. And if we are to understand the experiences of Venetians in the past, then it can be useful to find the gaps between the historical evidence and modern theories, and also the uncanny resemblances. I am less convinced than some that we can describe a past that is untarnished by the historical contingencies of present concerns. Of one thing I feel certain: print and new experiences of the world surely made early modern viewers more like us than they were before.

Chapter 1

From Myth to Metropole: Sixteenth-Century Printed Maps of Venice

In October 1500 the German publisher and trader Anton Kolb went before the Venetian senate to extol the 'new art of printing' demonstrated in his immense woodcut that he said would propagate the 'fame of this most excellent city' (figs. 3, 4, 9). Seeking an exemption from export duties given the extraordinary expenses invested in the project, Kolb highlighted the difficulties of producing the celebrated view:

> because it is he who three years ago had [to ensure that] that work, principally [resounding] to the fame of this most excellent city of Venice, was accurately and properly drawn and printed, and because many details from it are copied in other works, and because of the almost unattainable and incredible skill required to make such an accurate drawing both on account of its size and [the size] of the paper, the like of which was never made before, and also because of the new art of printing a form of such large dimensions and the difficulty of the overall composition, which matters people have not appreciated, not being able to estimate the value, considering the mental subtlety involved, and given that printed copies cannot be produced [economically] to sell for less than about three florins each, so that he does not in general hope to recoup the moneys invested: he therefore supplicates Your Sublimity that grace may be conceded for the said work to be exported and sold in all your lands and cities without payment of any duties and without any restriction.[1]

The supplication makes no reference to the designer, Jacopo de'Barbari, who probably met Kolb in Venice.[2] Instead, the publisher listed the technical feats, linking the mode of the representation to how the picture was intended to work; when reassembled, the printed sheets would produce a vision of the city seen from an imaginary point of view. Covering nearly four square metres, the print was a representational triumph, for both its size and its meticulous topographical detail.[3] Kolb intended to export the woodcuts throughout the dominion, furnishing an image of the Venetian capital in people's minds. Despite his appeal, the exemption from tariffs was denied; instead, he was granted exclusive rights of production for four years with permission to export the work 'to all places, paying the normal duty.'[4] Given the enormity of the project, the copyright must have been small compensation; the absence of emulators in the next few decades attests to the financial risks of the undertaking.[5] Nevertheless, authorization to export the print to a foreign audience indicates the senators approved of the striking image.

As this supplication indicates, developments in cartography and the new representational technologies of print and perspective drew attention to how the city was perceived. Woodcuts and engravings – produced in multiples, widely disseminated, and portable – provided the means to circulate new information about the world on paper. In turn, the increasing visibility of the world contributed to the growing awareness of boundaries between regions in early modern Europe. This new visual relation to the world outside focused Europeans on the city as the locus of cultural distinctiveness and on the ways in which identities within its boundaries were defined. A wealth of printed maps – sold as single sheets and incorporated into printed books – attests to the enormous popular interest garnered by city views in general and Venice in particular.

Located at the crossroads between the east and west, Venice was a destination for foreign merchants and pilgrims like Canon Pietro Casola, who wrote of his impressions when embarking on a pilgrimage in 1494. For Casola, the city appeared both 'well ordered and arranged' but also impossible to perceive as a whole: 'I cannot give the dimensions of this city, for it appears to me not one city alone but several cities placed together.'[6] Casola's reflections convey the visitor's conflicting experiences of the cityscape: the numerous islands seen upon entering the lagoon, the panoramic narrative of façades seen from the waterways, the seemingly incomprehensible network of *campi* (fields; the Venetian piazza), streets, and bridges experienced by the pedestrian, and the view of the contours of the city seen from the vantage point of any number of *campanili* (bell towers). These fundamentally different ways of perceiving Venice were brought together in the single remarkably coherent image designed by de'Barbari.

Sixteenth-century maps of Venice, and the de'Barbari view in particular, have drawn considerable scholarly attention. The maps have been catalogued, technical considerations debated, and their accuracy assessed. Cartography and the related pursuit of chorography, the art of exact description associated with city views, were underpinned by claims to objectivity associated with measurement and perspective. The circulation of printed copies and the practice of artists concealing their individual style furthered the notion that maps were unmediated reproductions of the local topography. In turn, these practices can often be found to magnify a range of ideological concerns that these same representational practices worked to conceal. Attempts to synthesize cityscapes were not without their strategic emphases and exclusions.

This chapter explores the conventions developed by printmakers within the broader context of changing notions of civic identity and space and time. Of particular interest are the ways in which these visual strategies organized viewers' relations to the city and thereby altered their perceptions of it. And this process fuelled the demand for images considered elsewhere in the book.

In the de'Barbari woodcut, with which the chapter begins, viewers were projected to a vantage point previously inconceivable. Yet the picture's mimetic resemblance to Venice also draws the viewer toward the particulars of the topography. The map emblematizes the relation between the collective and the individual during the years in which the republic's myths were being entrenched by state historians. The following section addresses the turn toward copper engraving for maps; viewers were encouraged to negotiate between the image and the legends, texts, and pictorial devices that surrounded city views. The image of the city became less detailed and more diagrammatic: an iconic and unchanging centre surrounded by the institutions that sustained it. By the beginning of the seventeenth century, the image of Venice was redefined; no longer a capital of an empire – a model that radiates from the core to the periphery – Venice was transmuted into a metropole, an image of the city in which all the world could be seen.

Jacopo de'Barbari's Bird's-Eye View

I have observed the said city is so well ordered and arranged.[7]

Pietro Casola

With its date boldly stamped at the top of the print, de'Barbari's famous woodcut of Venice declares its own historical importance, as if predicting its archetypal status among printed views of Venice, and even city views in general (fig. 3).[8] A monument of printmaking, the design required six pearwood blocks – each measuring 980 × 680 mm – into which the title was carved, like an epitaph, in large Roman letters with elaborate serifs. The blocks, recently restored for a millennium exhibition, were printed onto extraordinarily large folio sheets that when joined together measure 1.350 metres in height and 2.820 metres in length.

Displayed on a wall, and viewed from some distance, the landscape seems to emerge from the water, as if conjured from the sea by the eight wind gods that circle the islands. Like Venus, the islands appear to be 'floating among the waves of the sea,' as Marin Sanuto famously described Venice in his *De origine, situ et magistratibus urbis Venetae*: 'at the centre and summit of the sea she rests almost like a queen ... situated above the surging waters.'[9] Seen from this cartographic point of view – almost perpendicular to the city – the topography appears in plan, the city unpopulated, its geographic contours fixed in time, as the inscription states: 'At Venice 1500.'

Moving toward the surface of the print, the viewpoint shifts toward the south and the cityscape reveals itself (fig. 4). The topographical details have been projected from an oblique angle and the landscape to the north now appears in elevation as if seen from a low vantage point in the distance. At close range, it is the spectacular detail of the urban topography that comes into focus, a perspective that encourages viewers to investigate the gardens in the foreground, the façades of the palaces that line the Grand Canal, and the details of the riggings on the galleys that fill the basin of San Marco. Tiny figures of oarsmen emerge to animate the lagoon, adding to the striking contrast with the god's-eye view of the geographical contours.

The centre islands fill the sea as if inflated by the eight wind gods that circumnavigate the scene. The rays of wind direct viewers to the official civic centre and the *campanile* at Piazza San Marco, a focus that may explain why significant portions of the city have been excluded to the south and east. The islands of Torcello, Mazzabo, and Burano to the northwest are reduced 'to no more than modest satellites of the planet Venice,' as Elisabeth Crouzet-Pavan aptly puts it.[10] The vast lands of the terraferma – the Venetian mainland seen at the top of the sheets – have been compressed to a thin band at the horizon, the whole protected by the fortress of Alps that isolates the historical centre in the foreground.

Mercury, the messenger god of commerce and protector of trade and

Figure 3   Jacopo de'Barbari, *Venetie*. Printed by Anton Kolb in Venice, 1500. Woodcut, 135 × 282 cm [photo: Newberry Library, Chicago]

travellers, points the reader to the inscription that circles his powerful physique: 'I Mercury shine favourably on this above all other emporia' [MERCVRIVS PRE CETERIS HVIC FAVSTE EMPORISS ILLVSTRO].[11] From his cumulous support he gazes down at Neptune astride a monstrous dolphin who conducts the viewer toward the entrance to the city, a perspective for which the recently erected clock tower provides a focus. This new monument to measuring time marks the entrance to 'the mouth of the Mercerie,' the marketplace that Bernardo Giustinian described in 1493 as the 'bowels' of the city.[12] This narrow street leads toward Rialto, the commercial centre, and the wooden bridge that once spanned the Grand Canal. Rialto, the city's 'umbilical island,' is the pictorial and topographical centre of the woodcut. This foundational metaphor is supported by histories of the city's origins; S. Giacomo, the parish church at Rialto, was identified by authors as the site where the consuls of Padua supposedly established themselves during the *traslatio*, the exodus of refugees from the mainland.[13] Between Neptune and Mercury – also the mythical founder of civilization – de'Barbari establishes the picture's central axis around the corridor from San Marco to Rialto (fig. 3).

The long-standing reliance on Mark, the city's protector saint, has been abandoned in favour of these classical guardians, what might be called a new cast of patron saints, shifting the myth of Venice from east to west, from Byzantium to Rome.[14] Inaugurating a new myth of Venice, these statuesque *legenda* conflate the legendary values of the Roman republic with the grandeur of the empire. Without abandoning the Byzantine affiliation, Venetian humanists rediscovered their ancestors among the exodus from Rome after its fall.[15] If a new history of origins helped to compensate for their own loss of Constantinople to the Ottoman Empire in 1453, the antique provenance also rivalled claims to ancient origins celebrated by other Italian centres. The mythological framing of the islands in the woodcut suggestively links the birth of Venice with Roman republicanism, thereby iterating, in visual form, the Roman genealogy established by Bernardo Giustinian's *De origine urbis Venetiarum*. Published in 1493, *De origine* marks the birth of official civic historiography.[16] The development of a classical past was a complex process that changed throughout the century.[17]

Long-standing independence was attributed to the city's deceptive landscape since navigable routes to the city are concealed beneath the surface of the water. The physical facts of the topography are visible on close inspection, since human figures stand knee deep in the marshes.[18] However, it is Neptune's heroic body and trident, situated where the

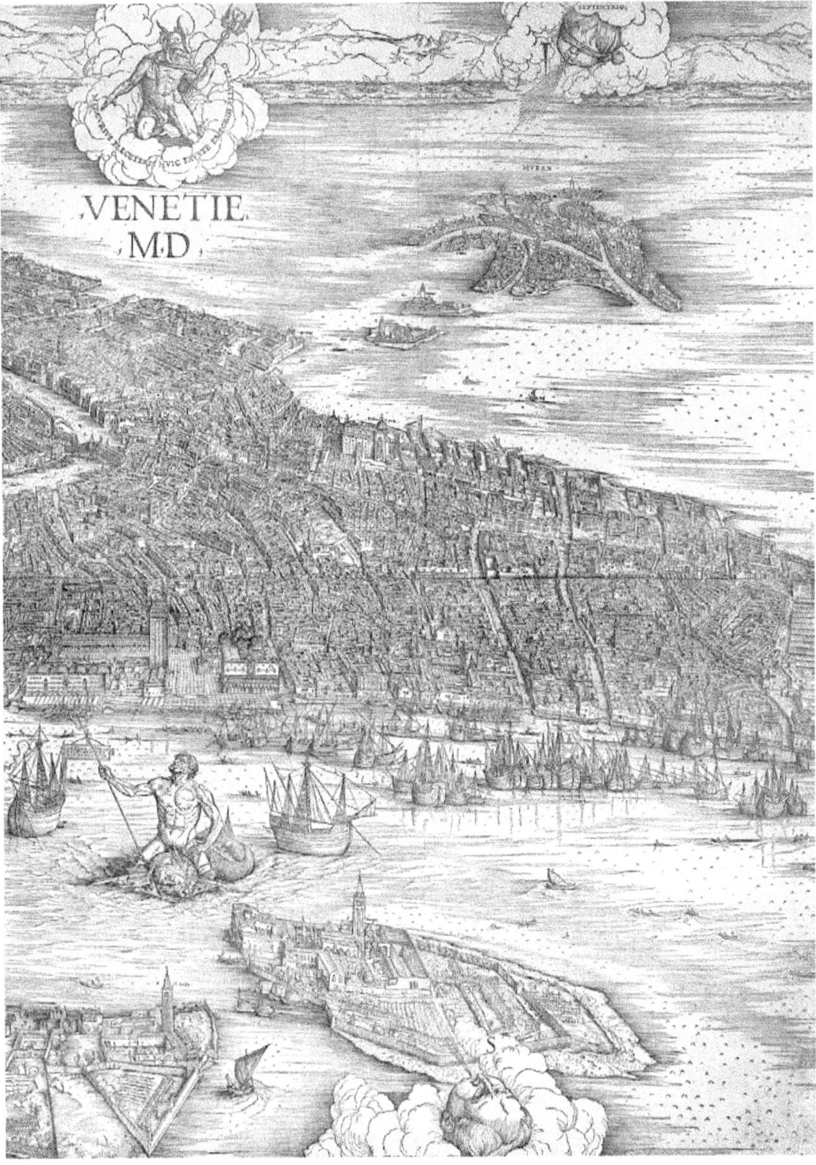

Figure 4   Detail, Jacopo de'Barbari, *Venetie*. Printed by Anton Kolb in Venice, 1500. Woodcut, 135 × 282 cm [photo: Museo Correr, Venice]

city's navigable canals converge, that shields the city's permeable landscape, a defensive posture repeated in the inscription on the antique tablet displayed by his trident: 'I Neptune reside here, smoothing the waters at this port' [AEQVORA TVENS PORTV RESIDEO HIC NEPTVNVS]. But the tablet also operates on another level, for its ansate shape corresponds to weights used by printmakers; the inscription then, may also be understood as an allusion to the artist's work of projecting the cityscape onto paper.

The Uses of Maps and Social Geography

Painted wall maps and manuscript charts served a symbolic and practical function for the Venetian state as decoration for the Palazzo Ducale and for the public magistracies of the republic, anticipating the subsequent importance of map production for governments throughout Europe.[19] Manuscript charts offered the most current information for navigation and colonial expansion, and accurate maps were often kept from the presses in order to protect the information from circulating.[20] For example, Cristoforo Sorte's maps for the Venetian state, produced at the end of the sixteenth century, were designed for a room that could be closed from the scrutiny of visitors.[21] These were made using both perspectival and orthographic projections. The latter charts geographical data in plan as if seen from an infinite distance and provides the kinds of information about peripheral areas and boundaries required for the business of government, trade, and war. Land surveys, coats of arms, and names were all used to substantiate claims to property and territories.[22] Because boundaries between countries were subject to change, however, these were rarely marked on printed maps. Instead, it was regions and particularly cities that provided stable points of reference.[23] In contrast to state and navigational functions of manuscript charts, printed maps fostered new ways of conceptualizing differences between here and there, familiar and unfamiliar, city and landscape. These oppositions were highlighted by the distinctive geographical terrain and walls that defined the Renaissance city.

Assessments of the de'Barbari woodcut have drawn attention to the accuracy of the detail, on the one hand, and its exaggerations and distortions on the other. To some scholars, the extraordinary naturalism indicates the map was the result of field data collected by a group of surveyors.[24] A cartographer at the end of the fifteenth century would have plotted relations between points by collecting distances and bearings. In open areas distances could be measured with cords or pacing (chains were adopted in the second half of the sixteenth century), while an astrolabe could be used to provide accurate data for distances within the field of vision by using trigonometry. Even at the end of the century, when space was becoming understood as a quantifiable concept, Sorte continued to collect data along existing routes and fields instead of using triangulation or abstract projections.[25] He would have plotted the geography orthographically and then rendered the landscape in perspective, a conventional rather than accurate mode that reflected artistic as much as topographical considerations.

Triangulation was known in the 1450s but not put into practice until 1513 in Strasbourg.[26] A pamphlet explaining the technique was published in Germany in 1528, and in Venice in 1546. Even were triangulation known in Venice and bearings calculated between towers, the absence of straight runs of land or water to measure distances between these points would have made it difficult to extrapolate sufficient data from which to produce an accurately scaled plan.[27] Although the role of scientific instrumentation in the production of the de'Barbari woodcut has not been excluded, the extant evidence and topographical complexities suggest the woodcut was a 'studio fabrication' drawn from a recent survey.[28] From 1485 to 1502, in fact, the cityscape was subjected to a thoroughgoing physical inspection, and this may have provided the data for the bird's-eye view.[29]

Earlier I noted that many of the islands – Casola's 'several cities' – were excluded by de'Barbari, who emphasized the integration of individual *contrade* (parishes/districts) instead. This structure was established by the twelfth century with each church functioning as a nucleus around which its dependents gathered. This insular organization, in turn, constituted the city's geographical syntax and had an administrative function. In other Italian cities the parish defined spatial associations between neighbours; in Venice, by contrast, there were a variety of social institutions and relatively high residential mobility that worked to limit both the power of individuals within the *contrade* and the political role of these neighbourhoods.[30]

Private local improvements were legislated by the public authorities. Expansion required the draining of marshes and lakes with both residents and the state benefiting from cohesive organic development and the concomitant improvements to the problems of swamps.[31] Permissions for drainage were granted in greater numbers for smaller extensions with equivalent concessions ensuring conformity. Numerous small extensions benefited the state by encouraging proprietorship; at the same time, the public authorities could demand that work be completed quickly or the concession could be revoked.[32] Equivalent expansion of adjoining properties was part of a communal process managed by the *vicini,* one of the public agencies that administrated development in the districts.[33]

Despite the absence of a systematic plan of expansion for the city as a whole, its growth demonstrates geometrical precision and even theoretical foresight. For example, the first concessions defined axes of expansion with development proceeding to the east and west of the old islands. This quadrated structure of early fifteenth-century growth can be seen on Giudecca in the left foreground of the 1500 woodcut (fig. 3).[34] Construction of new spaces was not without its conflicts; unlicensed draining and fraud, unsystematic development, and the tendency for the sources to exaggerate the system of public and private exchange attest to discordances. Nevertheless, as Elisabeth Crouzet-Pavan maintains, official controls were generally accepted and tensions absorbed.[35] With property neither the privilege of nor controlled by individual influential nobles, the state could deflect the interests of private contests onto civic initiatives. State control over concessions thereby suppressed the political control of individual families and the political influence of the *contrade,* while ensuring the latter were politically marginalized. Limits on private development continued through stringent building controls. Crucial to the uniformity of urban growth was the constant threat of erosion from the sea.[36] Regularizing the contours of the city was a practical requirement that yoked the image of the cityscape to public works and the political system, an alliance institutionalized with the Magistrato Veneto alle acque in 1501.[37]

The political power of the *contrade* was limited further by the growing employment of men in the business of government. Patricians and citizens were drawn from the districts to the city's official spaces, where they were employed in a variety of magistracies and agencies.[38] Centralization was concomitant with waning community ties between classes and the increasing identification of private spaces like parishes with women.[39] This female association may have been a factor in the absence of the *contrade* from Venetian civic rituals.[40] The Festival of the Twelve Marys provides a particularly striking example of how a ritual that once incorporated the districts could be appropriated by the state.[41] Each year, two parishes were given responsibility for festivities to commemorate the legendary rescue by men from the parish of S Maria Formosa of twelve young women who had been abducted with their dowries by outsiders. Local celebrations and spending by wealthy families fuelled rivalries between the *contrade*. The combination of potentially divisive spatial loyalties and the unruly atmosphere of the event during the thirteenth and early fourteenth centuries pressed the patrician regime to abolish the festival in 1379. In its new incarnation the event was modified into a ducal procession to S Maria Formosa and back to Piazza San Marco, thereby appropriating the festival and the centre of the Marian cult for the government.[42]

State encouragement of participation in the Scuole Grandi and Scuole Piccole (lay religious associations) deflected the focus from the parishes further, a tactic that fostered urban improvement and limited geographical allegiances.[43] The five Scuole Grandi fragmented residential allegiances by forging alliances between people from a variety of parishes.[44] Membership extended to a variety of ethnic groups and classes, and even in some instances to women, and in the Scuole Grandi, offices were the privilege of men from the citizen class. The Scuole provided an institutional framework in which *cittadini* could emulate the government's hierarchical organization from which they were constitutionally excluded. For Gasparo Contarini, the famous apologist of the Venetian republic, these institutions mirrored the patrician oligarchy as microcosms within the macrocosm, and thus served as a locus for channelling the aspirations of the *cittadini*.[45] The Scuole also fulfilled a number of charitable functions, and by the sixteenth century, as Brian Pullan has shown, they replaced the role of the parishes to become 'the mediating institutions between the rich and poor.'[46] In addition to social benefits to the state, the artistic and architectural projects of the Scuole developed sectors on the outskirts, embellishing a broad arc through the city from the south-west to the north-east.[47] Further, the participation of the Scuole Grande in civic processions necessitated the repeated presence of the members in Piazza San Marco, where they would progress in sequence, competing among themselves for the most elaborate floats.[48]

Although the *contrada* functioned as a unit of residence that 'identifies each Venetian without exception,' as Crouzet-Pavan states, many social institutions cut across this urban matrix.[49] Potential local political and social power for citizen and patrician men was redirected to organizations overseen by the state, and similarly all land expansion was subject to state control or surveillance. Local urban growth, the linked efforts of orderly expansion and public works to assuage the destructive potential of the sea, citywide organizations, and service to the state thereby worked together to reinforce associations between the parts of the city and its geography.

Print and Authorship

This tension between the *contrade* and the cityscape is embedded in and expressed by the 1500 woodcut's representational structure. First, while the use of perspective draws the viewer into the individual architectural details of each *contrada*, the replication of elements such as windows throughout the city constructs an image of uniformity. The vast size of the two parts of Piazza San Marco has been veiled by the blockcutter's hatching, thereby weaving these high-profile sites into the picture's homogeneous texture. Despite the emphasis on the entrance to the city – brought forward by the perspectival construction and viewpoint of the projection – the artist has attempted to present peripheral regions of the city with the same clarity of detail used throughout, thereby integrating each part into the whole.[50] When compared with modern modes of projection, the map has numerous inaccuracies, and many of these – the marginalization of the surrounding islands is one example – have been shown to emphasize particular sites. And yet, some of these distortions can be understood as symptoms of efforts to avoid privileging sites and to present instead a homogeneous republican fabric.

Such a strategy appears clear in a comparison with the famous view of Florence that had been engraved a generation earlier (fig. 5). Attributed to the engraver and mapmaker Francesco Rosselli, the view is known through the woodcut copy, the *Map with a Chain*, attributed to Lucantonio degli Uberti.[51] In both the Florence and Venice woodcuts, perspective was deployed as a means of organizing the viewer's perception of the city; however, in the view of Florence, well-known buildings were made to stand out from their context, to direct observers from landmark to landmark.

Both prints expose the tension between the rhetorical effects of perspective and the materiality of the medium, but this is used toward different ends. In contrast with the imaginary point of view constructed by de'Barbari, Rosselli presented Florence as if seen from the surrounding hills, using the illusion of the picture plane as an extension of natural space. Indeed, the artist situated in the lower right corner of the print has drafted the walls of Florence on his sheet, a tactic that calls attention to the play of levels of representation.[52] Transcribing what he sees with

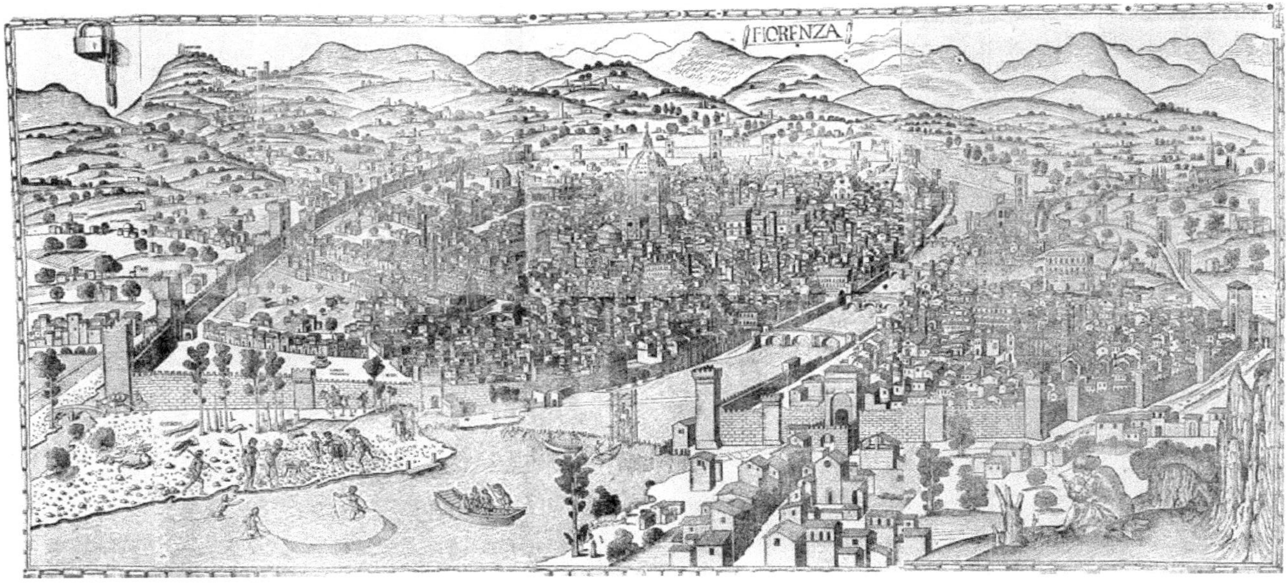

Figure 5   Lucantonio degli Uberti, *Florentia*. Woodcut copy after Francesco Rosselli's engraving, 1482. Kupferstichkabinett. Staatliche Museen zu Berlin [photo: Bildarchiv Preußischer Kulturbesitz]

his eyes, the figure authenticates, to use Louis Marin's concept, 'the real city [seen] from within the representation as we reader-viewers contemplate its cartographic representation from the outside.'[53] The replicative medium of print is crucial to this game of authorship as it asserts the relation between chorography and the *contra factum* (counterfeit), the art of exact description.[54] By illustrating himself in the process of describing the cityscape, the artist denoted the particular mode of chorography: an image of the city as a whole presented from a distant vantage point. Artists depicted the surrounding landscape and delineated the contours of a city's walls, as shown here, a process that facilitated visual comparisons between cities. Recognition depended upon replication, an effect magnified by the dissemination of multiple prints of the same visual concept. Both the mode and the medium consolidated an image of the city seen from a specific place, and the repetition of earlier models cemented its distinctive shape in the eye of the observer. The draftsman depicted in the foreground reiterates the overlap between the work of the chorographer and the medium of print. Seated inside the space of the representation, the figure doubles for the artist, reiterating both his earlier act of transcription and his presence there. The artist is both counterfeiter and counterfeited.

The city walls define the frontiers of Florentine citizenship, a message restated by the chain that surrounds the image. Each link reiterates the form of the walls, which are themselves connected together by towers to resemble the links of the chain that symbolically circumscribes limits of civic identity. If the draftsman inside this frame attests to his eyewitness perspective, the trompe l'oeil chain simultaneously throws authenticity into doubt. The padlock casts a shadow, whose transience signals the ephemeral status of print. Moreover, this gesture to the referent – to the presence of the object that caused the shadow – is another play on the act of representation. Similarly, the links of the chain, as duplicates, function as a signature for the printmaker's work. Falling on the sky, the shadow undermines the mimetic illusion constructed by the perspective view as it also signals the distance between the surface of the printed sheet and the lock that is situated closer to the space of the viewer. Drawn into the city by the veracity of the perspectival illusion on one side, the trompe l'oeil chain situates the viewer symbolically and figuratively on the outside. The *cartolino* that identifies Florence by name appears to have slipped, as if to challenge the association between the name and the identity of the image which is the claim of the *contra factum*.

In contrast to the print of Florence, in which the identification of buildings is facilitated by their rotated façades, the woodcut of Venice is overlaid with inscriptions and toponyms that play with the viewer's perception of surface and depth. For example, the Palazzo Ducale resembles the government building and it is identified by name with the letters PA LA CI VI. Carved into the woodblock, the label draws attention to the function of the map as a text.[55] The use of toponyms would have taught viewers how to interpret the woodcut, to recognize the relation between signifier and signified, between naming and seeing. The combination of image and text mobilizes the observer's movement across the surface of the picture plane.

Moreover, in contrast to the Rosselli design, in which the surface of the picture corresponds to the section through the visual pyramid according to the rules of perspective, the de'Barbari woodcut combines viewpoints that correspond to the two cartographic systems of representation described earlier. The perspectival axis situates the viewer high above the city from where the lagoon circles the islands as if city walls, a picture of independence enhanced by the centripetal force of the surrounding wind gods. Seen from this Olympian vantage point, Venice appears before the viewer as if conjured from the sea, as if a priori to the artist's work. Instead of the artist transcribing the city for the viewer, Venice, like Venus, appears from the sea as if fully formed, performing its own chorography, exposing itself.[56]

One effect of this cartographic auto-description has been persistent doubts concerning attribution. The absence of a name either on the print or in Kolb's supplication to the senate has provoked questions among scholars as to the identity of the artist. Not surprisingly, the extent of de'Barbari's authorship is less secure among those scholars favouring a scientific explanation than among those who interpret the woodcut as an artistic conceptualization.[57]

A number of historical and stylistic factors substantiate de'Barbari's involvement in the print, including the prominent caduceus held by Mercury, a trademark used by the artist in subsequent prints. Curiously, the function of the caduceus has prompted uncertainty since it already functions as an attribute for Mercury.[58] Because this is the first time the caduceus appears in a print designed by the artist, the iconographical evidence suggests that it is the mythical figure himself with whom de'Barbari identified. In a discussion of the etymology of hermeneutics – and Hermes, the Greek equivalent – Eric Hirsch explains that 'everything that belongs to the realm of understanding is attributed to him, particularly speech and writing.'[59] This association was reiterated in

1538, when Jacopo Sansovino included a sculptural relief of the ancient deity in the Logetta, a structure he designed for the Procurators, to signify the long history of 'letters and eloquence' in the Republic.[60] Furthermore, Mercury stands at the boundary between the imaginary and real, 'translat[ing] the infinite into the finite, the divine spirit into sensible appearance.'[61] From his lofty position in the print, the winged messenger communicates his dispatch by pointing to the inscription and the city that he has brought to light below. As de'Barbari's alter ego, Mercury literally and figuratively circulates his description through print in which the ideal and the real overlap.

This self-reflective engagement with both the medium and naturalism is brought forward by the faces of the wind gods, each of which is depicted differently. This unconventional practice of individuating the physiognomies of the winds highlights the analogy between geography and portraiture that circulated in editions of Ptolemy's *Geographia* (fig. 6).

> The aim of the chorographer is to represent only one part, as if one were to imitate or to paint only one ear, or an eye. But the aim of the geographer is to consider the universal whole in the guise of those who describe or paint the entire head. Therefore in all those figures or images that we propose to portray or represent, it is suitable firstly to accommodate and to arrange the primary or principal parts, and that these are duly situated, and with measurements and proportions that correspond sufficiently to their distance in sight, because either the whole or the particular are what one is able to sensibly understand.[62]

Allusions to both chorography and geography are evident in the map. For the latter, sources available to de'Barbari include the anthropomorphic winds that circled a map of the world from Francesco Berlinghieri's edition of Ptolemy's *Geographia*, first published in Florence around 1480 (fig. 7). Four wind gods surround a diagram of the world on a sheet from Hartmann Schedel's *Weltchronik* (*Nuremberg Chronicle*), a book that Kolb was selling in Venice before 1499 (fig. 8).[63] This cosmological model of the earth at the centre of the universe was typical of medieval *mappaemundi* in which Jerusalem was situated at the centre of concentric circles that signified the pilgrim's journey to the Holy Land.[64] An earlier Venetian example was designed by the Pizigani – mapmakers who worked in Venice – for their representation of Venice and Genoa, cities engaged in the battle of Chioggia (1380) for trading supremacy in the Mediterranean. Views of the two cities, identified by distinctive architec-

CHOROGRAPHIA QVID.

 Horographia autem (Vernero dicente) quæ & Topographia dicitur, partialia quædam loca seorsum & absolutè considerat, absque eorum ad seinuicem, & ad vniuersum telluris ambitum comparatione. Omnia siquidem, ac ferè minima in eis contenta tradit & prosequitur. Velut portus, villas, populos, riuulorum quoque decursus, & quæcunque alia illis finitima, vt sunt ædificia, domus, turres, mœnia. &c. Finis verò eiusdem in effigienda partilius loci similitudine consummabitur: veluti si pictor aliquis aurem tantùm aut oculum designaret depingeretque.

Figure 6   Peter Apian (Apianus, Petrus), after Ptolemy, *Cosmographia ... per Gemmam Frisium ... ab omnibus vindicata mendis* (Antwerp: Gregoria Bontio, 1550). Woodcut, 4° [photo: by permission of the British Library London] C.114.e.2.(2.)

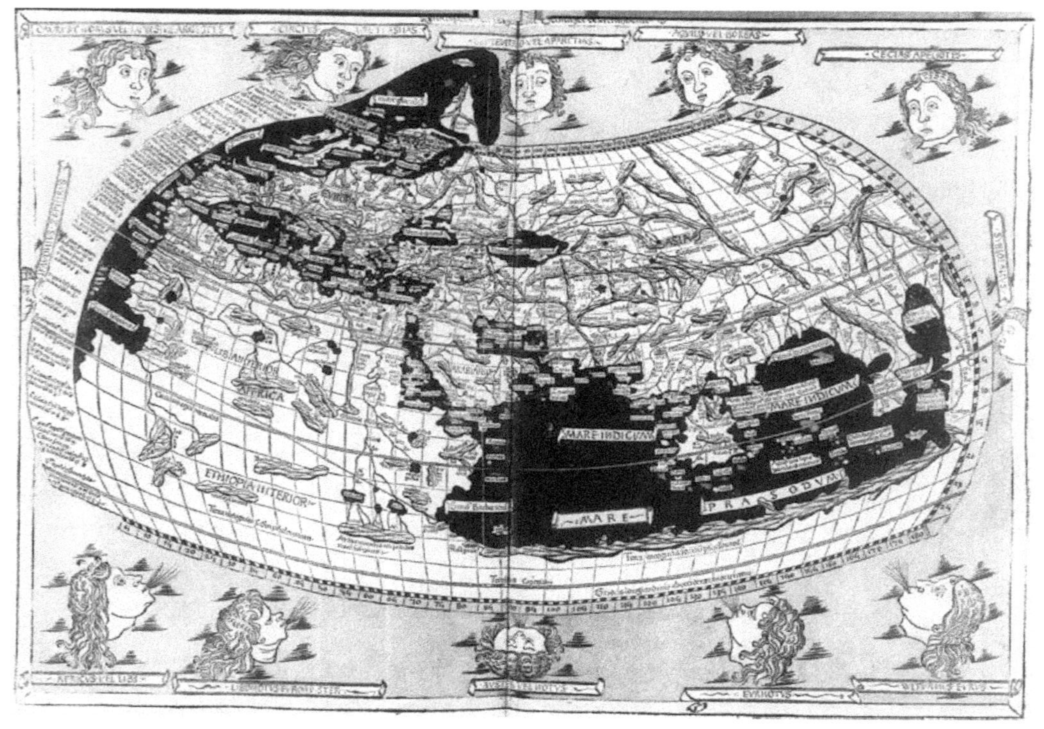

Figure 7   *World Map.* Francesco Berlinghieri, Marsilio Ficino, Ptolemy, *Geographia* (Florence: Nicolaus Germanus, 1482) [photo: Newberry Library, Chicago]

De sanctificatione septime diei

Onsummato igitur mundo: per fabricam diuine solercie sex dierum. Creati em dispositi z ornati tandé pfecti sunt celi z terra. Compleuit de gliosus opus suú: z requieuit die septimo ab opib[us] manuum suarú: postq[ue] cúctum mundú: z omnia que in eo sunt creasset: nó quasi operando lassus: sed nouam creaturam facere cessasit: cuius materia vel similitudo non precesserit. Opus enim propagationis operari non desinit. Et dominus eidem diei benedixit: z sanctificauit illú: vocáutq[ue] ipsum Sabatú quod nomen hebraica lingua requiem significat. Eo q[ue] in ipso cessauerat ab om̄i opere q[ue] patrarat. Un z Judei eo die a laboribus proprijs vacare dignoscitur. Quem z ante leges certe gentes celebrem obseruarunt. Jamq[ue] ad calcem ventum est operum diuinorum. Illum ergo timeamus: amemus: z veneremur. In quo sunt omnia siue visibilia siue inuisibilia. Et a domino celi: domino bonor[um] om̄iú. Cui data om̄is potestas in celo z in terra. Et presentia bona: quatenus bona sint. Et veram eterne vite felicitatem quera/mus.

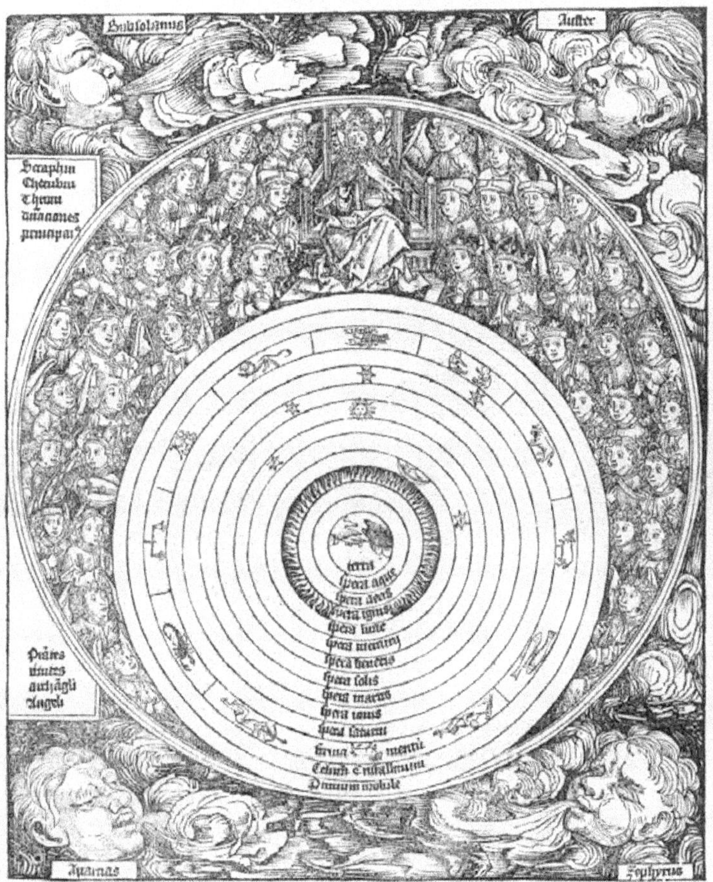

Figure 8   *De sanctificatione septime diei* (*Welt- und Sternenkreis*), Hartmann Schedel, *Nuremberg Weltchronik* (Nuremberg, 1493). Woodcut, folio [photo: Bildarchiv Preußischer Kulturbesitz]

tural monuments, like those seen on nautical charts, were each placed in the centre of their own worlds, represented as the concentric circles of cosmological diagrams. In the Kolb and de'Barbari woodcut, the theological frame of the cosmological view has been subsumed by the classical one, the islands of Venice substituted for earth, and the diagram of the planets reconfigured as a wind rose. Cosmology and cartography have been fused into a synchronic view of Venice as a world unto itself, the centre of the universe toward which the winds blow.[65] Seen from the eye of God, Venice appears as an exemplar of divine order.

One of the wind gods, seen at the far right, stands out on account of the specificity of the facial features (fig. 9). If the face of this Greek wind is a self-portrait, as Giuseppe Mazzariol and Terisio Pignatti suggested on the basis of a posthumous portrait of de'Barbari, the face might be understood as a signature.[66] Regardless of whether or not the face is a transcription of the artist's own reflection, it functions as an analogue for a range of activities associated with the woodcut: the artist's work of mimesis, the mirror image of the print from the block, and the notion of duplication inherent in both resemblance and the mirror. These are ideas to which I return in chapter 4.

Gesturing toward the city from a cloud, Mercury's own bird's-eye view directs viewers toward the evidentiary details of the cityscape. By mediating between the ideal and the real, weaving the parts into a stunning vision of the whole, de'Barbari becomes the mercurial trickster who slips between the visible world of the representation and the imaginary surface of the map. Thus it is not surprising that de'Barbari adopted the caduceus as a signature after making the woodcut, for it may have been through the making of the print that his own identity converged with that of Mercury.

Territories and Politics

The faintly adumbrated landscape at the upper edge of the woodcut minimizes the vast scale of the mainland territories (figs. 3, 4). The bird's-eye view thereby reinforces the city's historical origins and the significance of the sea while downplaying the extent of the state's dominion that claimed some 77,000 square kilometres at the end of the fifteenth century. This impulse is made clear when the de'Barbari woodcut, and printed maps of Venice in general, are contrasted with the miniature view that identifies Venice on a sixteenth-century Ottoman navigational chart; the Ottoman illuminator has reduced the central islands to a mere

Figure 9   Detail, Jacopo de'Barbari, *Venetie.* Printed by Anton Kolb in Venice, 1500. Woodcut, 135 × 282 cm [photo: Newberry Library, Chicago]

appendage of the sprawling and lush landscape of the terraferma.[67] This disjunction between the city's self-promotion – as the Serenissima, that most serene of republics – and the perception of outsiders points to mounting criticism that was directed toward Venetian expansion. The state was pressed both to justify and to refashion its image, a campaign manifested in the official histories of Marcantonio Sabellico and Bernardo Giustinian, penned in 1490 and 1493 respectively; with their detailed description and emphasis on mythic origins, both provide parallels for de'Barbari's pictorial expression.[68] Only a few years after the woodcut view was first printed, the military and expansionist aims of Venice were checked by the League of Cambrai, when all of Europe became uncharacteristically united in their opposition to the republic.

The city's political foundations at Rialto dominate these accounts.[69] Marin Sanuto celebrated the Venetian dominion in his *Itinerario,* but he omitted settlements outside of the centre in his *De origine,* a work, like the histories of Giorgio Dolfin and guide books of Francesco Sansovino, that misrepresented the gradual migration from the mainland in favour of an epic *traslatio* in which 'the second is born when the first dies.'[70] As a secure refuge, the singular geography provided the foundation for a myth that fused peace and liberty. 'Never conquered by any ruler,' as Girolamo Priuli explained at the beginning of the sixteenth century, Venice was '*virginea.*'[71] 'Preserved' from foreign domination, the republic was protected by the narrow canals of its anatomical landscape, a focus of the city's cosmogony.

The longevity of the republic was tied to the rejection of magnificence, a complex process of concealing emerging tensions in the service of presenting a unified image. As explained by Nicolò Zen in his *Dell'origine,* Zeno Daula planned 'for greater equality and similarity ... to leave the palaces and magnificent residences in order for the one not to overcome the other; fixing by law, that all residences should be equal, alike, of similar size and ornamentation.'[72] In the print, the emergence of the harmonious cityscape from the sea appears to be a manifestation of the republic's founding resolutions. Both the city's appearance in 1500 and its mythic origins were conveyed through the combination of the lofty view of the city's contours and its mimetic details; the present was made to emerge quite literally from the past, an effect that dramatized the teleology through which history and image appeared to be self-fulfilling.

During the years in which the wooduct was produced, the state was facing a number of pressures from both east and west. Waning economic and military power, dissolution of links to the sea, and factional struggles among patricians contributed to the city's shift from its traditional Byzantine orientation toward new interests on the mainland. The surrender of numerous eastern colonies, bank failures, and the discovery of trade routes by the Portuguese precipitated new industries and investment on the terraferma, changing not only the economic orientation but also the political orientation of the state.[73] Venetian dominance on the terraferma could be either justified or neglected as required by the aims of the writer. But an intriguing aspect of the woodcut is that it could do both. If, on one side, the subordination of the lagoon environment offered an antidote to widespread criticism of Venetian expansion, the fortress of mountains, moatlike sea, and impressive naval and mercantile activity could also assert the city's maritime power at a moment of crisis.

Little is known about who purchased the prints. Although five out of twelve sets from the first state are currently in Venice, inventories of Venetian households do not record the presence of local maps. We do know that the substantial cost of three florins would have limited the market to those of some wealth.[74] Moreover, Kolb's application for tax relief stipulated his aim of selling the prints 'in all your lands and cities.' Given the publisher's intentions to export the prints outside the capital, but within the dominion, the novelty of the view for Venetians, and the cost, perhaps the publisher targeted those Venetians buying palaces on the mainland. Although the complexities of territorial politics were surely not the driving force behind Kolb, a foreigner, and de'Barbari, a printmaker, nevertheless, some reflections on this historical context may provide insights into the perceptions of viewers in the years following the woodcut's production.

Noble status in Venice was the prerogative of 5 per cent of the population and traced through blood lineage back to the fourteenth century. In contrast to the peninsula, where noble blood was tied to landholding outside the city, the wealth of Venetian patricians developed through trade, and their prestige through building on the islands in the city. However, by the beginning of the sixteenth century nobles had developed a distaste for commerce that went hand in hand with praise for the princely life.[75] As the sharply observant Girolamo Priuli noted, not without a touch of acerbity, the terraferma provided greater comfort, honour, and glory:[76]

Before these forefathers of ours had the *terraferma* they devoted themselves to voyages and navigation to the great advantage and emolument of the city and they earned much money each year, and yet they were not renowned throughout the world and were regarded as fishermen. Whereas, having conquered the *stato* of the mainland, they have gained great reputation and name on that account and are much esteemed and appreciated and honored by the *signori* of the world and are respected by all.[77]

In the capital, by contrast, displays of wealth were limited by the Provveditori alle pompe, who legislated against lavish spending on banquets, birth festivities, decoration of houses, and sartorial display. A decree of 1495 cited the damage caused by 'excessive and fruitless expenses' and the danger of these private costs to the public interest.[78] Public and private architecture were under the purview of the Provveditori, who ordered in 1505 that estimates be provided for buildings, new or restored, in the interests of maintaining civic harmony. As a decree stipulated in 1514, the ornamentation of women and houses was potentially ruinous to nobles and citizens.[79] The state's mainland holdings, by contrast, offered spaces for the display of wealth limited by the density of the capital's urban context and censured by the myth of conformity and equality. Gentrification of the terraferma, in short, allowed the Venetian nobility to become 'territorial princes,' thus elevating themselves politically and socially.

Critics of these aristocrats, like Domenico Morosini, complained about their avarice.[80] Written between 1497 and his death in 1509, his treatise *De bene instituta re publica* develops a utopian image of Venice, but one that is always set in relation to the real city.[81] For Morosini, expansion on the terraferma is antithetical to his concept of the republic, which is instead tied to the city's maritime history.[82] Following his death, devastating losses on the mainland to the League of Cambrai, however short-lived, fuelled criticism against excesses of display on the terraferma and sumptuary legislation routinely included the mainland.[83] Doge Leonardo Loredan (1501–21), reiterating the deathbed plea made by his predecessor Tommaso Mocenigo a century earlier, called for Venetians to reaffirm their historical and spatial destiny with the sea.[84] In 1509 Priuli restated the need for a return to 'the sea and voyages of trade, and beyond the profit,' he urged, 'we will produce brave men, skilled in the use of the sea and in every other way, and perhaps this will be of more benefit to the Venetian Republic than the revenues of the *terraferma*.'[85] Where patricians benefited from a growing agricultural economy and the pleasures of an aristocratic lifestyle on the mainland, their status depended on their position in the city.

The double registers in the map might have resulted from pragmatic efforts to combine views of the city from its various *campanili*, with the distant view of the Alps as they appear when seen from the north. Nevertheless, their topographical and iconographic focus on the central islands and merchant galleys – the foundations upon which the Venetian patriciate had been established and defined – may have appealed to interests on both sides. The print even seems to accommodate this double focus. If the economic and social value of the terraferma is understated by the reduction of its vast expanse, the large scale of the image and the stereographic perspective (constructed as if seen by a standing figure) of the distant land constructs an impression of a horizon, expanding far beyond where the eye can see. Toponyms and naturalistic detail, moreover, ensure that locations on the mainland can be identified. If purchased by patricians for their mainland residences, the woodcut could have functioned as a form of pedigree, a sign of their Venetian identity. At the same time, the picture would have appealed to critics of the exodus since it reasserts those traditional values that were being undermined by this aristocratic ethos.[86]

It was a broader foreign audience, however, that may have interested the senate. Although they denied Kolb's appeal for an exemption from taxes, they stipulated that the prints could be exported beyond the boundaries of the dominion. Not surprisingly, perhaps, the visual emphases and exclusions could also be used to assuage critics of Venetian imperialism by redefining the city's image abroad. In the fifteenth century imperialism was justified as security against the expansionist aims of neighbouring principalities. Self-promotion as a peaceful republic was an antidote to the antagonistic boasting of conquests.[87] Indeed, Venice had already served as a model of political order and cohesiveness for Florence following the expulsion of the Medici in 1494.[88] It is the remarkable fusion of ideas that makes the woodcut extraordinary. The city could be interpreted as a powerful state with massive military resources, manifested in the expansive size of the Arsenale, and the centre of a trading empire, with its impressive fleet of galleys, *and* as an independent and isolated island, a utopia rendered with staggering presence by de'Barbari's dazzling realism.

Double Vision

Seen both from above and close at hand, the de'Barbari woodcut brings together the geographer's scientific interest in the plan and position of Venice with the chorographer's depiction of the city's form. 'Geographers,' explains Tommaso Garzoni, are those who imitate (as Claudius Ptolemy says) the design of all the Earth that is known to us, noting in plan, or on raised sections, lands and cities, not with their own form, as one makes in a design, but only with little signs, or round points, or small little squares, that imitate more rapidly the design, than a little sketch of the real site. And they are rather different to Chorographers because these actually paint and draw from nature the form and figure of places, and cities in particular, such as one would draw the land around Rome or around Naples. Besides this, chorographers attend more to the quality of places, representing their true figures and their likenesses. Geographers are the opposite, attending more to quantity, by describing sizes, sites, and proportion of distances.[89]

From the geographer's vantage point, the contours of the landscape appear fixed. Geographers considered the landscape in quantitative terms by organizing relations between autonomous sites, and by securing the location and identity of points on a map with names. By contrast, chorographers attended to the qualities of a city, its singular features that reflect the mobile gaze of human experience: the contingent spatial relationships of temporality. These are ideas associated with the body, and here, the toponyms identify places, such as the Venetian districts. As already suggested, these two representational modes overlap in the de'Barbari woodcut.

The large image is not only a representation of an ideal republic but a model of how this ideal operates. The naturalistic depiction would have encouraged viewers to progress through the city's *calle* that emerge with precise clarity from the web of marks made by the woodcutter's tool, traversing the map and choosing from a multiplicity of possible routes. The viewer's own movement across the vast surface of the print's details, glancing from place to place, corresponds to the temporality and particulars of lived experiences of the city in which identity is constituted by the accretions of perceptions absorbed through looking. As one moves away from the surface, however, the evidentiary quality of the cityscape dissolves. Instead it is the outlines of the city and the classical frame that come into focus, arresting the viewer's gaze. An ideal, unchanging image, Venice appears to be frozen in time, an impression reinforced by the presence of the name and date, which together reassert the picture's status as representation, as a sign.[90]

The Florence perspective (in fig. 5) celebrates the civic ideology of magnificence through architectural display, since key buildings are turned to face the viewer, who is positioned as if standing on the hill.

The single point of view provides an illusion of control, even ownership, of the object of representation, a perception, as Tommasso Garzoni would define it a century later, of sight as 'a powerful perspective ... [that] apprehends visible objects for its singular propriety.'[91] However, in the de'Barbari woodcut, the bird's-eye view is inaccessible; the distant point is always beyond that of the viewer, thereby thwarting control of the object. The structure of the representation situates the viewer within the perspectival cone of vision, as if he or she is standing inside a camera obscura, between the point of projection and the image inscribed on the surface. The god's-eye view of the geographer is used to construct a republican image that is both specific and expressly imaginary, and that also conveys the Venetian rejection of magnificence, the subordination of the individual to the collective. The double registers provide a visual expression of the state's urban policies and political ideologies that humanists would equate with the idea of *unanimitas,* which Margaret King defines as: 'the convergence of a multitude of wants and aspirations into a single will.'[92]

This synoptic structure of the bird's-eye view would have encouraged viewers to move between the general and particular, the 'harmonious totality' that Louis Marin identifies with utopic description.[93] The point of utopia, for Marin, is its existence *as* representation, a fiction that rationalizes rather than reconciles historical contradictions.[94] The two systems that operate in the de'Barbari view can never be synthesized; it is impossible to perceive the topographical particulars and the contours of the city at the same time. The eyewitness experience of the city resembles republican space in which the mobile spectator moves from place to place, free from the surveillance of the prince as theorized by contemporaries. By contrast, the distant view reveals that the subject's mobile agency is only an impression.[95] The pictorial representation of this Olympian gaze is not the view of the bird, nor is it analogous with the eye of the prince, since the viewer can never adopt the vantage point. Instead the overlapping registers in the picture resonate with Nicholas of Cusa's explanation of God's ubiquitous vision outlined in the Introduction.

Close up, viewers move through the city, like Cusa's monks walking in the church, while the high viewpoint recalls Cusa's description of the distant point in his geometrical diagram as a point of 'quasi-nothingness' (*prope nihil*) whose 'fecundity' enables a '*generation of a space.*'[96] The bird's-eye view might therefore be understood to suggest God's omnipresence as a field of vision.[97] This image resonates with Paolo

Paruta's later description of the universe in *Della perfettione della vita polit-ica*: 'Man is placed in this world as in a theater in which God sits as spectator of his actions.'[98] Paruta's interlocutor, Michele Surian, is defending active participation in civic life, and it is this phenomenological idea of the republic – the crowd in the street – that is brought together in the woodcut with the ideal one: the singular cityscape managed by the ruling elites.[99] Topographical and constitutional facts become mutually sustaining in this realization of an exemplary secular and independent state that anticipates Gasparo Contarini's 'orderly society which in turn reflects hierarchical cosmic order.'[100]

On one level, then, the bird's-eye view rationalizes the singularly Venetian construction of the individual as inescapable from the whole. On another level these two conceptual strategies verify the city's authenticity, for it was through the viewer's act of looking that the ideal and the real were made to overlap, each attesting to the facticity of the other.[101] Finally, the map's twofold system of visualizing the city inaugurates the cleaving apart of time and space that continues to unfold through the century.

Diagramming Space and Time

> There is needed ... a twofold map, [composed] of painting and writing. Nor wilt thou deem one sufficient without the other, because painting without writing indicates regions or nations unclearly, [and] writing without the aid of painting, truly does not mark the boundaries of the provinces of a region in their various parts sufficiently [clearly] for them to be described almost at a glance.[102]
>
> Fra Paolino Veneto

Anton Kolb and Jacopo de'Barbari's immense bird's-eye view became the touchstone for subsequent maps of Venice. And yet the sheer audacity of the representation – artistically and technically – precluded direct emulation in scale or detail. Although numerous views of Venice followed, the image was not copied closely until 1635, when it was engraved on a much-reduced scale by Matteus Merian and published in Cologne.[103] The combination of registers in one comprehensive representation was not to be repeated. Illustrators oscillated between resemblance and abstraction, but the diagrammatic clarity of the latter, facilitated by the use of copperplate engraving, soon replaced the former. In contrast to de'Barbari's phenomenological descriptiveness inside the representation, the viewer's experience of the city migrated to the frame that surrounds the image. Perceptions of the city became filtered through the legends, texts, perspective views, and processions that began to surround the image.

The Textblock and Copperplate Engraving

Between 1517 and 1525 the woodcutter and book printer Giovanni Andrea Vavassore followed de'Barbari's model.[104] The rhythmic fenestration of the latter has been replaced by a vigorous herringbone patchwork of rooflines and waterways; a concise textblock in Italian has been substituted for the classical iconography and Latin inscriptions: 'as you see depicted here in the middle of a maritime lagoon ... This city has an immeasurable number of people who come together from all parts of the world for trade.'[105] Vavassore's deictic address to the viewer – 'as you see depicted here' – parallels the mode of representation he deployed in the image; viewers can see for themselves that the city is filled with goods from galleys that have been spirited to the city by the enthusiastic efforts of the wind gods.

Vavassore's mimetic image was used later as a model by Matteo Pagan, who published two woodcuts of Venice of different sizes around 1560.[106] In a textblock on the smaller woodcut (410 × 585 mm), perhaps targeting a foreign audience unfamiliar with Venice, Pagan explained that a cartographer's work was 'to describe the site, the structure of the place, its origins, the inhabitants, and the prosperity of the place, and when the place that one is discussing is unknown, one strives to make it more clear to the eye and the mind of the viewer and reader.'[107] The small scale of the bird's-eye view required a selective description of the urban landscape in order to provide a clear image.[108] In the larger print (770 × 1652 mm), produced slightly later, Pagan attempted to illustrate the full gamut of the city's geography that he listed in the accompanying textblock: the six *sestieri*, seventy-two *contrade*, forty-four monasteries, and 450 public and private bridges.[109] For further information on dress and customs, Pagan directs his readers to the twelve-page guidebook *Le bellezze di Vinegia*, authored by Francesco Sansovino under the pseudonym of Anselmo Guisconi, published in 1556. The tract begins with a foreigner's impression of Venice as 'l'impossibile nell'impossibile.' Indeed, the visual disorder caused by the proliferation of details in the woodcut demonstrates the difficulty of translating the unique site and the particulars of the urban context into a single coherent image.[110] Sansovino constructed his pamphlet as a dialogue between a foreigner and a Venetian who guides the foreigner through the city, responding to his queries.

The use of textblocks points toward a shift in technology in the second half of the century, when engraving eclipsed the use of woodblocks for maps.[111] Text was an essential component of map production, both within the image and for legends, and it could be achieved with greater fineness and speed on copperplates both manually and with the use of letter punches. Despite the much lower cost of woodcuts, the rapidity with which an image could be engraved enabled changes in geographical knowledge to be rapidly circulated. For city maps in particular, engraving provided the means for small-scale detail and the use of text.

In Paolo Forlani's engraving of Venice, published by Bolognino Zaltieri in 1566 (fig. 10), the printmaker explains the convenience of the small format afforded by the technology. The fine detail, he boasts, invites comparison with his predecessors. Indeed, the two copperplates could be printed on a single large sheet (437 × 744 mm), which was a dramatic reduction from the six (and sometimes twelve) sheets required for the six blocks of de'Barbari's woodcut (1350 × 2820 mm).[112] The small format prompted a reconceptualization of the urban landscape and the use of topographical conventions. Individual residences were replaced with symbols, and verisimilitude was abandoned in favour of a visual clarity that highlights particular sites. Around Piazza San Marco, for example, landmarks are set into relief by expanses of white ground. As if dissecting de'Barbari's urban organism, Forlani exposed the structural skeleton and the tendon-like bridges that connect the parishes together. The accompanying legend, with more than 200 references, was literally riveted to the plate with the bird's-eye view, and this legibility contributed to the map's status as the model for printed views of Venice for the next fifty years.[113]

The use of a legend – a new invention – was explained the following year by Leandro Alberti. On the verso of his map of Venice, one of the many city views included in his *Isolario appartenenti alla Italia*, Alberti remarks on the impossibility of picturing all the bridges, churches, and details in a small format; 'however, we have supplied in part with this legend, a letter or number that corresponds to the church, or other thing that one wants; that number or letter then, one will find in the figure, and where it is, will be the place looked for; and conversely, having found the letter or number in the figure, and then located it in the legend, one will be able to know what place it is.'[114] The forty-nine toponyms functioned as a supplement to the small format, a key with which the viewer could link the sites in the picture to their names in the text.

In contrast to the de'Barbari woodcut, in which the vast scale and

Figure 10   Paolo Forlani, *Venetia*. Printed by Bolognino Zaltieri in Venice, 1566. Engraving, 437 × 744 mm [photo: Museo Correr, Venice]

complex detail elicit the physical movement of viewers, the key in the Forlani map compels the viewer to navigate between the image and the text. Roman numerals in the legend identify canals in the map that progress sequentially, tracing a path that enables the viewer to circumnavigate the islands visually. The Arabic numerals, on the other hand, identify the city's *contrade*, but these are ordered according to a different strategy. In contrast with the city's waterways, the Arabic numbers bear little relation to a pedestrian's movement; clearly the engraving was not intended to assist the foreigner's navigation within Venice. Despite Alberti's emphasis on the reciprocity between the image and the legend, it would take some time for a foreigner, having identified a district in the key, to locate the corresponding number in the bird's-eye view. Instead, and more easily, a viewer could select a number from the image and identify the site by name in the legend. In some cases, such as the equestrian statue of Bartolomeo Coleone (n. 134; near the middle of the map) or the buildings around Piazza San Marco, a visitor might recognize a monument seen in the city with its place in the map, and then identify it by name through the legend. Subsequent mapmakers did not repeat Forlani's exhaustive legend to the city's canals, *contrade*, churches, and specific monuments. Instead, it was the *contrada*, the unit of residence that identified every Venetian, that became the standard.

The symbolic function of this system is brought forward in Georg Braun's *Civitates orbis terrarum* (1572–1618). The six volumes included city views engraved by Franz Hogenberg and Simon Novellanus among others, and these were accompanied by descriptive texts in Latin that were later translated into German and French (fig. 11).[115] Braun was a friend, and Hogenberg a colleague, of Ortelius, whose atlas was published two years before the *Civitates*, an endeavour that corresponded in geographical scope and scientific interest. Venice and Rome are among those cities represented in the first volume, and the differences between them are revealing. The map of Rome concentrates on the city's ancient monuments that are listed in the key below. In the map of Venice, by contrast, viewers would select a number from the map and then match it to the name of the district in the legend, thereby incorporating the parts into the whole.

In the centre of this emblematic legend, the engraver has reproduced a detail from Matteo Pagan's famous woodcut of a ducal procession (fig. 12).[116] When joined together, the eight folio sheets (520 × 380 mm) create a woodcut that measures four metres long, a format well suited for the emphasis on the position of those in the cortege, which preoccu-

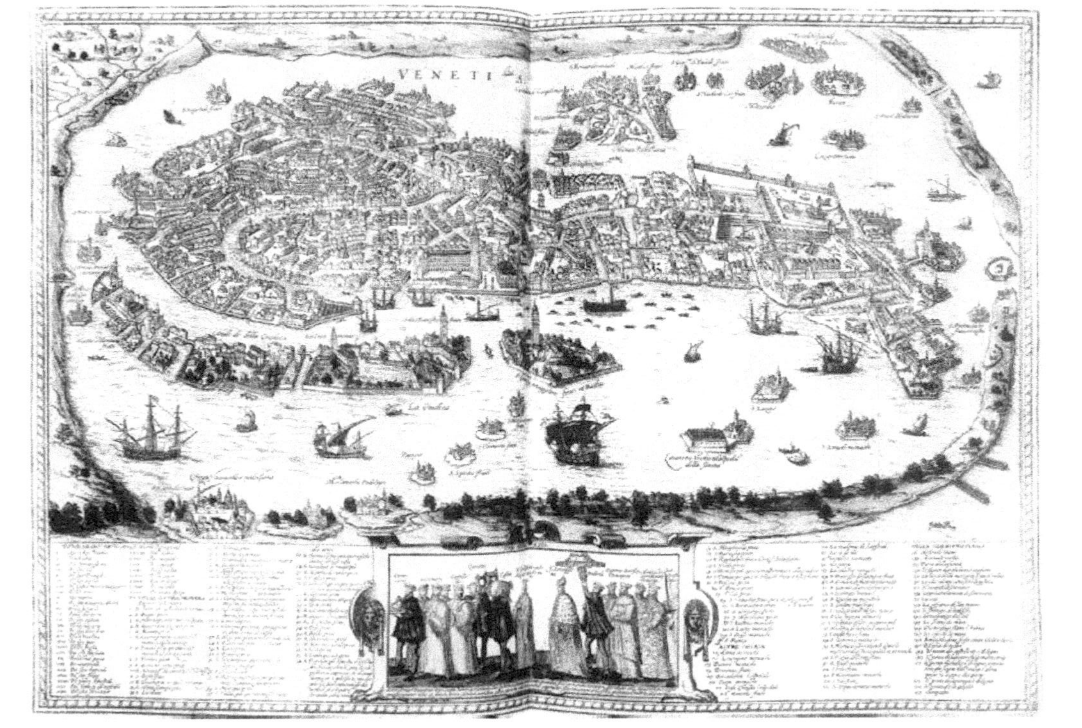

Figure 11   *Venetia*, Georg Braun, *Civitates orbis terrarum* (Cologne, 1572). Hand-coloured engraving, 337 × 482 mm [photo: Newberry Library, Chicago]

pied chroniclers. Above the arcades of the procurators' offices, which act as a metaphor for the orderly cortege, women and foreigners participate as spectators. Sartorial and symbolic accoutrements – the candle, *corno* (ducal cap), chair, cushion, umbrella, and sword – are depicted with Pagan's topographical eye, but these are also identified with labels for those unfamiliar with Venetian ritual. Moreover, since the patriarch and the doge did not appear together in the ducal processions repeated throughout the year, their presence here, with the Alexandrine gifts listed above, are signs of Venetian religious and political independence.[117] In the context of the Braun map, however, neither the patriarch, nor the *ballotino*, the young ducal attendant who signified the elected principle of the ducal office, are included (fig. 11). More important here is the political ideal of the republic; the doge – emblematic of the monarchical element of the constitution's mixed government and representative of the ruling nobility – is preceded by the grand chancellor, the single representative of the citizen class in the government. Instead of highlighting the doge's role as an elected figurehead whose power was rigorously circumscribed, the parade demonstrates the social structure of the republic and its political autonomy, ideals underscored by the Alexandrine gifts, list of districts in the legend, and the bird's-eye view, which has been altered accordingly. The terraferma and Lido, designed to mirror each other, contribute to an image of Venice as an autonomous and well-arranged universe.

Coupling the unique physical body of the city with its unparalleled political institutions was a familiar convention, and one that circulated widely in the introduction to Contarini's *De magistratibus et republica Venetorum* (1543).[118] For Contarini, it was the well-ordered institutions of the republic that enabled imperfect humans to subordinate their individual interests to the public good. These ideals were explicitly linked to the urban fabric of Venice, where the 'beauty and splendor' of the city's landscape were celebrated as physical manifestations of 'its excellent government.'[119] Contarini's reconstruction of the myth of Venice followed losses to the Ottoman Empire, bank failures, and the discovery of trade routes by the Portuguese at the end of the fifteenth century. More serious than these economic losses, however, was the diminished state of the city's military power, demonstrated by the League of Cambrai in 1509, to which Contarini responded when he formulated an idea of Venice that 'preserv[ed] that part of his *patria* which war could not destroy,' writes Elisabeth Gleason, 'and which had meaning far beyond its boundaries.'[120] Better than the utopian dreams of philosophers, as

Figure 12 Detail, Matteo Pagan, *Procession of the Doge and Patriarch of Venice*, c.1560. Woodcut, eight sheets, 520 × 380 mm [photo, Museo Correr, Venice]

Contarini proclaimed, the political order of the Venetian state 'reflects hierarchical cosmic order.' His teleological account of migration elevated the status of the founding families: 'the flower of nobility of all towns in the region of Venetia were assembled together.' Venice provided a living example of Contarini's reconceptualization of the state as a utopian republic. Numerous editions of his treatise proffered Venice as a model of government for the 'political education of Europe' in the latter decades of the sixteenth century.[121]

The cityscape published by Braun, with its list of districts in the legend and ducal cartouche, can be understood as a mutually sustaining triad that functions allegorically. To adapt William Empson's definition, the print impresses on the viewer the sense that the three levels 'correspond to each other in detail and indeed that there is some underlying reality, something in the nature of things, which makes this happen ... But the effect of allegory is to keep the ... levels of being very distinct in your mind though they interpenetrate each other in so many details.'[122] The system of *contrade* has become emblematic of the resident's fixed, immutable place in the Venetian *mondo*, a sign of the city's unique social and political geography. While Venetians were preoccupied with the complex details of rank and order, for the wider European audience to whom the *Civitates* was addressed, the engraving would have exported a myth of the city in which the individual districts were transmuted into the astounding cityscape through the wise stewardship of the government.

Both projects – Braun's *Civitates* and Forlani's bird's-eye view – were made possible by engraving. Although woodcuts were less expensive than intaglio because of the large number of sheets that could be printed from a block, engraving was faster, and thus responsive to a market fuelled by news, events, and geographical discoveries.[123] Indeed, Braun's engraving of Venice likely provided the impetus for Giacomo Franco's entrepreneurial idea. In 1597, Venetians and visitors witnessed the coronation of the dogaressa, the doge's wife, an event not seen in the city for four decades.[124] Franco produced three versions of the same bird's-eye view by altering the legend that initially accompanied it (figs. 66, 67). In the first version figures of the doge and dogaressa, framed by a cartouche, were inserted in the middle of the legend (fig. 66). As Giocondo Cassini has proposed, the generic figures suggest that Franco had not yet witnessed the event.[125] The absence of a dedication suggests Franco's enterprise was prompted by the incipient festivities and the presence of visitors for whom a view of the city as a souvenir would be enhanced with an image of the ducal couple. This was replaced with two miniature details of the event in the second version, and in the third, the entire legend was replaced by two horizontal processions.

On the basis of information provided by the contemporary writer Vittorio Zonca, and given the reduced clarity of the map in the third version, the bird's-eye view could have produced close to a thousand impressions.[126] As Domenico Tempesti's seventeenth-century information suggests, Franco's workshop was unlikely to pull more than thirty large prints in a day, indicating that Franco would have required about thirty-three working days before the plate was likely to have needed retouching.[127] Since he produced other engravings of the festivities, and given that printmakers usually pulled only a few prints from a plate at one time, it is likely that the three versions of the map were produced over several months.

Evidently Franco benefited from the 1597 event as a way to sell prints from a plate in which the topography of Venice was substantially outdated. Indeed, Donato Rascicotti's engraving attests to Franco's strategy. Rascicotti incorporated recent changes to the cityscape – at the Arsenale, Fondamenta Nuove, Rialto bridge, and the library – to bring the map up to date (fig. 1). In the dedication, in fact, the printmaker asserts that his engraving improved upon earlier ones, clearly a reference to Franco's bird's-eye views.[128]

These engravings demonstrate the growing attention of printmakers to the details that had come to supplement the bird's-eye view. Faster and more flexible production methods enabled changes to be accommodated in the map and the frame, but speedier techniques and the accompanying potential for variety also prompted printers to copy each other. Rascicotti's 'improvements' of Franco's maps, in fact, were copied exactly by engravers in Siena and in Rome. Published with no dedication, these copies attest to a wide market for prints of Venice outside the city.

With their focus on the city's districts, ceremonies, and famous urban spaces, these maps provide information deemed appropriate to outsiders, according to the distinction drawn by Donato Giannotti in his *Libro de la Republica de Vinitiani*. Published in 1526–7 and 1540, the dialogue was reprinted throughout the century. 'A foreigner,' explains Trifone Gabriello, one of the interlocutors, 'must know the form of the administration and the relationship of the various parts with each other,' whereas 'a citizen should know a city's wealth, military capacity, geographical situation, exports and imports, and government.'[129] Nevertheless, local maps do not appear in the inventories of Venetian households; residents, even artisans, displayed geographical maps of the different parts of the world instead.[130] In a city filled with printsellers, however, Venetians would have become accustomed to seeing the distinctive shape of their native city. Moreover, numerous printed books provided locals with the opportunity to compare their city with those of others. The *Civitates* was only the most elaborate of the new genre of books of city maps that appeared in the second half of the century, many of which were published in Venice.[131] Giulio Ballino's *De' Disegni delle piu illustri città, & fortezze del mondo,* published in 1569, consists of fifty maps of cities and fortresses. His image of Venice was reproduced in numerous *isolari,* or island books, for which the city's insular topography was ideal.[132] Idealized even further than the *Civitates* bird's-eye view, the islands have become the centre of a geometric landscape. The cosmological symbolism evoked by de'Barbari's view has been transformed into a signature of Venice's singular identity.

Thomaso Porcacchi's hugely successful *L'isole piu famose del mondo,* first published in 1572, is another example of this genre in which the pictorial and written portraits of the city authenticate each other (fig. 13). As his account of Venice explains,

> therefore, by the great providence of God, this marvellous city is planted in the middle of the sea; between the sea and the lagoons there is a tongue of land called the Lido that defends it from the impetuous waves of the sea; formed in the shape of an arc, it extends a distance of 35 miles; in this way the city is closed from the mainland and defended by the Lido. And, moreover, this ground opens in five places in order for large and small ships that come from outside to enter and then to stop in the port, and also in order that these pools, around which the city is planted, are maintained full of water.[133]

The Lido, as Girolamo Porro portrayed it, protects the city from the 'impetuous waves of the sea' while providing a natural fortress with access limited to a few well-guarded points. Symmetrically opposed to each other, the terraferma and Lido provide striking visual evidence of the city's natural protection.

In 1607 Giuseppe Rosaccio, also the author of an *Isolario,* produced an extraordinary map of Italy in which all the principal cities of the peninsula are lined up along the lower edge sheet (fig. 14). The repetition of square frames calls attention to the distinctive contours of each city, a

DESCRITTIONE DELLA ISOLA,
ET CITTA' DI VINETIA
DI THOMASO PORCACCHI
DA CASTIGLIONE ARRETINO.

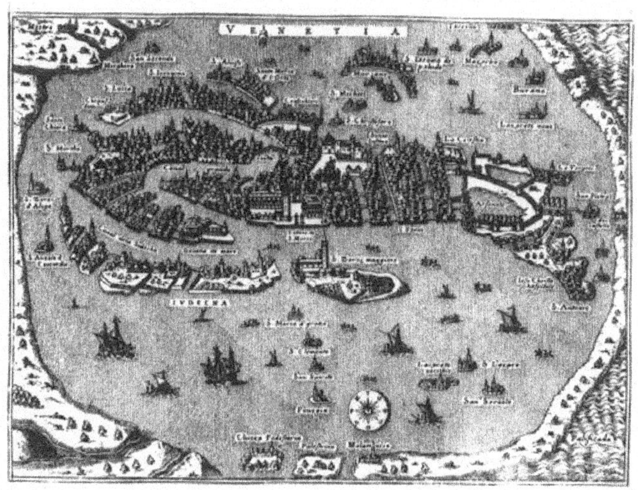

INETIA Città magnifica è posta in isola nel piu intimo golfo del mare Adriatico in mezo a stagni, & a lagune: & dalla parte di Leuante ha il detto mare, che si distende littoralmente fino a Capo d'Otranto per D C C. miglia, & uerso Leuante D. Da Mezogiorno, da Tramontana, & da Ponente ha parte del lito, che la serra: percioche questa marauigliosa Città piantata in mezo all'acque salse, per gran prouidentia di Dio ha fra'l mare, & le lagune, oue è posta, vna lingua di terra, chiamata Lito, che la difende dalle impetuose onde del mare: & essendo formato a guisa d'vn'arco; si distende per spatio di x x x v. miglia; in modo che la Città, o è serrata da terra ferma, o da questo Lito difesa. E' nondimeno questo lito aperto in cinque luoghi, per dare entrata a' nauili grossi & piccoli, che di fuora vengono, da potersi ridurre in porto, & ancho accioche gli stagni, oue la Città è piantata, si mantengano pieni d'acqua. La prima apertura è verso Tramontana, chiamata Treporti: l'altra in faccia di Garbino Lito maggiore:indi Santo Erasmo: poi i due Castelli: da' quali cinque miglia lontano è il porto di Malamocco, gia nominato Meduaco dal fiume della Brenta, così da' Latini chiamata, che quiui cadeua in mare: & questo è posto fra Sirocco, & Ostro, & dicono ch'era porto de' Padouani, all'hora

Lito di Vinetia.

A   che

Figure 13   Girolamo Porro, *Descrittione della isola et città di Vinetia,* Thomaso Porcacchi, *L'isole piu famose del mondo* (Venice: Simon Galignani and Girolamo Porro, 1576). Engraving, folio [photo: Newberry, Chicago]

format that would have inspired viewers to compare their own city with those of neighbouring locales.

Earlier I suggested that de'Barbari combined the fixed contours of cartographic description with the viewer's mobile eye that glances from place to place. Already in this woodcut inscriptions were used to single out places, prompting viewers to read the map as a text, to identify what they saw with a name. This process initiated a shift away from resemblance toward the use of textblocks to describe the visitor's movement through the city. In turn, these itineraries were transformed into legends with which viewers negotiated between image and text. The bird's-eye view was becoming a frame for the text, an abstract diagram that supplemented the narrative into which it was inserted. Chorography was itself becoming distinguished as a visual mode in contrast to the narrative function of chronicle. Moreover, in general, but not exclusively, these two modes were defined in opposition to each other and correlated to space and time.[134] Sight was becoming associated with places and chronicles with the movement of the body, a split to which growing attention to accuracy and the production of atlases contributed.[135]

By the end of the century, this division between space and time is given visual form in political *fogli volanti*, a new type of print (fig. 15). Giovanni Nicolo Doglioni's broadsheet is one example of this development in which the now iconic image of Venice is flanked by a register of all the doges (from 697 to 1585) and supported by a list of historical events from its legendary foundation in 407 to the year before the print was pulled: 10 April 1594.[136] As Doglioni explains, he has represented 'The City of Venice, with its origins, and government, and the succession of Doges, and all notable things that have occurred through the ages from the beginning of its construction until the present, thus arranged.'[137] Viewers are informed about the past and simultaneously placed in relation to it, an effect underlined by the dedication; not only the month but the day is noted. The temporal progress of events from line to line organizes the information spatially, a didactic mode analogous to that of paper memory theatres.[138] Indeed, Doglioni conveyed this concept in his comments:

> Dear readers. Because everyone, especially the nobles of this city (for whom the need occurs often enough in the discourse of their consultations), is able to recall the many notable deeds of Venetians with some effort, I have made the present little work in which I remind you, that those numbers from the left side of the lines are the years of Christ, and where there is a change

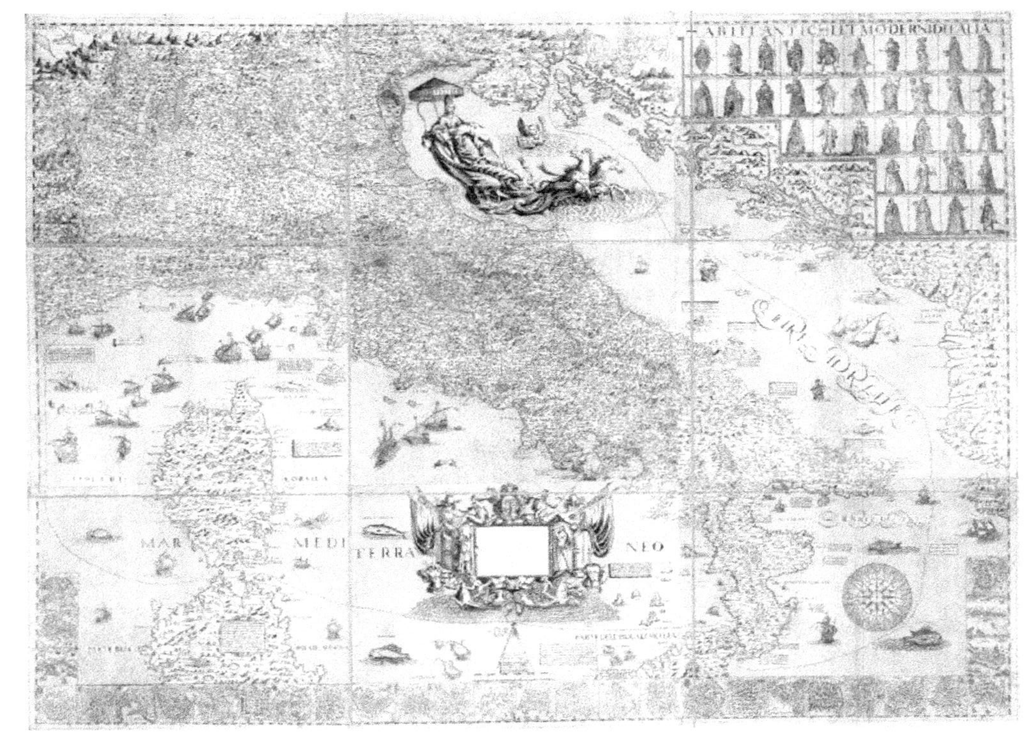

Figure 14   Giuseppe Rosaccio, *Abiti antichi et moderni d'Italia*, 1607. Engraving [photo: Bibliotèque Nationale de France, Paris]

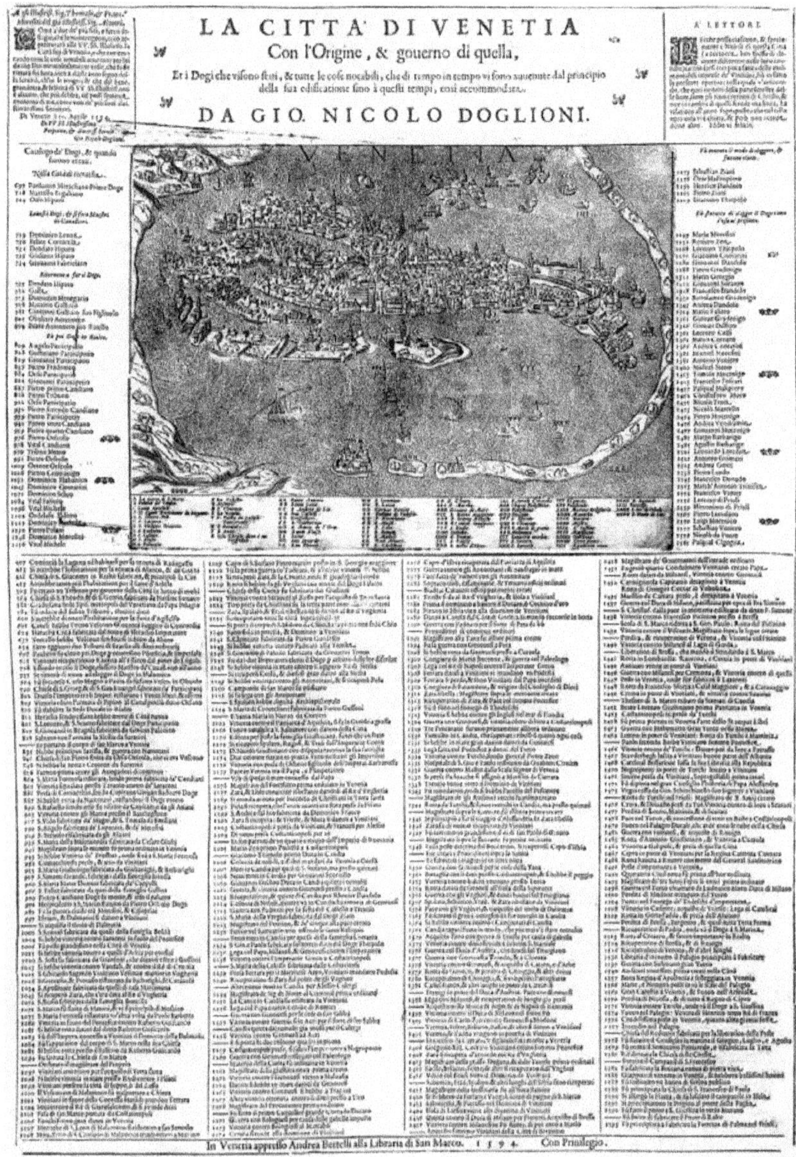

Figure 15   *La città di Venetia*. Text by Giovanni Nicolo Doglioni. Printed by Andrea Bertelli in Venice, 1594. Engraved map with letterpress [photo: Newberry Library, Chicago]

in those one sees a line that relates to the year above; everything else is clear, and therefore there is no need to say more about it.[139]

The chart was intended to provide a tidy reference sheet for Venetian nobles who needed recourse to the important events of the past and to the corresponding names of the doges, the kind of research that contributed to the formation of opinions, which was a social requirement.[140] Below the concentric circles of the cityscape is an abbreviated legend, vastly reduced from the immense compendia of possible itineraries provided by Forlani; the earlier relation between the parts and the whole has been reduced to an emblem of the republic with a list of names and achievements. The topography has been abstracted to resemble an oculus, which functions as a sign for the city's geographical location. Like a black hole, the fixed contours of the map recede into the distance of the diachronic frame that engulfs it. The image has been inverted into a pictorial caption for the text, fixing historical memory in space, a compact cosmology in which time continues but Venice stays the same.

With time and space cleaved apart, the random mobile eye of the person in the street is no longer accommodated in the printed map. But one final example suggests that this contingent experience of looking was translated into a new format. Figure 16 illustrates Venice as conceived by Giacomo Franco on the frontispiece of his album of engravings, *Habiti d'huomeni et donne venetiane* and *Habiti delle donne venetiane*, compiled around 1610. The bird's-eye view is now framed in a circular cartouche that resembles a convex mirror.[141] Emphasizing the desirability of the object, the mirror reflection focuses on the act of viewing, as if reflecting the image of Venice in the eye of the beholder. The frontispiece thereby allegorizes the Olympian view of the geographer's eye, an interpretation supported by sources for Franco's idea. Nicolas de Nicolay provides one possible source in the cosmological and global frontispiece he devised for his translation and elaboration of the Spaniard Pierre de Medine's *L'art de naviguer*, published in Lyon in 1554. Even closer is an image of a globe, complete with curvilinear shading, that was incorporated into an *impresa* on a 1574 frontispiece for *Philip II Rules the Four Continents* (fig. 17).[142] These ideas were translated by Franco into a new concept that he explains in a fascinating dedication that foregrounds the startling impact of the world's expanded geography:

Figure 16   Giacomo Franco, Frontispiece, *Habiti d'huomeni et donne venetiane* (Venice: Giacomo Franco, 1610). Engraving, 232 × 177 mm [photo: Museo Correr, Venice]

Here ... is the design that I send to your Serenity of the marvellous city of Venice in spherical form, a real portrait of the world, whose resemblance is so close to nature, and made by the arts, similar to the orb of the earth, those who well admire this design discover, from the height of a bird, the Arctic pole and the Antarctic and also from the East and the West with all the other parts that go around this world; similarly circled by water in a manner that seems the continent is entirely surrounded by the great ocean. What is it then to be deprived of the knowledge of cosmography, such that one does not know that the whole world is primarily composed of three parts, that is Europe, Africa, & Asia and that all parts in a continent are compiled in the appointed manner, as is this noble city; Geographers know without doubt that outside of our continent is America. One sees, even outside of the contained body of Venice, the Giudecca, in a guise that resembles the new world; the islands, and peninsulas with the reefs and shallows, each one mirrors the design that you will see corresponds in a true likeness to the appearance of the world map, as was said; I will say again that the districts are in such a number, as are the provinces of the world; but, having the will to make a major design of this form, & to locate all under its climate and degree, in height as in breadth, with the shape of the machine of the world (as I will make again) and with this drawn for your excellency to accept, and for your enjoyment together with the dress of Venetian women, with other designs of figures, which I have made for your curiosity, with the intention of making a large number of them.[143]

Franco has rotated the bird's-eye view of Venice about seventy-five degrees to the east and projected it onto a sphere, transforming the islands of Venice into the continents of the world. Giudecca with its *terra incognita* to the west represents the new world of America; Dorsoduro and San Polo are Europe; Cannaregio and Castello stand in for Asia and Africa respectively. Rialto occupies the position of Venice on world maps as the crossroads between continents. And San Marco is located on the crest of the globe, at the centre of the Venetian world, sited as the new Jerusalem.

In contrast to the beginning of the sixteenth century, when Venice was faced with losses to the Ottoman Turks in the Stato da Mar, and intensifying hostility from European powers, the end of the century could be perceived as a time of peace and opulence. As doge Nicolò Contarini proclaimed:

At the time, the Republic enjoyed the outward confidence of every Prince

Figure 17   Impresa (*Philip II Rules the Four Continents*), Luca Contile, *Ragionamento sopra la proprietà della imprese* (Pavia: Girolamo Bartoli, 1574). Engraving, folio [photo: by permission of the British Library, London] 635.1.26

and was, one might say, in open amity with all; moreover it abounded in all the things which the fertility of the land, the industry of man, and a suitable location usually bestow on a well-regulated commonwealth ... Trade flowed into the city from all parts, so much so in fact ... that she was deemed possibly greater at that time than she had ever been in days past.[144]

Throughout the sixteenth century, treaties and trade routes and growing competition challenged Venetian control over markets; nevertheless, Venetians continued to supply Germany and Northern Italy. However, between 1560 and 1600 increasing dependence on foreign vessels reduced the numbers of Venetian ships to half. 'Foreigners and strangers from remote countries have become masters of all the shipping,' reported the Venetian Board of Trade in 1602, and six years later concern was raised about flagging receipts from the German Fondaco because of 'the Flemings, the English, and the French, who now sail to the Levant to purchase silk, spices, cotton, and other commodities which they bring to Marseilles, Flanders and England, and from there to the Frankfurt fairs and other German localities.'[145] Protectionist legislation enacted by the state in 1602 and the loss of the spice trade to the Dutch in 1595 contributed to a recession.[146]

In spite of the fact that Venice was no longer the centre of the mercantile universe – indeed, perhaps because of this – Franco has reasserted the city's status as a metropole. Earlier printmakers had depicted Venice as a trading emporium, a model republic, and an icon of stability and liberty through sage patrician government. Franco has reanimated de'Barbari's double vision, but space and time – the abstract gaze of the geographer and the embodied experience of moving through the city – have been taken apart. For with this global vision, Franco introduces his book to the reader, who opens it to see the city's costumes, spaces, and civic rituals, to see the world *in* Venice.

Chapter 2

Costume and the Boundaries of Bodies

In 1574, returning from Poland to France as the new king, Henry III travelled through Italy. His visit to Venice prompted a flurry of publicity by chroniclers who described both the event and the appearance of the king in great detail. According to Marsilio della Croce:

> on Sunday morning ... his Majesty appeared in public dressed entirely in *Pavonazzo* (that is, [a sign] of his grief) of silk from Flanders, with a hat on his head in the Italian style with his veil, and a long cloak to his feet, a slashed jacket, stockings, a leather collar with a great ruffled collar of a very well fit shirt, perfumed gloves in hand, and on his feet, shoes and slippers according to the French usage.[1]

From the top of his head to his toes, the king's clothes were read as if they were a map of Europe, an account that highlights both the importance of costume and the interpretive skills deployed to comprehend foreigners.[2] As the image of the world expanded in the sixteenth century, so too did the function of costume. Costume books – a phenomenon that emerged across Europe during the second half of the sixteenth century – were one expression of the fascination with geographical classification. Venetians and visitors to the Veneto were particularly enthusiastic for this new genre; nine costume books were published there between 1540 and 1610, about a third of those produced throughout Europe.[3] Indeed, Venice was itself a 'theatre of the world,' where visitors could marvel at both local and foreign dress; as Giulio Ballino explained to readers of his book of city maps, Venice was 'inhabited by an infinite multitude of people who come together for commerce from various nations, in fact from all the world. They use all languages and are dressed in different ways.'[4]

As Della Croce's account of the king's attire illustrates, authors of texts attributed differences among garments to national styles. For example, Francesco Sansovino began his discourse on costume for his famous guidebook *Venetia città nobilissima* (1581) by explaining that 'costumes indicate the character of people.'

> We will see that the majority of Italians, forgetting about having been born in Italy, and following northern fashions, have given people the idea that they might appear as the French or the Spanish. And certainly this is to their damage, and their shame, and is a manifest sign of their lack of stability and firmness; those men who never maintained a perpetual and firm tone in their things have at times been taken over by other nations in the world. Only this city [Venice] has conserved itself in all times and in general is less corrupt than others. It is thereby a refuge for foreigners, who dream of introducing [constancy] in their homes and customs.[5]

If Spanish and French fashions were deemed threats to indigenous attire – a concern with rhetorical parallels to foreign domination of Italy – sartorial stability was claimed to be a cause of Venice's long-standing republican independence. Women were an important exception, however, and Sansovino began propagating this rhetorical commonplace as early as 1561 in his dialogue *Delle cose notabili che sono in Venetia.* As his Venetian guide explains to the foreigner, the gravity of male dress and the longevity of the republic were mutually constitutive; their classical black togas both reflected and contributed to a religious devotion to modesty and peace.[6] In contrast with the steadiness of men, however, the oscillating styles of women had required action: 'such licence had increased to such an extreme level that our senators came together to restrain such unbridled will with laws.'[7] The Provveditori alle pompe, the state's sumptuary legislators, had in fact targeted those 'damned inventions' that had invaded women's fashions and that were attributed to French styles.[8] As one commentator lamented, Venetians 'had avidly embraced the vices of foreigners,' because people 'are rare who are content with what they are born.'[9]

With widespread circulation of printed maps, Europeans had access to a world projected into images, and costume books followed this lead. Since borders between countries were subject to change in the sixteenth century, these were rarely demarcated in printed maps.[10] Instead it was cities that provided a stable point of reference, to which the appearance of printed collections of city maps in the second half of the century attests. The volumes of Georg Braun and Franz Hogenberg's *Civitates orbis terrarum 1572–1618* comprise the most elaborate example of this genre, but here too Venetian printers were especially industrious; Leandro Alberti's *Descrittione di tutta Italia* and Pietro Bertelli's *Teatro urbium italicarum* are two examples of collections published in Venice in the second half of the century.[11] In contrast to the fluctuating borders between nations, cities were clearly delineated by walls, fortifications, or water, and these boundaries could be easily translated into pictures. Accordingly, in the pictorial representation of costume, and in contrast with written descriptions, more often it was the city, or region, that became the principal frame of reference. After 1600, in fact, series of prints were devoted to the costumes of a single locale, including Venice, Danzig, Strasbourg, Augsburg, and Nuremberg.[12]

The format of costume books varies. In some cases a city is represented by a single figure. By contrast Cesare Vecellio used as many as sixty woodcuts to illustrate Venice, the city where he lived, and where his costume books were published in 1590 and 1598 (figs. 28, 35, 36, 44, 45, 47). Responding to the interests of locals and visitors, the place of publication is usually the most comprehensively represented. Vecellio was among those who presented a different costume on each page, but some illustrators engraved several examples on folded folio sheets in an atlas-like format (figs. 18, 21, 23, 25, 26). Both Abraham de Bruyn and Jean Jacques Boissard used the large sheets to demonstrate that costumes from a given location could be identified on the basis of shared visual characteristics.[13] De Bruyn's Danish attire is particularly indicative of this strategy, as seen in both the bell-shaped form and the vertical striations that embellish the clothes (fig. 18). Labels or brief verses are typically appended to the figures, but occasionally these are accompanied by lengthier texts, usually in the vernacular, and often translated into Latin, sometimes simultaneously. The use of Latin and multiple editions – often published in different cities – attests to the broad international audience for these early compilations.

Within these variations, costume books demonstrate that illustrators from across Europe shared similar interests, as explored below. Like atlases, costume books ordered the world by geography, rendering it legible and compact. This process of distillation, as I argue in what follows, compressed not only space but also time. Furthermore, the widespread dissemination of attire from distant locales, in combination with

Figure 18   Abraham de Bruyn, *Female Danish Costumes, Omnium pene Europae* (Antwerp: M. Colyn, 1581). Engraving, oblong folio [photo: by permission of the British Library, London] 810.k.2.(1)

the pictorial conventions used by illustrators, would have encouraged viewers to contrast the silhouettes of their own clothes with those of the depicted foreigners. This new experience of the world outside, moreover, seems to have sharpened the focus on local identities. Reducing a range of individual bodies to types, woodcuts and engravings of costumes codified differences, and as the case of Venice suggests, this process overlapped with local attempts to assert civic social categories. I begin with an analysis of woodcuts and engravings, exploring the sources and strategies followed by printmakers. The second section turns to the *album amicorum,* in which manuscript costume illustrations were collected by travellers to Italy from north of the Alps. Dozens of extant albums attest to the interest among those from Germany, the Low Countries, and to a lesser degree France, in European costumes in general, and Venetian ones in particular. These artifacts provide insights into the moral and allegorical function of costume illustrations. The lived consequences and social meanings of costume are considered in the third part of the chapter, where I turn to Inquisition and judicial cases. Finally, the last section explores the theoretical implications of the repeated exchange between images of clothes and their wearers.

Vicarious Peregrinations: Sources and Conventions of Costume Books

What incredible delite is take[n] in beholding the diversities of people, beastis, foules, fisshes, trees, frutes, and herbes: to knowe the sondry maners & conditions of people, and the varietie of their natures, and that in a warme studie or perler, without perill of the see, or daunger of longe and paynfull iournayes: I can nat tell, what more pleasure shulde happen to a gentil witte, than to beholde in his owne house every thynge that with in all the worlde is contained.[14]

Thomas Elyot

Figure 19 reproduces a folio engraving in which twenty-eight female costumes – from Rome to Calicvtica – are arranged in four horizontal rows. This epitome of international differences was engraved by Ambrogio (Ambrosius) Brambilla and printed in 1602, but Martino Rota was probably the inventor of the designs that were first printed in Rome in the early 1580s. Brambilla's folio was copied by Battista da Parma, and an extant example of the latter provides evidence of how the gridded print encouraged viewers to compare the attire. Battista's sheet was cut up into single figures that were then rearranged into groups of four and

Figure 19   Costume engravings by Ambrosius Brambilla (after Battista da Parma). First published by Claudio Duchet in Rome around 1590 [photo: by permission of the British Library, London] 146.i.10

pasted into the back of the so-called *Tailor's Book,* a collection of designs for costumes and pageantry from Milan, now in the Querini Stampalia Library in Venice.[15] Both the Brambilla and Battista engravings were pulled from copperplates that had been recut in order to extend their life, which indicates the popularity of the imagery.[16]

For all of his examples, Brambilla made use of the same profile, regardless of place of origin, thereby setting the sartorial characteristics into relief. The standard format not only designates costume as the marker of difference, but also calls attention to similarities among Italian and European costumes. Fantastic headwear and hemlines – the endless brim sported by Egiptia, the three-tiered tower on Arabica, the oval balloon of Calicutica's turban – highlight peculiarities imagined for distant lands. Located on the lowest tier of the print, and revealing their arms, legs, and breasts, figures from Africa and Asia are contrasted with their European counterparts, whose limbs are concealed by their dresses and their hands decorously occupied with some object. The relation between the contours of the costumes and the composition of the sheet as a whole would have highlighted bonds with neighbours. Viewers from Venice, for example, would have identified more easily with Roman or Florentine attire than with the more articulated garments worn by those from distant lands. The conventions would have enabled Italians to compare their clothing with that of other locales, screening out the details that protruded beyond the contained contours of those costumes found in European centres. On one level this accords with Kaja Silverman's assertion that a viewer identifies with images that are closest to the 'self-same body ... his or her stubborn clinging to those images which can be most easily incorporated ... The principle of the self-same body is consequently at the centre of all those varieties of "difference."'[17] In the sixteenth century, however, as demonstrated by hundreds of printed illustrations, it was less the body than what was worn over the skin that served as the locus of alterity. Those appendages and headdresses that extend from the profile are set apart, thereby drawing attention to nonconforming silhouettes. By making foreigners appear strange, an aspect of costume books that this single sheet serves to introduce, costume illustrations participated in the process of forging national boundaries.

Following his extensive travels throughout the Ottoman Empire, Nicolas de Nicolay, the French royal geographer, compiled his *Quatre premiers livres des navigations et pérégrinations orientales,* first published in

Lyon in 1567. Sixty 'portraits' of men and women from a variety of ethnic groups were drawn from life, as the author emphasizes in his preface (figs. 20, 52). Each social category is illustrated by a single costume that is identified by a label and explained in the accompanying text. Customs and habits of foreigners (including sexual practices, religious beliefs, and burial customs) were associated with the body, and these performative aspects of identity were described in the text. By contrast, the extraordinary sartorial display seen in the engravings provided the means to distinguish between bodies, to highlight cultural differences. The absence of landscape or architecture precludes any narrative, focusing the viewer instead on the attire. This strategy is suggested by Nicolay in his preface, where he explains the natural order of the world. In contrast to animals, which 'are confined according to species, and limited by their particulars and elements that are natural to them,' humans are able to extend their domain, discovering a world beyond 'the country of one's birth ... in all those habitable lands and navigable seas.' 'This is great evidence,' explains the author, 'that man is the only animal that was made [by God] for all the world.'[18] In the wake of discoveries of worlds unknown to Europeans, and in striking contrast with the regional variations seen in flora and fauna, the contours of the human body, unexpectedly and perhaps surprisingly, appeared to be universal. Thus, costume was charged with articulating geographical differences.

In the second half of the sixteenth century, printed costume books appeared across Europe in which illustrators called attention to the foreignness of distant lands by depicting an array of protruding appendages and headdresses that contrasted with the smooth contours of European attire. Serrated silhouettes came to designate the distinctiveness of Turks in costume prints, a visual strategy that contrasts with the emphasis on colour, size of turban, and length of beard that was deployed at the Ottoman court (fig. 21).[19] Moreover, although Nicolay often described the colours of the costumes, extant hand-coloured editions indicate that illuminators rarely followed the text.[20] Instead the contours and poses of the figures became archetypes, and these were replicated, even traced, in at least eight costume books published by 1601. (Compare fig. 20 with the fifth figure in figure 21 in the upper register, and figs. 51 and 52).

Differences in skin pigment are rarely shown, due perhaps in part to the medium that encouraged printmakers to emphasize surface patterns like tattoos and articulated profiles instead (figs. 21, 22). In some cases

Figure 20   Nicolas de Nicolay, *Janissaire allant a la guerre*, Nicolas de Nicolay, *Les quatre premiers livres des navigations et pérégrinations orientales* (Lyon, G. Roville, 1568). Engraving [photo: by permission of the British Library, London] 455.e.5

Figure 21   Abraham de Bruyn, *Turkish Costumes, Omnium pene Europae* (Antwerp: M. Colyn, 1581). Engraving, oblong folio [photo: by permission of the British Library, London] 810.k.2. (1)

images identified as Moors and Ethiopians provide exceptions to the generic body type, reflecting familiarity with visual images of their faces in Western art, the presence of North Africans as servants in Italian households, and the history of Moors on the continent.[21] Familiarity with pictorial conventions for depicting the black magus, for example, would have equipped Europeans with the cognitive framework to recognize some distinctive facial differences. The blackness of Ethiopians had long been attributed to their equatorial location, and given the practice of copying models by costume illustrators, the Ethiopian profile likely signalled geographical accuracy. However, the discovery of light-skinned peoples in equatorial regions of the Americas confounded ancient sources and prompted a range of theories to explain differences in skin colour, such as the kinds of food digested, latitude, and divine will.[22] Although sixteenth-century writers used the word 'race,' the meaning of the word was more closely analogous with 'nation,' in the sense of 'a group connected by common descent or origin.'[23]

The contemporary resonances of these terms are brought together by Jean de Glen in the preface to his costume book *Des habits, moeurs, cerimonies ... du monde*, published in Liege in 1601:

> The people of God came from the good race and sacred seed of the Patriarchs; according to scripture, corruption and depravation were imputed to intimacy and conversation with foreign nations ... How today can all the countries and nations so degenerated of candour and sincerity above all, except by a similar mingling with foreigners? And our country, which has become expanded so much from its first fullness, that like a Proteus, it changes every day; it diversifies itself and metamorphoses its costumes, habits, languages, and customs; again it sees the pleasures, voluptuousness, delights and vices of the more profligate nations?[24]

The text, magnified by de Glen's singularly acerbic mixture of xenophobia and religious morality, recalls Sansovino's warnings, cited above, about the contagious dangers of costume. Instead of facial features, it was 'costumes, habits, languages, and customs' that resonated as signifiers of race; physiognomy, as a signifier of race in its modern sense – as a sign of ethnic distinctiveness – was a concept not yet clearly articulated.[25] Instead, physiognomy was still associated with class or moral values and understood as external signs of the soul. Thus a misshapen profile could be used to signify an evil interior. Abraham de Bruyn exaggerated facial features of rural dwellers to distinguish them from urban

Figure 22   *Mulier Virgnie insule Habitatrix* and *Vir Virginie insule Habitator*, Pietro Bertelli, *Diversarum nationum habitus* (Padua: Pietro Bertelli and Alcia Alciato: 1594). Engraving and etching, small 8° [photo: by permission of the British Library, London] 810.c.2

ones, and in this case, physiognomy is coextensive with the form of classification designated by the costume (compare the robust faces of the peasants in figure 23 with the idealized ones in figure 25). Physiognomy is considered at greater length in chapter 4.

A variety of prejudices emerge in these early costume books, then, but it is religious ones that stand out. We have seen how the attire worn by Muslims was made to signal religious alterity; by contrast, the unclothed bodies of people from the New World could be used to represent a primitive stage of becoming European. This is the concept suggested by Hans Weigel in the introduction to his *Trachtenbuch* (1577), and illustrated by Jost Amman on the book's frontispiece (fig. 24).[26] The image in the centre of the page presents male personifications of the four parts of the world. To the left, the European man appears with no clothes, concealing his naked body with a bolt of fabric and holding tailor's shears. He gestures toward the semiclad figure of America, as if intent on attiring the man along with himself. Native North Americans presented Europeans with an image of their own genealogy in the likeness of Adam and Eve; the Spartan dress of inhabitants of the Americas could be seen as evidence of an early stage of development before conversion from paganism to Christianity and wearing of clothes. Pietro Bertelli was one of many printmakers whose figures of Virginia seem to have doubled as Adam and Eve (fig. 22). Costume illustrators followed Theodor de Bry's engravings made after John White's watercolours, and in this particular example, Pietro has misidentified the figures as male and female 'inhabitant[s] of the Virgin Islands.'[27] Amman made this idea of progress more explicit by incorporating a representation of the Fall above his personifications of the four continents (see detail at top of fig. 24). The prelapsarian figures of this new, now 'fourth part of the world' thereby served as a pictorial origin for a teleological history of costume in which time could be mapped across space.[28] Pagan cultures could be aligned with primitive Europeans, a view that bound the concept of the universal body to the notion of a universal Christian world. Indeed, a variety of writers claimed that it was the stability of Turkish costumes over time that attested to their moral intransigence.[29]

Copying and tracing were common among printmakers,[30] but in the costume prints these practices contributed to the meanings and didactic effects of the images. Abraham de Bruyn's *Virgo Veneta* (fig. 25, right), first published in Cologne in 1577, provided a source for Jean Jacques Boissard's *Virgo*, seen in his Lyon edition of 1581 (fig. 26, centre). In turn, Boissard's figure was traced by the engraver of a printed *album*

Figure 23 Abraham de Bruyn *Italian Country Folk, Omnium pene Europae* (Antwerp: M. Colyn, 1581). Engraving, oblong folio [photo: by permission of the British Library, London] 810.k.2. (1)

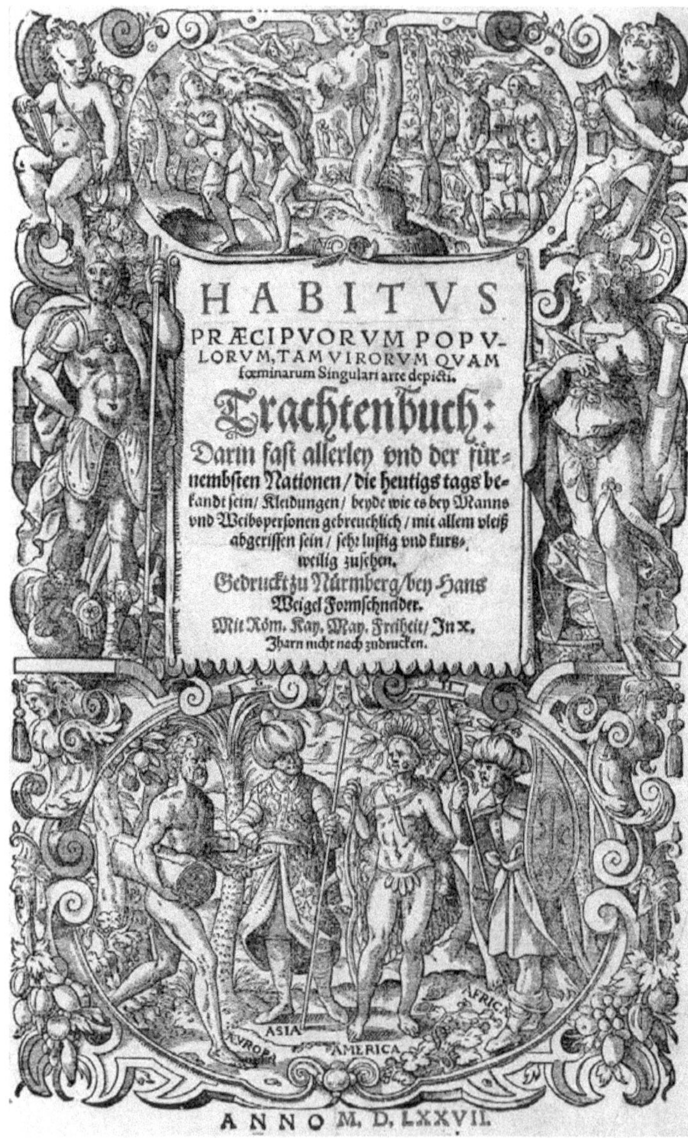

Figure 24   Jost Amman, frontispiece, Hans Weigel, *Habitus praecipuorum popu-lorum, tam virorum quam foeminarum singulari arte depicti* (Nuremberg, 1577). Woodcut, folio [photo: by permission of the British Library, London] C.119. h. 6

Figure 25   Abraham de Bruyn, *Venetian Women, Omnium pene Europae* (Antwerp: M. Colyn, 1581). Engraving, oblong folio [photo: by permission of the British Library, London]. 810.k.2.(1)

Figure 26   *Venetian Women*, Jean Jacques Boissard, *Habitus variarum orbis gentium* (Mechlin[?], 1581) Engraving, oblong folio [photo: by permission of the British Library, London] 146.i.10

Figure 27 *Virgo Veneta, Album amicorum, habitus mulierum omniu nationu Europae* (Leuven: Jean-Baptiste Zangrius, 1599). Engraving, oblong 8° [photo: by permission of the British Library, London] C.28.b.15

Figure 28   Cesare Vecellio, *Donzelle, Habiti antichi et moderni di tutto il mondo* (Venice: Sessa, 1598) Woodcut, 8°, 20 cm [photo: Newberry Library, Chicago]

Figure 29   *Virgo Veneta*, Pietro Bertelli, *Diversarum nationum habitus* (Padua: Pietro Bertelli and Alcia Alciato, 1594) Engraving, small 8° [photo: by permission of the British Library, London] 810.c.2

Figure 30   Manuscript sheet from a fifteenth-century model book, Rome [photo: Istituto Nazionale per la Grafica, Rome] Cat. no. 35. f. 8v FN 2824v

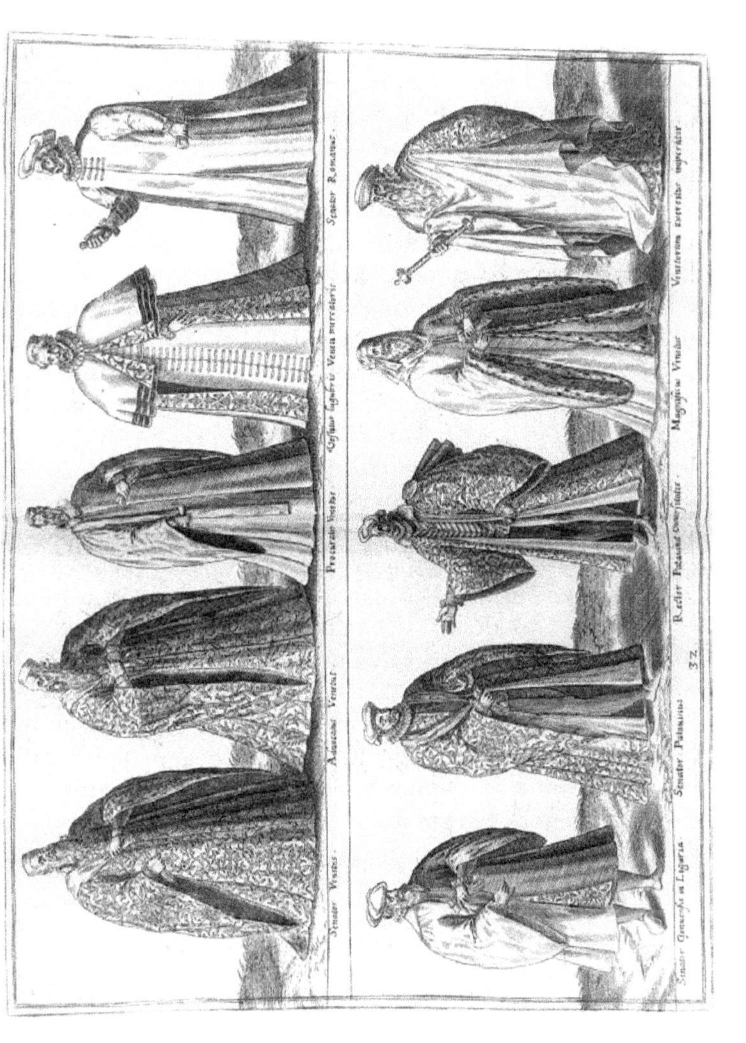

Figure 31 Abraham de Bruyn, *Italian Senators and Officials*, *Omnium pene Europae* (Antwerp: M. Colyn, 1581). Engraving, oblong folio [photo: by permission of the British Library, London] 810.k.2. (1)

amicorum, as evidenced by the identical scale and mirror image of the intaglio process (fig. 27). This form of book, to which I will return, was first published in Leuven in 1599 and subsequently reprinted in 1601 and 1605. Even the Venetian artist Vecellio adopted the figure for his woodcuts, using the familiar silhouette for both *Spose non sposate* (brides to be) and *Donzelle* (Venetian virgins) (fig. 28).[31] Copying was not always slavish however. For example, Pietro Bertelli, whose first volume of costumes was published in Padua in 1589, played with the contradictory image of marriageable girls who 'do walke abroad with their breastes all naked,'[32] but also 'go about,' as another visitor exclaimed, 'so completely covered up, that I do not know how they can see to go along the streets' (fig. 29).[33] Instead of distinguishing between the form of the body and the dress, the artist tailored the figure from parts, like a carapace. Headless, Pietro suggests to his viewers; a virgin is not a body in clothes, but a body of clothes. As these examples demonstrate, the meanings of the image were not bound to any original model; instead it was the representation of a concept that migrated, a concept that was crystallized in the outline.

Many characteristics of costume illustrations correspond to those seen in artists' model books. For example, the pages of a fifteenth-century northeast Italian manuscript are filled with allegorical and standing figures (fig. 30; compare with fig. 31). The sheet provides six models for depicting famous men, each of whom is separated from the other, arranged in two rows, and identified by a label.[34] The plain ground liberates the figures from any specific geographical setting, thereby facilitating their use as models by artists in different contexts. In the costume books, by contrast, these conventions were deployed for their clarity and cognitive value. As a means to compare and organize geographical differences, these representational concerns can be linked to the pictorial strategies used for scientific illustration.

As Abraham de Bruyn explains, the costume book was a vehicle of classification, a means to diagram the world's diversity:

Many knowledgeable people have put their interests to use to research and describe the situation of the four principal parts of the world, with the origins, customs, and conditions of the people there: a kind of endeavour that brings real satisfaction for enthusiasts and amateurs of science. There remains the true form and different modes of their attire which I have set as my work to represent as faithfully as possible by means of having received from some friends certain rare figures not yet known by the art of engraving or printing.[35]

De Bruyn's own zoological engravings attest to this mode of classification on the basis of visual characteristics; the specimens are organized according to their contours and surface texture, as if variations on a single species (compare figure 32 with figs. 31, 18, 25).[36] Capitalizing on the effects of block cutting and intaglio, these artists combined the art of the tailor with that of the scientific illustrator in a display of feathers, pleats, slashes, and ruffs. Brocade, lace, and other patterns ideally suited to the burin were substituted for scales and fur. Wings were exchanged for sleeves, gills for slashes, and armour for shells. The distinctive markings and the emphatic visual attention to the contours enabled costume to define the species, as it were, of the human genus.

Herbals and botanical illustration provide further insights into the function of printed costume books, since artists sought to diagram the 'unruly' New World with its unfamiliar vegetation.[37] Print media were ideally suited for illustrating morphological patterns, as David Landau and Peter Parshall state, the kinds of visible features that enabled botanists to produce a structural taxonomy.[38] This development was initially hindered, however, by the process with which the illustrations were prepared for Otto Brunfels's *Herbarum vivae eicones*, an early botanical (1530–40; fig. 33).[39] Hans Weiditz, Brunfels's illustrator, carefully depicted the characteristics of an individual specimen in watercolour, and the woodcutters in turn reproduced these details with great precision for the printed volumes. Their attention to the particulars of a singular plant, however, limited the identification of the type in the field, a practice that instead required 'useful symptom[s] of identity.'[40] The scientific limitations of Weiditz's faithful copies become clear when compared with the new prototypes published by Leonhard Fuchs in his *De historia stirpium* (1542; fig. 34).[41] In contrast to the wilting specimen copied by Weiditz from the workshop table, Fuchs's representation of Verbena presents the general characteristics of the species; the exemplar is depicted as if a living plant, but its parts are arranged to aid identification: leaves, stems, roots, and flowers can be inspected from all sides in the single view.

By 1583, with the publication of Andrea Cesalpino's *De plantis libri*, the system of classification was itself altered. In contrast to Brunfels and Fuchs, who followed the tradition of organizing herbals on the basis of

Figure 32   Abraham de Bruyn, [Twelve plates of animals and insects, with descriptions in Latin verse] (Antwerp?: 1583?). Engraving, oblong 8° [photo: by permission of the British Library, London] 871.h.75

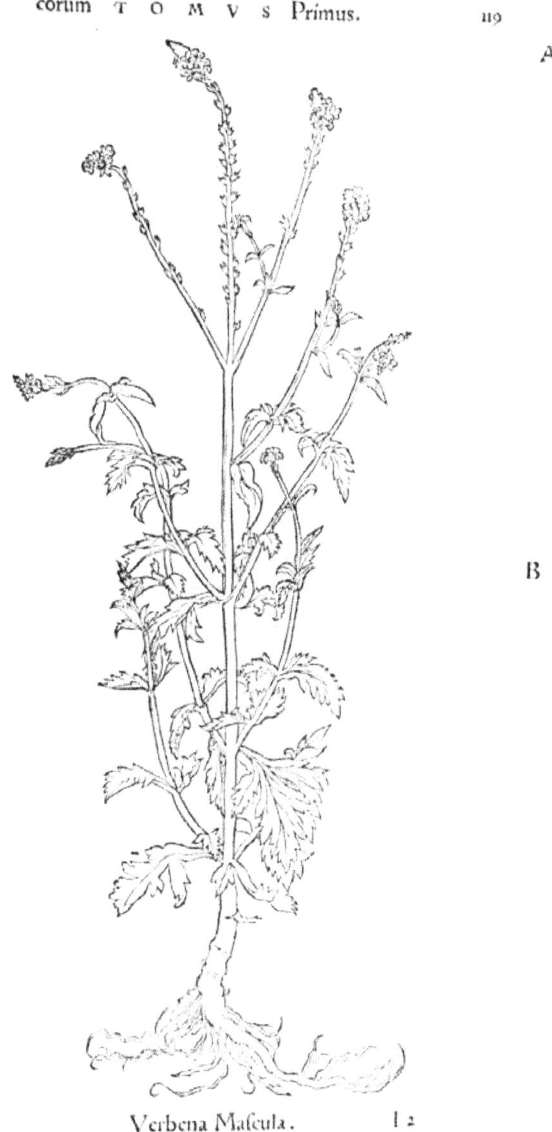

Figure 33   Hans Weiditz, *Verbena Mascula*, Otto Brunfels, *Herbarum vivae eicones* (Argentorati: I. Schottum, 1530–40) Woodcut, folio, 308 × 195 mm [photo: Osler Library, McGill University, Montreal]

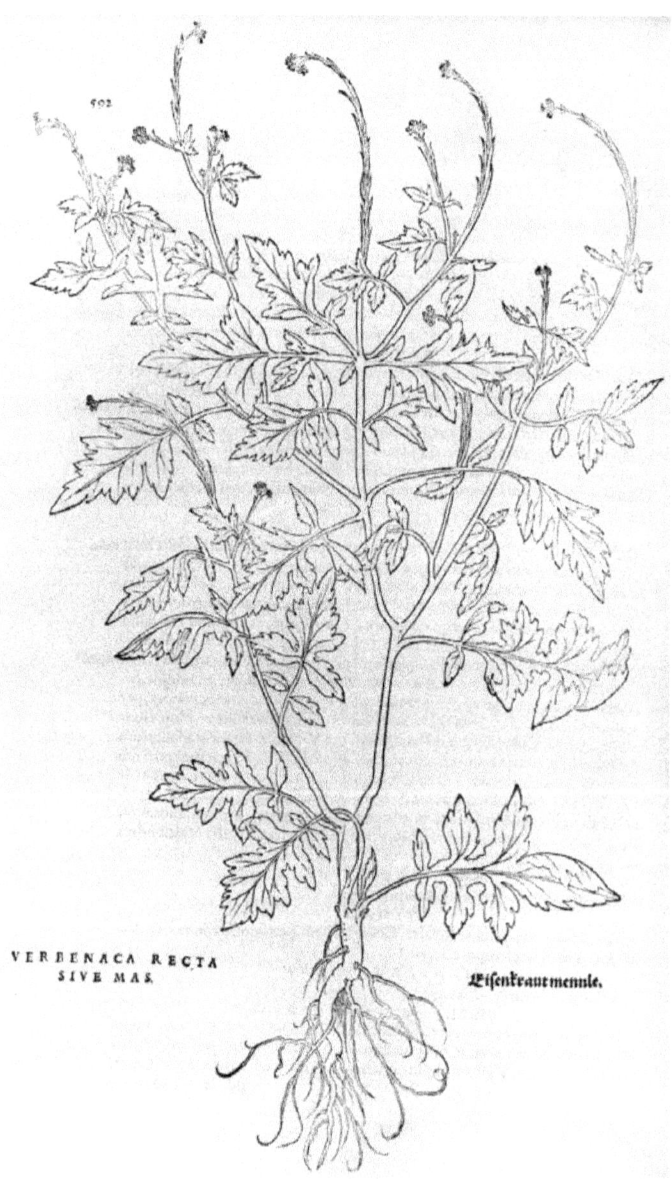

Figure 34   *Verbena Recta Sive Mas*, Leonhard Fuchs, *De Historia stirpium* (Basel, 1542). Woodcut, folio, 380 × 240 mm [photo: Osler Library, McGill University, Montreal]

medicinal properties, Cesalpino classified his plants on the basis of their physical characteristics.[42]

All of these authors illustrated male and female specimens, a mode of classifying sexual difference that is also characteristic of costume books; male and female types are almost always depicted on separate pages. In contrast to male figures, which are organized by profession (doge, senator, procurator), women are identified by their marital status (virgin, wife, widow) or in relation to their husbands' position (dogaressa, imbasciatrice, or procuratessa).[43] Courtesans and prostitutes were working women and thus exceptions to this paradigm. Vecellio classifies his example of these types according to a hierarchy of status that reflected the spaces in which they worked. Thus Vecellio contrasts the 'infamous places' inhabited by the street prostitute with the balconies on which courtesans can be seen soliciting clients (figs. 35, 36).[44] In a world viewed through theories of resemblance, men and women could be understood as parallel hierarchies; women were not different, just less developed, according to contemporary legal, theological, and scientific discourses. They were described as misbegotten: 'not in the ordinary course of Nature [praeter naturam],' as Cornelius Lapide put it, and 'not necessarily of the same species.'[45] Lacking the hot, dry humours found in men, women famously lacked reason. In the case of reproduction, this meant that it was women who provided the matter and men who contributed the form. An intriguing alternative to this Aristotelian wisdom is offered by the Venetian Giuseppe Rosaccio, cartographer, printmaker, and author who in his *Microcosmo* compares human reproduction to the generation of plants. The form of offspring 'is not made by the soul of the father, or of the mother, but by another, third [agent] that one finds inside the seed; and in order for this to be merely vegetative, without any capacity of imagination until its time is done, as we say, this [agent] only follows its vegetative movements ... doing nothing except perpetuate its species.'[46] Rosaccio's parallel between gestation and germination resonates with the broader tendency to find resemblances between plants, animals, geography, and costume, affinities that are highlighted by shared pictorial strategies.[47]

Botanical illustrators were consummate copyists, a result in part of the ephemeral nature of their models and the encyclopedic content of botanicals. Costume books required similar representational strategies.[48] In contrast to drawing from life – a practice subject to a range of contingencies, viewpoints, and the particulars of specific models, such as colour – print brought forward general characteristics, or essences.

Figure 35   Cesare Vecellio, *Meretrici Publiche*, *De gli habiti antichi, et moderni di diverse parti del mondo* (Venice: Damian Zenaro, 1590). Woodcut, 8°, 20 cm [photo: Courtesy John M. Wing Foundation, The Newberry Library, Chicago]

Figure 36 Cesare Vecellio, *Donne la Vernata*, *De gli habiti antichi, et moderni* (Venice: Damian Zenaro, 1590). Woodcut, 8°, 20 cm [photo: Courtesy John M. Wing Foundation, The Newberry Library, Chicago]

As more than one author explained, the graphic clarity of engraving made differences easily recognizable.[49] Moreover, classification, after Aristotle, considered substances rather than accidents, an approach that emphasized form, rather than smell or colour. Sight, which 'perceives the "essential" properties of a thing,' was becoming the criterion for classification, and the medium of print was the ideal means of expressing essences.[50] Not surprisingly, then, illustrators of botanicals and costume books typically filled the page with a single figure that was located close to the picture plane. Even when several costumes appear on a single sheet, these are arranged in rows as *exempla*. Placed on a low platform, or a generic patch of ground, the models are cut from their context like plants pulled from the ground; it is the contours and label of the vestments that signify topographical specificity, their rootedness.

Evidence of precisely this idea can be seen in Andrea Alciati's (Alciato) emblem book, a concept he popularized in the seventy-five editions of the book before 1570.[51] His series of moralizing images also served as albums in which their owners could collect signatures of friends, coats of arms, and also costume illustrations on the alternate empty leaves. Gathered toward the end of Alciati's 1564 edition are a number of pages with botanical illustrations that parallel the visual format seen in the costume books (compare figs. 37 and 35). Each plant has been extracted from the ground, identified with a Latin label, and surrounded by an elaborate frame.

The repeated use of frames, combined with the scientific and printmaking conventions discussed thus far, call attention to the category of identity designated by the costume. In contrast to the body as the means to convey moral values – an idea codified by Alberti in his treatise *On Painting*, and familiar to contemporaries from the Neoplatonic notion that outward appearances of bodies were an expression of interior moral worth – here the figures are cut from any narrative context in which their actions or movements could be interpreted.[52] The use of frames emphasizes the isolation of the figures and focuses the viewer on the vestments.[53] Instead of the body as the site of the moral good, in these representations it is the costume that is put forth as the locus of moral virtue.

Even the rare exception to the geographically isolated costume figures can be seen to prove the rule. In the volumes of the *Civitates orbis terrarum*, the first of which was published in 1572, Georg Braun compiled an atlas of the world's cities. Many contributing artists incorporated figures in the foreground that were copied from costume books.[54]

Figure 37   *Arbori. Cipresso,* Andrea Alciati, *Diverse imprese accommodate a diverse moralità* (Lyon: Gulielmo Rouillio, 1564) [photo: by permission of the British Library, London] Egerton 1215

To make the geographical fit clear, illustrators employed a number of devices to make the forms of local attire analogous with those of the topography. In the stereographic representation of Bilbao (fig. 38), for example, the dresses of the women in the foreground and the rolling hills around the city were made to emulate each other. Moreover, the poses and earlike appendages of the women's headdresses conform to those of the adjacent donkeys. Throughout the atlases of the *Civitates*, illustrators adjusted the costumes, architecture, topography, and even local livestock to demonstrate geographical commensurability.

By giving visual form to civic sartorial practices, costume books can be compared to chorography, the exact description of a city presented from a distant vantage point. This was clearly the parallel being drawn by Giuseppe Rosaccio, the author of the *Microcosmo* cited above, in his 1607 engraving of Italy (fig. 14).[55] The map is surrounded by 'ancient and modern costumes,' which fill the upper right of the sheet, and city views that frame the lower edge. Each image is individuated by the lines of the grid, which order the costumes and encourage comparisons between them. The publication of costume books was contemporary with the circulation of city views in printed collections, as noted earlier. By examining printed plans, viewers would have learned to recognize the distinctive shapes of cities: their walls, harbour, or fortifications.[56] Rosaccio's map informs viewers of the differences between places, and by bringing together city views with costume illustrations, the engraving demonstrates the shared pictorial and cognitive conventions of both.

Restating the title of Vecellio's costume books, Rosaccio's caption describes the figures as *abiti*, the contemporary term for costume. Derived from the Latin *habitus*, or aspect, the word signified the ways in which apparel invested bodies with meaning through the quality of the fabric and the tradition and conventions attached to dress.[57] The word is also defined as *contegno*, meaning attitude and behaviour and thereby conveying those attitudes to which people are inclined habitually or innately. *Abiti*, then, identified those aspects of clothing that were aligned with place, and these were the ideals inscribed in the costume prints: the social roles and characteristics that distinguished regional diversity across time. The Italian word *costume*, by contrast, meant custom, and suggests attitudes that are learned and adopted: how the wearer expressed claims about his or her status, education, or profession.[58] As the *art* of dressing, *costume* accentuates the theatrical aspect of clothes, how individuals styled themselves. These were the modes or fashions – adopted customs – that changed over time.

Figure 38   *Bilvao*, George Braun, *Civitates urbis terrarum, II* (Cologne, 1575). Hand-coloured engraving, folio [Courtesy Edward E. Ayer Collection, The Newberry Library, Chicago]

'Fashion,' for the modern theorist John Carl Flugel, 'in its more exuberant moments is seldom content with the silhouette that Nature has provided, but usually seeks to lay particular stress upon some single part or feature.'[59] In contrast to Flugel, who identifies changes to the contours of attire with fashion – the historical shift from breasts, for example, to legs – in the costume books, the silhouette signals the fixed contours of identity. The visual vocabularies used by the costume illustrators were more closely analogous to modes of representing flora or fish than what we today might expect for fashion. As in contemporary scientific illustrations, the costume prints were not attempts to represent particulars but to establish archetypes: an 'image which "floats" among the individuals of the species.'[60] Identity, in particular those visual features that enabled recognition, was still rooted in the concept of being identical to, or the same as, something else.

Travelling Books and the Meanings Invested in Costume

Printed costume books offered armchair travel, that pleasure Thomas Elyot describes in the epigraph cited earlier 'to beholde in his owne house every thynge that with in all the world is contained.' By contrast, manuscript illustrations of costumes were collected in small books that travelled with their owners across geographical boundaries. Small and portable, the *album amicorum* emerged as a contemporary phenomenon in which university students, merchants, and travellers from north of the Alps collected signatures, mottoes, and painted imagery, including coats of arms and costumes, as they moved between universities and other centres. The concept, as one owner of a printed album translated, provided 'Blanks, or Void Spaces for our friends, Adorn'd with the habit or dress of the Women of all the Country's in Europe, together with Blank Scutcheans Engrav'd in Copper, wherein may one very Conveniently paint their Cyphers or Coat of Arms.'[61]

The *album amicorum* first appeared in the 1550s among students, many from Wittenberg, embarking on academic peregrinations to universities in Bourges, Orléans, Besançon, Paris, Leuven, Leyden, Padua, Bologna, and Siena.[62] The concept expanded to a variety of professionals including merchants, artists, and artisans.[63] The majority of sixteenth-century books, however, come from Germany because of that country's vibrant education system that included travel to foreign universities.[64] Italians were not themselves owners of albums but their costumes appear in dozens of extant examples. The particular interest in

Venice, where there was no university, offers clues for understanding the function of costume illustrations more generally.

Early examples were typically small printed religious or emblem books in which blank sheets were provided for the owner to collect signatures and illustrations.[65] Editions of Andrea Alciati's *Emblemata*, the emblem book referred to earlier, and Philipp Melanchthon's *Loci communes theologici*, were the most popular choices. Jean de Tournes's *Thesaurus amicorum*, published before 1558 in Lyon, was the first book to target this market directly.[66] Sources for the visual imagery found in the albums include a wide variety of printed books including the earlier German *Stammbücher* (friendship albums) and *Wappenbücher* (books of coats of arms). These reflected the vogue among young nobles for collecting the date, signature, and arms of prestigious celebrities.[67] In *Wappenbücher*, costume figures, especially female ones, were used to frame escutcheons, many of which were left blank for owners to fill in. This convention appears in later manuscript and printed albums (fig. 39), but increasingly costumes and family coats of arms were separated from each other, indicating that costume was signifying in new ways (figs. 40–2). Detached from the escutcheon, and often alone on the page, the painted figures – located close to the picture plane and identified by a label – resemble those that would later appear in printed books.[68] In some albums, blank pages were surrounded with elaborate frames to add lustre to the owner's collection of inscriptions.

The use of the word 'album' to designate a list of autographs first appeared in a French dictionary in 1714, but its origins appear to have been the Roman word *album*, which signified the blank wall on which messages like those for announcing public games were posted. In a general sense, album referred to a list.[69] This idea is evident in the ordering of the books, for despite the apparent randomness with which images, dates, and signatures appear, there is always some organizational criterion, which often reflects the status of the signatory. For example, autographs of Fuggers, a family of wealthy German merchants, and patricians, are typically found toward the beginning of the books.[70] Signatures were often accompanied by mottoes, usually in Latin, and often Ciceronian in tenor, thereby marking the owner's humanist aspirations. Proverbs in a variety of languages could be incorporated alongside the Latin comments as signs of both international and elite interests.[71] By the middle of the seventeenth century, however, the modern vernacular languages came to predominate. The initial quest for 'nobility of blood,' evident in the *Wappenbücher*, had shifted toward an emphasis on 'nobility

Figure 39   Two female costumes with escutcheons dated 1574. Manuscript, watercolour, gouache, ink [photo: by permission of the British Library, London] Egerton 1191

Figure 40   *Duca di Venetia* from the *album amicorum* of P. Behaim from Nuremberg with a signature dated 1576. Manuscript, watercolour, gouache,
ink [photo: by permission of the British Library, London] Egerton
1192

Figure 41   *La dodesca di Venetie* with signature dated 1575 from an *album amicorum*. Manuscript, watercolour, gouache, ink [photo: by permission of the British Library, London] Additional 15699

Figure 42   *Duchessa Venetiana* with signature dated 1576 from an *album amicorum.* Manuscript, watercolour, gouache, ink [photo: by permission
of the British Library, London] Egerton 1191

of spirit,' thereby merging patrician values with humanist ideals in what one scholar has called 'the noble cult of friendship,' a coterie that may explain the dearth of women's signatures.[72] Family arms and signatures of colleagues – presented in the company of emblems, costumes, allegories, portraits, comic figures, and famous sites – asserted a relation between the visible and intellectual worlds in which their owners lived.

The inscriptions provided testimony of an owner's acquaintances and thus fulfilled a variety of functions. An illustrious signature could provide opportunities; like a passport, it could open doors.[73] Reflecting upon the motivational ideas conveyed in the pictures, texts, and comments inscribed by their professors and colleagues, students were offered moral guidance while being incited to intellectual vigour as directed by humanists.[74] To paraphrase Melanchthon, the books encouraged industriousness through their combination of inscriptions, which furnished wise teaching on one side and knowledge of the character and biographical details of the contributor on the other.[75] Moral guidance was the goal of Johann Theodor and Johann Israel de Bry, who offered pictures of positive *exempla* to emulate and 'coarser' behaviour to avoid in their *Emblemata secularia* (1611).[76] A third edition, published in 1614 in Frankfurt, continued this pedagogic track; the title encapsulates the function of the albums in general: *Pourtraict de la cosmographie morale … une centurie des plus belles inventions … pour presenter et corriger les moeurs.* As collections of names, albums could serve as memory aids and also as a list of absent individuals to whom one could toast when drinking socially.[77] Indeed, in the preface to his *Stamm-oder Gesellenbuch,* first published in 1579, Sigmund Feyerabend opined that *Schädtbücher* (books causing mischief) might be a more accurate description than *Stammbücher.* 'Many an honest man,' he assures his audience, 'considers making use of such a "Stammbuch."' This one, he contends, will even benefit the reader; 'indeed, he will see himself in it as in the Socratic mirror, and will find what defects in himself he must improve.'[78] Already in his *Bibliorum,* printed in 1571, Feyerabend advances morality and self-betterment; the printed models of coats of arms – to be embellished by the owner and his friends – are interleaved with illustrations of biblical stories identified by Latin captions. One of these volumes, owned by Conrad Weis, includes a manuscript costume illustration of a Venetian noble in a fur-lined toga that is signed by Weis's friend Cavilo Scheiner '1586.'[79]

What was the function of such an image amid a variety of hand-painted arms and allegorical figures? And what does this context suggest about the meanings of costume? Typically flashy and painted in brilliant gouache colours, the vestments appear to have been drawn from life, an impression furthered by meticulous attention to tailoring and textiles (figs. 39–42).[80] For example, the doge cuts an elegant figure in his ermine cape, gold cloak, and swish red robes with their wide, *alla dogalina* sleeves, painted to resemble luxurious velvet (fig. 40). With their poses and sophisticated rendering of foreign dress, the paintings might seem analogous with modern fashion plates. However, their function was significantly different.

Understanding the role of this imagery is complicated by the vast number of albums, each of which is a unique record of an individual's life, travels, and friendships. And yet, with the exception of the vivid colour, the representational conventions of the painted figures are remarkably similar to those in the printed costume books (compare, for example, figs. 43 and 44). A single figure, usually identified by a Latin label, often fills a page, and the absence of any setting renders the shape of the costume central. Costumes and poses are repeated in different albums by different hands, attesting to the use of manuscript or printed models instead of painting from life.

In contrast to print, however, manuscript illustrators could more easily accommodate changes in fashion such as the spiral *corni* into which Venetian women bound their hair at the end of the sixteenth century. The hand-painted pictures could thereby command a certain currency, as if individuals seen in the flesh. Artists of these sartorial souvenirs combined conventions and gestures known to them from models with an attention to the materiality of costume. This was a naturalistic mode of 'conterfeiting,' as Peter Parshall explains the term, used to claim 'the truth of the eye-witness account.'[81]

Many of the Venetian types sought by collectors, moreover, were the elite and the infamous: the doge, dogaressa, and courtesan. The popularity of the dogaressa in these albums bore little relation to the real experiences of visitors, however. Between the public festivities for the coronations of Zilia Dandolo Priuli in 1557 and Morosina Morosini Grimani in 1597, when many manuscript and printed illustrations considered here were made, there were few, if any, ceremonies in which the dogaressa could have been seen in public. Zilia Dandolo would remain in the Palazzo Ducale only until 1559, when her husband died. War with the Turks precluded any ceremony for dogaressa Loredana Marcello, the wife of Alvise Mocenigo (1570–7), and she died in 1572. Sebastiano Venier, Mocenigo's successor (1577–8), died before a procession could

Figure 43   *Cortegiana Venetiana* from an *album amicorum*. Manuscript, water-colour, gouache, ink [photo: by permission of the British Library, London] Egerton 1191

Figure 44   Cesare Vecellio, *Cortigiana, De gli habiti antichi, et moderni* (Venice: Damian Zenaro, 1590). Woodcut, 8°, 20 cm [photo: Museo Correr, Venice]

be staged for his wife. Therefore, when many of the illustrations were being painted, there was no dogaressa for visitors to see (figs. 41, 42). Even the Venetian Vecellio, who could have seen the 1557 event, which he describes toward the end of his 1590 text, follows models seen in the albums and northern printed books for the pose and lavish brocade vestments, veil, and jewelled *corno* worn by the dogaressa (see figs. 45 and 25).[82] Although past centuries left no visual record, he explains to the reader, 'I believe nevertheless that their costume is similar ... to those that ancient matrons used to wear.'[83] Consequently, instead of women seen in the streets, for northern collectors of Venetian costumes what mattered was likely the dogaressa's allegorical function as 'a feminine symbol of domestic virtue,' a personification of the apex of patrician luxury, constancy, and the ideal wife.[84] The manuscript illustrators do not identify the figures by name; instead of portraits of historical individuals, the images can be explained more effectively as representations of moral values.

The Veiled Virgin and the Courtesan were equally popular among owners of albums. Where the Courtesan, in Margaret Rosenthal's words, 'embodied the city immersed in luxury, spectacle, disguise, commercialization, voluptuousness, and sensuality,' the Virgin signified Venice's immaculate origins, chastity, and republican longevity, all preserved from foreign domination.[85] Thus the Dogaressa, Virgin, and Courtesan, in tandem with the male types – Doge, Senator, and Rettore (governor) – responded to the image of Venice as it was perceived by foreigners, as modest, veiled, concupiscent, exotic, sober, and austere.[86] By collecting foreign types alongside the signatures and arms of their associates, travellers could use these albums to shape their own experiences of the world into a moral cosmography.

This potential for flexibility and invention in content is also evident in the form of the visual imagery. In some cases, the albums were illustrated by their owners, but the elaborate coats of arms and foreign costumes were more often painted by professionals, as demonstrated by the appearance of figures in the same style in different albums.[87] The professional quality of many of the painted illustrations indicates they were probably produced by document illuminators and printmakers for whom the use of pattern books was a familiar workshop practice.[88] Drawing on a repertory of models, artists could paint costumes from different cities, often in the same album. In the famous Botticin codex in Padua, the painter constructed a parade of civic vestments by simply changing a sleeve or a collar, or adjusting the neckline of his otherwise generic male and female patterns.[89]

Figure 45   Cesare Vecellio, *Principessa, ò Dogaressa, De gli habiti antichi, et moderni* (Venice: Damian Zenaro, 1590). Woodcut, 8°, 20 cm [photo: Museo Correr, Venice]

Copying is also evident in early collections of manuscript costumes, a related form of visual imagery that anticipates artistic practices seen in both the friendship albums and the printed costume books.[90] For example, Sigmundt Heldt began his series of paintings in 1560, the year after he acquired an office in the administration of motto writers in Nuremberg.[91] Several of Heldt's images resemble those seen in Christoph Weiditz's hand-painted *Trachtenbuch*, begun in 1529, when he commenced his travels to Spain and the Netherlands.[92] Resemblances among the two artists' European costumes demonstrate that both men were copying prototypes that had remained constant for decades.[93] These manuscript compilations bring to the fore conventions seen later in printed costume books: the use of models, consistent scale, clear contours, the absence of a geographical setting, and the use of a label. Indeed, the graphic style of Weiditz's painted costumes, as Theador Hampe has proposed, suggests the artist intended to publish his codex.[94]

Travellers could obtain illustrations before departing for foreign parts; signatures, inspirational proverbs, and paintings likely served as memories of one's home. As Max Rosenheim has suggested, the signatory may have contributed to the cost of these illustrations, a hypothesis that is furthered by autographs made in the spaces around the paintings, as if to designate proprietorship of the image (figs. 39–42).[95] Some albums, on the other hand, include empty pages with captions denoting a costume; these blank sheets demonstrate the owner's anticipation of a figure that was never acquired. These lacunae are especially intriguing because they indicate there was a desire to collect particular social types.

The conventions in the albums and those found in printed costume books can be compared to the emblem book, a genre that is often aligned with moral concerns. However, beyond the association already drawn between costumes and social and moral types, there are also structural parallels. Alain Boureau has called attention to the communal and political function of emblem books. He attributes their success to the ways in which they distilled experience into visual images, thereby enabling the world to be classified and ordered.[96] By formalizing an idea, legend, or experience into an image, an emblem shifted the locus of meaning away from 'resemblance' toward 'representation.'[97] This turn toward abstraction necessitated that viewers learn meanings instead of recognizing the referent through its mimetic resemblance to something else. In contrast with naturalistic representation, emblem books translated political, moral, and communal concepts into allegorical figures (fig. 46). For example, the full-page allegories *Detractio* and

Figure 46   *Detractio* and *Veritas* from the *album amicorum* of Hieronymi Holtzschuher from Nuremberg. Manuscript, water-colour, gouache, and ink [photo: by permission of the British Library, London] Egerton 1201

Veritas are typical of those seen in emblem books and friendship albums, in which abstract ideas are personified by female figures.[98] Each stands on a patch of ground, holding her attributes. A label identifies what she symbolizes at the top of the page. The accumulation of painted costume illustrations by travellers may have operated similarly; the figures were valued for the *ideas* they emblematized. The migration of Venetian types into what were essentially moral guidebooks brings to the fore those concepts that were important to foreigners about Venice. Instead of Venetians seen in the streets, the images are labelled diagrams, 'walking Ideas,' that owners, or their friends who commissioned the paintings, added to their collections.[99]

This allegorical function is also evident in printed costume books since here too costume is the signature of the identities that constitute the social type (status, space, profession, gender, and sexuality).[100] This interpretation is furthered by the existence of costume books, albums, and single sheets that illustrate female costumes exclusively. For example, in 1586 Feyerabend published Jost Amman's *Im Frauwenzimmer,* a costume book consisting of female figures. Both the German and Latin editions were dedicated to women, indicating the use of female models may have anticipated female readership.[101] However, the emphasis cannot be ascribed only to audience, given the long-standing convention of using female figures to personify cities. In Amman's famous *Book of Trades,* published by Feyerabend in 1568 with poems by Hans Sachs, it is only men who are depicted. Another example is Ambrogio Brambilla, the engraver of the single-sheet of female costumes discussed above (fig. 19), who used the same gridded format for his etching *Street Sellers of Rome,* all of whom are men.[102] Although friendship albums were owned by men almost exclusively, these were embellished with female figures, sometimes exclusively, as the owner of a printed *album amicorum* translated: 'Adorn'd with the habit or dress of the Women of all the Country's in Europe.'[103] Instead of readership, then, it seems to have been the allegorical efficacy of the female body that encouraged its appropriation for geography, an emphasis that also corresponds with the use of female figures in emblem books. Personified as a female body, the physical terrain of a city could also be conflated with physiological notions discussed above, and with female sexuality. Not surprisingly, perhaps, it was the Venetian Dogaressa, the Veiled Virgin, and the Courtesan who were favourites: signs that the city's long-standing survival as a republic remained intact and yet open to the traffic of commerce and foreigners. Instead of fashion plates, the illustrations were gathered, like the signa-

Figure 47   Cesare Vecellio, *Spose in Sensa*, *De gli habiti antichi, et moderni* (Venice: Damian Zenaro, 1590). Woodcut, 8°, 20 cm [photo: Museo Correr, Venice]

tures of friends and acquaintances, as emblems of the moral imperatives registered in dress, the kind of imperatives being negotiated by the signatories and owners themselves as they travelled between cities.

Legislating Visibilities

For foreigners, as I have been suggesting, pictorial representations of costumed figures functioned as icons of the republic, whose meanings were fixed over time. For the Venetian state, by contrast, costume was a sign of identity – profession, status, faith – and the legibility of this system of visual classification required continual surveillance since transgressions, such as unlawful extravagances or changing one's clothes, disrupted the social order. Morever, Venice's singularity, as Francesco Sansovino and others noted, was a result of the presence of 'people from the most distant parts of the earth who come together here ... to deal and trade.'[104] And sorting out these foreigners required ensuring that their attire was consistent with their identities. Yet the dangers of travel in the sixteenth century forced merchants and wayfarers to change their clothes, names, and even faith. Instead of something inalienable and bound irrevocably to the self, identities could be adopted as voyagers moved between cities.[105]

In what follows I consider evidence from Venetian judicial processes that aimed to sort out the meanings invested in clothes, their social expectations, and the identities of those who inhabited them. I begin with problems raised by individuals who changed their clothes, then turn to an unusual arraignment in the Venetian colony of Crete; in this case, the clothes were the same, but the body that wore them changed.

As a trading crossroads, and with its reputation for religious tolerance and independence from Rome, Venice in the sixteenth century was composed of a complex mosaic of ethnic groups. Protestants from Germany and Muslims from the Ottoman Empire passed through the city, residing with their communities that had been established in particular neighbourhoods. Germans were housed at the Fondaco dei Tedeschi (1505–8), and an equivalent structure to contain the Turkish community was considered by the senate throughout the century, although not instituted until 1617.[106] Jews had been official residents since 1382, and in 1516 they were confined to the ghetto. The ghetto and its inhabitants could be viewed as a parish, as separate but different, as parts of 'a single, coherent order.'[107] On the other hand, as Randolph Head explains further, the Jews represented a threat to this unified image: 'Judaism was itself formless, but always threatening to the foundations of order.'[108] The issue became more complex with the arrival of Jews and Muslims from the Iberian peninsula – beginning in 1492 – many of whom had been forced to convert to Christianity. Marranos, a disparaging term used to describe converted Jews, were expelled from Portugal when it was annexed by Philip II in 1580.[109] Morescos – Arabic Muslims who had been forced to adopt Christian customs – were pushed out of Spain throughout the century and eventually expelled in 1609. It was in this context, complicated by the arrival of 'New Christians,' that the Venetian Inquisition in 1547 began its investigations 'of apostasy and Judaizing.'[110] Numerous Venetian Inquisition cases document the interrogation of visitors suspected of converting from Christianity to Lutheranism, Judaism, and Islam.

Since the Fourth Lateran Council in 1215, it had been decreed that Jews were to be distinguished from Christians in order to prohibit sexual relations between them. In Venice, one way of distinguishing Jews was the colour of their hats.[111] The official process 'of keeping Jews in what was considered to be their proper place,' as Benjamin Ravid has shown, required continual efforts by the state to ensure compliance. There were many exemptions granted by the state for groups of Jews, and also numerous attempts to circumvent the sign of the coloured hats.[112] For example, Brian Pullan cites the trial of Righetto Marrano, who evidently carried both yellow and black hats to be exchanged at a moment's notice.[113] A Spaniard complained of a Jew from Rialto, Consalvo Baes, whom he accused of changing his clothes: 'scoundrel, cheat, you did business with me in the dress of a Christian and now you dress as a Jew!'[114] However it was baptized Christians, suspected of changing their faith, who could be accused of heresy, and changing one's costume was material evidence.

For many witnesses at heresy trials, as Randolph Head explains, *biretta zhalla* (yellow hat) and *biretta negra* (black hat) became convenient shorthand for Jew and Christian.[115] Gian Giacomo de Fedeli was among those investigated for wearing both. During his trial he was asked if he went to mass, confessed, and took communion. He explained that he lived as a Jew in Venice, but when travelling outside the city, 'I lived as a Christian and I was confessed and communicated and went to mass.'[116] Questioned if he wore 'a yellow hat to such offices,' he replied, 'No, sir, I went out of the land to Bressa [Brescia] ... and there I wore a black hat.'[117] Outside the capital he traded his Jewish clothes for those of a Christian. The inquisitors were neither familiar nor interested in Jewish doctrine, but the defendant's clothing furnished them with evidence from everyday experience. For both judges and witnesses in legal trials, the costume of suspects was used as evidence 'to decide their real identity, and to condemn them if it conflicted with their primary, sacramental identity.'[118] A subject's 'real identity,' then, was determined by the performance of certain rites that marked the individual's affiliation with a community, but also, and this is crucial, identity depended on the proper alignment between an individual's actions and his or her appearance.[119] The Inquisition sought to define the boundaries between religious groups, and costume was charged with stabilizing identities.

In one early trial, the defendant was asked if he was presently a Jew or a Christian, to which he replied: 'Though I live as a Jew internally, externally I am named with the Christian (crossed out) name of Tristano de Costa.'[120] Asked whether this was a Jewish or a Christian name, he responded, 'When my father gave me this name, he said [it was] because [it would] be so much the better that he called me this name.' Warned that he must answer the question of whether he was a Jew or a Christian, he stated, 'I do not do the actions of a Christian.' Tristano's reference to his 'actions' corresponded with the inquisitors' interests in the ways in which religious identity was performed. Instead of interrogating individuals about their beliefs, the judges focused on the rituals – baptism in particular – and 'everyday patterns of behavior.'[121]

The merchant Andrea, the subject of another case, was born in Florence to Jewish parents and named Abraham, but later moved to Ferrara, where he was baptized and adopted his Christian name.[122] When he travelled to Turkey, he wore the clothes of a Jew; in Ragusa, he transformed himself into a Christian. In Venice, where he lived in the ghetto, he was tried for heresy. Here too, the proceedings focused on the colour of hat; Andrea explained his transmutations as follows: although baptized, he was forced to live as a Jew by his father. Indeed, his inheritance depended upon his Jewish identity, necessitating that he live in the ghetto and wear the red hat, now the colour that identified a Jew.[123] Whatever Andrea's 'real' faith, the exigencies of his life and his profession required that he fit in. The case thereby suggests that identities – even religious or ethnic ones – were not yet conceptualized as something intrinsic to the self.

But herein lay the problem, for as Head explains, 'the Signoria resolved the tension between commercial advantage and religious purity by insisting that every individual should be clearly and unambiguously assigned to only one religion.'[124] The value of such Inquisition cases, as Head stresses, does not lie in the information they provide about religious communities but in the concerns they reveal regarding how these groups were distinguished from Christians.[125] Where judges in the Spanish Inquisition came to the trials already certain of their conclusions on the basis of established stereotypes, the Venetian inquisitors investigated ambiguity. Thus, as Brian Pullan explains, 'neither [the judges], nor the Venetians they summoned as witnesses, had any clear idea of what they were looking for, and were generally prepared to be surprised.'[126] Moreover, in religious directives after the Council of Trent, costume was described as a sign and the wearer's adherence to the costume's meaning signified its effect. The aim was congruence between the sign and the referent, between, for instance, a cleric's habit and his pious actions. The comportment of the wearer was to become habitual and thereby in turn to invest the costume with its meanings.[127] As the Inquisition records indicate, it was the perception of a gap between the costume and the performance that preoccupied the inquisitors.

Venice was a departure point to the east, and travellers to the Levant often relinquished their native dress in favour of Ottoman attire. Venetians en route to Constantinople dressed as Turks for protection, and perhaps to signal the threshold between the two cultures. For example, the artist Gentile Bellini returned in Ottoman dress following his work for Mehmed II, whose portrait he painted in 1481.[128] The *bailo*, the Venetian ambassador, and his retinue were given robes of state by the Grand Vizier and the sultan.[129] Even before departing from Venice, however, the *bailo* and his family might appear for their journey attired in Ottoman costume.[130] After the unexpected defeat of the Turks at Lepanto, the triumphant Venetian soldiers returned to Venice dressed up as Turks.[131]

Nevertheless, the distinction between dressing as a Muslim (*da turco*), appearing as one (*far turco*), or turning into a Muslim (*farsi turco*) was a crucial one.[132] These concerns are demonstrated in a brief sketch of an early seventeenth-century case in which three men, Fra Giovanni Fecondo, Giovanni Lopez, and Bartolomeo Derera – from Barcelona, Madrid, and Seville respectively – arrived in Venice dressed as Christians.[133] Outcast and impoverished, they were offered support by the Muslim community at the Fondaco (*casa de Turchi, Ghetto*), where, according to witnesses, they shaved their heads and traded their Christian clothes for Turkish ones. Guided to a merchant galley bound for Constantinople, they were arrested, 'dressed as Muslims (*da turchi*) and wearing turbans,' and accused of converting to Islam.[134]

The two Giovannis, a friar from the order of hermits of Saint Augustine and a soldier, initially identified themselves as Morescos, Muslims forced to live as Christians in Spain, but both later confessed to having been baptized. Fra Giovanni then asserted that he wanted 'to be a Muslim (*far turco*) on the outside, and not to renounce his faith in his heart.' When the Turks were sleeping, he testified, he would secretly make the sign of the cross, adding that he had negated his faith 'only with his mouth and not otherwise with his heart.'[135] Bartolomeo initially denied being baptized, accounting for his Christian dress as mere ceremony, but he later recanted, stating 'I became a Turk (*farmi turco*), but not with my heart, because I am a Christian.' Presumably compromised by his early testimony 'of having experienced being Christian only ceremonially,' Bartolomeo, like Fra Giovanni, was sentenced to the galleys on suspicion of heresy.[136]

By contrast, Giovanni Lopez denied either dressing as a Turk (*da turco*) or becoming one (*farsi turco*), and he was released. He confessed only to shaving his hair and eating meat on two Fridays but asserted that he had had no intention of giving up his faith. Indeed, he claimed to have urged Fra Giovanni to return to the Christian faith. Giovanni Lopez was freed on the condition that he was forbidden from all dealings – especially those of faith – with Turks or other infidels. Costume, like eating meat on Fridays and circumcision, was evidence of having *acted* as a Muslim, and clearly legislated religious identity required a correlation between one's faith on the interior and how one appeared to others on the outside.[137] For the inquisitors, then, to dress like a Muslim was a symptom of having becoming one.

In contrast to these cases in which costume was interpreted as a sign of identity, an unusual case of *travestimento* (disguise) turned the process inside out. In 1594, the Quarantia Criminale investigated a denunciation that was sent to the doge from Zuanne Semitecolo, the councillor of Retimo (present-day Réthimnon) in Crete, where a peasant, Frangia Cudumini, was accused of having impersonated the Venetian governor. The masquerade – for the man was seen in the red clothes of a Rettore (governor) – was allegedly staged by the vice-governor Pesaro 'in his palace where he dressed a peasant in his red cloth, with a *Romana* (a long robe) and a round cap.' Wearing the red cloak, and escorted from the palace by soldiers, the peasant attracted a crowd that followed him to town. The soldiers reportedly encouraged the charade by exclaiming 'here is the Governor Falier,' whom they mocked by striking the impostor in the face with a cap. 'When I saw this,' lamented Semitecolo, 'I was filled with the greatest pain, considering it an ugly act made against a noble.'[138]

In response to the accusation, a lengthy and secretive investigation attempted to ascertain how Cudumini came to wear the red clothes, his intentions regarding the masquerade, and the response of those who saw him in the garments. Great attention was paid to this *Romana* during the process, the long robe that was worn by some nobles in Venice and identified with the uniform of Venetian governors in the provinces.[139] The cloak was not the black one worn by nobles, Cudumini specified to the magistrates, but a *pretina*, a long robe closed in front with many buttons, 'like that worn by you.'[140] Stranded in Retimo, he explained, and possessing only a single shirt and pants, he had asked the vice-governor for something to wear. Since the only old clothes he had were red, he directed Cudumini to take them to a lawyer, who would give him two lire for them. On account of the cold, he donned the jacket and cloak. 'Were you not able to imagine,' asked one official, 'that those clothes were not suitable for a peasant like you and that wearing them publicly would have conveyed the impression that you intentionally imitated the dress of the governor, because everyone would come with admiration to see you?'[141] However Cudumini denied these accusations and any knowledge of the significance of the attire. Indeed, he asked, cleverly, how he could have imagined the effect, since he had never worn the costume before?

Repeatedly witnesses were asked to confirm if they heard the words reported by Semitecolo: 'here is the true governor Falier,' or any other 'rude exclamations' (*villania*). Cudumini denied hearing such words, although he added that he could not understand French or Greek, the languages spoken by those in the crowd. Whether the entourage followed the impostor because they misidentified him as the governor, or whether they were co-conspirators in the masquerade was never determined and the case was closed. Either way, it was the alleged complicity of the vice-governor and soldiers and the symbolic affront to the Venetian state that was at stake, to which the secrecy and a final letter to the doge may attest. Following the investigation, Semitecolo wrote to the doge 'to justify his actions, having been moved by his zeal for public dignity.' He defended his assertion that 'the peasant knew the truth,' and worse, that 'the boor masqueraded in the *Romana* of red silk and Magistrate's hat by order of the Illustrious Bartolomeo Pesaro, now Vice-governor [and] in public places this peasant impersonated the Illustrious Falier, the Governor of Retimo: a display of derision and mockery, that showed the Illustrious Vice-governor's lack of respect.'[142]

The councillor's concern highlights the anxiety caused when there is a disjunction between costumes and the bodies that wear them, a gap between the performative function of clothes and the performance. Under normal conditions, the *Romana* had a constitutive function; by dressing in the red robes of a governor, the wearer was transformed into a representative of the government in the same way that performatives, such as 'I pronounce you' or 'I invest you,' change a person from one state into another.[143] The structure in which performatives operate remains relatively stable because the conditions within which the words are stated are highly codified and conventionalized, and maintained by the ideological and legal armature within which they operate. The costume represents that institutional power, which is only personified by the governor, magistrate, or priest. In Venice, this authority could be turned upside down and mocked during carnival, but when Cudumini donned the red cloak in the colony of Crete, neither the symbolic order in which it functioned nor the conditions for inverting this order were in place. Although the investigators did question the impostor's complicity in the performance, it was the soldiers' participation in the masquerade that was significant. Repeatedly witnesses were asked if they heard the words 'here is the governor Falier,' or 'here is the *real* governor,' as if Falier were himself the impostor. These words recall the labels in the costume books, but in this case, although they identify the symbolic function of the costume, they also point to its failure.

Cudumini's masquerade – whether intentional or not, and whether recognized as a *travestimento* by the crowd – failed, according to the councillor, because he was an illiterate peasant: 'with an aquiline nose, marked with a black scar on the left and another in the middle of this nose that crosses to the right; he looks to be fifty-six although he says he is sixty; he is crudely dressed with pants of rough white fabric, a shirt with no jacket and a black Dalmatian cap with boots of black leather.'[144] He might have appeared to be the governor, his clothes fitting into the symbolic system, but it was his body – the scars, wrinkles, and facial features – that did not fit, revealing a symptom of the 'real,' what Slavoj Žižek describes as the 'relation between symbolic identification and the leftover, the remainder, the object-excrement that escapes it.'[145]

This lack of fit between the governor's clothes and the peasant's body, and the alleged accompanying mockery, point to ideology's unwritten rules. Judicial procedures, sumptuary legislation, and registration were intended to clarify identities, but these institutions also depended upon the mechanisms that potentially subverted their meaning: the exchange of clothes, cross-dressing, disguise, and the temporal fluctuations and ambiguities of fashion. Courtesans who dressed as noble women, Jewish merchants who changed their hats, and the visitors who dressed as Turks, undermined stability, yet these transgressions also enabled the state to display its control over identities. By contrast, secrecy in the *travestimento* investigation suggests the masquerade was more subversive because it revealed the danger of making the unwritten rules public; by undermining the authority of costume, the charade threatened Venetian control in the colony. In this case, the threat of the performance lay in potentially exposing the clothes for all that they were: the material remainder of their symbolic function.[146]

Incorporating the Body

The cases discussed above highlight the gaps between the symbolic meanings invested in costume and the bodies that wear them. These were precisely the openings that sumptuary and registration legislation attempted to sew up, the lack of fit that the iterative work of regulating identities sought to conceal. Clothes signified through social exchanges the space between the performance and the expectations of the audience, between how the viewer styled himself or herself and what was perceived as innate. This final section turns to the effects of printed costume imagery on the body. By considering the ways in which clothing mediated between visual images and the body, I propose that the formation of identities increasingly depended upon the skin's function as a threshold between the body and the images through which the self was constituted.

Earlier in this chapter I suggested that the pictorial conventions of costume illustrations – graphic clarity, emphasis on contours, isolation of the figures from a specific context, copying of models, and the reproductive mode of production – reduced a plethora of differences into recognizable types that would have encouraged a range of individuals to identify with the same image. In so doing, costume illustrations located identity in the representation, in the identical image that circulated through print. I have also posited that this process would have altered the ways in which identities accrued to individuals. On one level, the conventions encouraged viewers to compare their costumes with those of others, thereby cementing civic and geographical associations. In contrast to long-standing familial and corporate affiliations, viewers were prompted to find their place within a world now catalogued by dress. On another level, as proposed in this last section, learning to compare pictures of costumes must have drawn attention to the effects of viewers' own clothes. Costume may thereby have come to function more forcefully as a threshold between individuals and their social experiences.

As emblems of moral and social types, the costume illustrations circulated images of ideals. The upright poses in the prints – generic and repetitive – would have furnished viewers with unified body images, 'stabilizing images' that would have called attention to their own posture.[147] Recognizing the distinctive silhouette of the figures would have further sharpened viewers' awareness of their own corporeal boundaries, a scenario that recalls Jacques Lacan's infant who identifies with the contours of the gesticulating body in the mirror.[148] In contrast to the infant, who mistakes its image for itself, the small-scale figures in the prints are exemplars. As models, they would have facilitated the identification of many individuals with the same image, a process encouraged by the labels that interpolate the viewer as a member of a group, as a senator, nobleman, religious, or matron.[149] If identity with one's family, parish, confraternity, and guild was characteristic of late medieval identity, the labels in costume books construct a cast of social roles in which the categories have shifted from the local *contrada* or parish, to the city as a whole. Profession, gender, and ethnicity have moved into the foreground. Abraham de Bruyn's *Italian Senators and Officials*, for example, display the subtle variations seen in the collective pattern of their uniforms (fig. 31). These sartorial signatures are what distinguish a people from other regions, and in the context of de Bruyn's atlas of vestments, printed costume books participated in constructing something resembling a new global order.

The costume illustrators circumnavigated bodies, displaying them from all sides for an observer who is often acknowledged by the gaze (or a veil in response to the gaze) of the figure in the print (figs. 28, 43, 44, 47). The absence of any narrative setting emphasizes this exchange between seeing and being seen, thereby drawing the attention of viewers to their own postural image, to the fact that the sensate body, in Lacan's words, is 'looked at from all sides.'[150] As we have seen, this mode of representation parallels contemporary scientific illustration; here, the depiction of the posterior view – with the characteristic 'tail-like appendage' – would have reminded viewers that they too were *in* the picture (fig. 47). These new experiences must have altered the ways in which individuals saw themselves by aligning the single point from which a person sees, with the place 'from which the subject will see himself ... *as others see him.*'[151] Identified by the image, viewers would have become both the viewing subject and the object.

And yet, if the representational conventions support identification of individuals with the civic community, concerns with legislating identities in Venice make it clear that the system was not seamless. In this case, Lacan's theory of the screen is suggestive, understood here as that threshold through which the subject negotiates its place within the social order: what the subject 'gives of himself, or receives from the other, something that is like a mask, a double, an envelope, a thrown-off skin.'[152] All of these analogies stress identification with something external to the subject's own body since the subject mistakenly identifies itself with the contours of the figure in the mirror or the image. Because of the misalignment between the subject and the ideal reflection, this exchange is analogous to a garment that is continuously being adjusted to fit.[153] The fit between the costume and the wearer – the extent to which the social type in the prints and the viewer's experience of his or her own body converged – would have been measured by social exchanges, the 'symbolic ratification' needed to acquire an image as a part of the subject's identity.[154] Significantly, the transformative impact of this exchange would have depended upon the novelty of the *repeated* experience of looking at images in tandem with the didactic effect of the visual conventions.

Lacan stresses the infant's misidentification with the specular image, a projection of the self into the social order that is facilitated by the presence of the mother, who legitimates the infant's acquisition of the image as a part of its identity; the mother also holds the infant, 'support[ing] the perspective chosen by the subject in the field of the Other.'[155] This symbolic figure is intriguing in relation to the costume books, since the images seen in the prints addressed both the viewer's visual *and* sensate perceptions. The label might have ratified the viewer's identification with the external image, which may in turn have called attention to the materiality of the viewer's own costume, the extent to which it constrains, shields, or exposes the body. However, in contrast to Lacan's 'other who emerges at the expense of the self,' the sheer novelty and accessibility of these prints, and the process of learning to compare oneself with others, would surely have intensified viewers' experiences of their own clothes.

The generic figures in the prints can be understood as ideal images, but their constitutive effects – the extent to which they would have shaped identities – would also have depended upon the materiality of costume. Costume illustrations invested moral values, ideality, and social roles in the clothing that surrounded the body. But on the body, costume is more than a frame; instead, clothing is the mediating surface through which the bodily and fragmented ego is integrated with the representations that sustain it.[156] The body, through its interaction with other objects, is continually constituted through touch, a model that accounts for the ego's sense of 'both "sameness" and "otherness."'[157] The former, defined by Silverman as proprioceptivity,

> can best be understood as the ego component to which concepts like 'here,' 'there,' and 'my' are keyed ... muscles which effect the shifting of the body and its members in space ... proprioceptivity would seem to be intimately bound up with the body's sensation of occupying a point in space, and with the terms under which it does so. It thus involves a nonvisual mapping of the body's form.[158]

The weight of the body in space and the experience of its surface are organized by imaginary and material representations – images and clothing – that support, orient, and individuate it.

Where Lacan stresses the container at the expense of the body – the subject's misidentification of its self with the unified body in the image – Didier Anzieu's account of the skin ego develops the inverse relation. The skin is the threshold between individuals and their social and psychic experiences, the boundary between the self and others, and a 'site of interaction with others.'[159] The skin, as a 'mirror of reality,' protects and relays the experience of the world that is in turn expressed on it, and through it, as for example, scars, wrinkles, and clothing – haunted by the traces of the wearer – enable individuals to be identified.[160] For Anzieu, individuation – the development of the ego and consciousness – occurs through tactile sensations. By touching oneself – an effect felt through dress – the subject experiences itself as both subject and object, the double sensation of the ego as both 'I' and 'self.'[161] Exerting pressure on the skin, moreover, clothing sustains the subject's self-sensation, distinguishing the wearer from recognizing himself or herself merely 'as a member of the species.'[162] This impression of being in one's body provides what the externality of the mirror image cannot: 'the apprehension on the part of the subject of his or her "ownness."'[163] The subject's identity, then, following Anzieu, is managed by imaginary *and* material representations, by the overlapping effects of ideals that circulate in images and the physical limitations imposed on the body by clothes.

In contrast with Lacan's *Gestalt* body image – that moment in the mirror stage when the subject sees itself prior to its symbolic structuration – Anzieu, Silverman, and others emphasize the subject's 'perception of the boundaries of the body.'[164] Here, the emphasis is on the relation between the stabilizing representations seen by the subject and those fragmented images of bodily experience which are shaped by 'the interests others take in the different parts of our body,' interests that are shaped by 'social exchange.'[165] Clearly, these were the kinds of investments in the body that were prompted by costume illustrations. As the interface between an individual's tactile experiences and the social roles seen in the prints, clothing may have come to reinforce the limits of the subject's own body. By enveloping the body as a second skin, costume takes on this boundary function, either securing or revealing areas of the body, an attachment to the skin through which clothes can acquire denotative meanings, such as those signified by gloves or shoes.[166] Costume not only changes the appearance of a body's shape, it also extends the wearer's experience, as for example, the famous platform shoes worn by Venetian women would have altered their visual and physical access to the world.

Costume also envelops the body as a second skin, thereby individuating the subject. If Venetians increasingly came to see themselves as they were seen by others – a historical process encouraged by print, as I have been positing – the interest among Venetian women in changing the contours of their bodies offers some material evidence. Fashions in the latter decades of the century required women to negotiate the pavement in remarkably high shoes; they revealed their breasts, covered their faces, padded their bodies, wore men's pants beneath their skirts, and bound their dyed blond hair into vertical spirals. As the traveller Fynes Moryson exclaimed, 'The women of Venice weare choppines or shoos three or foure hand-bredths high ... shew their naked necks and breasts, and likewise their dugges, bound up and swelling with linnen, and all made white by art ... their haire is commonly yellow, made so by the Sunne and art, and they raise up their haire on the forehead in two knotted hornes ... And they cast a black vaile from the head to the shoulders, through which the nakednesse of their shoulders, and neckes, and breasts, may easily be scene. For this attire the women of Venice are proverbially said to be Grande di legni, Grosse di straci, rosse di bettito, bianche di calcina: that is tall with wood, fat with ragges, red with painting, and white with chalke.'[167] By the end of the sixteenth century, Venetian women seem to have been intent on both transforming their silhouettes and making themselves more visible.

Paradoxically, then, the very process of reducing singular differences into types may have contributed to the subject's emergent interiority, the fictive sense of individuality. On one level, the representational conventions facilitated identification with a particular group by showing people what constituted the difference. In turn the generic social types seen in the pictures could have had a prosthetic function, shoring up viewers' bodily posture by calling attention to the material constraints of their own clothes and the boundaries of their own separate bodies.[168] On another level, the experience of looking at costume illustrations, as if looking in a mirror, may have encouraged viewers to imagine themselves as images, an experience that would have overlapped with social exchanges. The materiality of costume, as a threshold between the self and the world – an experience magnified by these prints – may have fostered a new kind of subject, as both an object and an 'I myself.'[169]

The costume books, sumptuary laws, guidebooks, and chronicles reveal the potential for disorder and the threat of fashion. And yet, contemporary efforts to control clothes may also have furnished viewers with the means to manage their own identities, for by learning to see oneself as an image, Venetians were being instructed in the representational weight of their own bodies, gestures, and poses: their style. Vecellio, de Bruyn, and Boissard, among others, show where bodies fit into the world by classifying their clothing, by rooting costume in space. But in practice, the viewers of these books had bodies, and it was in part the temporality of the body that destabilized the vestimentary system.

Chapter 3

Allegory, Order, and the Singular Event

A small perspective view of the entrance to Venice from the lagoon is juxtaposed with a personification of the city (fig. 48). A beautiful young woman, adorned with a crown and holding a sceptre, floats in a chariot drawn by a pair of splendid sea horses. 'The beautiful persona of the queen of the Adriatic,' as David Rosand has described the personification of Venice, 'delighted the vision of foreign observers as a perpetual declaration of the extraordinary, visible proof of divine intervention in the political affairs of men.'[1] The allegorical vision in the foreground is identified by the sword and scales of justice that are carried by two winged cupids. The latter allude to Venus, whose famous beauty and miraculous birth from the sea was used to signify the cityscape.[2] The sceptre and crown symbolize the goddess of Rome and the Virgin Mary, who represent the city's lineage to the ancient republic, divine origins, and immaculate state: 'never conquered by any ruler,' as Girolamo Priuli put it.[3] Giacomo Franco's small engraving, from his series of costumes, urban spaces, and rituals, *Habiti degli huomeni e donne*, thereby capitalizes on a range of associations invested in the allegorical concept of Venetia, whose beauty stands in, by metonymy, for the city's dazzling architecture. As Franco explains in the caption:

> This is the most fecund of all homes
> Venice: and such that he who sees her marvels
> to see the world collected in this small space.[4]

The text recalls the image of Venice from the frontispiece of his book, where the city is transformed into a globe of the world (fig. 16). Introduced by this cosmological vision, Franco's series evokes an atlas in which

Figure 48   Giacomo Franco, *Questa è d'ogni alto ben nido fecondo Vinetia, Habiti degli huomeni et donne venetiane* (Venice: Giacomo Franco, 1610). Engraving, folio [photo: Museo Correr, Venice]

the parts of the world have been substituted for urban spaces; as he explains in the dedication, the book of engravings is itself 'the world collected in this small space.' Moreover, the concept of the city as a globe, as described at the end of chapter 1, doubles as a convex mirror, reflecting an image of the city in the viewer's eye seen from the Olympian gaze of the geographer. The perspective view of the city behind the image of Franco's personification of Venice similarly allegorizes the outsider's experience of the city as a vision (fig. 48). The analogy between the body of the woman and the desirability of the cityscape is intensified by the perspective construction that simultaneously propels and returns the viewer's gaze along the shuttle between the distant and vantage points.

This ubiquitous perspective of the Piazzetta also appears in the window behind Franco's engraving of the doge (fig. 74). The source for the print is Leandro Bassano's portrait of Marin Grimani, painted following his election as doge in 1595 (fig. 49).[5] An active patron of the arts, Marin Grimani commissioned several portraits of himself and his wife, Morosina Morosini. Two of these, painted by Jacopo Tintoretto in 1579, illustrate the more familiar use of landscape seen through the window. Instead of nature, Leandro and Franco depicted the Palazzo Ducale, Library, columns of justice, and the Loggetta, thereby invoking patrician leadership, knowledge, justice, and eloquence.[6]

In the pendant portrait of Grimani's wife, by contrast, Leandro represented the *campo* of the family parish, with its cistern and church (fig. 50). Through this association of Morosina Morosini with the family *casa*, Leandro conveyed the boundaries that restricted women from public life. Urbanization and participation by men in citywide confraternities and the growing employment of men by the state functioned to marginalize social groups and areas of the city, as discussed in chapter 1.[7] Waning community ties between classes in the parishes and a narrowing group of influential noble families was concomitant with intensifying centralization. Patrician women in particular, on the other hand, were bound to the house and retained ties to the parishes, the private female sphere depicted by Leandro.[8] But he also pictured how women were understood to perceive the city, for the perspective seen through the window is also different. Looking down to the *campo* from inside the house, the viewer sees the city from the vantage point of a woman.[9] Here, the window convention, adapted from its earlier narrative function as a supplement to the viewer's identity, aligns the singular body of the sitter with a collective and gendered concept of space that bound vision to identity.

Figure 49   Leandro Bassano, *Marin Grimani*, c.1595. Oil on canvas, 1340 × 1111 [photo: Gemäldegalerie, Dresden]

Figure 50   Leandro Bassano, *Morosina Morosini*, c.1595. Oil on canvas, 1340 × 1111 [photo: Gemäldegalerie, Dresden]

These are ideas brought forward in prints generated by two unusual events: the battle of Lepanto in 1571 and the coronation of Dogaressa Morosina Morosini in 1597. At the beginning of the century, collective participation in ceremonies was a means of cohering civic identity, but toward the end of the century processions were drained of their local symbolic meanings and transformed into lavish displays, an overflow of civic self-promotion choreographed for the eyes of prestigious foreigners.[10] Prints widened the audience and extended the life of these otherwise ephemeral displays. For both the military contest and the dogaressa's procession, printmakers developed modes of reportage to illustrate time and space.

In late medieval Venice, communal identity was forged through ceremonial events that brought together the city's sacred and secular institutions.[11] Parading through symbolically invested sites and routes constructed what Edward Muir has described as 'an unusually vibrant and durable civic patriotism.'[12] More than other centres, ceremony in Venice demonstrates continuity with medieval traditions, a process that was used to absorb individuality. By eschewing change, working to eliminate festivities that threatened political stability, and bringing others under state control, the ceremonial occasion became institutionalized as a demonstration of the myth of consensus with individuals subsumed into their place within the rigid Venetian social hierarchy.[13]

Already, with the construction of the myth of Venice prompted by the league of Cambrai in 1509, the ducal procession came to be the mere performance of a text, the 'repetition of the script formally actualized,' as Matteo Casini describes it.[14] In Venice, this structural consistency was manifested in the ceremonial tomes in which the bare facts of events provided the 'baseline' against which future events were measured.[15] It was changes to conventions that provoked commentary, even in familiar rituals, and the extraordinary and the unusual that came to be reported. Marin Sanuto, for instance, documented copious details regarding participants in festivals, listing names, titles, and costumes, but his account of the events themselves attends to permutations in the order of processions.[16]

Rituals fulfilled diverse sacred and social functions that both provided a focus for and elicited the sentiments of viewers. Moreover, exchanges between viewers and participants were integral to the efficacy of the ceremonial event. For these reasons, rituals were often venues in which conflicts between social groups could be played out.[17] Ducal coronations, for example, were events in which custom intersected with familial ambitions, and efforts to assuage the splendour prompted by the latter were ongoing.[18] By the second half of the century, ceremonies were increasingly a locus for contests between the city's ruling oligarchs, and as aristocratic display intensified, *communitas* was drained from festivities.[19] The focus had shifted toward the framing of processions: the costumes, ephemeral architecture, chronicles, prints, and commemorative imagery. This might be explained as an 'urge to allegorize,' a fundamentally political operation according to Fredric Jameson, which 'comes less as a technique for closing the text off and for repressing alleatory or aberrant readings and senses, than as a mechanism for preparing such a text for further ideological investment.'[20] The visit of Henry III in 1574 offers a striking example of this process through the transformation of local Venetian festivities for a foreign audience.[21] For the king, who had participated in the Bartholomew massacres only two years earlier and who was returning to a country in civil war, travel through Italy was necessary to ensure his safe arrival in France. A lavish spectacle by the Venetians would signal their approval and thereby assist his political survival. For the Venetians, there was the advantage of reasserting their political interests with France.[22] For both parties it was publicity generated by the event, more than the festivities themselves, that was crucial: the dissemination of printed chronicles and images of Venetian homage to the new ruler.[23] As Egon Verheyen has noted, the speed with which printed pamphlets were translated from Italian into French and other languages for a wider European audience attests to this process of 'image building.'[24]

This process was also at work during the arrival of four Japanese youths in Europe in 1585, whose presence generated a flurry of printed chronicles, despite the relative lack of interest among Europeans, as I discuss in the following chapter. Newly converted to Christianity by the Jesuits, the ambassadors proposed a visit to Venice to see the famous Corpus Christi festivities.[25] Despite initial reluctance by the Venetians to host the embassy on account of the low social status of the Japanese, the government capitalized on the opportunity with unusally lavish festivities designed to counter the state's own diminished significance on the world stage. Emptied of their local import, and transmuted into performances for a foreign audience, festivities became a means of projecting an image that disguised reality.

Printed pamphlets recounted the otherwise temporary architectural splendour and elaborate staging. If these printed chronicles and engravings had the effect of buttressing declining mercantile and military prestige, they failed to disguise what contemporaries saw as the relation between lavish festivities, increasing decadence, and distaste for commerce. In 1612 the English ambassador Sir Dudly Carleton reported on the manifest decay of Venice, 'because they here change theyr manners, they are growne factious, vindicative, loose, and unthriftie,' buying land and 'giving themselves the goode time with more shew and gallantrie then was wont.'[26] A growing preoccupation with private advancement meant that sons were being reared as gentlemen rather than merchants while soaring dowries effectively restricted marriage to a single daughter with the others 'thrust ... into Convents.'[27] Modern commentators have thereby stressed the correlation between displays of wealth on the one hand and political decadence on the other.[28] This climate of dissemblance and aristocratic posturing encouraged the loss of patrimony and brought about a fractious and economically differentiated patriciate.

If 'the power of ritual,' as Patricia Fortini Brown explains, 'lies in its repetition,' that power migrated from the procession into representations designed to forge an impression of the event in the minds of a broad audience.[29] Already competition between rulers contributed to the elaboration of representations as fashionable spectacles, a practice fuelled by the surge in printed chronicles, popular pamphlets, and engravings. 'Reactivat[ing] the object reproduced,' to adapt Walter Benjamin's concept, prints transformed the ephemeral into something material.[30] Of interest here is how this reinvestment extended beyond the original event through a chain of visual representations. In contrast to chronicles, which related the order and explained the meanings of processions to readers, visual representations distilled a range of embodied experiences into a single perspective. The medium itself – widely disseminated, iterative, conventionalizing – would have contributed to this process. Venetians, as viewers inhabiting those spaces, may in turn have come to imagine themselves more distinctly within the visual field of others. Some time ago the Venetian historian Sergio Bettini pointed to the crux of the matter when he stated, 'The ceremonies, the liturgies, the commemorative feasts represent the necessity of a people to identify entirely with an image in order to be transformed from the inert subject of history into the actor of history: in *dramatis persona.*'[31] If print encouraged Venetians to see themselves as they were seen by others, this process may also have transformed those subjects into agents.

Venice and Mars: Representing Vision and History in the Battle of Lepanto

On 9 September 1570, the Venetian-controlled city of Nicosia on the coast of Cyprus fell to the Ottoman Empire.[32] Following a protracted siege of the inland city of Famagousta, the Venetians surrendered. During the subsequent martyrdom, recounted by a chronicler who was close at hand (and whose retelling was serialized in popular pamphlets), the Venetian officials were dismembered, and the governor, Marcantonio Bragadin, flayed alive, his skin stuffed with straw and raised on a mast as an effigy of the Venetian loss.[33] The illustrator for an anonymous pamphlet responded to the event with a picture of retributive justice (fig. 83).[34] The fleshy, undefined, but sumptuously decorated body of the sultan Selim is about to be snared by Charon for his attack of Cyprus. To the right, the heroic nude body impaled on a stake, with its allusions to the crucified body of Christ, transforms the Venetian governor into a new Christian martyr for a revived crusade against the Turkish infidel. I use the story of Bragadin here in order to highlight the charged resonance of the surface of the body and its uses in the construction of the opposition Venetian/Turk. The physical proximity of the Ottomans provoked Venetians to re-imagine them: to construct an image of the Turk that rendered the empire more distant. The complex system of popular, elite, and official representations produced in Venice around the war reveals anxieties about spiritual and masculine identity.

Confronted by the spectre of war, and pressed into action by the crusading fervour of Pius V and his war against heresy, the Venetians eventually joined the Holy League with the papal fleet and the forces of the Holy Roman Empire to defeat the Ottomans at the battle of Lepanto. For Venetians, whose territorial dominance in the Adriatic had been eroded by the Turks since the end of the fifteenth century,[35] the unexpected victory was a moment of rejuvenated pride. The sheer volume of pamphlets and popular prints generated by the event appears today to be completely out of proportion with what was the proverbial political reality: the Turks had severed a limb, but Venice had 'only shaved the beard of the Sultan.'[36]

Despite the facts of war for Venice – the loss of Cyprus, the massive toll of lives, and financial reparations paid to the Ottoman Porte (court/government) for the peace of 1573 – the short-lived victory was projected into the public consciousness for decades after.[37] Printmakers capitalized on widespread interest in the war, producing over 200 pamphlets with poems, sonnets, dialogues, and songs in Latin, the vernacular, and a variety of dialects.[38] Allegories, portraits, and depictions of the battle were among the visual expressions that could be seen in diverse formats and locales.[39] Prints could be purchased from printsellers in the streets for news and as souvenirs; allegories were constructed as tableaux vivants in processions; paintings were displayed in the streets during carnival; and portraits of patrician men in armour were commissioned for patrician homes and the official spaces of government. More than twenty single-sheet bird's-eye views of the battle were produced, in which printmakers reconstructed specific details as if sketched during the contest itself. Correspondence between Giorgio Vasari and Cosimo Bartoli indicates that printed views were used by artists to depict the battle in paintings.[40] However, the prints also shed light on other forms of visual imagery. The pictorial strategies – perspectival and cartographic – deployed in the engravings provide some clues about a broader rearticulation of the relation between the individual male subject and collective identity.

Perceptions of the Turks

Despite the Venetian community in Constantinople, and the presence of subjects of the Porte in Venice, infrequent travel perpetuated the long-standing negative view of Turkish culture. Venetian humanists learned Greek and Arabic, but there was little interest in Turkish, a language associated with a culture of 'barbari' in the fifteenth and sixteenth centuries.[41] With Venetians' scant knowledge of the language, experience of Turkish culture was vicarious and filtered through diplomatic reports, histories, and printed imagery of their costumes and customs that were beginning to appear in travel narratives and costume books. In Constantinople, merchants and even the *bailo* often depended on interpreters, sometimes Greek speakers, or youths who learned the language for trade.[42] News of these youths converting to Islam provoked calls for surveillance by anxious Venetian families.[43] At the same time, men were abandoning the Venetian territories, as the *bailo*'s secretary wrote in 1562, 'in order to earn in four months on the galleys of the Grand Turc what they earn in an entire year on the galleys of your Lordship.'[44] Senate deliberations over allegiances, in particular in the territories, were punctuated by cases of 'abjuration,' 'flight,' 'denial of faith,' and 'betrayal.'[45] The apparent ease with which religious identities could be adopted – a concern magnified by the work of the Council of Trent and the Venetian Inquisition – fomented spiritual anxiety.[46]

The military and political machine of the Ottoman Empire had generated admiration and emulation among European rulers.[47] Of particular interest to the Venetians was the elevation of Islamic law as an *Instrumentum regni*, the *carta segreta* of their imperial success, as the ambassador Matteo Zane put it, the means 'to deceive many particularly foolish people.'[48] This syncretic aspect of Ottoman rule functioned as a means to garner popular support and to galvanize the troops, who saw their territorial expansion as a *gazâ* or religious war.[49] For Venetians, their own shrinking imperial landscape furnished evidence of Turkish military prowess; in 1516 the loss of a ship had provoked Girolamo Priuli to assert 'the Turks are valiant men and the Christians are whores.'[50] But more typically, as Paolo Preto explains, the Venetian ambassadors propagated a less positive image, citing 'the discontent of the subjects, internal divisions, avarice, effeminacy, corruption in private and public life.'[51] After the war, although the Turkish fleet was fully restored in 1573, Marc'Antonio Barbaro related that the empire was 'in large part weak, uninhabited, and ruined' and its soldiers exhausted from an 'odious and spoiled life.'[52] These kinds of aspersions were pressed into service by popular poets in the prophetic literature that exploded around the contest. There was a striking correspondence between religious hatred and political language.

Religious antagonism was fuelled by diplomats, who turned their attention to exterior manifestations of the Muslim faith, in particular the contradiction perceived between private religiosity and visible expressions of piety. A popular insult, for instance, was that one 'swears, drinks and smokes like a Turk,' all practices forbidden by Islamic law.[53] Observance of restrictions against wine, gaming, blasphemy, respect for religious sites, and individual charity were cited as displays of dissimulation that concealed the facts of practice – that Turks were believed to drink wine, to gamble, to curse – and thus intensified the scandal.

The emperor Selim became emblematic of this new stereotype. Where Francesco Sansovino wrote with admiration for the sultans and Süleyman in particular, the author attacked Selim. The latter was 'all given to voluptuousness, corruptor of his laws, without faith, and one who does not keep his word.'[54] Contrasting his dissoluteness to his exemplary father, Sansovino questioned Selim's patriline, asserting that he was the illegitimate son of a Hebrew friend, planted by Süleyman's Hebrew mistress. Selim appears again in Sansovino's *Informatione*, an illustrated tract addressed to Christian soldiers in 1570. Below a generic costume figure titled *King of the Turks*, he asks his readers: 'Encountering such alterity, such pompousness, such major haughtiness, how can one represent this Turk to our eyes?'[55] With the renewed threat at Cyprus, Sansovino pressed the Venetian senate to move against the Ottoman Turks in a 'just' war whose successful outcome had been widely prophesied and enjoyed enthusiastic public support.[56] The author's more characteristic admiration for Ottoman military *virtù* was superseded by a pointed religious rhetoric.[57]

Sansovino illustrated the text with woodcuts of Ottoman military men to show his readers that the Turks were made 'of bones and flesh like you' (fig. 51).[58] On the one hand, the figures set forth physical commonality, while on the other hand, the Ottomans' costumes appeared 'strange' – a perception encouraged by the text – and provided Venetians with visual indicators of the 'evil and bestial' natures of their adversaries.

Sansovino assured his readers of the veracity of the images by maintaining these were drawn from life. In fact, these woodcuts were copied after engravings that circulated in a costume book, *Les quatre premiers livres des navigations et pérégrinations orientales*, discussed in the previous chapter (fig. 52). Following his extensive travels throughout the Ottoman Empire, Nicholas de Nicolay, the French royal geographer, compiled this collection of sixty figures of men and women from a variety of ethnic groups, whose customs are described in the accompanying texts.

For Sansovino, however, it was the absence of a European class system that fuelled his diatribe, as his description of the Azamoglan makes clear: 'uncouth and boors, they are for the most part wicked and bestial, and ordinarily hate Christians to death to whom they cause every sorrow and insult; but the amazing thing is that they do not acknowledge either father or mother, like true barbarians and peasants.'[59] He warns his readers that the Turk 'would murder the nobles.'[60] Although a monarchy, the Ottoman Empire was closed to the privileges familiar to European aristocrats. Ottoman subjects were slaves to the sultan, an aspect that provoked Venetians to parallel the Ottoman Empire with ancient Rome, and to contrast the general slavery of the people with the exclusive ruling class that formed the basis of Venice's mixed form of government. In radical opposition to Venice's castelike social structure with its privileges based in genealogy, all male subjects could aspire to the position of sultan. Social equality facilitated the Porte's geographical expansion in feudal lands, and for those who converted to Islam, Ottoman meritocracy offered social mobility.[61] In contrast to the sultan, whose position reflected his military sagacity and political shrewdness, the Venetian doge was a figurehead – usually elderly – elected by his peers for his equanimity instead of his ambition. This difference at the top of the two systems was complicated further by the republic's efforts to shore up its image on an international stage dominated by princes and

Figure 51   *Delo*, Francesco Sansovino, *Informatione di M. Francesco Sansovino a Soldati Christiani* (Venice, 1570). Woodcut [photo: by permission of the British Library, London] 1312k.15

Figure 52   *Delly*, Nicolas de Nicolay, *Les quatre premiers livres des navigations et péré-grinations orientales* (Lyon: G. Roville, 1568). Engraving [photo: by permission of the British Library, London] 455.e.5

monarchs, a concern highlighted in the grand ducal promotion of Cosimo de'Medici in 1569.[62] Within Venice the growing wealth of the citizen class had begun to rival the status of the patricians.

Sansovino's pamphlet reveals his admiration for the martial prowess of the Turks; however, an Ottoman victory at Cyprus threatened the loss of property, and more significantly, the Venetian ruling structure. The Turks' rejection of blood descent and the equality given to children regardless of birth undermined the very foundations of the oligarchs, whose exclusive authority was legitimated by noble ancestry.[63] If the woodcuts helped to foment both military fervour and popular aggression, the tension between sameness and difference expresses a contradiction felt by the Venetians in the face of the Turks, who were too familiar to be made exotic.[64]

Confronting the Turk

Despite the threat to Venetian possessions in the Stato da Mar exposed by the siege at Cyprus, the state resisted joining military forces with the Holy League. War threatened economic ties with the Porte, a concern that prompted secret negotiations with the Ottomans and even an offer to abandon the League after it was signed.[65] Pressure from the pope had forced Venice to join the League, which was concluded on 20 May, proclaimed at St Peter's on the twenty-fifth, and celebrated with a mass at the Church of San Marco and the Corpus Christi procession.[66] At home, the event was designed to garner popular support and spiritual assistance. All the Scuole Grandi, monks, priests, ambassadors, and senators left the church and entered the *cortile* of the Palazzo Ducale before beginning to traverse the piazza. Following the announcement to a silent crowd, a cacophony of instruments, artillery, and bells began to sound, the latter continuing for three days.[67] To its foreign allies, the procession projected an image of solidarity.

Giacomo Franco's well-known engraving of the parade illustrates the *apparati* (displays) carried by men on which various tableaux vivants demonstrated a united front against the Turk (fig. 53).[68] According to a printed pamphlet that describes the procession, the floats began with the *Gran Turco*, in which three youths dressed as Saints Peter, James, and Mark – the papacy, Spain, and Venice – launched a collective assault on a dragon with their swords. Another float presented personifications of Faith, Hope, and Charity to symbolize the signatories of the League, the former holding a globe to signify a universal Christian world. Prophe-

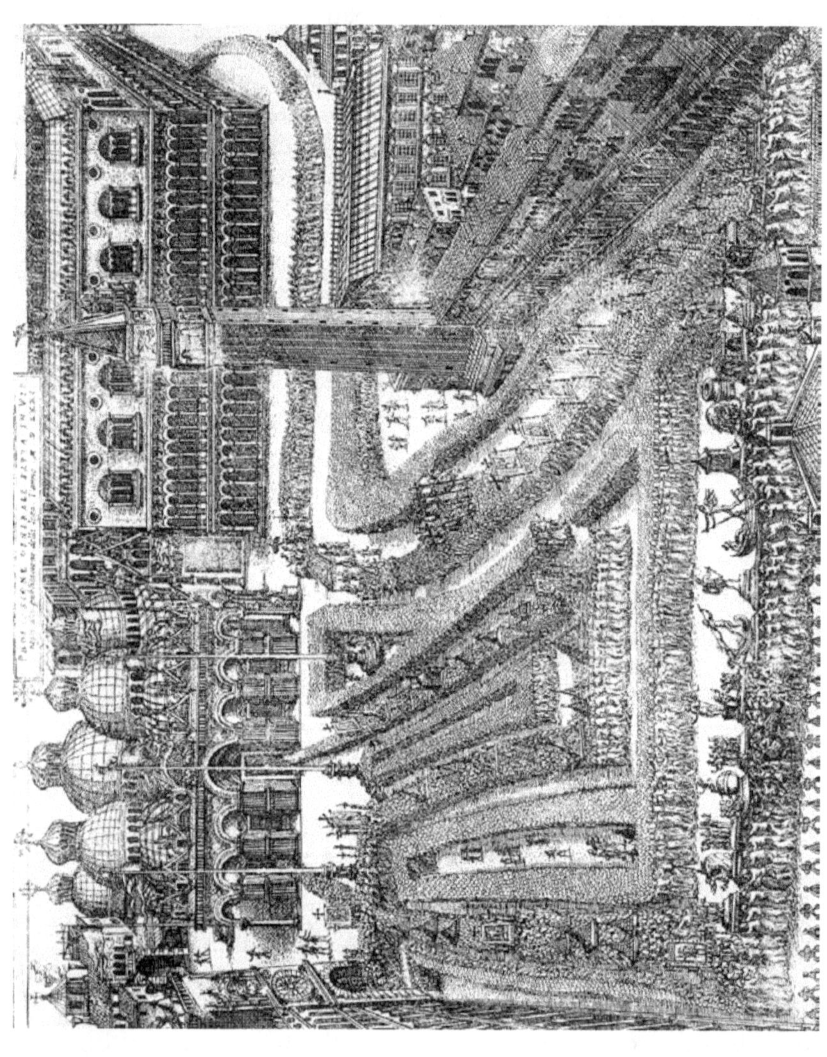

Figure 53   Giacomo Franco, *Processione generale fatta in Vinegia alla publicacione della lega. L'anno M.D. LXXI*, Venice. Engraving [photo: Newberry Library, Chicago]

cies in anticipation of the war had augured for the mass conversion of the Turks and the end of Mohammedanism; contemporary rhetoric referred to a 'just war' on the grounds of exactly this claim.[69] Another tableau repeated the theme of the Holy League with three youths wearing painted masks impersonating the pope, doge, and emperor. Venice was also personified, but associations with the female body of Venus were temporarily abandoned; instead the city was represented by Neptune, who stood triumphantly on a half-shell harnessed to a pair of seahorses. The last of the floats, according to the pamphlet, conveyed 'a bark rowed by a naked moor with wings and horns to signify Charon carrying off a Turk.'[70] Franco altered the order for his engraving, locating this Dantean scene front and centre instead.

The tableaux in the procession played out the city's collective fears by embodying them. Indeed, dozens of printed pamphlets have been described as an 'antidote' to a demoralized public, a kind of collective illusion that united the classes and was driven by an 'aggressive proselytism' fired with the 'spirit of the crusades.'[71] The procession would have mobilized popular support through its presentation of a refracted image of reality. Idealized and ephemeral, ceremonial events intensified the sensate experiences of viewers. Participants in processions would carry tableaux vivants on which actors appeared frozen like sculptures. When the parade stopped, the actors would begin to move, at which point participants became members of the audience. In turn, spectators in the piazza and balconies could be viewed by those moving in the cortege. In this way spectacles co-opted viewers, providing the means to physically structure the relationship between an audience and a performance. Franco's engraving of the Holy League suggests this reciprocal involvement of the ritual event, as densely packed swaths of observers are woven together as if integrated elements of the same procession, a concept of collectivity underscored by the presence of a few individuals scattered among the crowds. Seen from a vantage point on the façade of S Geminiano (no longer extant), the print provides a bird's-eye view of the parade as a whole with details of the floats in the foreground.

The solemnity characterizing the account of the publication of the League in the ceremonial register contrasts dramatically with the triumphant news of the victory.[72] On 19 October, Venetians heard a cacophony of gunfire, musical instruments, and cheers from the arriving fleet. A first glance sparked fear among the spectators, for the ships were adorned with Turkish spoils and arms, and the men aboard were dressed as Turks. However, the disguise only added to the pleasure of the surprise, as many fell to the ground and cried in happiness. Stepping into the costumes of their adversaries, the Venetians seem to have signalled their triumph over the image of the enemy.

The destabilizing effect of repeated threats of war after Malta in 1565, combined with the surprising victory – made larger in view of the risks – lifted the inferiority complex of Venetians.[73] As John Hale put it, 'if the sense of relief was exaggerated it was because the Venetians felt themselves to be freed from a neurosis as well as from an enemy.'[74] The catharsis, fuelled by an explosion of representations, was a catalyst for redefining the fiction of republican thought. This tradition was built upon a gendered construction of historical causation: the republic survived by relying on the *virtù* of its citizens, and *virtù* was a decidedly masculine conception. The battle served to refocus attention on republican male identity in general, and patrician men in particular.

Republican identity could be represented by Venice personified as a woman. In theory, a male viewer does not identify with the female body; this distance enables the personification to embody an abstract concept, which thereby directs the viewer's imagination toward an idea that cannot easily be represented.[75] For example, in Palma Giovane's *Allegory of the League of Cambrai*, painted for the Sala del Senato, Venice with her rampant lion staves off the onslaught of her adversary personified as Europa with her bull (fig. 54).[76] The female figures stand in for the collective work of war, their bodies decorated with the accoutrements of male authority, as Leonardo Loredan, the reigning doge, oversees the contest.[77] Depicting the battle of Lepanto, however, prompted different representational strategies, as suggested by the tableaux vivants seen in the procession. In Paolo Veronese's *Allegory of the Battle of Lepanto*, for example, the Virgin, surrounded by saints and angels, hovers close to the picture plane above a view of the war painted in perspective with a distant horizon line (fig. 55).[78] In contrast to the fading daylight visible in the distance of the gulf, the luminescence in the upper register is spiritual instead of physical, omnipresent instead of temporal. Promontories on either side define the geographical specificity of the engagement below the ethereal vision, whose divine intervention is signalled by the flaming arrows of an angel that conjoins the scenes. Veronese reconstructs the event using two distinctive visual registers: the allegorical and the historical.

This pictorial strategy can be traced to printed bird's-eye views that offered viewers a 'true representation' of the battle, an assertion bolstered by claims to cartographical accuracy and the timeliness of print

Figure 54   Palma Giovane, *Allegory of the League of Cambrai*. Venice, Sala del Senato, Palazzo Ducale. Oil on canvas, 380 × 460 cm [photo: Alinari]

Figure 55   Paolo Veronese, *The Battle of Lepanto*. Venice, Gallerie dell'Accademia. Oil on canvas, 169 × 137 cm [photo: Alinari]

(see figs. 56–7). Engraved maps could be rapidly produced and widely disseminated, thereby promising speedy visual access to news. Cartographic techniques and visual conventions had been adopted for depicting land battles, and these – the bird's-eye view, use of toponyms, and sketchy figures – were deployed for the 1571 confrontation.[79] The site was known from geographical maps, and printmakers identified the gulf by indicating the fortresses on either side of the entrance. Although the entire battle lasted only a day, engravers reproduced every stage of the event, developing a mode of reportage that claimed the veracity of the eyewitness report.

In one of the earliest printed maps of the conflict – dated 16 September 1571 and published by Antoine Lafréry in Rome – the draughtsman has contrasted the straight rank of the Holy League with the famous Turkish crescent formation of the Ottoman fleet. The text describes a reconnaissance: 'Warning, eight galleys of the Christian fleet went scouting today and having noticed the fleet of the enemy, they had to return immediately to their Squadrons.'[80] The sheet was drawn in anticipation of the battle, with no geographical landmarks, and thus the print is a theoretical map, abstracted from both time and space.[81] As the printmaker explains: 'We presume the Turkish fleet will come at us in this way.'[82] According to some accounts, the Ottomans largely abandoned the crescent formation in the altercation; nevertheless, the distinctive shape functions as a sign for the Ottoman fleet in the maps in general (fig. 56).

The cartographic point of view is also used for maps produced following the battle; but from now on the geographical locale is specified and the vessels depicted on the sheet are often counted and identified by type. In figure 56, the illustrator locates the event in space by indicating the site at the top of the sheet. The text in the upper left corner marks the date of the victory: 'the battle occurred on the 7th day of October, 1571, the day of Santa Giustina at 17 hours.'[83] In the centre of the sheet, the author pinpoints the time illustrated in the image: 'One of the heavy ships, which was first I do not know, since every one claimed to have been first, fired a gun into the midst of the enemy's fleet, and all the rest followed [that example].' Despite conflicting oral reports, the engraver has identified a ship by the smoke from the fired canons, a tactic that draws the viewer into the action, with the result that it is difficult to maintain a view of the whole.

In one of Giacomo Franco's engravings, the viewer is pressed to negotiate even more forcefully between the bird's-eye view of the whole and

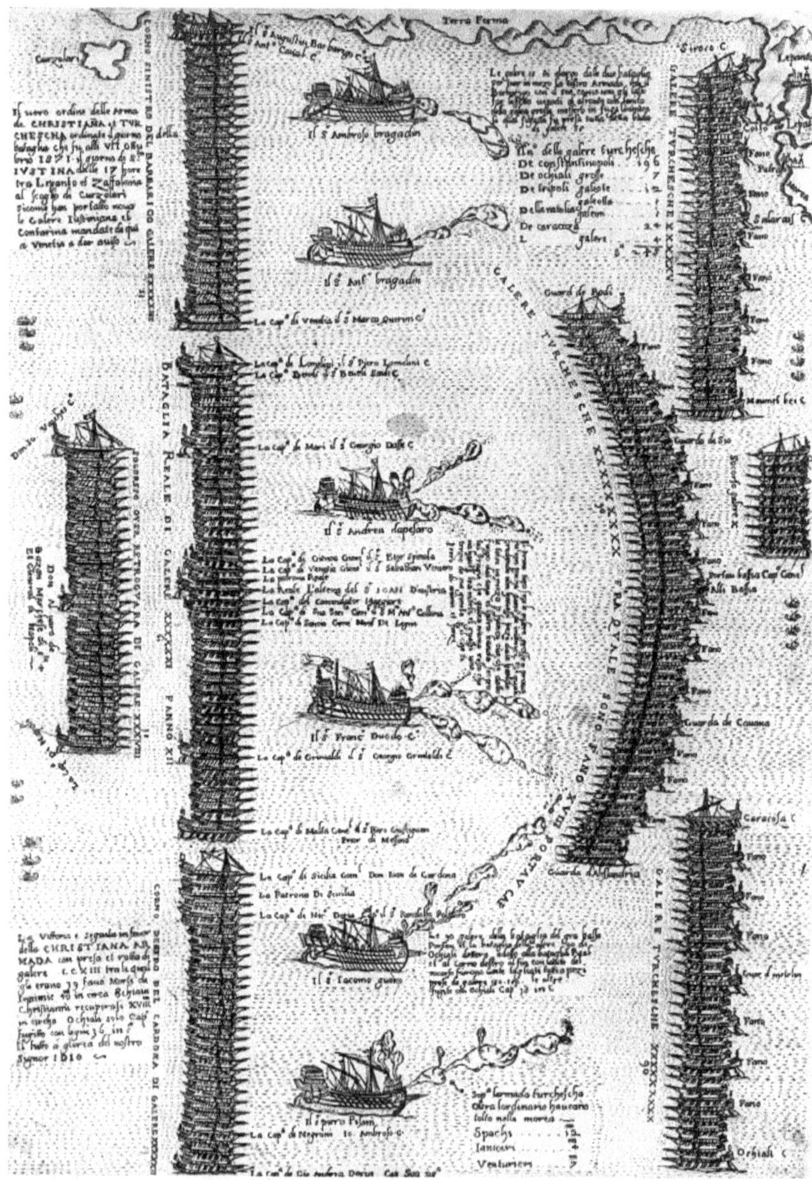

Figure 56   *Il vero ordine delle Armade Christiana et Turchescha.* 1571. Engraving
[photo: Newberry Library, Chicago]

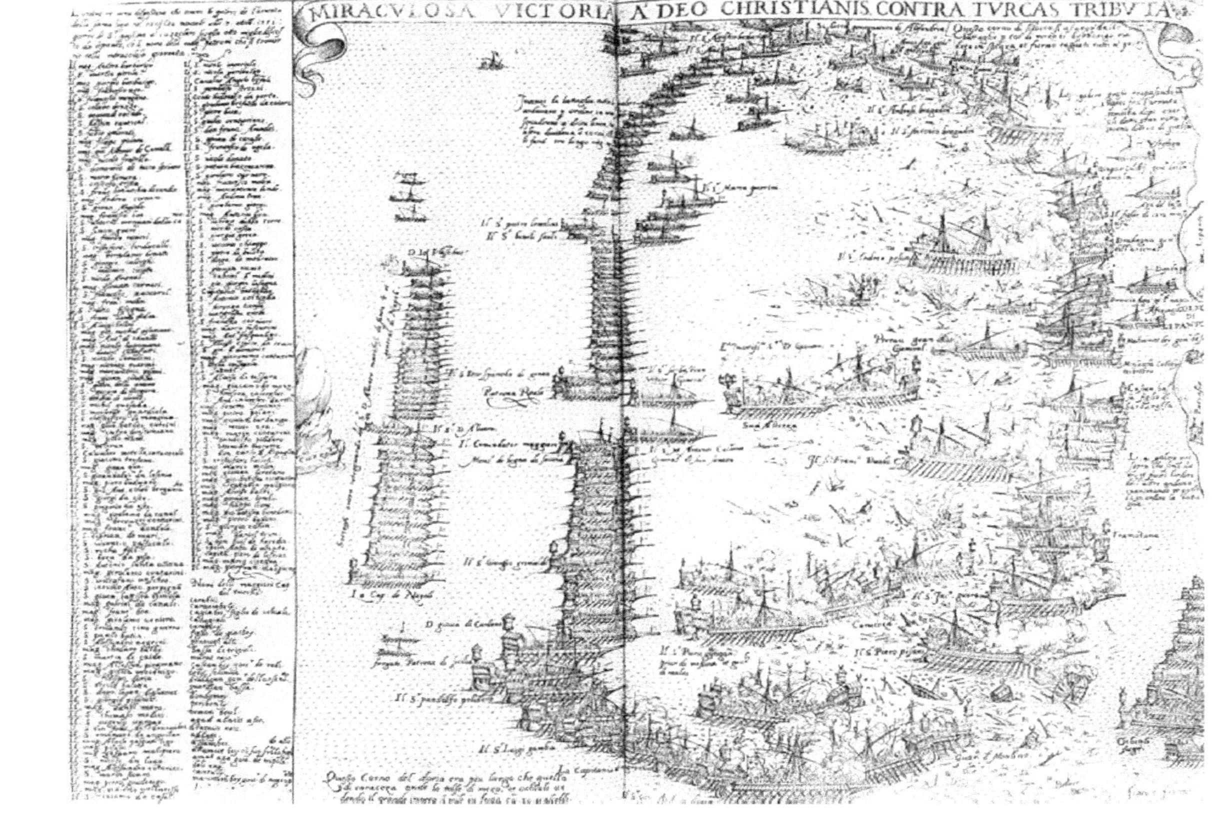

Figure 57 Giacomo Franco, *Miraculosa Victoria à Deo Christianis. Contra. Turcas Tributa.* 1571. Engraving [photo: Museo Correr, Venice]

the close-up particulars of the battle (fig. 57). The geographical frame, toponyms, and inscriptions cue the viewer, locating the historical event in space. In constrast to his perspectival view of the procession – that distills a range of potential experiences to the same point of view – the detail of the contest and toponyms insist on close scrutiny and encourage the viewer to explore the page furtively, even to count the bodies in the water. The formation of the Turkish Armada is largely subsumed into this chaotic narrative, which appears rapidly drawn, as if to imply it was sketched on site instead of reconstructed from accounts weeks later. This contrasts with the transcendent and atemporal Olympian view of the whole that locates the eye as the centric point of a perspectivally ordered field of vision.[84] This striking tension between the two visual registers is, in fact, addressed by Lafréry in a note to 'curious readers' on one of his maps of the war.[85] 'Do not be surprised if in our map one is not able to recognize a thing as fixed and stable, because by the time the stupendous battle was finished, infinite mutations had been made, and in such a way, that as each part was fighting the other, they became attached together, with every one demonstrating his own *virtù*.'[86] This unusual coexistence of the gaze and the glance translates between the event in the past and the viewer's act of looking in the present, resulting in a fiction of reportage that constitutes a relation between the past and present.[87]

The vessels are no longer described by type and allegiance, but by the names of the commanders. In contrast to Franco's maps of Venice, in which the legend furnishes a list of parishes to aid the viewer's vicarious movement through the city, here the printmaker has provided a list of Venetian nobles. Below the Venetian patricians who commanded the galleys are the names of the Turkish captains unprefaced by any title, a gesture that highlights the noble status of the Venetians.[88] This conjoining of geographical and social space recalls the tradition of mapping as a means to reinforce dynastic claims, translated in the present context into a defence and reassertion of social hierarchy. These patricians are marked as individuals by their names, but that individuality only takes on meaning if it is understood as part of a lineage.[89] The practice of naming, combined with visual registers, calls attention to the acts of individuals within a particular historical moment, implying the way in which Venetians defined the self as both 'attached together, with every one demonstrating his own *virtù*' and part of a genealogical, traceable line. Indeed, despite the disorder pictured in many of the engravings, the names of key heroes – Agostino Barbarigo and Sebastian Venier – can always be found (top centre and middle of figure 57).

The Making of a Model

With the election of Sebastiano Venier, the general of Venetian forces at Lepanto, as doge in 1577, the redecoration of the Sala del Collegio in the Palazzo Ducale was altered to accommodate his votive painting.[90] Paolo Veronese's canvas is located above the tribune, where the doge would sit, sometimes flanked by visiting ambassadors, to hear from supplicants. In Veronese's chiaroscuro *modello*, Venier is depicted kneeling before Venetia, who holds the ducal *corno* as if preparing to crown him (fig. 58).[91] This display of self-aggrandizement was mitigated in the final painting, but the process had already begun in the *modello*, as scholars have pointed out, with the addition in the background of S Giustina and Agostino Barbarigo, whose body is shrouded by the Ottoman standard.[92] Giustina, the saint on whose day victory was achieved, was brought forward in the painting with her martyr's palm and blade, displacing Venetia from her central position to the right of Venier, and behind St Mark where she now holds the ducal *corno* as a symbol of the state (fig. 59). The prominence of Barbarigo, who died in valiant action at the age of fifty-five, subordinates Venier's individual achievement to the success of the group. This strategy is furthered by the visibility of the saint in armour to the left of Mark, probably Theodor, the Byzantine saint whose triumph over the dragon would have recalled Venice's domination of Constantinople before 1453. The expanded cast of well-armoured bodies draws attention to the military persona of the doge, whose prosthetic armour shores up his elderly body. Seventy-five years old during the battle, and with no military experience, he was transformed into a masculine ideal, like a serpent who discarded his old skin, as one contemporary described him.[93] Both Venier and Barbarigo had continued to fight despite being wounded by arrows, Barbarigo dying from a hit to the eye. In the painting, their shimmering metallic bodies deflect penetration, ideas underscored by the grisaille figures of St Sebastian and Giustina who flank the scene.

Prior to Venier's election, it was Alvise Mocenigo who was to appear above the tribune, and Jacopo Tintoretto's *modello* for his votive painting, with military galleys in the distance, celebrates that doge's role in the conflict. However, when Mocenigo's painting was displaced from the prominent site by Venier's, the role of the former was redesigned. The fleet of ships, once intended for Mocenigo's votive picture, migrated, as it were, into the background of Veronese's painting.[94] With Faith and Giustina in the foreground of Veronese's new composition, the bat-

Figure 58   Veronese, *Modello* for the votive painting for Sebastiano Venier, Collegio. 30 × 40.7 cm. British Library, Prints and Drawings, inv. 1861-8-10-4 [photo: Copyright of the British Museum]

Figure 59   Veronese, *Allegory of the Battle of Lepanto* (Votive painting for Sebastiano Venier). Oil on canvas, 285 × 565 cm, Sala del Collegio, Palazzo Ducale [photo: Museo Correr, Venice]

tle in the background (the Ottoman standards can been seen from close up) serves as visual evidence of their intercessory power. As in his earlier canvas presenting the battle (fig. 55), Veronese has deployed two registers. In the foreground time has been collapsed into an allegory that conjoins the present, through Barbarigo and Venier, to past Christian warriors and martyrs figured by Theodor and Giustina; this immobile scene, presented on a shallow architectural stage, is supported by the narrative that frames it: the temporality of historical achievements.[95]

In contrast with aerial perspective in which the background dissolves, here the detail draws the viewer into the narrative of the landscape, making it impossible to maintain visual control of the whole. Following the conventions elaborated in the maps, the unusual and persistent coexistence of these two perspectives – the universalizing view from outside and the close-up view of the participant – works to locate the spectator in two temporal and spatial contexts simultaneously, a visual manoeuvre that parallels the peculiarly Venetian construction of the individual as inescapable from the whole. The battle becomes the historical antecedent for the votive drama staged in the foreground: Christ's victory at Lepanto is relayed through the intercession of Giustina to Venier and his troops, bringing the painting within the parameters of the official program of the palace decoration as a whole: a display of collective acts of *virtù* and divinely sanctioned leadership.[96] Following the fire of 1577, Girolamo Bardi, a Camaldolese monk from Florence, was charged, alongside Venetian advisers, with the program for the Sala del Scrutinio and the Sala del Gran Consiglio. In his printed guide, *Dichiarazione di tutte le historie,* Bardi leads the reader through the political and military battles depicted in the paintings. The text functions as a list of historical events, the individuals involved, and their deeds. With this guide the reader 'can more easily imitate these famous heroes, in order to leave an honoured memorial of their operations to the posterity which will be born in future ages in this most Serene Republic.'[97] If the painting preceded Bardi's program for the redecoration, as Terisio Pignatti believes on the basis of stylistic grounds, the moral imperative of the canvas – to prompt emulation – may have provided the impetus for the iconography of the Palazzo Ducale as a whole.

'A Virtue of the Greater'

Two days before the battle, the soldiers remained anxious, as Agostino Barbarigo reported to Sebastiano Venier, then general of the Venetian fleet, who recorded the meeting: 'That evening the most illustrious Barbarigo, talking to me, told me that they did not want to fight, but pretended [to desire it].'[98] Responding to these concerns, Venier addressed the troops before they sailed into battle. He did not preach a new crusade; instead, he reiterated the ideas propagated by Francesco Sansovino, noted earlier. 'I will show them,' warned Venier,

> in what danger they will find themselves, and what will be needed, that we will put all our force in order to defend our wives, children, and goods from an enemy that admits neither counts, nor knights, nor gentlemen, but only merchants, and people [*popoli*] who follow the court to make good points: [the enemy] admits boors, that work the earth, taking from one and the other, goods and children, and shaming the women according their appetite.[99]

An Ottoman victory threatened property but, more significantly, under-mined the very foundations of the oligarchs: their lineage. The apparent ease of adopting another identity that the confrontation brought to the fore – registered on the surface of body by costume or by religious conversion – was the opposite of Venetian blood identity. The oblivious-ness of the Ottomans to blood lineage was especially offensive because it failed to create a connection between the ruling nobles and the people, Gasparo Contarini's vision of political life: the 'intelligent minority against the ignorant crowd.'[100] Venier's disdain for the *popolani* and mercantilism – traditions of Venetian republicanism – also parallels Paolo Paruta's ruling-class mentality: his conviction that the nobility was none other than 'a virtue of the greater.'[101]

Like many of Venier's portraits – the large number is surprising in the context of Venetian *mediocritas* (moderation) – Giacomo Franco's printed likeness brings the ideas discussed above into sharper focus (fig. 60). The portrait was sometimes included, as was Franco's map of the battle, in his series of engraved costumes and rituals. Significantly, this is the only portrait of an individual – identified by name and likeness – that Franco incorporated.[102] Despite the advanced years of the sitter, he is depicted upright and potent, his body buttressed by the carapace of armour that sheathes it. Venier holds the commander's baton and he is placed to the left of a window, perhaps following Tintoretto's half-length portrait now in Vienna.[103] In both the painting and Franco's engraving, the conventional function of the landscape seen through a window has been given a double function. On one level this representation of war as

Figure 60   *I Capitani G[e]n[er]ali dell'aramata Venettiana*, Giacomo Franco, *Habiti degli huomeni et donne venetiane* (Venice, 1610). Engraving, folio [photo: Museo Correr, Venice]

landscape serves as a conventional supplement to the sitter's identity by illustrating the battle over which he wielded command. On another level, it also illustrates that 'ignorant crowd' of the Venetian republican body.

Lepanto furnished the means to redefine the 'regulating fiction' of Venetian republicanism by conjoining aristocratic rule with the collective performance of masculinity.[104] It was not only the iconographic meaning of representations of the battle of Lepanto that conformed to official representational needs, but the operative mechanisms that structured visuality, that linked vision with time. If the state benefited from popular aggression – fuelled by stereotyping practices that circulated in dozens of printed pamplets – that concealed anxiety over religious conversions, defections, and military prowess, it was the political ideal of noble blood that was expressed in the visual representations.

Rank and Display: The Coronation of Morosina Morosini Grimani

Figure 1 is a map of Venice printed by Donato Rascicotti at the end of the sixteenth century. The bird's-eye view of Venice is accompanied by a small perspective view of the Piazzetta, a view of Rialto, and two processions, one above the other. The upper register presents a detail of the Corpus Christi procession in which senators used to progress in the company of pilgrims en route for Jersualem. Dangers of travel halted the annual pilgrimages from Venice, but the concept was maintained by having the poor stand in for pilgrims. Below these male figures is a female procession with the dogaressa and a collection of women of various marital states. There were only two processions for the wife of the doge in the sixteenth century, in 1557 and 1597, and the event would be abolished in 1645, when the possibility arose again. Although Rascicotti does not refer to the 1597 event by date, or to Morosina Morosini, the wife of Marin Grimani, by name, the print clearly references this extraordinary occasion. The map follows Giacomo Franco's bird's-eye view that he produced for the event, but Rascicotti brings the cityscape up to date and fills the basin of San Marco with festive vessels that appeared in the procession, improving on Franco's earlier prints, as he implies in his dedication to Francesco Morosini. Although this engraving was a response to the unusual festivities for the dogaressa in Venice, Rascicotti subsumed the specific historical event into an image of the Venetian *mondo* as a whole. In the introduction I used the print to highlight the combination of points of view and the overlapping system of representations: the spatial (the bird's-eye view, perspectives, costumes), temporal (the legend and the processions), and performative (the costumes and processions). Here I consider this question in more detail. I also explore the unusual emphasis on patrician women in public, and the potential conflict this exposes between rank and moderation. By the end of the century *mediocritas*, the republican ideal, was coming under pressure, and the prints and paintings generated around the coronation draw attention to aristocratic display.

Morosina Morosini's procession also brings patrician women into the picture in a new way. In theory, access for patrician women to public spaces in Venice was severely curtailed as if following Juan Luis Vives's famous guide for maidens, wives, and widows. In the first book on Maidens, the chapter 'How She Will Behave in Public' observes that a woman 'will appear in public on occasion, but as rarely as possible.'[105] As if too open-ended a formulation, he adds (citing Thucydides): 'It is wrong for young women to be seen in public,' recommending that 'a woman should live in seclusion and not be known to many.'[106] 'Married women,' moreover, 'should be seen more rarely in public than unmarried women.'[107]

Public spaces, especially in Venice, were more often associated with courtesans, and not only by foreigners. Venetians regularly complained that courtesans could be mistaken for patrician women. As a proclamation noted in 1543, prostitutes appeared 'in the streets and churches, and elsewhere, so much bejeweled and well-dressed, that very often noble ladies and women citizens [of Venice], because there is no difference in their attire from that of the above-said women, are confused with them, not only by foreigners, but by the inhabitants [of Venice], who are unable to tell the good from the bad.'[108] Similar concerns were raised by Cesare Vecellio, who had explained to readers of his costume books that prostitutes were forbidden from wearing pearls in public to avoid confusion.[109] Nevertheless, he admits, it is difficult to recognize the difference between married women and courtesans on account of the similarity of their apparel and jewellery. Laws targeted their garments, forced them to register, and confined them to Rialto, away from churches, the city's ritual spaces, and those areas frequented by patricians.[110] On at least one occasion, patrician women themselves pressed the government to reassert the visual signs that distinguished them from courtesans, as Sir Henry Wotten noted at the 1617 festival of the Ascension.[111]

While prostitutes were often singled out in sumptuary legislation, the dogaressa was routinely excluded from restrictions.[112] Prostitutes functioned as illicit embodiments of Venetian *lusso,* but it was the body of the dogaressa that was legitimized as the centric point of ceremonial display. These two types functioned as two sides of female Venetian identity as it was perceived by foreigners: on the one hand, the chaste consort of the doge who was the symbolic centre of Venice, and on the other, the courtesan, who was a cipher through which the republic was viewed.[113] The coronation may have been an opportunity for noble women to assert their presence in the city.

Vicentino's Painting

A large canvas painted by Andrea Vicentino commemorates the coronation in May 1597 of Dogaressa Morosina Morosini, the wife of Doge Marin Grimani (1595–1605) (figs. 61, 62).[114] Vincenzo Scamozzi's famous floating *teatro del mondo* is depicted to the right; with its cluster of columns, it echoes the style of the library seen on the left, whose parade of columns, accentuated by the oblique viewpoint, reiterates the orderly procession underway in the centre. Viewers filling the balconies and arcades of the architecture survey and also participate in the spectacle, as the dogaressa, framed by a temporary triumphal arch, observes the viewer outside the representation.

In her famous gold dress, Morosina Morosini stands out from the crowd;[115] Vicentino has highlighted her pivotal position with one of the columns of justice, whose cylindrical shape accentuates the hingelike effect of her body from which the narrative in the painting unfolds. A second pyramidal composition overlaps the lavish and lively scene; the dogaressa is positioned between the allegorical figure of Justice that crowns the prow of the *Bucintoro,* the state ship in the left foreground, and the personification of Venice as Justice located above the arch. The latter establishes the apex of a pyramid that joins the figures to a tableau vivant on the right in which a woman dressed up as Venice sits under a ducal *baldacchino,* her gestures replicating those of the allegorical sculptures.[116] The gold costumes of these allegorical figures mirror the luminous dress worn by Morosina Morosini, thereby underscoring the symbolic function of the dogaressa in the republic. With the vessels from the procession by sea in the foreground and the Palazzo Ducale in the background, the focus on the dogaressa's disembarkation suggests the transformation of the doge's wife into a symbol of the state, a metamorphosis for which the triumphal arch functions as a threshold.[117]

I will return to the painting shortly, but first a synopsis of the proces-

Figure 61   Andrea Vicentino, *Disembarkation of the Dogaressa Morosina Morosini Grimani from the Bucintoro and Her Progress toward the Triumphal Arch*, c.1597. Venice, Museo Correr. Oil on canvas [photo: Museo Correr, Venice]

Figure 62   Detail, Andrea Vicentino, *Disembarkation of the Dogaressa Morosina Morosini Grimani from the Bucintoro and Her Progress toward the Triumphal Arch*, c.1597, Venice, Museo Correr. Oil on canvas [photo: Museo Correr]

sion itself, in particular how the chroniclers reported on the women and their costumes. The *Bucintoro*, filled with women for this rare pageant, was accompanied by a plethora of allegorical *macchine* in a procession along the Grand Canal toward Piazza San Marco, where a canvas and stucco triumphal arch was erected at the end of a temporary wooden bridge. Descending from the state ship, the doge's wife and her cortege entered the city through the arch emblazoned with inscriptions and sculptures that celebrated Morosina Morosini on the lagoon side and her husband on the other with heraldry that equated Venetian prosperity with his wise stewardship. Decorated with painted landscapes of Venice's empire and insignia that proclaimed the nobility of the two families, the arch presented an iconographic program of almost dynastic proportions.[118] Indeed, the dogaressa's extraordinary regal presence in the numerous history paintings and engravings seems more closely aligned to court ritual than republican ideology, a suggestion to which her attendant dwarfs, depicted in Vicentino's painting, contribute (fig. 62).[119]

Three days of festivities included *regatte* and war games. Mock naval contests were staged between the Dutch and the English, and the popular 'wars of the fists' (*pugni*) were transformed into formal performances with the Nicolotti and Castellani factions fighting on the Ponte dei Carmini, according to a chronicler, 'with grand decorations, dressed in various uniforms and liveries ... to the sound of trumpets and drums.'[120] The dogaressa's approach to the city from the sea, the triumphal arch that dramatized her arrival, and the staging of martial battles presented the entry as if Morosina were a visiting foreign – even royal – dignitary. Contributing further to the courtly atmosphere were a variety of panegyrics, at least one of which described the couple as divinities.[121] This was the first *insediamento* for which such encomia were commissioned, a development far from the moderation sought by the senators, who would abolish the procession at the next occasion in 1645.[122]

It was precisely this kind of monarchical posturing that the protocols for the coronation had been designed – in characteristic Venetian fashion – to guard against. If a new doge's wife was still living, she moved into the Palazzo Ducale with her family until his death, when her public persona was terminated. Her move to the palace was celebrated a year after her husband's election in order to mitigate familial aggrandizement and royal associations that a joint coronation had the potential to facilitate. The restrictions imposed on the doge's family in the *promissione ducale* were ceremoniously presented to the dogaressa at the family house by officials at the commencement of the procession. Following the oathtaking at her family palace, the dogaressa departed for her new residence in the Palazzo Ducale. Later, at the high altar of San Marco, she swore to obey this list of limitations that underlined her status as a figurehead.[123] In contrast with the routinely circumscribed role of the doge, however, the rarity of this unusual event magnified its significance.[124]

Sumptuary laws were not suspended as they usually were for visits by foreign dignitaries and as they had been for the entry of Henry III.[125] Nevertheless, in spite of attempts to constrain extravagances, the program managed to exceed all precedents. The impression created by the spectacle was one of sumptuous luxury 'never seen before,' a claim writers rarely failed to make.[126] If restraint promised republican sobriety, the exemption of the dogaressa and her family from luxury laws enabled them to shine more brightly among the cortege and the crowd of spectators.[127]

The dogaressa was preceded by what seemed to one commentator to be more than 200 young women dressed in white with feather fans and elaborate pearl necklaces.[128] She was followed by married women, dressed, as Giovanni Stringa put it, 'not of white, but of another colour like green, dry rose, and deep purple, according to what suited their age.'[129] The piazza was embellished by patrician women, who received bouquets from twelve men who were sombrely dressed in black silk.[130] The chroniclers' detailed reports of the costumes of the women replicate the obsessions of sumptuary legislators. The women, supported by youths dressed as foreigners, undulated on high *zoccoli* (wooden platform shoes) that transformed the women, as contemporaries complained, into *gigantesse*.[131] The decorated bodies of the 'bel sesso' were employed as scenic backdrops for the 'austero Senato,' the grave male representatives of the state, while the physical beauty of the women, and their jewellery enunciated, by metonymy, the city's landscape and financial wealth.[132] The visual representations, with women filling the surrounding balconies, emphasize the decorative function of the women as 'mirrors of so many precious stones.[133] Indeed, it is this impression that characterizes Vicentino's painting.

Neither patron nor details of the commission for the painting are known. Although Marin Grimani recorded payments to artists, no document has been found pertaining to Vicentino's *Embarkation*. Nevertheless, it seems likely, given the personal significance and Marin Grimani's familiarity with Vicentino's work, that he and his wife – by then resident in the Palazzo Ducale – were behind the project. Grimani's extensive patronage included commissions for numerous portraits of himself and his wife, and the canvas similarly commemorates the role of specific individuals in the procession.[134] The canvas was likely inspired by Vicentino's recreation of *The Meeting of Henry III at the Lido* in 1593, which it emulates closely in scale and composition, as can be seen in an engraving produced soon after the work was completed (fig. 63). Michel Hochmann has suggested that Marin Grimani was probably instrumental in the planning of the redecoration of the Sala delle Quattro Porte, where the *Meeting* is displayed.[135] Even if he were not directly responsible, Grimani would have known the artists employed there since he commissioned subsequent work from them.[136] Although there are significant differences between the architecture in the *Embarkation* and the *Meeting*, the proscenium organization is remarkably similar (compare figs. 61 and 63). Floating vessels fill the foreground, and a wooden bridge to the centre left leads the observer from the *Bucintoro* on the left toward the temporary architectural structures. Even the scale and details of the triumphal arches – engaged columns, broken entablature, and attic story – resemble each other. Vicentino focuses on the arrival of the protagonist on the bridge, thereby highlighting the important symbolic moment of each event; gestures, glances, and sheer density of detail are used to construct an impression of spontaneity. However, the courtesans who embellish Henry's meeting on the Lido have been replaced by noble women in the *Disembarkation*.

The 1574 meeting with the king at the Lido – a carefully chosen site on the periphery of the city – was scripted to avoid the appearance of an *entrata*, the symbolic exaltation and domination of the city by the ruler.[137] In Venice, temporary architectural monuments were not constructed for visiting dignitaries in the centre of the city (at least until the second day of festivities) in order to guard against the political posturing that such structures afforded. Long-standing liberty – freedom from foreign rulers – was a constant in Venetian political discourse, and deliberations over protocols and the choice of site for the official meeting with the king were consequently intended to assuage any appearance of a threat to Venetian autonomy.[138] As noted above, the visit generated numerous chronicles and prints, including Francesco Bertelli's engraving of the ephemeral architectural accoutrements (fig. 64).[139] Francesco depicted the relation between the two temporary structures erected on the Lido, including the prominent Loggia, an architectural form associated with the nobility on the terraferma.[140] In Venice, this resonance was

Figure 63   M. Preys, *Il grande apparato* … (after Andrea Vicentino, *Henry III of France Disembarks at the Lido and Progresses toward the Arch Designed by Palladio*). Engraving with some watercolour, 345 × 455 mm [photo: Museo Correr, Venice]

Figure 64   *Il nobilissimo e superbo apparto fatto nel lido di Venetia …* (*Arrival of Henry III at the Lido*), G.D.M. inv. Printed by Francesco Bertelli in Padua, 1574. Engraving, 345 × 600 mm [photo: Museo Correr, Venice]

embedded in Jacopo Sansovino's Loggetta, which was erected at the base of the bell tower in 1538 during Doge Gritti's project of urban renovation for the Piazzetta.[141] Constructed of costly marbles for the procurators – the nine officials who, like the doge, were elected for life – the Loggetta was embellished with relief sculpture that projected an image of the state as the embodiment of justice and rulership over its dominions.[142] The new monumental axis from the Palazzo Ducale to the Loggetta – down the Scala dei Giganti, under the Arco Foscari, and through the Porta della Carta – fuelled the growing number of associations with ancient Rome; indeed, the classical staging cast the toga-clad oligarchs more forcefully as inheritors of Roman authority.

In this context, the Loggetta could only have been viewed by insiders as a public symbol of the oligarchy, 'a patrician club' according to Wolfgang Wolters, where prestigious foreigners could view ceremonial occasions.[143] Francesco Sansovino, the architect's son, described such an event in his guidebook: the 1557 procession for Zilia Dandolo, the wife of Lorenzo Priuli, the only other dogaressa to have a coronation during the sixteenth century. 'According to custom,' observes Sansovino, 'the triumphal progress went to the base of the Campanile near the Loggetta in which the ambassadors of the emperor, the duke of Savoy, and the duke of Urbino were [seated].'[144] The design of the Loggia for the visit of Henry III, and the concomitant aristocratic splendour, may have drawn upon Zilia Dandolo's coronation. In turn, these ephemeral stage trappings were reactivated in the official centre of Venice for Morosina Morosini's coronation, where the sequence of classical backdrops, with their attendant references to humanist learning, would have underscored the elite status of the performers.[145] This process may have encouraged reading the processions as linked celebrations of rulership.

Sansovino's architectural concept for the Piazza as a whole called for replacing the stalls that crowded the entrance to the city. In the 1580s, the senate relocated these structures, showcasing the new buildings on the western side of the Piazzetta instead. These are the structures Vicentino used for the backdrop of the *Embarkation*; the arcades on the library and the brilliantly illuminated Loggetta provide a parallel for the cortege of festively dressed women who have begun their progress through the Piazza. The concept recalls Matteo Pagan's large woodcut in which the arcades of the Procurators' offices frame the procession of the doge and the patriarch (fig. 12).

Franco's Prints

Vicentino's *Disembarkation* was only one of several canvases that aspired in scale and format to the pretensions of history painting. The coronation was also commemorated in portrait medals and celebratory prints that circulated Morosina Morosini's likeness and her name to a wide audience. Marin Grimani paid for medals to celebrate his election as doge in 1595 and the coronation of his consort in 1597. The following year, portraits of Marin Grimani and Morosina Morosini were used for the production of bronze medals, of which 112 copies were made.[146]

Printmakers were particularly enthusiastic participants. Giacomo Franco, for example, produced numerous engravings and maps framed with details of the festivities (figs. 65–7). Indeed, he generated prints in advance of the occasion and also after, thereby capitalizing on local interest and foreign visitors. As we saw in chapter 1, Franco devised alternative frames for a bird's-eye view of the city, benefiting from the coronation to sell copies of a map in which the topography was now out of date.[147] Even as late as 1610, he included engravings of the coronation in his book of costumes and rituals, *Habiti degli huomeni et donne venetiane*, transforming an unusual spectacle into the everyday. This extraodinary production of souvenirs and monumental canvases contributed to the prominence of Morosina's coronation as the highlight of her husband's tenure, as state and private interests came together to commemorate the couple's family names.

The novelty of this remarkable visual attention to patrician women in Venice, even the doge's wife, is worth underlining. Considered within the context of increasing aristocratic display in late sixteenth-century Venice, Franco's printed maps intimate some of the ways in which individual display and collective restraint were complicated by gender and sexuality.

The first version, in which the doge and dogaressa are framed in a cartouche, offers a clue to understanding how the map and the processions might have worked (fig. 66). The figures are presented as generic types, whose reciprocal gazes foreground the conjugal and family structure of the well-ordered city seen in the map.[148] In fact the couple were not ruling sovereigns, and thus the protocols were carefully scripted to forbid their appearance in public together.[149] The potential effect of this is suggested in a chronicler's anecdote which describes how on the third day of festivities, in the Church of San Marco, the clamour of the crowd was silenced by the presence of both the doge and the doga-

Figure 65   Giacomo Franco, *Il nobilissimo teatro deto il mondo* ... Venice, 1597. Engraving and etching, 402 × 518 mm [photo: Museo Correr, Venice]

Figure 66   Giacomo Franco, *Venetia*, Venice, 1597. Engraving, first version, 402 × 522 mm [photo: Museo Correr, Venice]

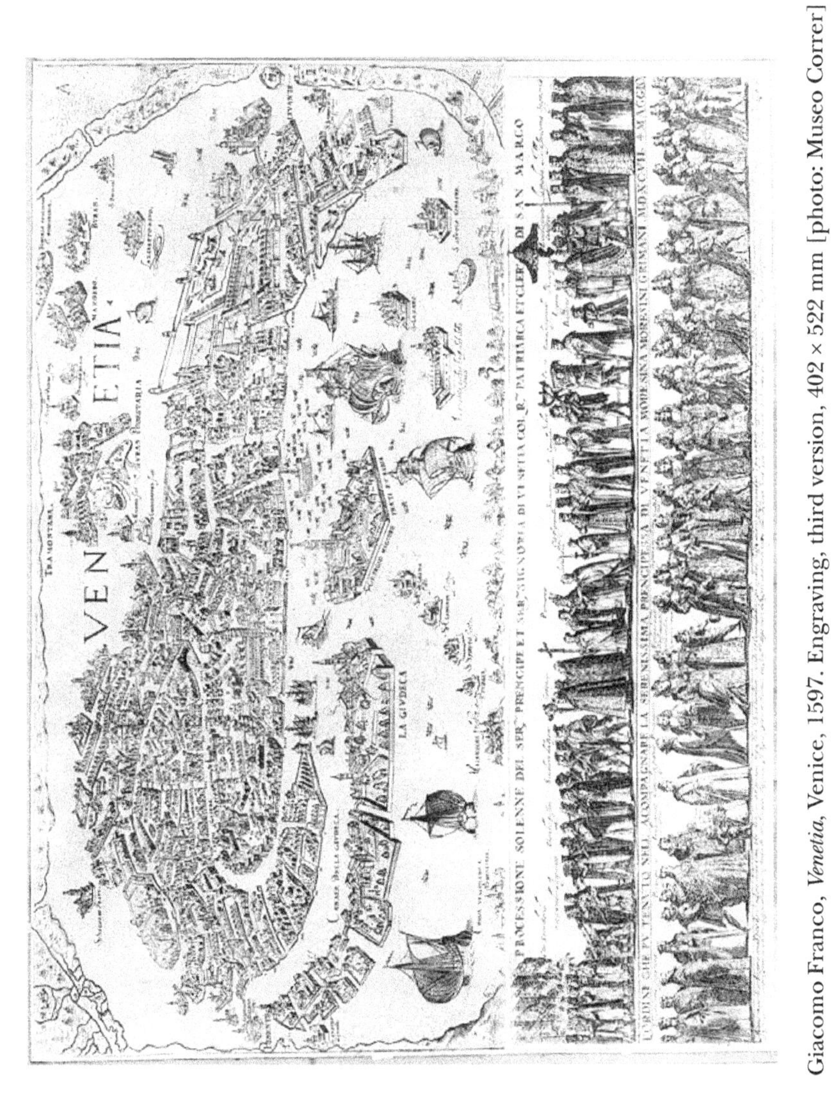

Figure 67   Giacomo Franco, *Venetia*, Venice, 1597. Engraving, third version, 402 × 522 mm [photo: Museo Correr]

ressa.[150] In the cartouche in the print, in which both figures wear the Venetian *corno*, the representation of the couple recalls dynastic mapping and the use of figures to suggest authority over geographic space.[151] On one side, the use of cartographic conventions that linked mapping with entitlement furthers an interpretation of the couple as sovereigns. This was an idea implied in the inscriptions and iconography that decorated the arch, as noted earlier. On the other side, the absence of their names or coats of arms combined with the small-scale standing figures encourages associations with costume books. In one example the doge and dogaressa appear on the same page of Jean Jacques Boissard's *Habitus variarum orbis gentium*, published in 1581. Franco's cartouche, moreover, resembles the grotesque frames used in book illustrations, particularly those Cesare Vecellio used for the costume plates in his *De gli habiti antichi, et moderni di diverse parti del mondo* (fig. 45).[152] Costume was a sign of civic and regional identity, and printed costume books, as I argued at length in chapter 2, called attention to the relation between clothing and categories of identity during the last decades of the century. Foreign and local sartorial distinctions were circulated throughout Europe in more than twenty costume books. Franco's combination of city view and local costume certainly recalls the format used by Georg Braun in the volumes of his *Civitates orbis terrarum* (figs. 11, 38). But even for those unfamiliar with costume books, the juxtaposition links the costume with the map in the mind of the viewer.

A festively dressed noblewoman accompanies the doge and dogaressa in the engraving, addressing the viewer directly, and a *scudiero*, a ducal attendant, stands to the left with a figure resembling the Cancelliere Grande (the representative of the citizen class is depicted in the third version of the map under the word ACOMPAGNARE; fig. 67). His attire also recalls the *Habito ordinario*, a robe worn not only by nobles, but also by citizens, who benefited, as Vecellio explains in his costume book, by association with patrician attire.[153] The incorporation of these figures from outside the ranks of the nobility may express collective participation in the ceremonial event, thereby mitigating an interpretation of the couple's appearance as ruling monarchs and underlining the dogaressa's (merely) symbolic role.

Because of the apparent ambiguity in the print – because the print suggests both specific agents and their symbolic roles – Franco's crowned couple was likely intended to associate the coronation with the Sensa, the annual festival during which the doge marries the sea.[154] Only a few days after the coronation, on the fifteenth of May, thousands would have participated in this watery wedding, a ceremony that drew on the gendered hierarchy of conjugal social relations to proclaim Venetian sovereignty. The inclusion of the *Bucintoro* in the map, and its ubiquitous appearance in Franco's prints of the festivities, would have furthered this association with the Sensa when the doge sailed on the state ship to the Adriatic. At the opening, the sea was ceremoniously inseminated with holy water by the Patriarch, while the doge threw a ring into the sea, proclaiming 'In signum veri perpetuique dominii.' Procreation with the sea symbolically legitimized colonial pursuits while proclaiming the city's own liberty from foreign domination.[155] A constellation of meanings invoked Venetian origins, prosperity, and fecundity, and the procession reaffirmed constitutional order, mercantile practices, control over the sea, and of course marriage and lineage, all demonstrated to foreigners who were regularly invited to participate.[156] The doge and his patrician officials travelled in the *Bucintoro* surrounded by smaller vessels that included people from all of the city's districts and islands, including children and women.[157] The floating procession with its centre surrounded by satellites, might have appeared to visitors, as it does in the printed map, as a metonymic symbol of the city as a whole (fig. 66). In Rascicotti's engraving, this cluster of vessels is even more prominent (fig. 1).

In the second variation, Franco replaced the cartouche with a pair of scenes illustrating two events from the festivities. In the upper register of the detail, he depicted a view of the lagoon with the floating *teatro deto il mondo* and festive war games. Both are depicted together in an engraving that circulated in his costume book (fig. 65). The teatro was the most elaborate of the wood and canvas floats; designed by Vincenzo Scamozzi, this was a hybrid structure in which the pedimented porticoes of Andrea Palladio's *Villa Rotonda* were adapted for an oval platform that was tethered to a fleet of monstrous fish. The pediments at the bow and stern of the float were painted with a *mappamondo*, and the cupola was crowned with twelve stucco figures holding signs of the zodiac.[158] Following humanist concepts, these centrally planned *macchine del mondo* represented the universe, their domes painted with scenes of the heavens. The floating theatre constructed Venice as a microcosm of the world and as a utopian vision seen from above.[159] The inscription refers to the forty male organizers of the ceremony who sailed aboard the float during the parade, but in the print Franco replaced the sombre figures with festively dressed females. Encased in a cage of columns, these *donzelle* provide a pictorial counterpart for the martial display staged nearby.

The combination of points of view – the bird's-eye view and details seen in all the variations of the map – bring together Ptolemy's distinction between chorography and cosmography (figs. 66, 67). 'Chorographers,' as Tommaso Garzoni explains, 'actually paint and draw from nature the form and figure of places, and cities in particular, such as one would draw the land around Rome or around Naples. Besides this, chorographers attend more to the quality of places, representing their true figures and their likenesses.'[160] By contrast cosmographers 'describe the nature, and ownership of lands, and things found there: costumes, peoples, and notable things that happen from time to time.'[161] This distinction is brought into sharper focus in the third modification to the engraving in which Franco replaced the legend with two parades presented as if arrested moments of the same festival (fig. 67). The combination of registers looks back to earlier sources: notably the view of Venice in the *Civitates orbis terrarum* (fig. 11). Processions were depicted in printed costume books, such as Pietro Bertelli's *Diversarum nationum habitus*, to which Franco had contributed designs. But no source that I have seen provides a precedent for the female retinue in Franco's engraving. Instead, it must have been the procession itself that inspired the idea. The prominent caption explains the event: 'the order that was kept to accompany the most serene Princess of Venice, Moresina Moresini Grimani, 1597, 4 May.'[162] Franco underlined the female cortege with a list of participants as if to insist on its facticity by accounting for those absent from this glimpse of a more spectacular and grandiose event. The banner highlights the singularity of the parade; however, the figures were still cast in accordance with the roles patterned in the costume books.

Costume and Cosmography

Vestments had long been a means of incorporating individuals into groups, and the captions of the costume illustrations express these codes of status, gender, sexuality, and profession. By the middle of the sixteenth century, however, as scholars have frequently noted, these categories of identity were increasingly threatened. For nobles in particular, the practice of restricting marriage had resulted in growing numbers of bachelors, inflated dowries, and unmarried women.[163] Reduced access to the patrimony was manifested in forced claustration for many women, both in convents and in the home as unpaid servants, so-called 'second-grade' virgins or 'secular spinsters.'[164] By the beginning of the seventeenth century, one writer commented on the 'confusion' and 'disorder' caused by women in convents; over two thousand noblewomen had been forcibly contained 'as though in public warehouses.'[165] If young women consented to monachization through family pressure, and from the lack of enforcement of regulations regarding dress and visits, Gregory XIII's move in 1580 to tighten the constraints of conventual life intensified the growing sense of defiance among patrician women. '[W]ith the rumor of reform in the air,' as Virginia Cox explains, 'some young women [were] boldly refusing to take the veil.'[166] By the end of the century women – if principally patrician women – were becoming understood 'as a distinct social (as opposed to simply biological) group.'[167] And, as Cox has argued, it was the 'status and identity' of noblewomen that the trend of restricting marriage among families most explicitly threatened.[168] Soaring dowries for a single daughter were one of the means by which the nobility garnered increasingly prestigious marriages, a practice that had the concomitant effect of decreasing the patrician population by limiting the number of legitimate births.[169] Late sixteenth-century Venice was confronted with the combined forces of these *monache forzate*, who seem to have considered 'themselves as in some sense standing outside the rules,' and the power afforded those women who were equipped with ever-larger dowries.[170]

In this context, family display overlapped with social mobility; indeed, the circulation of costumes in a second-hand clothing market facilitated disguise and the transgressions of sumptuary laws.[171] Vecellio addresses a related problem in his introduction, where he complains about the difficulty of classifying female dress: 'because women's clothes are subject to a great deal of change, and more variations than the form of the moon, it is not possible to explain all that one can say about it in a single description.'[172] The association of women with the temporality of fashion was a common refrain, as Tommaso Garzoni explained in his catalogue of professions. Given the 'never ending diversity of ornamentation, one can never learn about the shape of clothes which vary daily so much that tailors know less about them in their old age than when they began their trade ... Nevertheless, great judgement is required ... to satisfy everyone ... and women above all, who change their custom and style of dressing everyday.'[173] This discourse expresses the anxiety of legislators for whom, as Diane Owen Hughes writes, 'fashion changes bred worse than excess or extravagance, they bred disorder ... differentiation had got out of hand.'[174] Vecellio's book parallels official attempts to constrain the expressive potential of fashion by describing social and spatial boundaries for clothes. Visual enforcement of social categories became paramount, to which sumptuary laws attest.[175]

While excesses were largely attributed to women, it was their husbands who were reprimanded for the extravagant attire worn by their wives, and for excessive expenditures on weddings and banquets.[176] Although legislation ostensibly secured republican moderation, the laws established the very lines to be crossed, thereby fuelling family competition. Indeed, secret denunciations enabled men to accuse each other of display on the basis of the luxurious appearance of their wives. Both the sumptuary laws and the denunciation process highlight the complex relation between women as a measure of festive elegance and patrician status and attempts by those patricians to curtail ostentation.[177] The vicissitudes of women's attire preoccupied the Provveditori alle pompe throughout the century, a focus that deflected criticism by transferring the blame to patrician women who assumed the 'state function' of display.[178] Thus the oligarchs who instituted the luxury laws benefited vicariously from the prestige of their wives transgressing them.

In this charged context Franco's bird's-eye view, with its procession of bejewelled women in lavish attire, brings forward some of the social expectations and anxieties concerning the public appearance of women and rank (fig. 67). This problem of reconciling status with female ostentation appears in Francesco Barbaro's famous treatise *On Wifely Duties*: 'If [wives] are of noble birth, they should not wear mean and despicable clothes if their wealth permits otherwise.'[179] Moderation is crucial, however, since history shows that adorned women are seeking the attention of those other than their husbands. 'Sumptuous attire, magnificent clothes, and luxurious apparel' Barbaro continues,

> give pleasure to those who frequent porticos, open courts, and sidewalks or very often promenade through the whole city. Hence, it was wisely forbidden to the women of Egypt to wear ornate shoes so that they might be prevented from wandering about too freely. Indeed, if we were to deprive most women of their sumptuous clothes, they would gladly and willingly stay home ... Yet I think we ought to follow the custom ... that our wives adorn themselves with gold, jewels, and pearls, if we can afford it. For such adornments are the sign of a wealthy, not a lascivious, woman and are taken as evidence of the wealth of the husband more than as a desire to impress wanton eyes.[180]

In the print, the costumes and position of the men in the upper register indicate their status and profession. The parallel procession of the women, identified in Franco's labels as Dogaressa, Procuratessa, and Imbasciatrice, reflects this social order. This use of costume is explained by Vecellio in his discussion of the wives of governors: 'the wives of those gentlemen, who are sent to govern some city, are given the same name as their husbands, and are called Podestaresse, Capitane, and the like. In order for the special name to signify, it is accompanied with some form of dress according to dignity. And therefore, they appear very sumptuous, and with clothes conforming to the titles and to the rank.'[181] This concept was manifested in a variety of tropes. A woman was seen to conform, 'as has been said many times,' wrote Giovanni Battista de Luca in his *Cavaliere e la Dama*, to 'the quality of the husband, as if she were a kind of moon that received all its light and splendor from the sun, that is the husband.'[182] The trope echoed Luther's earlier assessment: 'for as the sun is more splendid than the moon (although the moon is also a most splendid body), so also woman, although the most beautiful handiwork of God, does not equal the dignity and glory of the male.'[183] Not only were women viewed as misbegotten men – 'not in the ordinary course of Nature [praeter naturam]' – they were 'not necessarily of the same species.'[184] As lunar reflections of the sun, women could be understood as subordinate to the genus, ordered in a hierarchy parallel to that of men that was illustrated, as if by design, in the print's horizontal registers. If the doge, was 'splendid like the sun,' as Giovanni Caldiera put it, the dogaressa was the body onto which this light shone: imprinted in the splendour of her costume and reflected back onto her husband.[185] In Franco's prints, the luxurious attire of the women, juxtaposed with the bird's-eye view, or with the *teatro deto il mondo*, can therefore be understood as an image of the Venetian cosmos (fig. 65). Indeed, as Garzoni noted, cosmography proper signified ornament, an equation etymologically linked with the decoration of bodies and the ritual presentation of a city.[186]

The order of the women conforms to the ubiquitous categories of maiden, wife, and widow that filled the pages of costume books, and were familiar from Vives's three books on female comportant. This was also the order in which the noble women progressed during Morosina's coronation, and female observers would have recognized the codified display of marital status signified by the women's costumes. Curiously, however, Franco's lively coronation detail may have hinted at a different order, for the female protagonists in the print do not entirely correspond with what one might expect given the private life, virtues of humility, and obsequiousness expected from the princess of Venice.[187]

Instead Donato Rascicotti's subsequent engraving (fig. 1), produced for the same event, seems a more fitting display of the stipulated decorum. In his dedication to Francesco Morosini, the printmaker explained his print was an authorized and corrected version of events.[188] Both the women and the city in the map have been reconfigured. The recently completed architectural projects – the Arsenale, Fondamenta Nuove, Rialto Bridge, and the library – have been included in the map.[189] At the same time, the women's roles have been more rigorously classified in their visual arrangement and labelled accordingly with the familiar captions as *Donzelle, Principessa, Matrone,* and *Gentildonne.* The dogaressa is still located in the centre, but she is no longer identified by name as Morosina Morosini. The young men, who had supported the young women on their precipitous footwear during the procession – a detail carefully woven into the fabric of the engraving produced by Franco (fig. 67) – are no longer present. Instead the bodies of the women in the Rascicotti engraving convey the moderation prescribed by writers such as Barbaro and Vives.

According to Vives, a woman should be 'contained, with the limbs held close to the body ... In her walk a woman should not be too hurried nor deliberately slow ... She should keep her eyes cast on the ground ... she will not speak save when it would be harmful to keep silent.'[190] 'A woman,' he explains, 'should give no sign in public of arrogrance or disdain or affected manners either by voice, word, gesture or walk.'[191] Vives's equation between public appearance and speech was reiterated by Barbaro. Referring to Plutarch, he notes 'It is proper ... that not only the arms but indeed also the speech of women never be made public; for the speech of a noble woman can be no less dangerous than the nakedness of her limbs.'[192] This concern with female behaviour, however, rallied alternative voices in the defence of women, and the resulting tension is evident in Stefano Guazzo's words: 'with all the authority that women today have over men, they can pride themselves [in the fact] that although withdrawn in their houses, they govern the city and public things at their will.'[193] All of these texts addressing comportment and dress would have overlapped with different forms of visual imagery, such as printed costume books, by calling attention to visual effects of clothes, posing, and the contours of the body. And it was in part this gap, between the role and how it was performed – between the image and the performance – that came to define the self.[194]

To return to the engravings, both Franco and Rascicotti parallel the singular cityscape with its social organization. However, the latter has removed signs of specificity, transforming the singular event into the general. With greater determination than in Franco's map, the classification systems operating in the map were designed to subordinate individual identity to the ideals of the city, to the ideal city. Nevertheless, if these visual representations functioned to make women reflections of the state, they may also have intensified viewers' awareness of the representational weight of their own bodies.

It is worth recalling that sumptuary laws were not suspended for the coronation. Grimani's largesse following his election may have contributed to resistance to a procession for his wife, which was delayed for two years, one more than the conventional pause following her husband's election.[195] Perhaps Leonardo Donà, one of the senators who was opposed to lavish aristocratic display, contributed to this delay; in any case, he certainly obstructed the event by attempting to tax the festivities and to curtail the numbers of foreigners.[196] Intriguingly, according to Andrea da Mosto, it was Morosina Morosini who pressed her husband to push for the coronation.[197] Perhaps it was not only anxiety over courtly aspirations that drove senators to restrict the coronation when the occasion next arose, but also fear of all those women 'coope[d] up.'[198] 'Open the door of the cage,' as one writer warned, 'and the bird is almost certain to fly out.'[199]

Chapter 4

Reproducing the Individual: Likeness and History in Printed Portrait Books

New Formats for Printed Portraits and Recognition

If printed civic imagery impressed upon viewers their roles as Venetian social types, in particular through their sartorial appearance, then what was the function of portraiture at the end of the Renaissance, a mode of representation usually understood to illustrate singular differences? In contrast to portraits, costume book models were generic mannequins and not identified by name or likeness. One exception that proves the rule, however, is the *Generale di Venetia* in Cesare Vecellio's *De gli habiti antichi*, published in 1590 (fig. 68).[1] As the author explains, he has depicted the general as Sebastiano Venier, whose valiant and upright performance during the battle of Lepanto made him an ideal model of Venetian manliness.[2] Despite being wounded by an arrow, Venier continued to command his fleet to victory, a feat magnified by the unexpected success of the Holy League against the Ottoman Empire in 1571. Because his actions exceeded the expectations of the role, he became a cultural ideal; the costume could no longer signify without his individual body.[3] Venier became 'a mirror,' as Pietro Contarini put it, 'for other Venetian nobles to hold up to themselves with respect to their Patria.'[4] Depicted in numerous portraits wielding the general's baton and clad in armour, even after his election as doge in 1577, Venier became the military type for male patricians to emulate in their portraits.

Costume books organize the world into professional, social, and religious categories – kings, captains, doges, popes, artists, sultans – and these are also the types that characterize printed portraits. Indeed, many producers of costume books – Jost Amman, Pietro Bertelli, Jean Jacques Boissard, Jean de Glen, Giacomo Franco, Enea Vico – also illus-

Figure 68   Cesare Vecellio, *Generale di Venetia, De gli habiti antichi, et moderni di diverse parti del mondo libri due* (Venice: Damian Zenaro, 1590). Woodcut, 8°, 20 cm [photo: Museo Correr, Venice]

trated series of portraits.[5] Sold as single sheets and bound together in books, the printed portrait was a burgeoning form in the last decades of the sixteenth century, particularly in Italy.[6] Multiples were not an invention of print, of course. Painted and sculpted portraits, medals, and coins had disseminated the likenesses of individuals as forms of political currency in antiquity, and these practices were revived in the Renaissance. Printed portraits continued to operate within this economy, through patronage for example, but the medium also fostered new publics for imagery. On one side, printmakers were responding to a market for images of famous men and women, while on another side, portrait books could be used to elevate the status of groups, such as artists, seeking fame.

Print fuelled the demand for news and portraits during periods of conflict. Medallions and printed portraits, for example, like those engraved by Agostino Veneziano, were produced in response to the contest between Charles V, Francis I, and Süleyman in Tunis in 1535. Similar imagery was generated by the battle of Lepanto, discussed in the previous chapter.[7] Inexpensive, ephemeral, and small in scale, printed portraits provided widespread access to faces never seen before. Moreover, street vendors and booksellers altered the conditions under which portraits were seen and established new audiences and uses for them. By the end of the seventeenth century, the ubiquity of printed imagery would become fodder for Giuseppe Mitelli's comic engraving of an 'itinerant printseller of war maps and prints' (fig. 69); the figures flanking the printseller complain 'we're full of news, go away, go away, we're fine as we are,' and 'I don't want to hear any more news, no, no, no!'[8] Displaying his wares – city views, broadsheets, and portraits – the printseller holds up the face of a Turk. As the engraving shows, prints made images widely available in which the face and shoulders of the sitter were the focus, precisely those parts of the viewer's own body that cannot be seen without the use of a mirror.[9]

Portraits of foreigners, celebrated figures from antiquity, and family members were commonplace in sixteenth-century Venetian households. The accumulation of goods, including paintings and printed books, was spread across social levels. Portraits were numerous and could be found throughout the house, from private commemorative images of women and mothers found in bedrooms, to the large portraits of standing figures seen in the more public entrances.[10] Images of foreign rulers were sometimes displayed with printed maps, furnishing a new cosmopolitan context for family portraits.[11]

Figure 69   G.M. Mitelli [itinerant printseller of war maps and prints], Bologna, 1688. Engraving, 272 × 198 mm [photo: copyright British Museum, London]

By the middle of the century, images identified as Turks (the nomenclature for Muslims rather than a specific ethnic identity) were also familiar sights on the walls of Venetian houses.[12] Roman emperors were another popular type, as recorded among the vast collection of paintings owned by Gasparo Segizzi, a painter of miniatures. He also owned a small gilded mirror that was hung among the portraits, probably adjacent to a portrait of Caesar Augustus.[13] Venetians were the only producers of good-quality plane mirrors – an industry they protected – until the middle of the seventeenth century, when lower costs made these novel objects conventional in European households.[14] A sampling of notarial records from 1569 to 1595 show that Flemish merchants shipped crates of mirrors, sometimes framed, from Venice to London, Cádiz, Seville, Lisbon, and Amsterdam.[15] A crate of mirrors was listed among the goods stored in the warehouses of one of these men, Francesco Vrins.[16] Thirty-three smaller cases inside the crate contained nearly 900 mirrors in two sizes.[17] His residence in Venice was filled with paintings, portraits, mirrors, and maps. The entrance, for example, was decorated with nine portraits, four of which were of relatives, a small mirror, and a large *mappamondo*. A room overlooking the canal contained a large mirror and two portraits including one of Vrins's wife. Three maps and a second *mappamondo* embellished the portego on the floor above. Although more common in the homes of the well-off, inventories of the last decades of the century in Venice attest to the growing presence of framed mirrors by the 1580s and their location, amid collections of portraits, suggests that residents may have seen their own faces reflected among those depicted in the surrounding images.

Portraits had long functioned as a form of cultic imagery – to make family members present and to confirm lineages.[18] Increasingly, professional connections could be established through shared representational conventions. Portraits of famous figures continued to serve as models, and printed portrait books, with their combination of likeness and biography, spring from this context. Since these likenesses were compiled into categories, usually profession, and identified by costume, coats of arms, and other external accoutrements, the genre indicates that individual identity was still, even at the end of the sixteenth century, subsumed within collective affiliations of family, status, and trade. Series of prints would therefore seem to question Jacob Burckhardt's parallel between portraiture and the 'birth of the individual.' Sixteenth-century selves, as Stephen Greenblatt maintains, were defined by the ownership of their words or actions and not their individual bodies.[19] As noted in the Introduction, John Martin has suggested that we should not disregard Burckhardt's ideas in their entirety.[20] Martin's research indicates a growing split between a sense of interiority, defined by sincerity and prudence, or dissimulation. As suggested here, it may have been the very process of serialization that contributed to the split identified by Martin, and to the impression of a modern subject whose identity is defined by its body. Portrait books may have responded to humanist beliefs that outward appearances were an expression of a person's soul, but as this chapter suggests, print participated in inverting this process by showing how the face came to constitute the characteristics that determined identity. In so doing, printed portraits, and the social practices with which they intersected, may have altered the ways in which identities accrued to individuals. The conventions of costume books, as we saw, prompted viewers to recognize differences between geographical, civic, and social types. Printed portraits reveal a similar interest in the legibility of signs; however in portrait books, as this chapter argues, the imagery calls attention to differences within the type. In contrast to costume books, in portrait books the type unfolds to reveal the individual.

The Face and the Map

At the end of the fifteenth century, as we saw in chapter 1, Jacopo de'Barbari surrounded his woodcut of Venice with heads of wind gods, each of which was rendered distinctively from the others (fig. 9). Perhaps, as suggested by Terisio Pignatti, the face of the Greek wind god to the right is a self-portrait of the artist; more certainly, the naturalistic physiognomy functions as an analogue for the mimetic accuracy of the cityscape. Moreover, with this face de'Barbari evokes Ptolemy, whose parallel between the work of the cartographer and the portraitist became a commonplace in the Renaissance. For Ptolemy, as we saw in chapter 1, the geography of the world was analogous with the human face, and its cities comparable with facial features (fig. 6).[21]

The aim of the chorographer is to represent only one part, as if one were to imitate or to paint only one ear, or an eye. But the aim of the geographer is to consider the universal whole in the guise of those who describe or paint the entire head. ...

[C]horographers attend more to the quality of places, representing their true figures and their likenesses. Geographers are the opposite, attending more to quantity, by describing sizes, sites, and proportion of distances.

Remarkably, de'Barbari has conflated both visual metaphors in the same bird's-eye view (fig. 3). Seen from an Olympian vantage point, and surrounded by wind gods, the woodcut follows conventions of printed *mappaemundi* (fig. 7); Venice is depicted as a world unto itself following Ptolemy's geographer, who delineates the entire human head. Yet every window and *calle* of the city is depicted with the portraitist's devotion to the eye or the nose in accordance with the chorographer's art of exact description. In this synoptic image, then, Venice was envisioned as both a face and a close-up.

Francesco Sansovino reiterated this double vision of the city in his 1561 guidebook in which he describes Venice as 'the eye of Italy.'[22] This physiognomic identity is suggested by Giuseppe Rosaccio, who exaggerated the scale of Venice on his map of Italy (1607; fig. 14). When the Italian peninsula was represented from above in maps, the profile was seen to resemble the face of Europe, and Venice – with its insular pupil centred in an iris-like lagoon – its oculus. This correspondence of the city's topography to a human eye becomes fixed in later sixteenth-century bird's-eye views in which distortions to the Lido and the terraferma create a symmetrical frame (fig. 13). Toward the end of the century, this iconic view appeared in a new format, surrounded by portraits of the doges, who are accompanied by brief biographies (fig. 70). In these political *fogli volanti* the 'natural likenesses' of the doges were seen to parallel the 'portrait of the marvellous city of Venice.'[23] The analogy between these two 'nobilissimi spiriti' was made by the friar Fulgenzio Manfredi and published by G. Battista Mazza and Gasparo Uccelli in 1598. One extant copy of their broadsheet was cut into parts and is now bound in a volume in the British Library (fig. 71). Manfredi compiled the compendia of civic history, events, and biographies of the doges, and his younger brother designed the portraits after those in the Ducal Palace. Figure 71 demonstrates how the distinctiveness of an individual's physiognomy is set into relief by the collective context.

Biography, likeness, and geography had been brought together earlier by Sansovino, who advocated the use of portraits of celebrated people in texts in the fourth book of *L'historia di casa Orsina*. Published in Venice in 1565, this early example of a portrait book consists of biographies and portraits of the Orsina family, many of whom had served the Venetian state. His introduction is cited at length because it introduces a number of overlapping themes to which I return throughout the chapter:

Figure 70 Francesco Vallegio, *Map of Venice with the Doges*. Engraving, etching, and letterpress, 565 × 955 mm, issued 1623–4 [photo: copyright British Museum, London]

Figure 71   Fulgenzio Manfredi, *Venetia,* detail from a *folio volante* (Venice: Battista Mazza and Gasparo Uccelli, 1598). Engraving, etching, 379 × 735 mm [photo: by permission of the British Library, London]

[V]iewers are often curious to identify in likenesses (effigie) those virtues about which they have heard celebrated [and] to exalt their fame greatly among the living world and among writers; thus one profits from the presence of esteemed people no less than from the memory of their honoured deeds; and, since for the student of history knowledge of cosmography is necessary with respect to places where the described events occur, so too does it confer much to that same history to have the images of those people about whom one reads in front of one's eyes for the evidence signalled and illustrated [in those faces]. Thus although having frequently seen for themselves that actions [of individuals] do not correspond to their faces, and that sometimes under beautiful faces one discovers dreadful and horrible thoughts, the reader will come to marvel ... [and] to contemplate the miracles that nature knows to produce in the countenances of man. And finding the forces of our souls implicated together with [Nature] in the making of the face, in the way that smell, taste, and colour are bound together in the making of a fruit, the judgment of human hearts is most undoubtedly found in the face. Now we have to note that in such clear images of the Orsina men one sees greatness and majesty in the countenance of the face, because they have spirit and military vigour, with open foreheads, and with mouths rather large for the most part, signifying men of much eloquence; and with truly real likenesses, clearly we are able to believe (in the absence of any other knowledge of their origins) that they are without any doubt, descendants from the highest and noble blood, if from the face (that it is truly the demonstrator of our souls) one can conjecture the greatness of generous, and lofty thoughts.[24]

For Sansovino, the portraits provide a frame for his histories that enable the reader to profit 'from the presence of esteemed people.' Significantly, he invests the image with new potential; the print is a mnemonic device, a way to recall the sitter's actions, his history. The portrait is charged with reviving the presence of an absent individual and with propelling the memory of that person into the present. Moreover, Sansovino directs his readers to the visual evidence of the sitters' faces; even if physiognomy cannot always be trusted as an indicator of character, the visual evidence of these engravings, he claims, demonstrates the virtuous and noble character of the men.

Sansovino sometimes begins by referring to the accompanying engraving, as in the case of Camillo Orsino da Lamentana (fig. 72):

This face, so dry and of an emaciated colour, demonstrative of the quality of a nervous man, and by nature agile and strong, is the true portrait of Signor Camillo Orsino, son of the preceding Signor Paolo, the one who had him reared in the honoured studies of military discipline under Nicola Orsino, Bartolomeo da Liviano, and Gian Giacomo Trìulci, who passed onto him his great expanse of authority, of prudence, and of faith.[25]

The man depicted in the portrait is indeed a gaunt figure, whose weedy beard exaggerates his lean face. But the figure is dressed in armour and looking toward the viewer with sharp eyes, and the text prompts us to interpret his gaze as incisive and his visage as a sign of vigour and assiduity.

Only eleven portraits of the Orsina are included, despite the preparation of the same oval frames for seventeen. Perhaps, as Cecil Clough has suggested, the six empty spaces indicate that no image could be found and that the rest were thereby 'deemed authentic likenesses.'[26] In those cases where there is no portrait, any description of the individual is cursory and general, indicating that Sansovino's account of the sitter's physiognomy was drawn from the likeness used for the plates. The clarity of engraving distinguishes the singularity of the face, and this in turn encourages the reader to scrutinize its topography, as Sansovino does, for evidence of the sitter's talents and actions. The face is like a map that can be read for signs of character, even ancestry. Like frontispieces, the portraits introduce the histories, distinguishing the life of one man from the actions of the next in the reader's mind.

The portraits stand alone in Giacomo Franco's album *Effiggie naturali dei maggior prencipi et piu valorosi capitani* (figs. 73, 84, 89, 96, 97), a series of thirty-five engravings first published together in 1596. Bringing together illustrious leaders from across the continent, the *Effiggie naturali* is an atlas of portraits. The parade of faces is ordered by status, and their rank identified by a plethora of authoritative symbols: sceptres, orbs, coats of arms, and batons. The album begins with the pope and progresses to the emperors, kings, and queen of Europe, including those of Persia, the Tartars, and the Turks. Archdukes and princes follow, with the doge of Venice as the transition between the more illustrious category of royals that precede him and the dukes of the Italian states that follow. Generals, military leaders, and counts form the rest of the contingent. A group of six plates with twelve Roman emperors was added to the expanded 1608 edition of fifty-five portraits.

For his likeness of the reigning doge, Franco used Leandro Bassano's

Figure 72   *Camillo Orsino da Lamentana*, Francesco Sansovino, *L'historia di casa Orsina* (Venice: B. & F. Stagnini fratelli, 1565). Engraving, folio [photo: by permission of the British Library, London] C.80.c.9

Figure 73   Giacomo Franco, *Marino Grimani Doge di Venetia, Effiggie naturali dei maggior prencipi et piu valorosi capitani* (Venice, 1596). Engraving, 4°
[photo: Biblioteca Nazionale Marciana, Venice]

portrait of Marin Grimani, painted after his election in 1595 (figs. 49, 73). For the printed portrait, Franco has faithfully copied the image of the doge, but he has omitted the window from Leandro's painting; Franco thereby focuses the viewer on this particular doge, whose likeness is identified by his family coat of arms.[27] His name is also inscribed in Roman letters, as if carved in the pseudo-parapet below, anchoring the printed image to the broader conventions of painted portraits. Grimani's death in 1605 prompted his omission from the 1608 edition of the album in which he was replaced with Leonardo Donà (reigned 1606–12).

The spectre of Grimani's presence however, remains in Franco's costume book, *Habiti degli huomeni et donne venetiane*, where he used the same painted portrait for his costume of the doge (fig. 74). Franco extended the body of the model to emphasize the ducal robes. A descriptive caption of the costume and the view of the Piazzetta and Palazzo Ducale have replaced the signs of the sitter's identity seen in the printed portrait. The referent has been reduced to a Venetian type emphasizing the costume and spaces inhabited by someone of his stature.[28]

The first portrait album appeared in Rome with the publication in 1566 of Marco Mantova Benavides's *Illustrium iureconsultorum imagines*, a collection of engravings of jurists by Nicolò Nelli and Cornelis Cort published by Antoine Lafréry.[29] Two years later, Lafréry also published the first portrait book, Onofrio Panvinio's *XXVII Pontificum Maximorum*, the likenesses and achievements of the post-Avignon popes.[30] The local ecclesiastical community and pilgrims to Rome provided a market for portraits of popes, and the city became the centre for the production of portrait books on other subjects as well.[31] Nelli reprinted twenty-four of the Benavides plates in Venice in 1567, when he transferred his business there toward the end of his career. Cornelius Cort was also active from 1565 in Venice, where Franco studied with him, and where he began his career by producing frontispieces and portraits for a variety of publishers.[32] Many printers operated in both cities. Pietro Bertelli was one of that family's 'printing dynasty' that operated in Venice, Rome, Padua, and Vicenza for several generations.[33] An engraver, publisher, and printer, Pietro had links to all these centres after extending the family business to Padua and Vicenza. His portrait book of sultans, *Vite degl'imperatori de'Turchi con le loro effiggie*, follows conventions established for Roman emperors, but the Vicenza printing in 1599 indicates he targeted a local audience that provided a market for both elite and popular printing houses (figs. 85, 87, 88). Pietro Bertelli's series of popes with

Figure 74   Giacomo Franco, *In questa habito si vede il Ser.mo Doge di Venetia ...,*
Habiti degli huomeni et donne venetiane (Venice:1610). Engraving, folio
[photo: by permission of the British Library, London]. C.48h.11 f.5

their coats of arms, *Effigie de sommi Pontefici dalla sedia d'Avignone ritornati a Roma fino a questi tempi*, was published in 1611 (fig. 75). Supplementing the post-Avignon focus is a list of the popes since Peter, into which a miniature engraving of Paul V, the reigning pope, has been inserted (fig. 76). The kings of France, illustrious ancients, and Roman emperors provided further categories for printmakers, including engravings of the latter made after portraits by Titian.[34]

All of these projects were spawned by Paolo Giovio's immense collection of painted portraits of renowned individuals once seen together in his palace, turned museum, in Como.[35] A humanist, Giovio was fascinated with *imprese* – those devices in which an individual's image and motto were converted into a symbol of his or her character[36] – and the portrait book, with its combination of image and text is an expression of this interest. Nevertheless, his two biographies – one of famous poets and philosophers, and the other of great warriors – were published without reproductions of his portraits in 1546 and 1551, perhaps, as suggested by Cecil Clough, because the quality of engraving was not yet adequate.[37] Giovio's plan to combine portraits with an account of the sitters' deeds appeared only posthumously, when Tobias Stimmer's drawings were used to illustrate two new editions of the *Elogia* and two portrait books.[38] The *Musei ioviani imagines*, published in 1577, brings together 122 octavo woodcuts made by Tobias Stimmer after Giovio's portraits (fig. 77). Significantly, Giovio subordinated concern for artistic style or aesthetics in favour of copies that could be traced back to a source, a preference, as Linda Klinger has demonstrated, for the portrait's function as a historical document.[39] The likeness was thereby objectified; instead of making the sitter present – the use of portraits as cultic imagery for family identity – the copy provided a form of historical distance.

Portrait books were also a response to the revitalization by Renaissance humanists of ancient theories concerning facial features and personality.[40] These ideas circulated in the medieval period and were rehearsed through the Renaissance. Toward the end of the sixteenth century, however, writers began to emphasize the process of reading the face and body as texts composed of signs. A striking example of this shift toward the semantic potential of the face is Giovanni Bonifacio's *L'arte de'cenni*, a text which aims to promote the 'mute eloquence of gesture' as a universal language.[41] As he explains, 'The concepts of our souls can be expressed in four ways, [with] signs/gestures, speech, writing, and

Figure 75   *Clemente VIII. Fiorentino, Effigie de sommi Pontefici dalla sedia d'Avignone ritornati a Roma fino a questi tempi* (Vicenza[?]: Pietro Bertelli, 1611). Engraving, folio [photo: by permission of the British Library, London] C.80.f.4

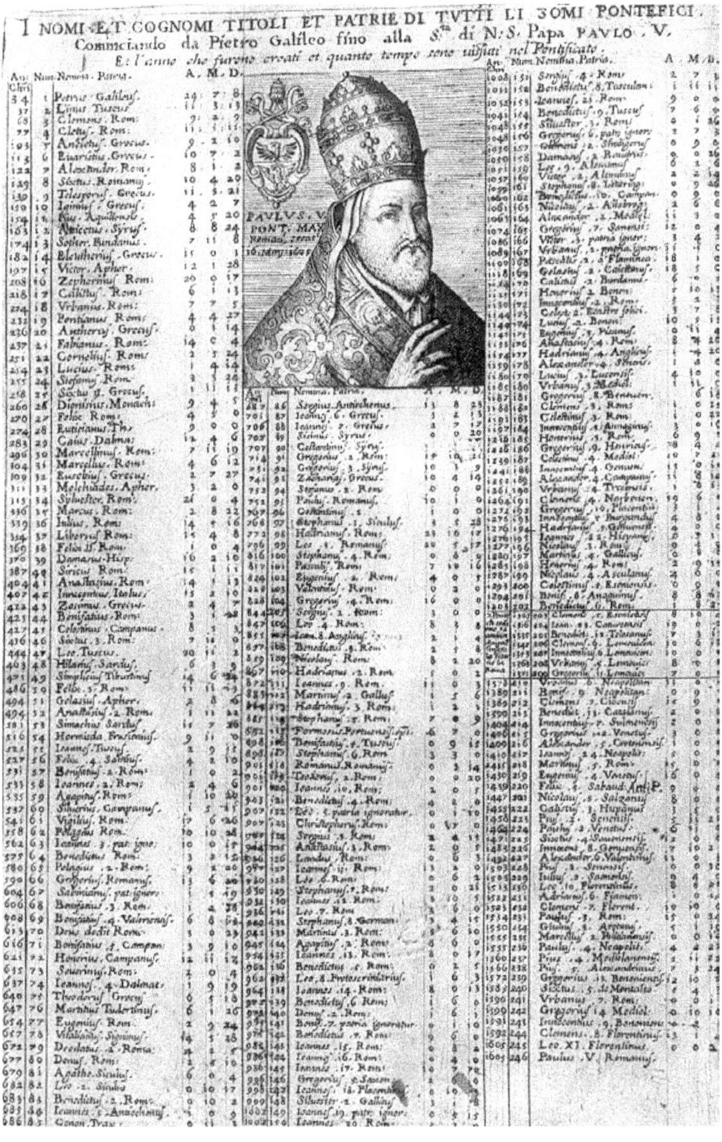

Figure 76   *I nomi et cognomi titoli et patrie di tutti li somi pontefici.* List of popes, *Effigie de sommi Pontefici dalla sedia d'Avignone ritornati a Roma fino a questi tempi* (Vicenza[?]: Pietro Bertelli, 1611). Engraving, folio [photo: by permission of the British Library, London] c.80.f.4

Figure 77   Tobias Stimmer, *Politianus*, Theobald Müller, *Musaei Joviani imagines artifice manu ad vivum expressae* (Basel: Petri Pernae, 1577). Woodcut, 4° [photo: by permission of the British Library, London]

symbols.'[42] However, only the first of these modes of communication – 'the most noble, ancient, and sincere way' – can be understood by people of all dialects and foreign languages.[43] In support of his argument that 'all the nations of the world' can agree on the meanings of gestures, he cites the uses of them by European artists in paintings, asserting that such signs would be recognized by Asians and Africans alike. Nevertheless, the text is a didactic one, and readers are introduced to the physiognomic complexities of every single part of the body. This handy lexicon furnishes the tools to interpret differences between, say, a wink or a squint. Fifty-eight sections are devoted to the eye alone. For theorists of both physiognomy and gesture, the face and eyes were the most important carriers of meaning, and these external visible indices were considered to construe identity and personality.

Significantly, Giovanni Battista della Porta, the famous advocate of the science of physiognomy, was himself looking at portrait books.[44] For his *De humana physiognomonia,* first published in 1586, he drew on Tobias Stimmer's reproductions of paintings from Giovio's museum for his comparisons of human and animal facial features (figs. 77, 78).[45] In one example, Della Porta juxtaposes a portrait of Angelo Poliziano with the head of a rhinoceros. Giovio, in his written portrait of the poet, had already suggested an alignment between Poliziano's 'censurable habits,' envious personality, and unfortunate appearance, the latter caused by his 'excessive nose and sly look' (*l'occhio losco*).[46] Della Porta capitalizes on this aspect of Poliziano's physiognomy to illustrate his chapter on the nose, exaggerating his lengthy proboscis, eyes, and hair to resemble more closely the pointed horn and brutish features of the adjacent creature. Drawing on Giovio's assessment of Poliziano's personality, but not referring to him by name, Della Porta explains that 'A very large nose is proof of a man who takes over the work of others and who does not like things if they are not his own, and who laughs off those of others.'[47] A caption above the engraving, however, identifies the face: 'Reader, you have here the great nose of the Rhinoceros, from whose middle springs a horn, with the living likeness of Angelo Poliziano.' This deictic mode is used throughout the book to address his audience more directly and to point out features in the illustrations.[48] Moreover, the images themselves prompt the reader to compare the figures: to identify what the character of the animal implies about the adjacent human head, whose resemblance has been ensured by strategic manipulation (also see figs. 79 and 93).

Della Porta's project was inspired by the growing epistemological superiority of optics, by visual experience, and by the conviction that

LIBER SECVNDVS.   73

id quod à Galeno iisdem verbis est transcriptum. In Physiognomonicis verò ait: Videbit autem
vtiq; quis & canum optimos moderatas aures habere. Polemon & Adamantius : Quadrangulares
aures non excedentes magnitudinem , virilem hominem & bonum manifestant. Adamantius virilem, & egregijs sensibus præditum dicit. Conciliator eadem. Sed satis inepte transfert. Lœuus op-
timas aures ita describit . Semicircularis conuexa linea in medio aliquantum ex parte conuexa
versus centrum, magnitudine mediocres, capiti decenter adhærentes, & mediocriter pilosæ ; sicn.
seminalem virtutem, quæ eas efformauit , fuisse pollentem, & optimam iudicatur, vt Albertus ex
eo refert. Mediocres aures Augustum habuisse refert Suetonius: vnde præclaris moribus ornatus,
& animi dotibus præpollens à scriptoribus designatur.

DE NASO: *Cap. VII.*

NASVS in facie sensibilis est, hæc siquidem pars hominem præ cæteris, formosum
deformemq; reddit. Estq; in eo varietas maxima, vt nõ sit alia facierum distinctio,
quàm per nasum. Aristoteles Animalium libro hæc habet de naso: Pars faciei nasus:
cartilagineã partem, quæ nares discriminat, interseptum vocamus, vtrumq; mea
tum inane. Eius initium est à glabra, interstitium inter supercilia constitutum. Pars
ima est, vbi nasus delatior in aures se fundit. Adnotandum præterea quandam esse
proportionem faciei partium ad totius corporis partes , & sibi inuicem correspondere , aut men-
sura , aut quantitate , aut signis.

Habes hic lector Rhinocerotis ad viuum effigiatum nasum magnum, à cuius medio cornu procedit.
& Poliuani vera effigies.

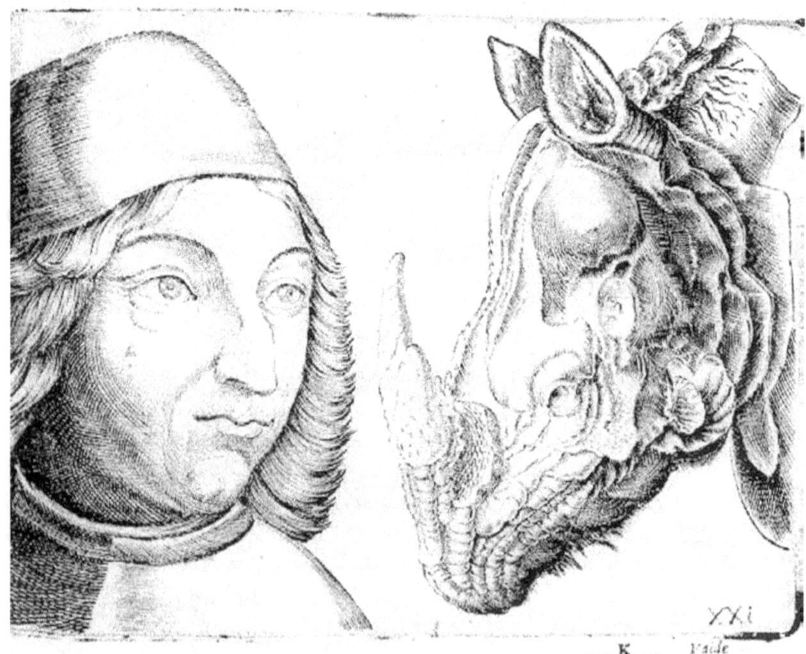

Figure 78   Giovanni Battista della Porta, *De Naso, De humana physiognomonia libri IIII* (Naples: Tarquinium Longum, 1603) [photo: Osler Library Montreal]

describing phenomena could also be used to explain them.[49] Following widespread belief in the Renaissance that the virtues of plants could be construed on the basis of their outward appearance – the so-called doctrine of signatures – Della Porta pursued animal and human physical characteristics, even illustrating in pictures how flora, fauna, and humans resemble each other.[50] In a range of tracts, and employing various comparative analyses, he uses images and texts to demonstrate that chiromancy (palm reading), phytognomony, and physiognomy could all be deciphered for signs of character. Physiognomy, he explains toward the end of the first book, is 'a science that studies the signs that are fixed in the body, and accidents that transform into signs, [that teaches how] to investigate the natural habits of the soul ... The name of Physiognomy one could almost say means the law or rule of Nature; that is, by a certain rule, norm, and order of Nature one recognizes from the form of the body the passion of the soul.'[51] Size, shape, and lines visible on the exterior were deemed to reveal interior truths.

Nevertheless, for Della Porta (and Francesco Sansovino, as noted in the passage cited above), physiognomy is never the only means of understanding character; nor should a portrait alter the historical facts of an individual's actions. Portraits of Messalina and Faustina, the wives of Claudius and Marcus Aurelius, are used to make this point. As Della Porta tells the reader in the caption, the likenesses are based on portrait busts and medallions found in his brother's museum, and the depiction of the women facing each other in profile confirms this antique source.[52] In contrast to Poliziano, and in the absence of zoological clues to their character, to the untrained eye the portraits reveal little of the two women's infamous temperaments; nor does Della Porta's description bear much resemblance to the illustrations. He begins with Messalina, who in addition to being remarkably hairy, had 'a delicate and thin face and neck ... large, lascivious, and deeply set eyes, [and] a chin turned up toward her nose ... and blond hair, as Juvenale writes.' We also learn of how Messalina forced other Roman women to emulate her own depraved behaviour:

> The example of her lechery surpassed all Roman women of her time ... Going by the name of the prostitute Licisca, she used to enter in the morning, staying all day in the practice; at the end of the evening she used to leave, tired, but her lechery not yet satiated; and she sought to be paid for her work. These and other of her deceitful works are written by Suetonius and by Dio Cassius.[53]

Faustina 'was also full of hair, thin, and with similar features and habits; she would even lay down with gladiators and other lowly people; the histories are full of all these things.'[54] Readers learn that a beautiful face is not necessarily evidence of a good interior; instead, it is an individual's actions that are the key to her or his personality, and these histories are described in texts.[55] However, if Della Porta's account of Messalina indicates her attractions, his strange description constructs her as a monster. The reader learns to interpret abundant hair, wide eyes, a pulled-back mouth, and pursed facial features as signs of a dangerous sexual drive and deceitfulness.

Following the usual array of Arabic, Aristotelian, and other antique sources, Della Porta divides the face and body into parts to explain their meanings, but these syntactical units are then reassembled and the meaning of the whole interpreted using his 'syllogistic' method.[56] This helps to explain the repetition of the same engravings in different sections of the book. For example, the pairing of the lion and his human type is deployed to illustrate the forehead, a sign of magnanimity (fig. 79).[57] As the caption in the Italian edition states: 'Here below is presented the human forehead of a squared shape similar to that of the lion with an exact [visual] description; you are not fooled by the similarity.'[58] The same image is also used to illustrate sections such as 'the flattened nose,' and 'delicate lips in a grand mouth.'[59] In contrast to earlier ideas, in which a leonine face was a sign of a lion-like personality, Della Porta's method claims to distill the essence of the individual from a combination of character traits. Significantly, he sought to explain what the small differences between faces elucidated about individuals. He instructs readers to survey the faces of individuals as they would a map. Crucial to the argument of this chapter, the pictures themselves bring forward a new cognitive role for the image since the paired physiognomies, like those faces reproduced in the portrait books, urge the viewer to compare their countenances.

Thus if Della Porta's theories were bound to the Renaissance world of resemblances, where Michel Foucault situates him, the mode of representation initiates those processes of discrimination in the viewer that Foucault assigned to the classical age.[60] Broken down into its constituent parts and then reassembled, the face is transformed into discourse. This concept of the face *as* representation – comprised of features whose meanings are learned, and read, instead of recognized *as* something else – emerges against the backdrop of the portrait's function to resemble the sitter, to make the sitter present in 'flesh and

34   DE HVM. PHYSIOGN.

In hac figura mediæ magnitudinis caput inter reliqua cum leonino capite contemplare.

Caput mediocre :

A RISTOTELES *commendat Alexandro Magno caput mediocre, & intra men-*
sum constitutum, cum Polemon, & Adamantius mediæ magnitudinis caput laudent.
Id videtur Leoni comparandum, ipse enim ad corporis rationem, moderata capitis ma-
gnitudine est: vt apud Aristotelem videre est, leonis formam describentem.   Albertus ad hæc.
Moderatum caput indicat ingenium, & sensum, aliquando tamen timidum, & liberalem,
sed ego non timidum, sed audacem, & magnanimum ad leonem relatum.

Prima hæc tabella in dextra sui parte non naturalem capitis formam refert, in qua anterior eminentia perit, posterior
tumet sinistra vero secundum capitis innaturalem formam, in qua postica pars deperditur; anterior gibba.

Figure 79   Giovanni Battista della Porta, *Caput mediocre, De humana physiognomo-*
nia libri IIII (Vici Aequensis, Iosephum Cacchium, 1586) [photo:
Osler Library Montreal]

blood' according to the contemporary topos professed for painted portraits. At the end of the century, print troubled the notion of resemblance, as I suggest here, translating and altering its function.

As proposed in chapter 2, sixteenth-century Europeans were more attuned to nuances of costumes and customs than facial features. They identified behaviour with facial characteristics, but this practice followed physiognomic theories of similitudes as well as ancient and medieval medicine and physiogology, which attributed differences to the balance of humours within bodies. Thus a forbidding countenance was a sign of a villainous interior; red hair, an indication of a fiery temperment; and brutish features a sign of peasants. Yellow skin was a symptom of a choleric personality – an individual with too much yellow bile – and not yet of race as we understand the word today.[61] Prejudices against ethnic groups, especially Jews and those described as Turks, or Muslims, were well ensconced, but as I hope to suggest below, these stereotypes circulated in language and not yet in facial features. What I want to bring forward here is a crucial difference between how the west looks at faces today and some of the ways in which Europeans were looking at faces before the modern contours of race or ethnic differences had been fully drawn.

To introduce this problem I turn to the visit of the Japanese youths to Italy in 1585, since this encounter provides insights into perceptions of difference before these were filtered through established representational conventions. In contrast to the Turks, who were deemed to be immutable in their faith and their costumes, Europeans were confronted with young converts to Christianity who changed their clothes throughout the journey. They travelled in European attire, donned Japanese national costume for ceremonial events, and often wore a combination of both. This sartorial confusion, I propose, combined with the range of identities attached to the Japanese, prompted closer attention of the chroniclers to the bodies of the youths and to their physiognomy. A wealth of sources reveals the struggle faced by writers who tried to describe these unfamiliar faces. This textual evidence, considered together with the absence of visual imagery, indicates that artists could only depict facial features as signs of ethnic difference once they recognized them as such, and that process required the repeated experience of comparing faces.

Describing the Japanese

With the arrival of an embassy from Japan, chroniclers were confronted with foreigners never seen before on European soil.[62] Not surprisingly, the costumes of the Japanese sparked curiosity; these were described in numerous printed *relationi,* and in one case a woodcut provides a 'Portrait and clothes of those Indians who arrived in Rome on 23 March 1585' (fig. 80):

> They wear two long dresses, the outer one sleeveless, the inner one with sleeves, which go over the shoulders and the breast down to the belt, as the Carthusians or the friars of St Francis of Paula use, but without [a] hood, all in white silk, embroidered in various colours with leaves and lines and drawings of birds and other animals; jewels in the Arabian fashion; a felt hat, a cap with the golden plait and a pleated-collared shirt, both in the Spanish way; a silk belt holding a weapon; a venerable face, of the same colour as an African, short of stature and roughly eighteen years of age.[63]

The woodcut follows conventions established in printed costume books discussed in chapter 2: a caption identifies the figure who stands close to the picture plane, and the absence of any narrative setting highlights the silhouette of the apparel. The comparison with classical vestments resonates with contemporary catalogues, such as Abraham de Bruyn's 1578 *Imperii ac sacerdotii ornatus,* in which dozens of cassocks are illustrated and classified by religious order.[64] The mélange of kimono and Spanish shirt pictured in the woodcut, and efforts to describe the body of the Japanese in the text, introduce the representational dilemma brought forward by the embassy.

Despite seventy-eight known printed chronicles of the embassy, this was the only visual record of their attire to appear in the pamphlets. A perfunctory woodcut from Rome and a small grisaille fresco in the Teatro Olimpico in Vicenza are among the few visual records of their presence. Jacopo Tintoretto was commissioned by the Venetian senate to paint portraits of the Japanese, but these are no longer extant, if in fact they were ever completed. The lack of images of the Japanese is especially surprising in Venice, where the state staged a lavish festival for the visitors, and where foreign visits, such as the entry of Henry III in 1574, fuelled the production of popular prints. Cesare Vecellio's woodcut of Japanese attire is the best-known record, and this was published later in the 1598 edition of his costume book, *Habiti antichi et moderni di tutto il mondo* (fig. 81).

Perhaps the most intriguing images are the amateur miniature portraits collected in Urbano Monte's manuscript, where he included

Figure 80   *Effigie, & habito di quei Indiani arrivati a Roma li 23. Marzo 1585, Avisi venuti novamente da Roma delli XXIII di Marzo* (Bologna: Alessandro Benacci 1585) 20 × 14 cm [photo: Biblioteca Nazionale Marciana, Venice]

paintings of the youths to show that 'there is little difference among them.'[65] The youths are depicted in three-quarter format by an amateur hand, in western dress with Spanish collars and holding hats to match. Each is identified by name, title, place, and age in a bandarole above. Mancio Ito, nephew of one king, and sent by another, also holds a crown, in accordance with the standard use of portraiture to display rank and status. The Japanese are distinguished from their Jesuit escort, who wears a liturgical robe and cap and who appears older than the youths. Since the eyes of the youths are drawn as simple ovals, they appear more pointed than their Jesuit companion, whose eyes are circled with lines to indicate a heavy lid above and wrinkles below. Since his face is also rendered to suggest a faint beard, I suspect the artist was attempting to make the Jesuits appear older, instead of depicting the youths as Asian. Vecellio's Japanese figure, like the face of the woodcut from the *Avisi*, is similarly depicted with generic facial features; without his costume, there would be little to distinguish him from the parade of figures (fig. 81).

In her important essay on the embassy, Judith Brown argues that this absence of ethnic facial distinctiveness in the visual images is evidence of 'homogenization.' Redressing interpretations of the Japanese visit as a spectacle of exotic foreignness, she highlights the relative lack of interest in the youths. Instead of a confrontation with otherness, she maintains, Europeans were able 'to see the emissaries as extensions of themselves.'[66] In contrast to the darker-skinned Indians, who had proven difficult to convert, the Jesuits described the Japanese as 'white.'[67] For Brown, this whiteness is evidence that 'the emissaries were not so much alien beings as living confirmation ... of the European ability to attenuate and contain the exotic – to bleach away the difference.'[68]

But were there representational conventions available to Europeans with which to depict the Japanese? Since vision and representation are historically specific, could artists represent something never seen before, if seeing and drawing are mediated through the repertory of images that are culturally accessible to them?[69] Since this was the first encounter with the Japanese in Europe, and given the surprising absence of visual imagery, could Europeans 'bleach away the differences' before they had been constructed in the first place? The description of the ambassadors' clothes cited above demonstrates the problem: the chronicler saw the clothes and the body of the Japanese *as* something else, as an African Carthusian monk with a Spanish collar. Furthermore, commentators show uncharacteristic attention to the faces of

Figure 81   Cesare Vecellio, Giapponese, *Habiti antichi et moderni di tutto il mondo* (Venice, Sessa 1598). Woodcut, 8°, 20 cm [photo: Correr]

these foreigners and also diverse opinions about what it was that they saw. This unusual attention to physiognomy, then, offers evidence about perception before subjective descriptions had been transformed into representational conventions.

Costumes and Customs in Japan

The embassy to Europe was one of several strategies devised by Alessandro Valignano, the Jesuit Visitor,[70] to improve the success of the Society of Jesus in Japan. On one side, with the presentation of new Christians, he sought to elicit papal support for the work of the Jesuits in Asia; on the other, the event promised conversions once the Japanese returned with reports of European splendour. European leaders also capitalized on the visits by the young ambassadors to their cities, absorbing the event into what was a larger global contest over trading power and religious authority, as Brown has demonstrated.[71] From the perspective of the pope, Gregory XIII, who provided papal funds for the embassy, the presence of new converts promised to buttress the flagging Roman Church, battered by reformers in northern Europe.[72] News of the Japanese touching and kissing relics would instill religious fervour and provide visual evidence for the universal breadth of the Catholic Church.[73] For Philip II – king of Spain, and after 1580, of Portugal – converts from the Portuguese colonies offered political prestige. Although the Venetians were reluctant to host the Japanese, they postponed the feast of the apparition of St Mark for their benefit, using the elaborate festivities to counter the state's diminished significance on the world stage.[74]

It was Valignano's experience in Japan that prompted his initiative. Francis Xavier had already described the Japanese people as 'the best who have yet been discovered ... a people of very good manners ... [who] prize honour above all else,' and Valignano saw them similarly: 'The people are all white, courteous and highly civilized, so much so that they surpass all the other known races of the world.'[75] Valignano's enthusiasm for 'living with cultivated and intelligent people' contrasted with his perception of the Africans: 'a race born to serve, with no natural aptitude for governing.'[76] The Indians, although a 'base and bestial people,'[77] fared better, and here too, it was class that comes to the fore: 'they are miserable and poor beyond measure and are given to low and mean tasks ... as Aristotle would say ... [they] are born to serve rather than to command.'[78] On the issue of recruits, Valignano rejected Eurasians, 'because all these dusky races are very stupid and vicious, and of the basest spirits, and likewise because the Portuguese treat them with the greatest contempt.'[79] In contrast with the Africans and Indians, the Japanese appeared to be white, but enthusiasm by the Jesuits for the Japanese was evidently more about status than colour: in contrast to the low status of Asian 'rice Christians,' it was the higher classes of Japanese converts that mattered.[80]

Somewhat ironically then, the manners of the Japanese were compared to those of noble Europeans, whereas the boorish habits of the Jesuits had done little to encourage conversion to their faith.[81] To the Japanese, the customs and dress of the priests appeared barbaric, an impression caused by their lack of personal or household hygiene and their impoverished state.[82] Moreover, the Jesuits had demonstrated little interest in adapting to the customs of the country. Some of the priests maintained a self-satisfied posture, whereas to the Japanese they appeared ill-mannered and uneducated. That the Jesuits chose to stay in Japan furthered negative perceptions of Europe, for if as grand as the priests claimed, why would they have left their country and risked the dangers of lengthy travel? Despite some commonalities, as Valignano wrote, the Japanese are 'so different and opposite that they are like us in practically nothing.'

> The properties and qualities of this country are so strange, the mode of government of the state so different, and the customs and ways of living so extraordinary and so far removed from our own that they are difficult to comprehend even for those of us who have been living here and dealing with the people for many years. How much more difficult, then, to make them intelligble to people in Europe.[83]

Not surprisingly, for sixteenth-century Europeans, it was the customs and costumes that defined the Japanese: when they stand or sit, how they mount a horse, what they eat.[84]

Failure to observe local customs not only offended the Japanese but also lowered their estimation of the Jesuits. Valignano was convinced that higher numbers of conversions required the integration of the Jesuits into the local community and also remedying the perceptions the Japanese had of Europe on the basis of their encounters with the poor priests. After experiencing his 'first year mute as a statue,' Valignano began to educate himself by studying Japanese culture and learning their customs and language.[85] He proposed new rules of conduct for the priests including changing their dress, eating habits, and, in particular, learning the protocols of visiting and addressing the Japanese. 'More than other people of the earth,' he wrote, 'the Japanese observe an exact and detailed ceremonial in their costume, eating habits, relations with servants, in the organization of the house, the greeting of guests and in all these displays, according to social classes.'[86] This context required establishing a corresponding social hierarchy among the priests.

Significantly, Valignano distinguished between external ceremonial customs and the soul; in contrast to the visible manifestations of Japanese culture, he explained to his colleagues, 'we instead look for the saving of souls and internal virtue.'[87] Thus the priests were to become like the Japanese; they were instructed to constrain bodily movements, to avoid flamboyant gesticulations, and to moderate their tone of voice.[88] As a result, the rate of conversion improved, and by 1582, following thirty years of Jesuit missionary activity in Japan, there were some 200 churches and 150,000 Christians.[89]

The Japanese in Europe

Valignano's scheme for an embassy to Europe was an integral part of this process of cultural exchange:[90]

In sending the boys to Portugal and Rome our intention is two-fold. Firstly it is to seek the help, both temporal and spiritual, which we need in Japan. Secondly it is to make the Japanese aware of the glory and greatness of Christianity, and of the greatness and wealth of our kingdoms and cities, and of the honour in which our religion is held and the power it possesses in them. These Japanese boys will be witnesses who will have seen these things, and being persons of such quality they will be able to return to Japan and to say what they have seen. Since the Japanese have never seen our things they cannot believe us when we tell of them, but these witnesses will confer proper credit and authority on us, and thus they will come to understand the reason why the fathers come to Japan. At present many of them to do not undertand; they think we are poor people, of little consquence in our countries, and that we come to Japan to seek our fortunes, with the preaching of heavenly things as a mere pretext.[91]

Because of the lengthy journey (it would take five and a half years to travel there and back), young boys, aged twelve and thirteen, were picked for what was called the 'mission of four youths.' The embassy was made up of two ambassadors, the young princes Mancio Ito and Michele, and two nobles who came from the seminary at Arima: Hara, baptized Martino, and Nacaura, known as Giuliano. Their nobility was to improve the status of the embassy both in Japan and Europe.[92]

After they had seen 'the beauty and richness of our cities,' Valignano anticipated that the ambassadors would return with accounts of Europe as a place of grandeur. As witnesses to the prestige of the church that the Jesuits represented in Japan, the youths would assist the order's efforts to convert the Japanese. But ensuring the positive impression of the youths required circumspection. For example, Valignano instructed his colleagues to censor news of religious upheavals; the ambassadors were protected from unsuitable sights and behaviour by their vigilant chaperones and housed throughout the journey in Jesuit residences.

In contrast to the radical cultural differences experienced by the Jesuits in Asia, the encounter in Europe was much less charged. Censorship of the boys' experience resulted in less spectacular public ceremonies in most cities.[93] With their refined manners and familiarity with European languages, the Japanese did not stand out. Moreover, at the behest of their Jesuit hosts, they travelled in Western attire to avoid being noticed.[94] Already dressed in European clothes when they embarked, the youths carried their national attire for ceremonial occasions with the pope and other rulers. Western costume was also intended to disguise the youths; if they explained to their compatriots how they fit into European culture, Valignano believed there might be less resistance to the Catholic faith in Japan. Nevertheless, their clothing was recorded with characteristic punctiliousness in written accounts:

> They dress in fabrics of very light silk like taffetta or Ormesino, woven of various beautiful colours with different sorts of flowers, birds, and other animals from Japan; they wear half ankle-boots or Borzachini of a certain skin so thin and soft that they could be grasped in one's fist; they are coloured and bright, appearing of silk, all in one piece with a single opening that they lace with strings. The foot of these ankle-boots is in the style of those gloves that have the large finger separated, and the others united; the shoes are like those of the Capuchin monks, without heels and sharply pointed at the end: for *tomora*, they have a single cord that barely covers the end of the toe, in a manner that ... it appears impossible to walk in them; they wear a long dress of silk which is stuffed into their trousers in a sailor-like fashion, long to the heel, and united to the end in a way that it appears

one garment, and these are restrained with the garment over the sections so that it all appears to be a single suit; besides this, they wear a very large band of silk over the right shoulder and under the left arm in the style of our soldiers.[95]

Deciphering unfamiliar apparel required that writers move between sartorial vocabularies, translating Japanese terminology into an amalgam of clerical, marine, and military references with which Europeans were familiar. As Yasunori Gunji translates: '*hakema* are described as mariners' trousers, a *kataginu* as a sacerdotal tunic, a monastic garment ... with a military shoulder belt; *tabi* and *zori* can be compared respectively to little boots and to sandals.'[96]

Lorenzo Priuli, the Venetian ambassador to the pope, also compared the costumes of the Japanese to those of sailors, and described their headwear as Spanish.[97] In western attire, by contrast, they metamorphosed into Italians: 'they dressed in long Roman clothes with gold trimming all around and now they resembled many Bolognese doctors.'[98] The pope's gifts had included silk for western clothes to symbolize the universal dominion of the church.[99] Fitting in, however, was the subject of criticism by those, like Daniello Bartoli, a Jesuit writer, who argued that it was precisely their sartorial difference that mattered: 'that same strange Japanese costume of theirs in which they appeared did not serve curiosity as much as devotion, for in this [costume] they truly seemed to be a people who came from another world.'[100] For the embassy to be noticed, the youths needed to stand out.

Intriguingly, efforts to deflect unwanted attention through the use of western dress prompted closer attention to their bodies. As one writer observed, 'in regard to the body, their stature is very small and of an olive colour; they have small eyes, large eyebrows, [and their] noses are rather large at the end, but [their bodies evince] an innocent and noble aspect and with nothing barbaric.'[101] According to Nicolo Trevisan, by contrast, 'these Japanese are of a mediocre stature, pale of face, with large noses and fat lips in the style of Saracens and all their faces are so similar that it is difficult to know one from the other and they show themselves to be a people of good creation.'[102] If the colour of the skin of the Japanese appeared to be different from that of Europeans, there was evidently little agreement among commentators about what that colour was. According to the Venetian ceremonial secretary: 'they have faces that differ little from one to the other, and one gathers that almost all those from that country have rather brown flesh.'[103] The Venetian ambassador was more negative, describing their skin as 'the ugly colour of meat,' while 'swarthy' was the term chosen by Marcantonio Tolomei: 'Their stature is very short, they are of swarthy complexion, [with] a negro's profile, prominent eyes, dull and very small; it seemed as if they could not look up; a mouth with thick lips, as for the rest quite ugly.'[104] As we saw with their costume, their facial features were often described *as* somethinge else: their skin as the colour of meat, their noses and lips like those of Saracens, the profile of a black African. Not surprisingly perhaps, if Europeans could not distinguish between the faces of the youths, they could see that their faces were different from those around them.

Explaining this difference was more difficult, however. In contrast with the Africans and Indians, the Jesuits classified the Japanese as white. But in Europe, writers were looking at the Japanese through a different lens. Guido Gualtieri drew on the theory of the humours, attributing the change to their lengthy voyage. 'Although it is said that in Japan their flesh is white, and this is believable because of the great cold that there is there, nonetheless, in these [ambassadors] because of the length and discomfort of their trip, their flesh has gained color so that it rather tends toward an olive tint.'[105] Not unlike the discovery of light-skinned inhabitants in the 'fourth-part of the world,' the embassy exposed a gap in the long-standing theory that equated proximity to the equator with skin colour.

The Japanese visitors tested the representational system of Europeans because they fell between existing categories of identity: not fully noble in blood but noble in performance; dressed as both Europeans and Japanese; Christians but from far away; neither white-skinned nor dark. In western dress, the Japanese appeared to fit in; and yet this very commonality – the failure of the ambassadors' costumes to signify as foreign – provoked commentators to compare their faces with those of Europeans. Similarly, instead of Europeans seeing the Japanese through the lens of ancient physiognomical theories, in which the balance of humours or noble birth are seen to determine moral character, the disparate statements indicate there was no established vocabulary to predetermine their commentary. The absence of consensus indicates commentators were struggling – before ideas of racial difference had been clearly articulated in relation to bodies and physiognomy – to distinguish those differences that the costumes of the Japanese failed to.

In this context, the paucity of visual imagery and the western facial features in those images suggests that contemporaries were not trained to look for signs of ethnic difference in the human face. Even artists, who looked closely at faces all the time, looked at people through the repertory of visual representations in which they were immersed, and not all perceptions about racial differences had yet been codified into pictorial statements. Instead of intentional, discursive, or even subconscious processes of transforming the Japanese into Europeans, artists used the pictorial vocabularies available to them. It was not possible to 'bleach away the differences' until they had been sedimented in the first place.

Valignano's injunctions to the priests to become like the Japanese proved fruitful for the Jesuit mission.[106] Once the priests adopted Japanese habits and forms of courtesy, more Japanese began to convert to the Christian faith. Similarly, the paucity of visual imagery of the emissaries can be attributed in part to the fact that the Japanese, in their western attire, appeared to be European. The Ottoman Turks, by contrast, were seen to be intransigent in their faith, and this was ascribed to the differences seen in their costumes. Moreover, images of them were ubiquitious in the late sixteenth century. Nevertheless, here too I suggest that Europeans were looking at the faces of Turks before their features were racialized.

Reflecting on the Face of the Turk

If the human body was seen to be universal, as Nicholas de Nicolay proposed, and it was costume that rendered differences visible, then what about physiognomy? The consequence of this question is demonstrated by the title page of a popular pamphlet published in Venice after the battle of Lepanto in 1571, to which the printer has added a small, bust-length portrait of a man with the name 'Selin' (reigned 1566–74; fig. 82).[107] Although the figure is clearly identified as a Turk by his turban and beard, it is the caption and not the crude facial features that identified the sultan held responsible for the war. Despite the generic quality of the woodcut, the image clearly agitated at least one reader, who slashed the face of the sultan with a pen as if wielding a knife.

In another woodcut, a title page printed around 1575, Selim – again identified by name – is about to be snared by Charon as retributive justice for events following the siege of Famagousta on Cyprus (fig. 83).[108] Following capitulation to the Ottoman fleet, as one eyewitness recounted, the Venetian Provveditore Marcantonio Bragadin was flayed alive by order of the sultan's general, and his skin was stuffed with straw and

Figure 82   *Capitolo a Selin imperator de Turchi: Delle feste et allegresse ch'ei faceva in Costantinopoli ... della presa del'isola di Cipro* (Venice[?] 1580[?]). Woodcut, 12° [photo: by permission of the British Library, London] 1071.g.7. (81)

Figure 83   *[ ] et ultima desperatione de Selim Gran Turco per la perdita della sua armata* (Venice: 1575?) [photo: by permission of the British Library, London] 1071.g.7.(85)

raised on a mast as an effigy of the Venetian loss.[109] In the print, the heroic nude body of the Venetian skewered on the stake sets into relief the fleshy, undefined, but sumptuously decorated body of Selim. Once again, the reader's presence is evidenced by the defacing of the sultan, whose head is literally excised from his body below. Clearly, there is a distinction to be drawn between faces and bodies in the construction of the opposition between Venetian and Turk.

The face evidently resonated in significant ways. Nevertheless, these meanings did not yet accord with modern notions of race in which ethnicity, physiognomy, and identity coalesce. Even though printed images and texts expose a number of prejudices, these were directed toward performative aspects of group identities, like faith and customs. Turkish stereotypes about group behaviour – preconceptions and oversimplifications forged by repetition – circulated widely, but these moved through language and were signified by actions and costume. In the sixteenth century, stereotypes about group behaviour were not yet ascribed to distinctive facial features.

Exchanges

The demand for portraits of Ottomans grew during periods of conflict, as noted earlier. However, this trend did not account for the production of portraits of Turks in the Veneto in the last quarter of the century. Instead of conflict, it was the sultan's ascension to power that prompted Giacomo Franco to engrave a portrait of Mehmed III (1595–1603; fig. 84). Relatively stable relations developed between the Venetians and the Ottoman Porte after 1573, and Mehmed had confirmed the peace in December 1595.[110] Remarkably, by the beginning of the seventeenth century, the Turks were even described as saints, albeit in contrast with the evils of the Spanish and the Jesuits during the interdict of 1606–7.[111] Franco's commemorative portrait conveys a certain respect for the reigning sultan, who is surrounded by a veritable catalogue of accoutrements of regal splendour and military leadership. Indeed, a year later the engraving was published in his *Effiggie naturali* referred to above. In 1599, the portrait appeared in another context when it was copied by Pietro Bertelli for his series of portraits, *Vite degl'imperatori de'Turchi con le loro effiggie*, published in nearby Vicenza (fig. 85). Both of these collections presented images of Ottoman and other Muslim rulers in new ways. Each series presents a general type – leaders and sultans – consisting of individuals who held those positions.

Figure 84   Giacomo Franco, *Sultan Maumet III*, *Effiggie naturali dei maggior prencipi et piu valorosi capitani*. Venice, 1595. Engraving, 12° [photo: Museo Correr, Venice]

Figure 85   *Meemet/Maumet.III*, Pietro Bertelli, *Vite degl'imperatori de'turchi con le loro effiggie* (Vicenza: G. Greco, 1599). Engraving, 4° [photo: by permission of the British Library, London] 583.i.9

Franco filled the background of his engraving of Mehmed III with narrative details that frame the face in the foreground (fig. 84). The fantastic coat of arms in the cartouche, sceptre, and chains were attributes of authority foreign to Ottoman culture; instead these signs addressed a European audience.[112] Since Mehmed II (reigned 1444–6 and 1451–81), the sultans had exploited western symbols of portraiture and regalia to demonstrate their status to Europeans.[113] Yet by the middle of the sixteenth century, the growing religiosity and seclusion of Süleyman (reigned 1520–66) initiated a turn away from the west and the patronage of western artists in favour of Islamic traditions. Religious and political struggles between the Sunni Ottomans and the Shi'ite Safavids in the east also contributed to the cultural shift, although Selim II would continue to pressure Europeans in military engagments until his death in 1574.[114]

Despite the increasing establishment of geographical and cultural boundaries, or perhaps because of this, Venetian interest in the appearance and customs of the Turks intensified. Citizens and immigrants to the city, such as Sansovino, were becoming engrossed with their former lands now controlled by the Porte, a preoccupation that prompted the state in 1556 to commission Paolo Ramusio to write a history of the conquering of Constantinople by the Venetians and French in 1204.[115] Moreover, beginning in the the mid-sixteenth century, an immense variety of materials on the Turks was published in Venice, including histories, travel accounts, chronicles, plays, and costume illustrations.[116] Sansovino's histories provide a good example of enthusiasm for the subjects; his series *Gl'annali turcheschi overo vite de principi della casa othomana* was published in 1571, and several editions of his *Historia universale dell'origine et imperio de turchi* appeared between 1560 and 1600.

The production of portraits of Ottomans accompanied the flourishing market for printed material on the Turks throughout Europe. Franco incorporated several military leaders from Islamic lands into his 1596 *Effiggie naturali.* In the same year Jean Jacques Boissard's portrait book *Vitae et icones sultanorum turcicorum* was published by Theodor de Bry in Frankfurt am Main, and Domenico Gigliotti included Turks in his series, *Ritratti di cento capitani illustri ... con li lor fatti in guerra brevemente scritti,* with engravings by Aliprando Capriolo.[117] *Prosapia vel genealogia imperatorum turcicorum,* a brief history of the sultans in German verse, illustrated with woodcut portraits, was published in Straubing in 1597 (fig. 86). And in 1599, Pietro Bertelli published his *Vite degl'imperatori,* a compilation of full-page portraits of the sultans that are accompanied by biographies (figs. 85, 87, 88). These collections are not without

Figure 86   *Appendix* (*Mehmet III*), *Prosapia vel genealogia imperatorum turcicorum,* (Straubing, 1597). Woodcut, 8° [photo: by permission of the British Library, London] 555.a.17

precedent. In 1567, Nicolò Nelli engraved portraits of the sultans for Sansovino's broadsheet *Sommario et alboro delli principi othomani*, made in response to the empire's 'incomparable' and even 'invincible' force, and dedicated to the Venetian *bailo* Vittorio Bragadino.[118] An epitome of the sultans' achievements flanks the branches of a family tree on which portrait medallions, circled by their names, have been arranged. Print was not the only medium. Fourteen bust-length painted portraits of the sultans were made following the ascension of Murâd III (reigned 1574–95). The portraits, now in Munich, have been attributed to Paolo Veronese's workshop (fig. 91).[119]

What brought about this interest in portraits of Muslim leaders in the last quarter of the century? Since the fall of Constantinople in 1453, Venetians had continually faced the erosion of their earlier territorial dominance throughout the Mediterranean. The situation stabilized, however, in the late sixteenth century, mitigating anxieties that had threatened the economic and social security of Venetians for generations. The most important events included the victory of the Holy League at Lepanto, efforts by Venetians to maintain good relations following their private peace agreement with the Ottoman Porte in 1573, and the turn toward the east by the latter.[120] As a result, in spite of Ottoman introversion, there were growing numbers of Turkish, Bosnian, Albanian, Persian, Anatolian, and 'Asiatic' businessmen in Venice after 1573, most of whom were identified by the rubric 'Turk.'[121] Foreigners in the city, especially Muslims, were subjected to regular attacks by Venetians, requiring efforts by the senate to protect them. The commitment made finally in 1617, to house these groups in a Fondaco, a combined residence and warehouse, was a response to continued antagonism toward these outsiders.[122]

In this context, evidence of new uses of printed portraits is particularly intriguing. For in spite of aggression toward Turks, images of them were becoming familiar sights on the walls of Venetian houses. Two paintings – one of a male sitter, and the other of a female ('doi quadreti con Turcho e Turcha') – were recorded in the home of a barber.[123] A small portrait of a Turk (*Turca retratta*) was among the possessions documented in the house of the craftsman Andrea Faentino. The display of the portrait by an artisan, who was himself a foreigner, may have signalled his desire to adopt certain prevailing cultural attitudes in Venice.[124] Moreover, the presence of a portrait of Andrea himself indicates the complex functions and relations that were played out between portraits and viewers in Venetian homes.[125]

Figure 87   *Mahometto II*, Pietro Bertelli, *Vite degl'imperatori de'turchi con le loro effiggie* (Vicenza: G. Greco, 1599). Engraving, 4° [photo: by permission of the British Library, London] 583.i.9

Portraits in general, but also generic portraits of Turks, played a distinctive role in the articulation of Venetian identity. What was the relation, then, between hatred toward Muslims in the streets of Venice, and the purchase and display of images of them in Venetian houses? In the last decades of the sixteenth century, the Venetian government, inquisitors, and artists in Venice organized the body into a legible system of discrete parts that drew attention to the nature of the sign, to how it signified and was registered optically.[126] In this environment of increasing attentiveness toward the visible appearances of people, the interest in images of Turks by Venetians is revealing.

Ancient theories about physiognomy circulating in the fourteenth century continued to be rehearsed throughout the Renaissance. However, toward the end of the sixteenth century, writers began to emphasize the process of reading the face and body as texts composed of signs, a thesis articulated in Sansovino's introduction cited above.[127] The shift reflects a new interest in visual experience, precisely the kind of experience facilitated by print. Moreover, claims to objectivity were advanced by engraving during the decades in which physiognomists were teaching viewers how to read the human face as though it were a text.

Copies and Likenesses

Paolo Giovio's collection in Como extended to Ottoman artifacts, and these, including his Turkish garments, resided in a special 'sala de'Turchi,' a room that may have displayed some of his portraits of Ottomans and their allies.[128] Seven Ottoman sultans and several other military leaders appear in Theobald Müller's *Musaei Ioviani imagines artifice manu ad viuum expressae*, published in Basel in 1577 (fig. 92).[129] Two of Stimmer's woodcuts of sultans – Bâyezid I (reigned 1389–1402) and Çelebi (one of Bâyezid's four sons from the Interregnum; reigned 1403–13) – served as models for Pietro Bertelli's *Vite degl'imperatori*. In Müller's publication the faces of the men appear on both the verso and recto of the sheets, enabling viewers to compare the physiognomies of sitters, such as Mehmed II and Giuliano de' Medici, who appear adjacent to one another. Furthermore, the elaborate frames connect the group together as a general type, thereby highlighting differences within the type. Pietro's quarto engravings similarly accentuate the singularity of each sultan (figs. 85, 87, 88). The large scale of the likenesses (*effigie*), almost half life size, and the modelling of the faces command the attention of the reader, as does the direct gaze of the most recent sultans. This

Figure 88   *Selim I*, Pietro Bertelli, *Vite degl'imperatori de'turchi con le loro effiggie* (Vicenza: G. Greco, 1599). Engraving, 4° [photo: by permission of the British Library, London] 583.i.9

fiction of the sitter's presence is emphasized further by the absence of elaborate frames like those used by Müller and Stimmer. In their books, the flamboyant frames highlight the act of re-presenting Paolo Giovio's museum for circulation in print.

Pietro turned to several sources for his sultans, including Franco's *Effiggie naturale*. In contrast with the heroes that comprise the earlier *Musaei Ioviani imagines,* Franco's album is a roster of reigning princes and captains, as explained in his dedication to Giovanni Battista Borbone, Marquis of Monte S Maria, and Captain General of the Venetian infantry:

> I have collected and engraved the most natural likenesses that I was able to of the major princes and of the most celebrated captains of our age ... having in consideration the conspicuous and glorious nobility of princes here portrayed, and together, the celebrated and famous virtue of the others; I do not believe it possible to dedicate the said collection to another more worthy than your eminence; you, with your illustrious ancient nobility joined together with noteworthy merits and the immortal splendour of proper virtue, are justly able to escort such a glorious series of heroes, and to conduct them into the view and consideration of the world.[130]

With its theme of 'captains of our age,' the title of the series – *Effiggie naturali* – resonates beyond standard rhetorical conventions regarding the lifelikeness achieved by painters of portraits.[131] Printmakers repeatedly stress the living presence of the sitters, usually identifying the images as likenesses (*effigie*) instead of portraits (*ritratti*).[132] Others stress their efforts to obtain models for which the sitter was believed to have posed. In 1624, Giacomo Crulli di Marcucci asserted that his collection of portraits represented the popes from life (*da naturale*) since the 'likenesses' were copied from 'medals, and paintings, with the most possible diligence.'[133] Even if Marcucci exaggerated, for he also used prints as sources, his claims underscore the iconic function of printed portraits. Some publishers even acknowledged their debt to earlier printed portraits, for the same reason.[134] Franco's sitters, however, were contemporaries. Thus when Pietro Bertelli copied Franco's engraving of Mehmed III, the authenticity of the reigning sultan was guaranteed precisely because Franco's series consisted of contemporaries (figs. 84, 85).

In 1597 the same engraving was transformed into a small woodcut medallion for the German portrait book *Prosapia vel genealogia impera-*

torum turcicorum (fig. 86). The portrait of Sinan Bassa, the sultan's captain general, also copied from Franco's album, is a '*Contrafactur*,' as the text above the small oval image states (figs. 89, 90). Lifelikeness lost in the translation from engraving to woodcut was compensated for by the counterfeit, a naturalistic mode used to claim 'the truth of the eyewitness account.'[135] Woodcut copies could be inserted into inexpensive reprints as generic portraits, in some cases the same portrait being used for different lives.[136] Repetition itself provided, in Cecil Clough's words, 'a patina of authenticity.'[137] The very fact that a portrait was a copy attested to its lineage. Paolo Giovio, for example, referred to his museum as 'true portraits ... faithfully copied from the original'; these copies were the paintings he commissioned of a standard size from the originals he had collected over thirty years.[138] The circulation of Stimmer's woodcut copies of Giovio's portraits in 1577, moreover, seems to have spurred collectors to commission painted copies.[139]

Although copying was an integral part of compiling these series, the process was clearly selective. Pietro Bertelli only reproduced two of the seven Ottoman sultans published in the 1577 *Musaei Ioviani imagines*, as noted earlier. When Pietro copied Franco's print of Mehmed III he deleted the background, but he also altered the sceptre wielded by the sultan and the cartouche, details that indicate the image is neither traced nor a mere copy. The small changes mark the artist's intervention and gesture toward the fiction of the printmaker's own presence before the sitter. The series of bust-length portraits of the sultans, now in Munich, furthers the suggestion that models were altered in the studio in order to create the effect of lifelikeness. In some cases it is the representational convention that implies authenticity. For the portraits of Mehmed II and Süleyman, for instance, the artist has adopted the profile poses familiar from a range of models, but the details of the faces are rendered with spontaneity. Only one of the Munich portraits, a profile of Bâyezid II (reigned 1481–1512; fig. 91), bears much resemblance to the sitter in Giovio's painting of the sultan, who turns instead toward the viewer, as seen in Stimmer's reproduction (see fig. 92). If Giovio's model served as a prototype, the painter from the Venetian workshop has transformed it.

None of these Venetian artists seems to have drawn on portraits by Ottomans, who were themselves pressed to turn to western examples for their portrait albums, a genre initiated by Sayyid Lokman and Nakkas Osman in 1579.[140] Limited access to the sultan and prohibitions against figurative representation necessitated that artists search outside the

Figure 89   Giacomo Franco, *Sinan Bassa, Effiggie naturali dei maggior prencipi et piu valorosi capitani* (Venice: Giacomo Franco, 1596). Engraving, 4° [photo: Museo Correr, Venice]

Figure 90   *Ware Contrafactur Sinan Bassae, Prosapia vel genealogia imperatorum turcicorum* (Straubing, 1597). Woodcut, 8° [photo: by permission of the British Library, London] 555.a.17

Figure 91   School of Veronese, *Baiazeth II*. 1580s. Oil on canvas. Alte Pinakotek, Munich [photo: Alte Pinakotek, Munich]

Figure 92   Tobias Stimmer, *Baiazeth. II*, Theobald Müller, *Musaei Ioviani imagines artifice manu ad vivum expressae* (Basel: Petri Pernae, 1577). Woodcut, 4° [photo: Thomas Fisher Rare Book Library, University of Toronto]

empire for models for their illustrated genealogies. A likeness 'was considered a "reflection" of the person, devoid of his soul,' and thus Islamic artists conveyed information about historical and fictive persons through iconographic conventions and compositional devices such as seating arrangements.[141] Until the nineteenth century, as Esin Atil explains, 'all representations of rulers were executed from memory and based on accepted models of an ideal type' authenticated by research into the individual's 'physical characteristics.'[142]

In printed costume books, almost every image of a Turk was derived from Nicolas de Nicolay; for Book I of his *Diversarum nationum habitus*, first published in 1589 in Padua, Pietro traced the engravings of Abraham de Bruyn, who had himself used Nicolay's archetypes as a source. Although similar genealogies can be drawn for individual printed portraits,[143] producers of portraits appear to have resisted copying entire series in order to assist in the fiction of the sitter's singular presence.

The mechanical process of reproduction worked together with the precision of copperplate engraving to render the singularity of the likeness legible. These were the 'clear images' about which Sansovino enthused in his Orsina history, stressing the claims to objectivity made by the art of engraving. Franco was among those popular printmakers who altered his mode of working the plate, even erasing his style, in accordance with the subject matter. In his *Effiggie naturali* every portrait is marked with *Franco Forma*. The printmaker usually differentiated between those works he designed – signed with *f* or *fecit* – and those that he published, and often engraved himself, on the copperplate, identified with *forma* or *formis*.[144] *Forma* referred to his process of inscribing the plate and his proprietorship over the dissemination of the image.[145] Thus he seems to have distinguished between an original design and the business of print: the work of making copies and control over their mechanical reproduction. In this light, the use of the term 'likeness' (*effigie*) comes into sharper focus. Pietro Bertelli and Giacomo Franco clearly intended to assert the presence of the sitters in the images. Their engravings can be understood following the conventions of icon painting in which the presence of the sitter is ensured by the repetition of gestures, naturalism, and by the suppression of the artist's style. Hans Belting has described the transition from icons to art – from resemblance to representation – in the Renaissance: 'The new presence *of* the work succeeds the former presence of the sacred *in* the work ... the presence of an idea that is made visible in the work: the idea of art, as the artist had it in mind.'[146] The collections of images considered here indicate a reversal of this formulation since the artists have subordinated their style in order to replicate the original, the individual depicted in the print. Yet, this is not merely a return to earlier practices; instead the likeness of the sitter is produced in the work of printing, through the printer's work of reproduction. Instead of erasing the relation between resemblance and the referent through the artist's mediation, what Belting would refer to as the loss that is art, the printed portrait authenticates the referent through its very reproducibility, an idea emblematized by the mirror image pulled from the plate, the indexical sign of the printing process.

Acting and Appearances

Venice was a departure point to the east, and travellers adopted identities as required, changing their names and dressing in local costume. Clearly legislated religious identity, however, required a correlation between the performative attributes of identity – those concepts more easily described in texts – and how one appeared to others on the outside. For judicial authorities, as discussed in chapter 2, circumcision and the eating of meat on Fridays were evidence of acting like a Muslim, and costume a sign of that identity.[147] Efforts to distinguish between external appearances and internal character also provided fodder for popular representations of Turks. *La Turca* was the title of two plays that were published in Venice in 1597 and 1606, the latter a satire by Giovanni Battista della Porta that was probably penned in the 1570s.[148] The author's fascination with appearances drives the plot of this cross-dressing comedy that hinges on the ways in which bodies seem to, or fail to, signify. Set on the island of Lesina, then a Venetian outpost off the Dalmatian coast, the play begins with two old men, Gerofilo and Argentoro, each planning to marry the other's daughter, Clarice and Biancafiore. The wives of the men had been abducted by Turks, to whom the elderly *inamorati* express their gratitude *in absentia* as they describe the looks and personality of the women to each other with comic, if brutal, flare.[149] Argento's lengthy account of his wife Gabriana's facial features – 'a physiognomy more of a cow than a woman' and with 'the mustache of a baboon' – recalls the author's famous comparisons of human faces and animals that fill the editions of Della Porta's *De humana physiognomonia* (fig. 93).

Gerofilo's son Eromane, already secretly wed to Clarice, and his friend, Eugenio, the lover of Biancafiore, set out to rescue the girls by

LIBER   SECUNDVS.   51

nu à vultu pudore. Sunt qui ex partis huius signis quibusdam vaticinia aucupantur, quos me-
tapofcopos dicimus, nulla tamen iniuncta nostris mentibus necessitate, sed lubentia potius qua-
dam, & procliuitate ex sanguine, & spiritibus physicis.

In hac tabella obuia, est magna hominis frons, insigniuimus etiam bouine frontis forma,
in qua relata magnitudo conspicua est, sic & cetere peculiares frontium
similitudines seriatim tabellulis preponentur.

Magna frons.

ARISTOTELES animalium libro ait. Frons magna segnitiei plena. Galenus
in eo libro, quod animi mores corporis temperaturam sequantur, idem ex eo transferens,
eadem quoq; Plinius ex Trogi sententia, stulte eum deridens refert. In suis verò Physiognomonicis. Illos, quibus frons valdè magna ignauos, seu timidos esse coniicit, quod in bobus
similiter se habeat. Polemon. Magna frons maiori ex parte secordiam signat. Adamantius non magna, sed plana. Mendax textus, qui Aristoteli, & ceteris contradicit. Rha-
ses in Almansore idem confirmat, Albertus, Conciliator, & eiusdem farine homines. Mele-
tius Philosophus, immodica fronte preditos hebetis, & obtusi ingenij esse ait. Cuius naturalis
causa esse potest materiei vbertas operationi inobediens, & quod anterior pars cerebri phlegmati-
ca sit, vnde spiritus debilitantur, ne suis operationibus frui possint. Virtus enim minus
restricta debilior.

Magna, carnosa, & lenis frons.

ARISTOTELES in Idea Iracundi, ascribit ei frontem magnam, & carnosam, &
lenem. Sed Polemon, & Adamantius eodem loco, paruam, carnosam,
& lenem.

F   2   Parua

Figure 93   Giovanni Battista Della Porta, *Magna Frons, De humana physiognomonia libri IIII* (Vico Equense: Iosephum Cacchium, 1586) [photo:
Osler Library, Montreal]

dressing up as Turks and abducting them at night. In the meantime, we learn that the old men had refused to pay the ransom for their wives, which is why Gabriana informed their Turkish kidnappers of their husbands' whereabouts. Preparing to rob and enslave the husbands, the 'real' Turks, Dergut and Hebraim, arrive at Clarice's house, where they speak with her maid, who appears on the balcony. Since the maid is aware of the charade, and assumes the Turks are Eromane and Eugenio, she advises them that Clarice is waiting for them with her jewels. Dergut misinterprets their eagerness as the behaviour of prostitutes, calling the maid a *Ruffiana* (a procuress). Hearing this surprising insult, the maid questions whether the voice is in fact that of the young lover. However, the shrewd Dergut realizes they have stumbled into a plot and convinces the young woman to join them with her cache. When she is tied up and ravished by Dergut, she asks him if by dressing in the costume of a Turk he has taken up their customs.[150] Throughout the play such ethnic stereotypes are expressed in actions and costumes instead of physical features.

Since the streets of Lesina that night are filled with 'false Turks,' Eugenio and Eromane become separated from each other. The latter, mistaking Dergut for Eugenio, hands over his sister Biancafiore. Two scenes later, and before he realizes his mistake, Eromane comes across Dergut, once again mistaking him for his friend, who he believes has so skillfully impersonated a Turk. At this compliment, Dergut laughs and declares Eromane his slave.[151] At the supposed jest, Eromane also laughs: 'Ah, ah, ah; how you pretend to be the Turk with such noble kindness (*gentilezza*); if I had not seen you cross-dressing with these eyes, I would judge you to be a true Turk, since you have the gestures and the comportment.' At this Dergut asks rhetorically, 'You would recognize if I were a Turk, or only dressed as one?' No one could be a more convincing imposter of the Turkish race, responds Eromane, since 'you attack so well with your hands.'

Finally, when Eromane realizes that instead of liberating his betrothed he has handed her over to the Turks, Clarice explains why she was deceived: 'The desire to be with you, and the costume of the Turk fooled me; as soon as he appeared, I went to him right away, recognizing the clothes (*vesti*) of my Lord, not the person.'[152]

However convincing Dergut's performance, the end of the play reveals he too is an impostor, born a Christian, but taken by the Turks and circumcised. Not only Italian, but of noble Venetian blood, he is identified by his father, now the governor of Lesina, by a scar on his forehead. Signs of authentic identity like noble blood and scars could not be exchanged like clothes or faith. *La Turca*, with its comic exaggerations, draws on the fact that contemporaries stereotyped Turks on the basis of how they were deemed to act as a group.

Official and popular Venetian accounts provide further evidence that Turkish stereotypes circulated in language, and these were related to customs and practices and not facial characteristics. Dergut Rais, for example, the single historical character in the play, was based on the Turkish corsair Dragutto Rais, who was legendary for his harassment of Italy.[153] In his *relazione* to the Pregadi in February 1553, the *bailo* Bernardo Navagero reported that Dragutto Rais was as 'greedy as are all the other Turks.' This comment was echoed in Jacopo Ragazzoni's report to the senate in 1571 on Selim: 'by nature he is very greedy as all the Turks are universally.'[154] Turks were characterized as licentious and lacking in masculine *virtù*, on one hand, but violent and barbaric on the other. Phrases such as 'to swear, drink, smoke like a Turk' or the combination of associations 'Turk – assassin – dog – heretic' (*Turco-assassino-cane-eretico*) indicate that prejudices targeted acting like a Turk and not looking like one.[155]

According to Ptolemy, as Della Porta reports in his *Fisonomia*, 'Arabs are great thieves, with double souls, fraudulent, with a servile soul, unstable, and desirous of profit.'[156] Although Della Porta introduces ancient theories that attributed differences in character, customs, and physical appearance to geography, climate, and the configuration of the stars, his own analysis focuses on the particulars of faces. Since a raven has a curved nose and the character of a thief, this facial feature is typical of domestic servants, who steal money and cutlery, or a prostitute, who robs a silver vase. Moreover it is individuals from history who provide evidence: 'Catilana had a similar nose, and he was ambitious, avaricious, rapacious.'[157] A hooked nose – a sign of magnanimity and regal poise – is illustrated with the head of the eagle and the profile of the Roman emperor Servio Sulpicio Galba (ruled 68–9 CE). A parade of famous men, such as Constantine, is brought forward as evidence that a hooked nose distinguishes rulers and heroes. Significantly, the list includes several rulers of Muslim nations, including Mehmed II, who had a 'hooked and notable nose, that almost reached his upper lip; and he had a great soul.'[158] Both Selim I and Süleyman figure in the text; the former had an 'arched nose, was very munificent, emulating the great Alexander. Also Suliman, son of Selim, had a hooked nose, [and was] a warrior and splendid.'[159] Despite the spurious geographical stereotypes rehearsed by Della Porta in his introduction, these are not central to his 'new physiognomy,' defined as those signature traits that marked individuals. If visual imagery has trained modern viewers to interpret a hooked nose as a Semitic feature – as a sign of both physiognomic and ethnic identity – sixteenth-century viewers were only beginning to relate the actions of individuals to their facial features.

If portraits of Ottoman Turks called up stereotypes about group behaviour, it was the turban that brought these ideas to mind instead of facial features. In the case of series of portraits, as we have seen, it was the authenticity of the likeness that was crucial. In this context, two of Tobias Stimmer's woodcuts provide examples of how contemporaries might have interpreted their faces. Both Haireddin (Horuccius Pirata; fig. 94), a Muslim, and his captain, Sinan the Jew (Sinas Judaeus), are depicted in profile, which highlights their crooked noses and pointed chins. Their turbans contribute to the articulated silhouette of their portraits. Significantly, the likenesses of the two corsairs were carefully copied from a painting once in Paolo Giovio's museum, in which the two men appear together (fig. 95).[160] The men's articulated profiles thereby attest to the status of the copies as truthful portraits. In contrast to modern perceptions of the portraits as racial types, contemporaries more likely equated the craggy features – the furrowed brows and arched noses exaggerated by Stimmer for visual effect – with their singularly predaceous dispositions than with racial types.

What stands out in Pietro's book, and this is typical of the genre, is not the similarity of the faces of the sultans, but the remarkable differences between them. The genus – identified by the turban – is divided into the species of individuals, with the character of each described in the text. Middle Eastern faces seen in the prints of Stimmer, Pietro Bertelli, and Giacomo Franco offer little evidence of geographical or ethnic distinctiveness familiar from modern racial stereotypes. Instead, the repetition of the turban foregrounds the features that distinguish one from the other.

What seems crucial here, however, for understanding the mechanisms initiated by the format, is that the reader is enlisted to look for the signs of the biography in the likeness. Franco's iconic image of Mehmed III, as noted earlier, is supported by a military parade and stately procession that appear in the background (see fig. 84). When Pietro copied the image, this temporal frame migrated into the biographical text that accompanies the portrait (fig. 85). As a result of the simple dark

Figure 94   Tobias Stimmer, *Horvicivs Pirata*, Theobald Müller, Musaei Ioviani imagines artifice manu ad vivum expressae (Basel: Petri Pernac, 1577). Woodcut, 4° [photo: by permission of the British Library, London]

Figure 95   Anonymous, *Two Corsairs* [photo: Art Institute of Chicago]

ground, the viewer is forced to concentrate on the face of the sultan and to compare his facial features with the physiognomies of the other sultans pictured in the book. When considered in relation to the abbreviated histories of the sultan's deeds (*attioni*), the facial distinctiveness of each sultan becomes evidence of his singular personality read in the text. Substantive details of military pursuits are interwoven with a scintillating synopsis of the sultans' characters and customs: the strangling of male siblings by the ascending sultan, sexual appetite, and of course the seraglio. Pietro rarely makes explicit correlations between the likeness of the sultan and his biography. One significant exception is Mehmed II (fig. 87). Once again, the portrait is an attentive replication of a model; Mehmed's features were well known since Costanzo da Ferrara introduced his likeness in his fifteenth-century medals. The sultan's profile was reproduced in many paintings, including those made by Ottoman artists. However, in contrast to Della Porta's description, cited above and repeated here, Pietro is more inimical: the sultan had 'a face of an ugly yellow colour, with fierce eyes, arched eyelashes, and a nose so hooked that it seemed on the point of touching his lips ... He was notably cruel in war as in peace, since for the smallest reason he would murder those young men in the seraglio that he had loved lasciviously.'[161] The birdlike eyes and nose, and skin colour imputed to yellow bile and choleric personalities, are associations culled from the Renaissance world of resemblances and humours. Even though Pietro understands Mehmed as a choleric type and his countenance as a sign of his villainous character, this step of combining actions with distinctive facial features lays the groundwork for the future ascription of physiognomy to alleged collective behaviour.

On a structural level, then, portrait books, with their distinctive serial format and combination of image and text, prompted viewers to forge connections between both the actions and character of individuals and their facial features. It was the accompanying text and not the countenance that identified a sitter's character. However the portrait became a means to confirm that history.[162] The process was thereby similar to pictures of famous men and women used by Della Porta in his *Fisonomia*, whose faces are used to confirm the preconception in the text, 'a synthetic expression or memory-image of a biography,' as Lina Bolzoni explains the relation between Giovio's biographies and his painted portraits.[163] If initially the face is a way to remember the biography, in turn viewers learn to distinguish between faces. Moreover, the format compels the reader to compare the image to the text, to find in the visage of Selim II his predilection for pleasures, or to search for signs of virility in Mehmed III (fig. 85). The sultan's face becomes fused with his history in the reader's mind, his face a distinctive landscape. The turn of the head, forehead, eyes, and nose become both signs and symptoms of the actions described in the text. An inscription identifies each sultan further, specifying the referent, whose name is printed twice again on the same page in movable type. His facial features become a signature of his singular personality.

Self-Reflections

Della Porta was proposing a 'new physiognomy,' a method designed to explain what the differences between faces elucidated about individuals. According to his 'doctrine of signatures,' marks imprinted on the surface of the body could be deciphered as signs of identity. To collect evidence for this doctrine, Della Porta visited jails and morgues, where he measured the heads of criminals and took casts from the feet of corpses.[164] Not surprisingly, perhaps, he recommended the study of physiognomy as a means to choose one's friends.[165] Following ancient sources, Della Porta compares faces and comportment with those of animals. But instead of generalizations about personality, he insists that we look at all the signs.[166] The face is divided into parts and these syntactical units are translated following the character traits of animals in order to distill the essence of the individual. By transforming the face into a text, he teaches his audience how to read.

In addition, Della Porta suggests that by examining the faces of others we can reflect upon our own personality. Like poets and painters, he explains, we can identify the habits of others, but also, by looking at ourselves in the mirror, we can reflect upon our own physiognomies in order to correct our imperfections.[167] And this points to new functions for printed portraits. In the increasingly aristocratic culture of Europe, dissimulation was the modus operandi, and the desire to interpret human nature went hand in hand.[168] Moreover, a variety of Renaissance discourses recommended miming named actors.[169] As Francesco Sansovino advocated in his Orsina history, readers could profit from the study of famous men. Significantly, Sansovino concludes his history with a portrait and biography of his patron, Pietro Giordano Orsina, Duke of Bracciano. If this worthy man initiated the history, he is also the living hinge between past and future generations.[170]

Giacomo Franco's albums of major princes and valorous captains offered viewers a parade of illustrious contemporaries worthy of emulation. In a striking mirroring of identities, Franco incorporated his dedicatee, Giovanni Battista Borbone, into the album as the twenty-sixth of his 'glorious series of Heroes' (fig. 96). The Marquis of Monte S Maria could reflect on his own image inside the collection as his patronage of the series as a whole served to escort the 'captains of our age' before the eyes of the world. Instead of progressing through the series of portraits as if reading a narrative, the captain of the Venetian infantry would have found himself subsumed into the series, seeing himself.[171] For all viewers of the series, the myriad faces gazing back would have reminded them that they too could be seen as if a picture (figs. 84, 89, 96, 97). Franco's album, with its distinctive historical frame, must have compelled viewers to reflect on their own faces and also their singular role in history.

With engravings of rulers from England to Denmark and Russia to Portugal, Franco constructed an atlas of faces from twenty-three states of the world. As we have seen, the Ottoman Porte had begun to consolidate its western borders, and by the end of the century a new concept of Europe as a geographical and cultural entity was becoming articulated.[172] A concise expression of this development can be seen in the two editions of Cesare Vecellio's costume books, published in 1590 and 1598. In the first series he explained: 'In our day, Europe comprises all those parts of the world in which the Christian faith is recognized, and some parts of the country of the Turk.'[173] In the expanded 1598 edition, however, published with a parallel Latin text for an international audience, the costumes are organized into ten books; the Turks are now one of these ten nations. On one level, the collections of faces described in this chapter coincide with the array of projects that sought to order geographical, sartorial, religious, and linguistic differences as the European image of the world expanded. The inclusion of Turks, Persians, and Tartars into Franco's album participates in this process of geographical classification.

On another level, these portraits of leaders of Islamic regions are being presented as role models. Until the middle of the sixteenth century, the sultans had adopted western signs of prestige to signal their status to Europeans. Franco has reappropriated this convention, transforming his Ottoman captains and Muslim heads of state into models of European nobility. Since the fifteenth century, the military and political machine of the Ottoman Empire had garnered admiration and emulation among European rulers.[174] The sultan and his generals were emblematic of this relationship between leadership and military *virtù*, and in the album they symbolize the role played by the individuals assembled there.

Franco's series, with its naturalistic engravings of living individuals and its distinctive global frame, must have stimulated viewers to consider their own place in time and space. By contrast, Pietro Bertelli's sultans progress through time, a concept highlighted by the accompanying genealogical chart. With their engraved likenesses, lists, genealogies, names, and achievements, these books call attention to the acts of individuals within history. For Venetians, these series of portraits may have reinforced the

Figure 96   Giacomo Franco, Gio. Battista del Monte Cap. Gnae della fant. della ser sig. ii Venetia (Giovanni Battista Borbone del Monte Maria, Captain General of the Venetian infantry). *Effiggie naturali dei maggior prencipi et piu valorosi capitani* (Venice: Giacomo Franco, 1596). Engraving, 4° [photo: Biblioteca Nazionale Marciana, Venice]

Figure 97   Giacomo Franco, *Carolo de Lorena Duca d'Umena*, Giacomo Franco, *Effiggie naturali dei maggior prencipi et piu valorosi capitani* (Venice: Giacomo Franco, 1596). Engraving, 4° [photo: Biblioteca Nazionale Marciana, Venice]

ways in which the self was defined as part of a genealogical traceable line.[175] Concomitantly, opening up the type into individuals may have disrupted the peculiarly Venetian construction of the individual as inescapable from the collective republican body.

Scholars have stressed the ways in which identity-making in the Renaissance compelled subjects to dissimulate, to adopt the mask or persona. By contrast, these series of portraits exhorted viewers to reflect on their own identities and their personalities. At the end of the century, viewers were learning to scrutinize the faces of others, but the Socratic mirror postulated reflexive speculation about the self. The multiplication of faces in prints in conjunction with the presence of foreigners in the streets must have urged Venetians to see themselves as others, to find their identity at a distance. This dual process suggests the unravelling of the categories of identity that defined the self and the emergence of a subject compelled to search, like Narcissus, for its identity in images.[176] The proliferation of printed portraits available in single sheets or bound in series multiplied the possibilities of identification, especially for male viewers. Ideal images of others would have functioned to shore up the coherence of subjects whose identifications with collective social types were becoming fragmented by signs of individuality. The split between self-reflection and finding one's identity at a distance meant that viewers would see images of what they would like to be while simultaneously striving for their own ideal. As a result, however, the images may have provoked the subject's aggression toward those ideals. For Venetians this narcissistic process was magnified by the exchange with Ottoman Muslims, who represented what Venetians admired and lacked, and also what they feared.

A vast array of representations and practices sought to classify and catalogue the Turks in order to designate what made them both the same and different. The Venetian state, through the Inquisition, worked to ensure that individuals were ascribed to a single religious identity. Costume was one way of marking religious identities that faces failed to reveal. And yet it was precisely these nonidentical features that appeared to be so easily reversed: the apparent ease of changing identity by cross-dressing or religious conversion.

By contrast, the faces of Turks held up a mirror to Venetians. Aggression directed toward the faces in the woodcuts, and to Turks in the streets of Venice, might then be explained by the rival of the image, by its stubborn exteriority.[177] This confrontation with the Ottoman Turks, the production of printed portraits, and attention to the grammar of the face worked together to establish the differences between individuals, and in so doing, the face was becoming constructed as discourse. By transforming likenesses into representations, this process provided the ground for the future ascription of facial sterotypes to ethnic groups. After the repeated circulation of identical images in print, and the alignment of singular facial features with collective behaviour (*costumi*), the correlation between racism and facial types would emerge out of sixteenth-century prejudices with greater visibility.

Nicolò Nelli, a printer of portraits cited earlier, produced a dramatic woodcut with the image of a Turk in 1571 (fig. 98). The profile accentuates the physiognomy of a rather unremarkable face, but the immense turban defines it as the face of a Muslim. The meaning of the print, however, only becomes clear when the image is viewed upside down. Seen from this direction the contour of the figure metamorphoses into the face of the devil. The print was made in response to the threat of war and it targeted the audience to which Sansovino directed his *Informatione*. The implication that the Turk is two-faced responded to the imminent threat, but it also serves as dramatic testimony to ongoing Venetian ambivalence.

Portraits in Time and Space

It was in Rome in 1600, when Ottavio Leone began dating his drawings of individuals, that serialization of portraits turned in a new direction.[178] Ottavio had been trained by his Paduan-born father Ludovico Leone in the art of drawing portraits *alla macchia*, 'so called,' explains their biographer Giovanni Baglione, 'because they are done after having seen the subject only once, and rapidly.'[179] These 'striking likenesses,' as Baglione described them, were sketched from memory in black and red chalk on blue paper; white highlights and rapid hatching for the costume add to the spontaneous effect. Ottavio numbered and dated some 400 of these portraits that he drew over fifteen years, with a consistency that indicates he retained the drawings for himself.[180] He had been increasingly attentive to the dates when he drew the likeness, and by 1615 he added the month and sometimes the day to the drawing.[181]

Some of the portraits share similar formats and are designed with illusionistic frames, such as ovals, used for poets and philosophers, and twelve-sided frames for artists. One seventeenth-century collector of the drawings in fact used this system of classification to organize the portraits into professions when he pasted them into an album, now in the Biblio-

Figure 98   Nicolò Nelli, *Turkish Pride*, 1572 [photo: Biblioteca Communale, Mantua]

teca Marucelliana in Florence. The frames indicate Ottavio planned to publish the portraits in accordance with the formula that characterized late sixteenth-century series of portraits explored above.[182]

In 1621 Ottavio began a new project for a series of etchings based on portraits of contemporaries, all of whom were active in Rome.[183] Before his early death, caused by the noxious process of etching, he had completed forty prints of artists, poets, mathematicians, and patrons. In contrast to his earlier plan, however, all of these professional categories were included in the same series. By bringing artists together with contemporary intellectuals, Ottavio's series would have established the equivalence of painting with poetry, a goal that followed decades of efforts to elevate the status of artists.[184]

Composed of living likenesses, the prints would have resembled Giacomo Franco's album. By contrast, however, the batons, orbs, sceptres, coats of arms, and narrative backgrounds that signify the identity of Franco's sitters have been omitted or at least underplayed. Instead it is Ottavio's 'striking likenesses' that become the sign of the sitter. No longer classified by profession, the printed portraits reproduce the presence of the sitters *in* Rome *qua* individuals.

The persistent conviction that outward appearances were symptoms of the soul was coming to define personality, but in so doing, the causal link was becoming inverted; facial features were becoming signs of identity – Della Porta's 'doctrine of signatures' – and this became the framework for relocating identity *in* the individual. Significantly the meaning of 'identity' underwent a dramatic shift during this period. Its Latin roots were *idem* and *entitas*, or 'same entity,' a meaning that corresponds with the sixteenth-century meaning of identity as 'absolute sameness'; 'the quality or condition of being identical in every detail ... Also the fact of being identified with.' By the middle of the seventeenth century, however, the term came to mean the inverse: 'the condition or fact of a person or thing being that specified unique person or thing, as a continuous unchanging property throughout existence; the characteristics determining this, individuality, personality.'[185] Instead of understanding individuals primarily through a network of external relationships – family, parish, profession, corporate affiliation – it was the boundaries of the body that were coming to define the self. And the face – through the processes of conjoining biography and physiognomy described above – was becoming a sign of an individual's personality.

Conclusion

The Signature

Francesco Vrins, the Flemish merchant encountered in the last chapter, exported an extraordinary range of merchandise from Venice to Europe. Following his death in May 1604, an inventory was made of his storerooms and personal goods that included a large number of portraits, mirrors, and *mappaemundi* that were displayed throughout his house. Surrounded by likenesses of family members and other portraits, one can imagine Vrins considering his own reflection in an adjacent mirror. The world maps seem especially appropriate for a merchant living abroad, as does a particularly intriguing record in the inventory: a set of Georg Braun's *Civitates orbis terrarum*, the grand atlases of printed city maps discussed in earlier chapters (figs. 11, 38).[1] The views in the books are framed with figures in local attire and accompanied with a text that explains each city's history and customs. Perusing the volumes, Vrins could explore the cities of Seville, Lisbon, Marseilles, and London to which he shipped goods. He could also compare his native home to Venice, where he was now a resident. For by seeing one's place in the world it was possible to examine one's relation to place and history, to put one's identity into perspective.[2] Print offered a way of imagining one's place in relation to what was outside: a vicarious experience of alterity that in turn contributed to the self's identification with the familiar.

For the printmakers who translated between the thing seen and the observer, this process of self-identification can be traced in the image. For example, at the top of the woodcut of Venice published by Anton Kolb in 1500 is a mountain pass that leads to Germany, Kolb's homeland, a reference that links the publisher of the print to the inscription of his place inside the representation.[3] In chapter 1, this idea is considered in relation to Jacopo de'Barbari's authorship; the lack of a name, in the documents or the woodcut, and the picture's extraordinary realism – the absence of a distinctive personal style – prompted debates about his involvement (fig. 3). Even the dominance of the caduceus, which became the artist's trademark, could be attributed to the iconographic significance of Mercury to the city instead of the artist. He did not adopt the caduceus as a signature until leaving Venice to work in Germany. However it may have been through the very process of crafting the image of the city seen from an Olympian height that de'Barbari came to identify with the constellation of associations ascribed to Mercury, the messenger who translates between the real and ideal. Living in Germany, and reflecting on his native place may have led him to adopt the attribute of Mercury as a sign of the messenger who brought forth a vision of the city from the sea (fig. 4).

Painters in Venice largely abandoned the use of signatures early in the sixteenth century since their identity began to be recognized by their distinctive style.[4] By contrast, Giacomo Franco, like many of the printmakers discussed in the book, adopted a naturalistic mode as a means to underpin claims to objectivity, and it is more often the characteristic serifs of his text that function as a sign of his hand, such as his cursive script, or the calligraphic signature with which he sometimes embellished his maps (fig. 66). In one of his maps of Venice, for example, the first letter of his signature, 'Giacomo Franco fecit,' is drawn out below into an interlace which fills the remaining space at the end of the legend and frames the date in which the print was made. As we saw, he usually differentiated between those works he designed – signed with *f* or *fecit* – and those that he published and sometimes engraved himself, on the copperplate, identified with *forma* or *formis*.[5] *Forma* referred to his process of inscribing the plate and his proprietorship over the dissemination of the image. Thus he seems to have distinguished between the composition of the image and the business of print: the practice of copying and his control over its mechanical reproduction. In this bird's-eye view, Franco did both, and the trace of his original inscription on the copperplate – repeated identically through print – circulated outside the city as a sign for his place of business.

Friendship albums, as we saw in chapter 2, moved with the traveller. These were used to collect autographs that were often underlined with dramatic and seemingly illegible calligraphy; as Max Rosenheim has shown, many of these flourishes should be read as 'manu propria.'[6] The manuscript words, or their abbreviation, are literally the trace of the signatory's own hand. The collection of names of individuals, accompanied by the date of the signature, personal motto, and coat of arms, became separated from the place in which the person had inscribed it. Since a signature is never exactly the same but carries the trace of the individual, the albums can be understood as collections of places: a network of sites or *topoi*.

In the earlier travellers' albums, the phrases were usually in Latin, but by the end of the century, these came to be transcribed in the 'modern' vernacular languages.[7] Crucial to this process was the visibility of this shift, to which the signatures in the albums attest, for alphabets began to express national differences in visual terms (fig. 99).[8] As the use of Latin waned, the moral universe of humanist associations seen in earlier albums was being reconfigured; the inscription was beginning to carry the signs of national identities.

Marks made by owners also appear in printed costume books, and these provide some evidence of how the books were used. For example, the owner of a copy of Pietro Bertelli's costume book, now in London, translated the Latin captions into English (fig. 22). The printed *album amicorum*, discussed in chapter 2, is another example. The owner translates the function of this book from Latin into English in his lavish cursive script: 'Adorn'd with the habit or dress of the Women of all the Country's in Europe.'[9] The owner experimented with styles of writing throughout the book, including all the letters of the alphabet on one page (fig. 27). On the same sheet he transcribed 'Virgo Veneta' repeatedly, and he also wrote the text in English – 'Venetian Virgin Veil'd' – in a different font. The empty shield on the coat of arms has been filled in, perhaps by a different hand since the inscription at the top right gives a name, 'Aeneas Lowe,' and states the words 'Yours Received by your Friend – together with a Bill.' This page, with its experimental interlaces and flourishes, indicates that the owner was inspired to emulate the engraver's hatching.

Portrait books, as explained in chapter 4, encouraged viewers to consider an individual's likeness in relation to his or her history, even to find the signs of the sitter's achievements and character in his or her face. In contrast to the function of painted portraits to memorialize the sitter, printed portraits had a mnemonic function, for they enabled readers to remember whose biography belonged to whom. As I posited, the face was itself becoming the signature of the self, a sign of the indi-

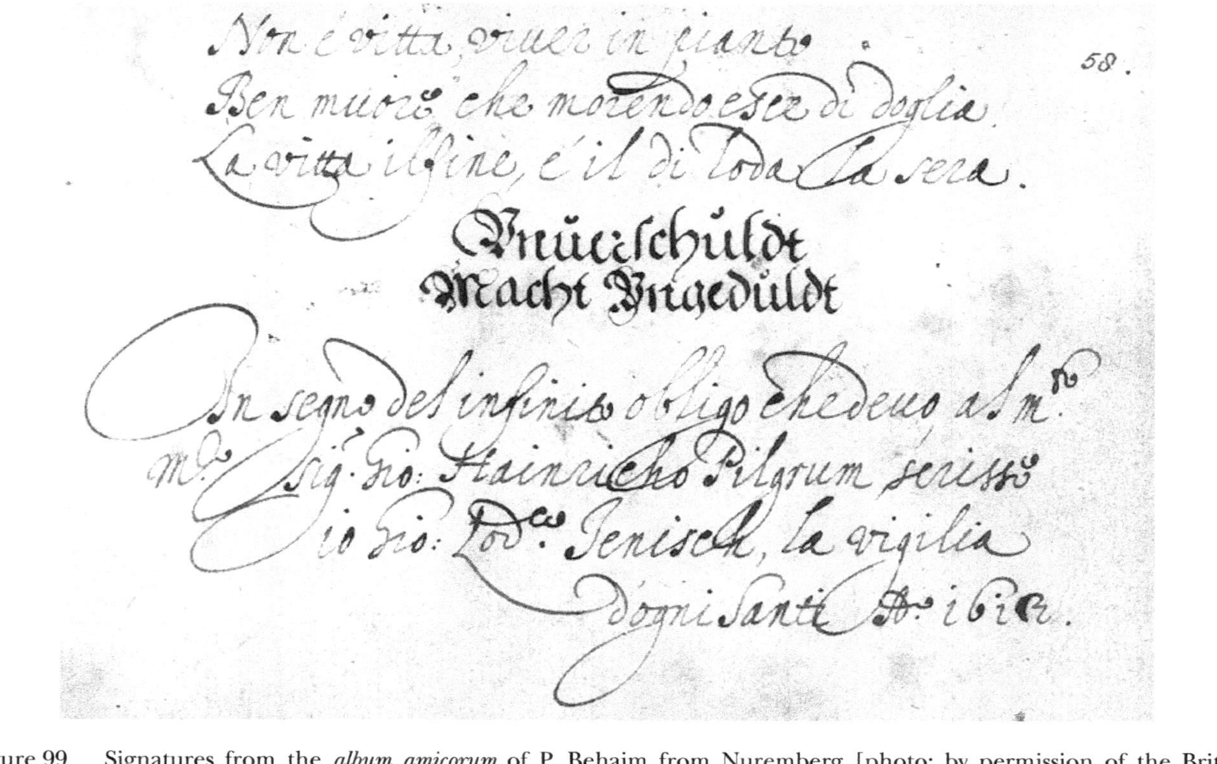

Figure 99   Signatures from the *album amicorum* of P. Behaim from Nuremberg [photo: by permission of the British Library, London] Egerton 1192

vidual's singular personality. Printed portraits, city views, and costume illustrations altered how the city was perceived and, in so doing, located the subject in two places simultaneously. As a result Venetians were prompted to identify with the image, the signature, the gaze of others, the mirror.

Perspective and Identity

Ottavio Leone's printed portraits, to which I turned briefly at the end of chapter 4, provide evidence of a shift in the meaning of identity by the beginning of the seventeenth century. In contrast to affiliations with one's family, parish, occupation, and confraternity, the categories that characterized late medieval identity, Ottavio's proposed series consisted of individuals drawn from diverse professions who all inhabited the same time and city. Significantly, Ottavio incorporated himself in this collection of intellectuals along with many of his colleagues, a strategy that signals his claims for his own status among the group of illustrious individuals (fig. 100).

The mode of representation also points toward a change in understandings of perception. Ottavio's portraits were made 'alla macchia,' drawn rapidly from memory, a process that demonstrates, as Giovanni Baglioni remarked, the artist's skill for conjuring an image of the sitter in his mind, and then projecting it onto paper.[10] These 'striking likenesses' were etchings, a process that enabled him to draw directly on the plate. Thus the representation of the sitter was no longer copied from earlier sources – that lineage which authenticated the likeness – or mediated by the labour of a blockcutter or engraver. Instead it was the artist's impression of the sitter, a vision imprinted in his mind from life, that Ottavio drew on the medium coating the metal plate.

Baglione's description of the method in which an image was refracted through the eye of the artist corresponds with what was a new understanding of sight: the epistemological change brought about through the development of print and the plane mirror. Optical experiments, like those made with mirrors by Giovanni Battista della Porta, contributed to Johannes Kepler's 'principle of refraction.'[11] First, the object seen is transmitted through the eye, where it is imprinted onto the retina. In turn, this image is reflected back to the pupil by the optic nerve, at which point it is recognized by the viewer's mind. Significantly, this final cognitive phase no longer required a theory of resemblances, that mode of understanding the world through concordances between the

Figure 100 Ottavio Leoni, *Self-Portrait*. Etching, Kupferstichkabinett. Staatliche Museen zu Berlin [photo: Bildarchiv Preußischer Kulturbesitz]

microcosm and the macrocosm that characterized Renaissance think-ing. Instead, recognition was relocated inside the mind of the viewing subject. Consequently a face seen in a mirror no longer resembled the viewing subject. Instead, as René Descartes would have understood it, the image was decoded by the rational mind of the viewer, who recognized that the image was a representation, a result of his or her singular point of view that is reflected in the mirror. This emerging modern subject, traditionally identified with Descartes, is thereby confirmed by its unique perspective on the world.[12] Instead of identity being understood through the world of resemblances – 'the fact of being identified with' – Ottavio's portrait project indicates a new understanding of 'a person ... being that specified unique person.'[13] The reflection was turned back on the subject and interiorized as a part of its own identity.

Baglione's account of Ottavio's projected likenesses resonates with the concept Erwin Panofsky formulated in his famous *Perspective as Symbolic Form*, first published in 1939. Panofsky sought to demonstrate that perspective is an expression of the culture that produced it by identifying perspective with the *concetto*, that projection of the Idea formed in the artist's mind.[14] Perspective offered Panofsky the means to differentiate between the subjective world of the ancient Greeks and the objective and universal world-view he saw in the Renaissance. He begins with an account of how the material practices of artistic production led to the epistemological foundations of perspective. However his idealism pressed him to see the artist as the causal agent, to invest artists with the ability to project objective categories into the subjective realm of sense perceptions.[15] For Panofsky, perspective enabled the 'objectification' of 'subjective' perceptions, and perception, therefore, is determined by 'the laws which the artistic consciousness "prescribes" to the perceptible world.'[16] The artist – as both a product of artistic practices and a consciousness that prescribes perceptions – seemed to Panofsky to correspond with the 'mental habits' of Renaissance culture, since in perspective the artist's viewpoint – the projection of the artist's idea in the *concetto* – and a means of organizing objects according to the viewer's subjective perceptions, appear to converge. Thus perspective is deemed 'a factor of style' rather than value, even a symbolic form in which the reality of space and the perception of space are reconciled.[17]

For Hubert Damisch, like Panofsky, perspective is both a mode of representation and a model of consciousness.[18] However, in contrast to the self-certainty of Panofsky's artist, empowered by his perspectival gaze, Damisch's assessment of perspective provides a critique of the unified and rational subject who looks out at the world. Instead of defining perspective as a bridge between a culture's subjective perceptions and cognitive epistemologies, for Damisch, geometric proof asserts the opposite: that perspective has nothing to do with the culture that produces it. Like geometry, perspective is self-evident, exposing itself in the mirror with which Brunelleschi demonstrated it. According to his biographer Manetti, Brunelleschi painted a view of the Baptistery, more or less perspectival, onto a small, square panel which was then positioned opposite a mirror-like surface. Looking through a small hole in the back of the painting, a viewer would see the picture of the Baptistery reflected in the mirror, an arrangment which propelled the viewer to the place from which Brunelleschi had projected the image onto the panel. Looking into the perspectival apparatus, explains Manetti, 'You thought you saw the proper truth and not an image.'[19] Because the viewer's body was partially concealed behind the panel, the experience of seeing would have been detached from the experience of his body, and thus the truth, as Manetti saw it, was in the image reflected in the mirror. Damisch's analysis calls attention to the eye of the viewer, for the hole through which the viewer looks would also have been reflected in the mirror. This eye, for Damisch, is the other (you) who looks back and defines the subject (I). The perspectival apparatus thereby splits the subject between the place it occupies behind the panel and its phantasmatic double on the other side of the mirror. Through this experience of seeing oneself as the subject of another's gaze, the experiment was a demonstration of the emergence of the subject in the symbolic order. No mere metaphor for modern subjectivity, perspective becomes the organizing structure of consciousness through which the subject is constituted by representations that are external to itself. Where Panofsky's structuralism moves him toward a synthesis of epistemology and art, Damisch's structuralism insists on the exclusion of the historical and material conditions of the demonstration.

Damisch's analysis follows that of Jacques Lacan, who was himself looking at Renaissance pictures.[20] For Lacan, because experience of our bodies is fragmented – we can only see and touch parts of our bodies at one time – the subject is forced to search for its identity in images that are external to it. This process occurs in the imaginary, or mirror-phase, that moment when the gesticulating infant begins to identify with the image it sees in the mirror. The mirror reflection produces the subject by eradicating the ego's self-assuring specular image and substituting a fictive alternative.[21] But this misidentification of the infant with its reflection is ratified by the mother, in Lacan's later formulation, who holds up the infant's body before the mirror. Like the mother, perspective functions as a prosthetic device that stabilizes the body within the symbolic order, within the field of vision of others. Similarly for Damisch, perspective structures perceptions of images and even orients the subject's experiences of the world.[22] Thus perspective *is* the symbolic order of modern visuality; the subject can attempt to resist the ways in which it organizes the field of vision, but such attempts only call attention to its omnipresence.

Kaja Silverman brings forward two aspects of Lacan's theorization of the visual field referred to in chapter 2. First, she proposes that Lacan's concept of the screen be understood as the repertory of historical representations through which the subject sees itself. Projection, recognition, and misidentification are always mediated by the representations that are culturally available to viewers.[23] Second, in contrast to both Damisch and Lacan, for whom the subject's consciousness and identity are constituted by representations that are external to the body, Silverman emphasizes the role of the body in identification and the historicity of that process. It is this reciprocity between the body and the image that the prints in this book bring forward.

These theoretical accounts of the ways in which identities are constituted and mediated through the visual field were already formulated, in part, by Nicolas of Cusa in the fifteenth century. In the Introduction I discussed Cusa's efforts to visualize God's gaze by using a painting of the face of Christ. Since the eyes of the painting seemed to follow the monks wherever they walked in the church, the experiment demonstrated that the men were always within God's field of vision, within the symbolic order. Moreover, their identities were ratified by the presence of each other. If Lacan's gaze and Damisch's perspective evoke Cusa's account of God's omnivoyance, it is worth recalling that Cusa's idea was also a response to the perspectival paintings with which he would have been familiar.[24]

Beginning with Cusa's concept of the gaze, still anchored to a cosmological view of the world, this book has endeavoured to trace some of the ways in which printed images participated in the changing status of the Venetian subject. With the importation of Ptolemy's system of mapping to Italy at the beginning of the fifteenth century, one could see the world from a place outside, as an object.[25] The widespread circulation of printed civic imagery in the sixteenth century similarly prompted Venetians to look for the signs of their identity in images, outside of their phenomenal experience. By intensifying the visual exchange with foreigners – an audience constructed through the circulation of prints – Venetians may have come to see themselves as they were seen by others.

New formats and uses for printed visual imagery shaped the ways in which individuals interpreted the world and negotiated their place within it. Because the content and conventions deployed by printmakers overlapped with social practices, printed imagery may have helped to secure ideological values that were central to Venetian cultural life, such as noble status, masculine *virtù*, religious identity, and appropriate forms of female comportment. Print was central to this claim, for it would have been the repeated identifications of sixteenth-century viewers with representations that cemented and regulated identities. The iterative work of securing identities was a process that sought to conceal the *loci* at which these 'regulatory fictions' were transgressed.[26] This change signals the threshold at which the performative veers toward performance, that moment when the expressiveness of bodies created anxieties about categories of identity. For the very process of being named, of acquiring a normative identity, also produces a resistance to that norm. A subject can never fully identify with a norm, and it is the failure to incorporate the image as a part of the subject's own identity that produces the resistance to it.[27] As Venetians came to understand their place within the world through images, and to negotiate their embodied experiences through images, so too were they instructed in ways to manage their own identities. Perhaps it is not surprising that by the late sixteenth century, *Venezianità*, or being Venetian, was becoming analogous with dissimulation.

Notes

Introduction

1 'Car comme la Geographie est l'oeil naturel et la vraye lumiere de l'histoire: tout narré sera tousiours obscur, et ne sçauroit on bien comprendre aucun discours pour vray qu'il feust, si lon ne cognoist premierement les lieux, l'humeur du people, et la qualité du pays duquel on entend parler.' Lancelot du Voisin, *Les trois mondes*, 35v–36r. Tom Conley's translation, *The Self-Made Map: Cartographic Writing in Early Modern France*, 280–1.

2 For examples of cities, islands, and alphabets, see: Georg Braun and Franz Hogenberg, *Civitates orbis terrarum 1572–1618*; Benedetto Bordone, *Isolario di Benedetto Bordone*; Tommaso Porcacchi, *L'isole piu famose del mondo*; Francesco Sansovino, *Ritratto delle più nobili et famose città d'Italia*; Theodor and Johann Israel de Bry, *Alphabeta et characteres, iam indè à creato mundo ad nostra usq.*

3 Ester Pastorello counted 453 printmakers and sellers. *Tipografi, editori, librai a Venezia nel secolo XVI*. On printing in Venice, see BMV, IT VII (2500–12077), Schedario di Horatio F. Brown, *Privilegi Veneziani per la stampa*, 1529–97; Emmanuele Antonio Cicogna, *Corpus delle iscrizioni di Venezia*; Maria Cristofari, 'Editori vicentini del XV e XVI secolo,' in Neri Pozza, ed., *Vicenza illustrata*, 179–88; Roberto Fulin, 'Documenti per servire alla storia della tipografia veneziana'; *Matricola dell'arte dei stampatori e librari di Venezia* with additions by E. Cicogna *Scritte lettere Affari*; Giacomo Moro, 'Insegne librarie e marche tipografiche in un registro veneziano del'500'; Anna Maria Petrioli, 'Stampe popolari venete del cinquecento agli Uffizi'; P. Ulvioni, 'Stampatori e Librai a Venezia nel Seicento'; Fernanda Ascarelli and Marco Menato, *La tipografia del'500 in Italia*, 321–470; Pozza Neri, ed., *La stampa degli incunaboli nel Veneto*; N. Pozza, 'L'editoria veneziana da Giovanni da Spira ad Aldo Manuzio. I centri editoriali di terraferma,' in *Storia della cultura veneta. Dal*

primo Quattrocento al Concilio di Trento, 3 vols, 2: 215–44; Maria Cristofari, 'Editori vicentini del XV e XVI secolo' in *Vicenza Illustrata*; Ester Pastorello, *Bibliografia storico-analitica dell'arte della stampa in Venezia*.

On pictorial printmaking in Venice see: Michael Bury, *The Print in Italy, 1550–1620*; Gert Jan van der Sman, 'Print Publishing in Venice in the Second Half of the Sixteenth Century, 235–47; David Landau and Peter Parshall, *The Renaissance Print*; Marino Zorzi, 'Stampa, illustrazione libraria e le origini dell'incisione figurativa a Venezia,' 690–2; Paolo Bellini, 'Stampatori e mercanti di stampe in Italia nei secoli XVI e XVII,' 19–45; Carlo Pasero, 'Giacomo Franco, editore, incisore e calcografo nei secoli XVI e XVII,' 332–56; Prince Victor Masséna Essling, *Les livres à figures vénitiens de la fin du XVe siècle et du commmencement du XVIe*; Roberto Fulin, 'Documenti per servire alla storia della tipografia veneziana,' 84–219.

On the publishing industry, see Horatio Brown, *The Venetian Printing Press: An Historical Study*; Paul F. Grendler, 'Form and Function in Italian Renaissance Popular Books,' 451–85, and 'Il libro popolare nel Cinquecento,' 211–36; Brian Richardson, *Print Culture in Renaissance Italy: The Editor and the Vernacular Text, 1470–1600*; Dennis E. Rhodes, *Silent Printers. Anonymous Printing at Venice in the Sixteenth Century*; Martin Lowry, *The World of Aldus Manutius. Business and Scholarship in Renaissance Venice*; Ivo Mattozzi, 'Mondo del libro e decadenza a Venezia (1570–1730),' 743–86.

4 'Vivendo io in cosi Illustre, & chiara Città come è questa, la qual senza alcun dubbio si puo chiamar il Theatro del Mondo, & l'occhio d'Italia.' Francesco Sansovino, *Delle cose notabili che sono in Venetia libri due. etc.*, dedication. All translations are author's own, unless noted otherwise.

5 Francesco Sansovino, *Dialogo di tutte le cose notabili che sono in Venetia*; Sansovino, *Delle cose notabili*; Elena Bonora, *Ricerche su Francesco Sansovino: imprenditore, librario e letterato*, 174.

6 'singolare oltre a ciò, perche essendo commoda a tutte le nationi cosi vicine come lontane, ci concorre dalle piu longinque parti della terra ogni gente (onde ci si veggono persone differenti et discordi, di volti, di habiti, et di lingue, ma però tutti concordi in lodare cosi ammiranda città) per trafficare et mercantare.' Sansovino, *Venetia città nobilissima e singolare*, 3v.

7 'Diciamo, dunque, che l'uomo in questo mondo è messo quasi in certo teatro, nel quale siede Dio spettatore dell'azioni di lui: però, suo ufficio è di ben imitare con le proprie le divine operazioni, e con tale imitazione cercare quanto più può di rassomigliarsi a Dio.' Paolo Paruta, *Opere politiche*, vol. 1, 134. William Bouwsma's translation, *Venice and the Defense of Republican Liberty*, 208; see also 199–223. Also see Gaetano Cozzi, 'La società veneziana del rinascimento in un'opera di Paolo Paruta: *Della perfettione della vita politica*,'

in *Ambiente veneziano, ambiente veneto: saggi su politica, società, cultura nella Repubblica di Venezia in età moderna,* 155–83.

8 Peter Heylyn, *Single Works. Microcosmus, or a Little Description of the Great World. A Treatise Historicall, Geographicall, Politicall, Theologicall,* 115.

9 On this concept see Gasparo Contarini, *La Republica, e i magistrati di Vinegia … nuovamente fatti volgari, etc.* On the body politic in the Renaissance, see Leonard Barkan, *Nature's Work of Art: The Human Body as Image of the World.*

10 Sansovino, *Venetia città nobilissima e singolare.*

11 Bonora, *Ricerche su Francesco Sansovino,* 94–5; 188; 169–70.

12 On the myth of Venice, see James Grubb, 'When Myths Lose Power: Four Decades of Venetian Historiography'; Edward Muir, *Civic Ritual in Renaissance Venice,* 1–61; Myron Gilmore, 'Myth and Reality in Venetian Political Theory,' in John Hale, ed., *Renaissance Venice,* 431–44.

13 'eccelso governo.' Sansovino, *Venetia città nobilissima,* 3v. Bonora, *Ricerche su Francesco Sansovino,* 163, 183.

14 Giocondo Cassini, *Piante e vedute prospettiche di Venezia (1479–1855),* 78; Lionello Puppi, ed., *Architettura e utopia nella Venezia del Cinquecento: Mostra, Venezia, Palazzo Ducale, Luglio–Ottobre 1980,* cat. 7, 55; Juergen Schulz, 'The Printed Plans and Panoramic Views of Venice (1486–1797),' *Saggi e memorie di storia dell'arte* 7 (1970), 26, 59, cat. no. 53.

15 Henri Lefebvre, *The Production of Space,* 13.

16 Cassini, *Piante e vedute,* 79.

17 Louis Marin, *Utopics: Spatial Play,* 207.

18 See Max Jammer, *Concepts of Space: The History of Theories of Space in Physics,* chaps 1–3.

19 Walter Ong, *Orality and Literacy: The Technologizing of the Word,* 73.

20 Ibid., 14. On space in antiquity see 7–26.

21 Ibid., 16–17.

22 Jammer, *Concepts of Space,* 27–8. Grosseteste's view of God through space and light explained instantaneity as the 'basis of extension in space,' in which he reduced 'the creation of the universe in space to the autodiffusion of light' (38).

23 Jaspar Hopkins's translation, *Nicholas of Cusa's Dialectical Mysticism: Text, Translation, and Interpretive Study of* De Visione Dei, 115; 18.

24 The citations are taken from the preface of Cusa's *De icona,* also known as *De Visione Dei sive De icona,* excerpted and translated by Michel de Certeau, 'The Gaze Nicholas of Cusa,' 11–12; For Hopkins's translation, see *Nicholas of Cusa's Dialectical Mysticism,* 110–17.

25 Cusa begins his *Complementary Theological Considerations* by questioning the suitability of disseminating the text he had written on mathematics, *Mathe-*

maticis Complementis, which he had sent to Pope Nicholas: 'as if at my advanced age and at my station in life I were permitted to write to the head of the Church about mathematics, without that work's usefulness, symbolically, in regard to the theological befigurings. Therefore, I will endeavor to transform the [mathematical] figures of that book into theological befigurings in order (to the extent that God grants) to behold with mental sight how it is that in the mirror-of-mathematics there shines forth that truth which is sought in and through everything knowable – shines forth not only in a dimly remote likeness but also with a certain bright-shining nearness ... These theological matters are better seen with the mind's eye than they can be expressed in words.' Cusa, *Nicholas of Cusa: Metaphysical Speculations: Six Latin Texts*, trans. Jaspar Hopkins, 5; de Certeau, 'The Gaze,' 14.

26 de Certeau, 'The Gaze,' 15.

27 Cusa describes the distant point of his geometrical diagram as a point of 'quasi-nothingness' (*prope nihil*) whose "fecundity" enables a '*generation of a space.*' Italics in original. In de Certeau, 'The Gaze,' 14–15. Also see Lyle Massey, 'Anamorphosis through Descartes or Perspective Gone Awry,' 1161–2.

28 On Cusa's *De icona* in relation to the 'individual,' see Ernst Cassirer, *The Individual and the Cosmos in Renaissance Philosophy*, 35–7; de Certeau, 'The Gaze,' 6.

29 James Elkins, *The Poetics of Perspective*, 14–15.

30 Ibid., 107.

31 Federico Commandino, *Federici Commandini Urbinatis in planisphaerium Ptolemaei commentarius*. On Commandino's proof of perspective and the 'progression away from dependence on actual objects and toward a nongravitational, "isometric, homogeneous" modern sense of space,' see Elkins, *Poetics of Perspective*, 108–11. On the anachronistic understandings of perspective in relation to space see ibid., esp. 12–29.

32 Skelton, 'Introduction,' in Braun and Hogenberg, *Civitates orbis terrarum*, xiv.

33 Elkins, *Poetics of Perspective*, 90; on the treatise see 89–96.

34 Giorgio de Santillana, *Reflections on Men and Ideas*, 158; also see 159–60.

35 This followed Copernicus's contention 'that it would be much simpler to attribute motion to the contained body than to the container.' Jammer, *Concepts of Space*, 73; see 69–73. As Jammer notes, the separation of time and space was not theorized until Newtonian physics; Elkins, *Poetics of Perspective*, 24.

36 A twenty-five-year privilege was granted on 7 March 1598 to 'Donà Rasicotti per le stampe di Rame in foglio reale a otto per foglio con le città più illustri, et la perspettiva della Piazza di S. Marco verso S. Ziminiano, et anco in legno delle misure, et forme fatte da lui che saranno in numero di fogli cento.' BMV IT VII, 2500 (12077), 917–18. On the print see Franco Barbieri and

Guido Beltramini, eds, *Vincenzo Scamozzi 1548–1616*, 219; Giorgio Bellavitis and Giandomenico Romanelli, 83; Puppi, ed., *Architettura e utopia*, 100.

37 Patricia Fortini Brown, *Venetian Narrative Painting in the Age of Carpaccio*, 165–91.

38 Me ti valor, me la virtu circonda / E giusta e forte in terra e in mar io regno / D'armi d'arti d'erroi, Madre feconda.

39 In the text Scamozzi writes: 'sono le fabriche per habitatione de gl'Illustrissimi Signori Procuratori fra tutte le fabriche di Europa incomparabili, per il sito, per la grandezza, per la forma, e per l'Artificio. Furono incominciate dall'Illustrissimi Signori Procuratori di San Marco con spesa publica l'Anno 1583 e l'Anno 1597 furono approbate dall'Eccellentissimo Senato sotto il Serenissimo Doge Grimani, che si dovessero seguire secondo il Modello di Vicentio Scamozzi Architetto di tanta opera, & contra l'openione di molti Emuli.' On the print see Barbieri and Beltramini, eds, *Vincenzo Scamozzi*, 219. On the Procuratie, see Andrew Hopkins, 'Procuratie Nuove in Piazza San Marco (1581),' in Barbieri and Beltramini, eds, *Vincenzo Scamozzi*, 211–16; Gabriele Morolli et al., *Le Procuratie Nuove in Piazza San Marco*, 13–116; Manfredo Tafuri, *Venice and the Renaissance*, chap. 7.

40 The project for the Procuratie (completed in 1616) and renewal of the Piazza were seen as a means to reassert 'the sovereignty and autonomy of the state.' Tafuri, *Venice and the Renaissance*, 165–6. Initially, the design was to conform to the existing two-storey elevation of the library in order 'to exalt the church of San Marco,' explains Tafuri, 'an emblem of the Republic's autonomy' (167). Following a survey, however, Vincenzo Scamozzi's model was selected, and by 1587 his scheme prompted the committee to suggest the library be raised a storey to conform to the new Procurators' offices. Vincenzo Scamozzi's proposal, with its geometrical rigour and *all'antica* style, initiated a protracted political contest. Ibid., 168. On the architect's interest in perspective, see Scamozzi's *Discorsi sopra le antichità di Roma*. Marc'Antonio Barbaro and Jacopo Foscarini were supporters of Scamozzi's Romanist style. Leonardo Donà – with his rigorous anti-Roman and anti-luxury views – became the project's chief adversary, since the triumphal style would only enhance aristocratic pomp. In 1587, efforts were made to abandon the project by pointing out its impact because it would overshadow the Church of S Marco. Tafuri, *Venice and the Renaissance*, 168–71. Scamozzi's plan was temporarily defeated. However the debate reemerged with the ducal election of 1595 in which both Jacopo Foscarini, who had supported the Scamozzi plan, and Donà, who rejected all aspects of it, were candidates. The third, Marin Grimani, who won the election, put forth a compromise of two instead of three storeys, which set the project in motion again. Ibid., 175. It is this to which Scamozzi refers in the text that was appended to the 1599 print.

41 On *perspectiva naturalis*, the medieval geometry of angles associated with optics, see Elkins, *Poetics of Perspective*, 48–50, 68–9.

42 'Il soggetto di questa scienza son le linee visuali, ma di esse son due specie, l'una è di quelle, per le quali procedono i raggi retti, i quali non si restono, nè rifrangono; e mediante liquali si fa l'atto del vedere diritto, o (come dicono i prospettivi) la visione retta, et l'altra è di quelle linee, per le quali caminano i raggi, che si reflettono, o si rifrangono, & mediante le quali si vede obliquamente, & (come dicono gli istessi Perspettivi) si fa la visione obliqua, Indi son nate due parti della prospettiva, secondo ch'ella considera queste due sorti di linee visuali & quella parte che considera la prima schiera, è stata detta Optica, cioè prospettiva semplicemente ma quella, che s'ha tolto per soggetto il secondo ordine e stata chiamata specularia si da'latini, come da volgari, della quale parliamo in un discorso particolare. Cerca l'Optica, overo Prospettiva si considerano sei cose principali. cioe il vedere, la cosa visibile, il mezo de vedere la specie visibile, il visibile raggio, & il modo del vedere ... Questo viso non e altro, che una potestà perspettiva, la qual apprende gli oggetti visibili per sua proprietà singolare; appartenendosi all'occhio propriamente di vedere, si come dice Macrobio nel settimo de Saturnali, alla ragione di giudicare, & alla memoria di ricordarsi. Questo viso e il più certo quasi di tutti i sensi, perche discerne da lontano tutte le cose pertinenti a corpi, come il colore, la quantità, la figura, il moto, la positione, la distanza, o intervallo.' Tommaso Garzoni, *La piazza universale di tutte le professioni del mondo, nuovamente formata*, 293. John Martin counts twenty-nine editions by the 1650s. 'The Imaginary Piazza: Tommaso Garzoni and the Late Italian Renaissance,' in *Portraits of Medieval and Renaissance Living: Essays in Memory of David Herlihy*, 443n6.

43 For some modern considerations, see Maurice Merleau-Ponty, 'The Primacy of Perception,' in Maurice Merleau-Ponty, *The Primacy of Perception and Other Essays on Phenomenological Psychology, the Philosophy of Art, History and Politics*. Jacques Lacan follows Merleau-Ponty by stressing the passivity of perception: 'the phenomenologists have succeeded in articulating with precision, and in the most disconcerting way, that it is quite clear that I see *outside*, that perception is not in me, that it is on the objects that it apprehends. And yet I apprehend the world in a perception that seems to concern the immanence of the *I see myself seeing myself*. The privilege of the subject seems to be established here from that bipolar reflexive relation by which, as soon as I perceive, my representations belong to me.' *The Four Fundamental Concepts of Psycho-Analysis*, trans. Alan Sheridan, 80–1; also see 71–2; Kaja Silverman, *The Threshold of the Visible World*, 169. This is also key to the mirror-image, which for Lacan is less reflective than constituent of the subject, and thus can be understood as

those images through which the subject sees the world and him or herself. In this way, the subject's identity is constituted by external representations and only knowable through representations. Lacan, 'The Mirror-Phase as Formative of the Function of the I,' in *Mapping Ideology*, ed. Slavoj Žižek, esp. 94.

44 'quantunque il nostro intelletto dal suo nascimento divino sia, nondimeno, mentre quaggiù abita tra queste membra terrene, non può fare sue operazioni senza l'aiuto de'sentimenti del corpo; co'l mezzo de'quali tirando dentro all'anima l'imagini delle cose materiali, a sè stesso le rappresenta, e secondo quelle ne forma i suoi concetti; nè parimente alle contemplazioni spirituali per sè stessso, ma svegliato dagli oggetti sensibili, suole innalzarsi.' Paolo Paruta, *Della perfettione della vita politica*, 1: 116; Bouwsma, *Venice and the Defense of Republican Liberty*, 206.

45 Walter Ong, *Orality and Literacy: The Technologizing of the Word*, 73.

46 John Hale, *The Civilization of Europe in the Renaissance*; Peter Sahlins, *Boundaries: The Making of France and Spain in the Pyranees*; Fernand Braudel, *Civilization and Capitalism 15th and 18th Century*, vol. 3: *The Perspective of the World*.

47 Hale, *Civilization of Europe*, 15. Richard Helgerson, *Forms of Nationhood: The Elizabethan Writing of England*, 108. Conley, *The Self-Made Map*.

48 Helgerson, *Forms of Nationhood*, 122.

49 For Conley 'the self's emergence is evinced where discourse and geography are coordinated, and the self becomes autonomous only (1) when it is fixed to an illusion of a geographic truth (often of its own making) and (2) when it can be detached from the coordinates that mark its point of view, its history, its formation, and the aesthetics and politics of its signature.' *The Self-Made Map*, 6.

50 John Martin, 'Inventing Sincerity, Refashioning Prudence: The Discovery of the Individual in Renaissance Europe.'

51 Jacob Burckhardt, *The Civilization of the Renaissance in Italy: An Essay*, 81.

52 See Stephen Greenblatt, *Renaissance Self-Fashioning from More to Shakespeare*; Natalie Zemon Davis, 'Boundaries and the Sense of Self in Sixteenth-Century France,' in *Society and Culture in Early Modern France*; Richard Trexler, 'Introduction,' in *Persons in Groups: Social Behavior as Identity Formation in Medieval and Renaissance Europe*. .

53 Greenblatt, *Renaissance Self-Fashioning*, esp. 1–10. Also see Norbert Elias, *The Civilizing Process. The History of Manners and State Formation and Civilization*, trans. Edmund Jephcott.

54 Alasdair Macintyre, *A Short History of Ethics*, 121–2.

55 Ibid., 122; 126–7.

56 Ibid., 128.

57 Stephen Greenblatt, 'Psychoanalysis and Renaissance Culture,' in David

Quint and Patricia Parker, eds, *Literary Theory/Renaissance Texts*, 216; Leo Spitzer, 'Notes on the Empirical and Poetic "I" in Medieval authors,' *Traditio* 4 (1946) 414–22. Greenblatt questions the value for the sixteenth century of psychoanalysis, as exemplified by Freud, because it is the key to the individuated self.

58 Greenblatt, 'Psychoanalysis and Renaissance Culture,' 215, 218.

59 Ibid., 216.

60 Ibid., 218.

61 See Natalie Zemon Davis, *The Return of Martin Guerre*, esp. 85.

62 John Martin, 'Inventing Sincerity,' and 'Spiritual Journeys and the Fashioning of Religious Identity in Renaissance Venice.'

63 See Silverman, *Threshold of the Visible World*, 92.

64 Anthony Pagden, *European Encounters with the New World*; Judith Brown, 'Courtiers and Christians: The First Japanese Emissaries to Europe,' 872–906, esp. 879 and 885, and notes 27–9; Eldred Jones, *Othello's Countrymen: The African in English Renaissance Drama*; Winthrop Jordan, *White Over Black: American Attitudes toward the Negro, 1550–1812*; Wolfgang Neuber, 'The 'Red Indian's' Body: The Physiognomy of the Indigenous American between Exoticism and Learned Culture in the Early Modern Period,' 93–107, and Sonia V. Rose, '"The Great Moctezuma": A Literary Portrait in Sixteenth-Century Spanish American Historiography,' in Karl Enenkel et al. eds, *Modelling the Individual: Biography and Portrait in the Renaissance*, 109–32.

65 Since Carlo Pasero's 1937 essay on Franco in *Bibliofilia*, there has been only the occasional notice. Pasero, 'Giacomo Franco,' 332–56.

66 Hayden White, 'The Fictions of Factual Representations,' in *Tropics of Discourse: Essays in Cultural Representation*, ed. Hayden White, 121–34; Michel de Certeau, *The Writing of History*, trans. Tom Conley; Natalie Zemon Davis, *Fiction in the Archives: Pardon Tales and Their Tellers in Sixteenth-Century France*; Peter Burke, *The Historical Anthropology of Early Modern Italy; Essays on Perception and Communication*.

67 On readership and the uses of print, see Roger Chartier, ed., *The Culture of Print: Power and the Uses of Print in Early Modern Europe*, trans. Lydia Cochrane; *The Order of Books: Readers, Authors and Libraries in Europe between the Fourteenth and Eighteenth Centuries*, trans. Lydia G. Cochrane; *Cultural History: Between Practices and Representations*, trans. Lydia G. Cochrane; Rose Marie San Juan, *Rome: A City Out of Print*.

1 From Myth to Metropole: Sixteenth-Century Printed Maps of Venice

1 This document is published in R. Fulin, 'Documenti per servire alla storia

della tipografia veneziana,' 142. The translation is by David Chambers in Chambers and Brian Pullan with Jennifer Fletcher, *Venice: A Documentary History, 1450–1630*, 373. Juergen Schulz's interpolation of the Italian emphasizes the impact of print in the mind of the viewer: 'the printed plates of the view, when joined together in the beholder's imagination, will allow him to reconstitute the image of the city in his mind.' 'Jacopo de'Barbari's View of Venice: Map Making, City Views, and Moralized Geography before the Year 1500,' 473.

2 On de'Barbari, see Jay A. Levenson, 'Jacopo de'Barbari and the Northern Art of the Early Sixteenth Century.'

3 The blocks, once displayed in the Museo Correr, were recently restored. See Jacopo de'Barbari et al., *A volo d'uccello, Jacopo de'Barbari e le rappresentazioni di città nell'Europa del Rinascimento*. On the woodcut also see Deborah Howard, 'Venice as a Dolphin: Further Investigations into Jacopo de'Barbari's View'; Piero Falchetta, 'La misura dipinta: Rilettura tecnica e semantica della veduta di Venezia di Jacopo de' Barbari'; Giocondo Cassini, *Piante e vedute prospettiche di Venezia (1479–1855)*, 40–5; Juergen Schulz, 'Jacopo de'Barbari's View of Venice,' 425–74 and 'The Printed Plans and Panoramic Views of Venice (1486–1797),' *Saggi e memorie di storia dell'arte* 7 (1970); Terisio Pignatti, 'La pianta di Venezia di Jacopo de'Barbari'; Giuseppe Mazzariol and Terisio Pignatti, *La pianta prospettica di Venezia del 1500 disegnata da Jacopo De' Barbari*. On the extraordinary size of the paper, see David Landau and Peter Parshall, *The Renaissance Print 1470–1550*, 16–17.

4 Sanuto evidently heard about the application but must have been absent from the proceedings for he incorrectly recorded Kolb's success in October: 'Noto, a di 30 di questo mexe, per la Signoria fu fato una termination, che, havendo Antonio Colb, merchadante todesco, fato con gran spexa far stampar Veniexia, qual si vende ducati 3 l'una, che possi trarle di questa cità, e portarle senza pagar dacio.' Marin Sanuto, *I diarii di Marino Sanuto*, vol. III, col. 1006. Schulz, *La cartografia tra scienza e arte*, 45; Chambers, in Chambers, Pullan, with Fletcher, *Venice: A Documentary History*, 373.

5 Landau and Parshall suggest this may explain the unusual absence of an inscription on the print recording the privilege. *Renaissance Print*, 300.

6 Pietro Casola, *Canon Pietro Casola's Pilgrimage to Jerusalem in the Year 1494*, trans. M. Margaret Newett, 125–6.

7 Casola, *Casola's Pilgrimage*, 128.

8 On the influence of the map, see Cassini, *Piante e vedute prospettiche di Venezia*, 44.

9 'et havendo descripto la sua origine, quivi *Domino gratiam concedente*, il sito, et cose memorabili vi scriverò. Questa tra le fluttuose onde del mar sta in mezo il vertice del pelago quasi come regina, mantiene il suo grande impeto, e

situado sopra le acque salse.' Sanuto, *De origine, situ et magistratibus urbis venetae ovvero la citta di Venetia (1493–1530)*, ed. Angelo Caracciolo Arico, 20.

10 Elisabeth Crouzet-Pavan, 'Venice and Torcello: History and Oblivion,' 419.

11 Schulz's translation, 'Jacopo de'Barbari's View,' 468.

12 Bernardo Giustiniani's 1493 *De origine urbis Venetiarum* is cited by Ennio Concina, *A History of Venetian Architecture*, 148; on Neptune, 82.

13 The transfer of the ducal seat from Malamocco in 697 cemented the symbolic value of Rialto. Crouzet-Pavan, 'Venice and Torcello,' 425. On the history of Rialto, see Roberto Cessi, *Venezia Ducale*, 155–92.

14 Edward Muir, *Civic Ritual in Renaissance Venice*, 24–5. Patricia Fortini Brown, *Venice and Antiquity*. On the coexistence of the eastern and western traditions, see Debra Pincus, 'Venice and the Two Romes: Byzantium and Rome as a Double Heritage in Venetian Cultural Politics.' Also see Crouzet-Pavan, 'Venice and Torcello.'

15 The birth of Venice is traditionally identified as 25 March 421, the feast day of the Annunciation to the Virgin.

16 Giustinian's *De origine urbis Venetiarum* was the first book to receive a copyright; it was granted in 1492. Angelo Colla, 'Tipografi, editori e libri a Padova, Treviso, Vicenza, Verona, Trento,' in *La stampa degli incunaboli nel Veneto*, 52. Venetian historiography was inaugurated by Sabellico and Giustinian. In 1516, Andrea Navagero became the first public historian to be nominated by the state. Colla, 'Tipografi,' 53. The post remained empty between Pietro Bembo's tenure in 1530 and that of Alvise Contarini in 1577. In 1580 the position was filled by Paolo Paruta, whose writing style and language reflected the humanist and patrician values associated with state historiography. See Elena Bonora, *Ricerche su Francesco Sansovino imprenditore librario e letterato*, 165n., 166–7. Also see Gaetano Cozzi, 'Cultura politica e religione nella "Pubblica Storiografia" Veneziana del'500,' in *Ambiente veneziano, ambiente veneto: Saggi su politica, società, cultura nella repubblica di Venezia in età moderna*, 13–86.

17 On the myth, see Brown, *Venice and Antiquity*, 263–84.

18 These human figures are adjacent to areas built well above the ground, a detail Bellavitis suggests may have operated on a parodic level. Giorgio Bellavitis and Giandomenico Romanelli, *Venezia*, 237.

19 See P.D.A. Harvey, *The History of Topographical Maps. Symbols, Pictures and Surveys*, 80. Richard Helgerson, *Forms of Nationhood: The Elizabethan Writing of England*, 146; Rodolfo Gallo, 'Le mappe geografiche del Palazzo Ducale di Venezia.' Juergen Schulz points to the tradition from 1479 to 1553 – perhaps dating back to the fourteenth-century doge Francesco Dandolo – of cartog-

raphers who decorated the Chiesola and ducal chambers with maps including the Venetian state, Asia, and America. 'Cristoforo Sorte and the Ducal Palace of Venice,' 205. On Antonio Leonardi's map of Italy in the Ducal Palace, see Lilian Armstrong, 'Benedetto Bordon, *Miniator,* and Cartography in Early Sixteenth-Century Venice,' 73. On the symbolic uses of geography in the Baptistery of San Marco, see Debra Pincus, 'Geografia e politica nel Battistero di San Marco: La cupola degli Apostoli,' in *San Marco: Aspetti storici e agiografici,* 459–73ff. For an introduction to mapmaking in Venice see Eugenio Bevilacqua, 'Geografi e Cosmografi,' in *Storia della cultura Veneta: Dal primo quattrocento al Concilio di Trento,* II: 355–74.

20 David Harvey, *The Condition of Postmodernity,* 247; J.B. Harley, 'Silences and Secrecy: The Hidden Agenda of Cartography in Early Modern Europe.'

21 Schulz, 'Cristoforo Sorte and the Ducal Palace,' 205.

22 On state mapping see, David Buisseret ed., *Monarchs, Ministers, and Maps: The Emergence of Cartography as a Tool of Government in Early Modern Europe.*

23 John Hale, *The Civilization of Europe in the Renaissance,* 33–5.

24 For this earlier interpretation see Mazzariol and Pignatti, *La pianta prospettica.* Schulz, 'Jacopo de'Barbari's View,' 430–1. Also see Bellavitis and Romanelli, *Venezia.*

25 Juergen Schulz, 'New Maps and Landscape Drawings by Cristoforo Sorte,' *Kunsthistorischen Institutes in Florenz* 20, no. 1 (1976): 116–19. Also see Roberto Almagià, 'Cristoforo Sorte e i primi rilievi topografici della Venezia Tridentina.'

26 Schulz, 'Jacopo de'Barbari's View,' 436.

27 In his 1970 essay, Schulz believed the woodcut's verisimilitude should be attributed to a scientific explanation. In view of the apparent absence of technical means available to Kolb and de'Barbari, combined with inconsistencies in the woodcut (notably the progressive compression of the cityscape to the west), he changed his opinion. Schulz, 'Jacopo de'Barbari's View,' 436–40.

28 Ibid., 439. On Schulz's view, see Lucia Nuti, 'The Perspective Plan in the Sixteenth Century: The Invention of a Representational Language,' 125n.64.

29 Elisabeth Crouzet-Pavan, *'Sopra le acque salse,'* 79–82, 137.

30 Edward Muir and Ronald F.E. Weissman, 'Social and Symbolic Places in Renaissance Venice and Florence,' in John A. Agnew and James S. Duncan, eds, *The Power of Place: Bringing Together Geographical and Sociological Imaginations,* 90–1. On the city's urban development see Crouzet-Pavan, *'Sopra le acque salse';* Schulz, 'Urbanism in Medieval Venice,' in Anthony Molho, Kurt Raaflaub, and Julia Emlen, eds, *City States in Classical Antiquity and Medieval Italy,* 419–45.

31 Crouzet-Pavan, *'Sopra le acque salse,'* 71–2.

32 Ibid., 73–89, esp. 84–5.

33 Ibid., 79–82, 137. Draining was extensive from 1329 to 1445. At this time the *vicini* were introduced into the parishes; they were agents, not residents, and functioned as proprietors. The other two groups were the Commune and the magistrates of the Piovego, nobles whose visual inspection of potential sites preceded the handing out of concessions. This function was transferred to public works from 1485 to 1502, when the city was inspected in its entirety. Ibid., 72–80, 89.

34 Ibid., 90. As evidence of foresight, Crouzet-Pavan cites the council's anticipation in 1254 of a waterway and bridge between the old and new islands on Giudecca (93).

35 Ibid., 93, 116, 131–2, 151.

36 Ibid., 91–2.

37 Ibid., 131. On the symbolic function of St Mark and Venice's 'battle with the sea,' see Muir, *Civic Ritual*, esp. 98–9; Crouzet-Pavan, 'Venice and Torcello,' 424–5.

38 Muir and Weissman, 'Social and Symbolic Places,' 91–2.

39 See Dennis Romano, 'Gender and the Urban Geography of Renaissance Venice'; *Patricians and Popolani: The Social Foundations of the Venetian Renaissance State*, 156n.37. One symptom of these social changes was a shift in local bequests to the poor as increasingly these gifts became controlled by the state (152–4 and n. 26). On the house as 'a visible sign of family honor,' see Thomas Kuehn, *Law, Family, and Women: Toward a Legal Anthropology of Renaissance Italy*, 124. On domesticity and the visibility of women, see Diane Owen Hughes, 'Representing the Family: Portraits and Purposes in Early Modern Italy,' 31–3. On Venice's factional and social geography, see Robert Davis, *The War of the Fists: Popular Culture and Public Violence*, esp. 33.

40 Muir and Weissman, 'Social and Symbolic Places,' 81–103.

41 On the festival, see Muir, *Civic Ritual*, 135–56; Lina Urban, 'I ludi mariani ossia la festa delle Marie, in *Processioni e feste dogali: 'Venetia est mundus,'* 29–50.

42 Muir, *Civic Ritual*, 153–4. Brian Pullan, *Rich and Poor in Renaissance Venice: The Social Institutions of a Catholic State, to 1620*, 153. Pullan notes that the parishes may also have lost their significance as populations dropped because of the plague (n. 43).

43 On building carried out by the mendicant and conventual orders, see Crouzet-Paven, *'Sopra le acque salse,'* 97–115.

44 On the basis of Sansovino's estimates, Richard Mackenney notes that 'over 70 churches are represented in each Scuola, though it is clear that the two which seemed biased toward lower social groups had a tendency to express a

certain neighbourhood solidarity.' Here he is referring to supra-parochial Scuole. *Tradesmen and Traders: The World of the Guilds in Venice and Europe, c.1250–c.1650,* 56. See his appendix II for a breakdown of Scuole membership; also see 49. Also see Brian Pullan, 'Natura e carattere delle Scuole,' in Terisio Pignatti, ed., *Le scuole di Venezia,* 9–26; *Rich and Poor in Renaissance Venice.* On the Scuole and visual imagery at the turn of the century, see Patricia Fortini Brown, *Venetian Narrative Painting in the Age of Carpaccio.*

45 See Gasparo Contarini, *La Republica, e i magistrati di Vinegia ... nuovamente fatti volgari, etc.,* trans. E. Anditimi.

46 Pullan, *Rich and Poor,* 153. In view of their membership – only about 10 per cent of the city's population – the extent of their impact on social welfare remains uncertain. See Mackenney, *Tradesmen and Traders,* 49; R.C. Mueller, 'Charitable Institutions, the Jewish Community, and Venetian Society. A Discussion of the Recent Volume by Brian Pullan' ; Pullan, *Rich and Poor,* 33–187.

47 Concina, *A History of Venetian Architecture,* 155; Donatella Calabi, 'Images of a City "in the Middle" of Salt Water,' in Edoardo Salzano, ed., *An Atlas of Venice: The Form of the City on 1:1000 Scale Photomap and Line Map,* 21. Also see P. Brown, *Venetian Narrative Painting;* Pignatti, ed., *Le scuole di Venezia.*

48 Lina Urban Padoan, 'Apparati scenografica nelle feste veneziane cinquecentesche.' Adriana Boscaro, 'La visita a Venezia della prima ambasceria giapponese in Europa,' *Il Giappone, anno V.*

49 'La *contrada* identifie sans exception chaque Vénitien.' Crouzet-Pavan, *'Sopra le acque salse,'* 84. Business at the parish level was carried out by priests, commoners whose secular role seems to have been aligned with the administrative function of the *contrade.* Muir and Weissman, 'Social and Symbolic Places,' 91. Mackenney explains that the parish church was 'tied to an unusually democratic way of life in that local residents elected their own priest.' 'Many of the altars,' however, 'were maintained by brotherhoods, the *scuole,* which often had nothing to do with life of the parochial community.' *Tradesmen and Traders,* 47. Boholm notes that the *sestieri* were represented following the election of the doge when he was presented in the church of San Marco. By contrast, 'the chiefs of the *contrade* were expected to gauge the reaction of their parishioners.' Åsa Boholm, *The Doge of Venice: The Symbolism of State Power in the Renaissance,* 137.

50 According to Calabi, by masking the 'empty areas, lacerations and deformities ... the shreds of an urban fabric which was never to be closely woven,' the map 'seems to justify' the pervasiveness of the system of controls and thus resecure 'their permanent "marginal" status.' 'Images of a City,' 21.

51 Mark Zucker describes the artist's technique as 'just about as impersonal as that of an early Italian engraver can be, its very lack of individuality and idio-

syncrasy having prevented him, until recently, from being credited with the engravings themselves.' Adam von Bartsch, *The Illustrated Bartsch*, vol. 24, part 2, ed. Mark Zucker, 5. On Rosselli, see Roberto Almagià, 'On the Cartographic Work of Francesco Rosselli'; Lucia Nuti, 'The Perspective Plan,' 113–15; G. Fanelli, *Firenze*, 77–86.

52 Nuti, 'The Perspective Plan,' 114–15.

53 Original is italicized. Louis Marin, *Portrait of the King*, 178.

54 Peter Parshall, '*Imago contrafacta*: Images and Facts in the Northern Renaissance.'

55 See Michel de Certeau, *The Practice of Everyday Life*, trans. Steven Rendall, 92.

56 On Venice personified see chapter 3; also see David Rosand, '*Venezia figurata*,' in David Rosand, ed., *Interpretazioni Veneziane. Studi di storia dell'arte in onore di Michelangelo Muraro*, 182; *Myths of Venice: The Figuration of a State*, 26–46, 97, 100–8, 114–17, 130, 138, 147.

57 Cassini, who summarizes the historiography of attributions, has reservations concerning de'Barbari's authorship of the whole. *Piante*, 44.

58 For Landau and Parshall the caduceus is included because of Mercury's symbolic importance to the city, and thus it 'can hardly be taken as an effective gesture of self-promotion.' *The Renaissance Print*, 45.

59 E.D. Hirsch is citing August Boeckh, *The Aims of Interpretation*, 18n.159.

60 'in questa Rep.la eloquenza ha sempre havvuto gran luogo, & gli huomini eloquenti vi sono stati in numero grande & in sommo grado di riputatione: ho voluto figurar Mercurio, come significativo delle lettere & della eloquenza.' Jacopo Sansovino is cited in his son's account of the Loggetta, *Venetia città nobilissima e singolare*, 111v.

61 Hirsch, *Aims of Interpretation*, 18. Also on Mercury, see Jean-Christophe Agnew, *Worlds Apart: The Market and the Theater in Anglo-American Thought, 1550–1750*, 20–4, 57.

62 'Il fine della Corografia è di rappresentare una sola parte, sì come chi imitasse ò dipingesse un'orecchia sola, ò un'occhio. Ma il fine della Geografia è di considerare il tutto in universale, alla guisa di coloro, i quali descrivono, ò dipingono tutto un capo. Percioche in tutte quelle figure, ò imagini, che noi ci proponiamo à ritrarre, ò rappresentare, convenendosi primieramente accommodare, et disporre le prime, ò principali lor parti, et che elle sieno debitamente situate, et con misure, et proportioni, che sofficientemente corrispondano alla lontananza della vista, perche, ò intera, et tutta, ò particolare che ella sia, possa tutta sensibilmente comprendersi.' *Geografia di Claudio Tolomeo*, 1.

63 Landau and Parshall, *The Renaissance Print*, 43.

64 The orientation of maps changed in accordance with uses. Medieval maps

were usually 'oriented' with east at the top, in accordance with the tradition of orienting European churches in the direction of Jerusalem. Nautical charts, on the other hand, were oriented toward the north, following the compass. See David Woodward, 'Medieval *Mappaemundi*,' in J.B. Harley and David Woodward, eds, *The History of Cartography*, esp. 286–307. On Portolans, see Tony Campbell, 'Portolan Charts from the Late Thirteenth Century to 1500,' in Harley and Woodward, eds, *History of Cartography*, 371–461; Ugo Tucci, 'La Carta Nautica,' in S. Biadene, ed., *Carte da navigar: Portolani e carte nautiche del Museo Correr 1318–1732*, 10, 19. On city views in nautical charts, see Giandomenico Romanelli, 'Città di costa. Immagine urbana e carte nautiche,' in Biadene, ed., *Carte da navigar*, 20–32.

65 P.D.A. Harvey comments on the change between the thirteenth-century Hereford map of the world, in which Jerusalem was located at the centre, and a map of the universe produced by Heinrich Loriti (c. 1510) in which he placed a perspective view of his home in Glarus Switzerland at the centre. *The History of Topographical Maps*, 83.

66 The idea draws on the resemblance between the wind god and a seventeenth-century painting by Georg Fennitzer after a self-portrait of de'Barbari. Mazzariol and Pignatti, *La pianta prospettica*, 8, 10.

67 See the view of Venice in the Deniz Atlasi, Walters Art Museum. I am grateful to Piero Falchetta and to the Walters Museum for this reference. For an example of the more typical city view of Venice, see the nautical chart of Giovanni Xenodocos da Corfù in Giandomenico Romanelli and Susana Biadene, *Venezia piante e vedute: Catalogo del fondo cartografico a stampa*, 52.

68 Charles Hope and Jane Martineau, eds, *The Genius of Venice 1500–1600*, 392. On Sabellico and Giustinian see Colla, 'Tipografi,' 52–3; on de'Barbari's descriptive image and Patricia Fortini Brown's concept of the eyewitness style, see Deborah Howard, 'Venice as a Dolphin'; on the 'eyewitness' style see P. Brown, *Venetian Narrative Painting*.

69 See Crouzet-Pavan on the genealogy of this tradition. 'Venice and Torcello,' 418–23.

70 Ibid., 419. Sansovino, *Venetia città nobilissima*, 3v–4. Sanuto's *Itinerario* is a diary of his travels through the terraferma, with histories of sites and sketches of the fortifications. Marin Sanuto, *Itinerario di Marin Sanuto per la terraferma veneziana*.

71 In the context of the League of Cambrai, Priuli writes in August 1509: 'li inimici, insuperbiti de una tanta victoria, *cum* lo Imperatore electo sarianno venutti sopra le ripe salse senza contrarietade alchuna et haverianno obtenuto il tutto fino al mare salso, et, vedendo li Venetiani fugatti, haverianno tentato et facto ogni loro forze in queste furie di prendere la citade veneta

virginela, mai stata subgiugata d'alchuno Signore, et destripare et ruinare il nome veneto, chome desideravanno' (240). The following month he states 'Et quantumque, o dignissimo et sapientissimo intellecto, se debia considerare che, atrovandossi questa digna et magna citade venetta situyta nel mirabille sycto suo, circumdata da aque maritime, et che quantumque sentivanno bombardare la citade patavina, come se dice, et li inimici sopra le ripe salse, pocho se poteva dubitare deli inimici per essere il transito da potere venire a Venettia molto difficille rispecto dele aque, che se questo mirabile sycto di questa virginea citade non fusse stato, *sine dubio actum erat de imperio venetto*, et solamente le aque d'intorno l'à preservatta, perchè chavali non possonno venire' (325). Girolamo Priuli, *I diarii.(1494–1512)*, ed. Arturo Segre (Bologna: Zanichelli, 1921–41), tome 24, part 3, vol. IV.

72 'per consiglio di Daulo, si fece un nuovo governo partendosi la provincia equalmente à ciascuno, et per aguaglianza, et similitudine si diliberò di lasciar i palagi, et le habitationi magnifiche, per non sopra farsi l'un l'altro; fermando per legge, che tutte le habitationi fossero pari, simili, di una medesima grandezza, et ornato, et il vestire con questo indifferente tra tutti; cosa, che fin al dì d'hoggi si osserva.' Nicolò Zen, *Dell'origine di Venetia*, 15. Jessica Levine's translation, Tafuri *Venice and the Renaissance*, 3. On Nicolò Zen, see 1–3.

73 Venice lost numerous outposts to Ottoman expansion between 1463 to 1479. Despite the acquisition of control over Cyprus in 1489 (lost in 1571), the last decade of the century saw further losses at Lepanto, Modone, Corone, Zonchio, and Negroponte in 1500. The years 1495 and 1499 saw bank failures. Alvise Zorzi, *Venice, 697–1797: City, Republic, Empire*; Alberto Tenenti, 'The Sense of Space and Time in the Venetian World,' in John Hale, ed., *Renaissance Venice*; Priuli, *Diarii*, I, 183, 198, 270; II, 26–7, 38; On relations with the Ottoman Turks between 1457 and 1500, see Domenico Malipiero, *Annali Veneti dell'anno 1457 al 1500*, vol. I, part 1. Also see Angelo Ventura, 'Le trasformazioni economici nel Veneto tra quattro e ottocento.' Nevertheless, the Levant maintained its mercantile and symbolic value for the Venetians. See Frederic C. Lane, 'Venetian Shipping during the Commercial Revolution,' and 'The Mediterranean Spice Trade: Further Evidence of Its Revival in the Sixteenth Century,' in Brian Pullan, ed., *Crisis and Change in the Venetian Economy in the Sixteenth and Seventeenth Centuries*, 22–46; 47–58.

74 Five of the twelve extant set of impressions from the first state are in Venice. Landau and Parshall, *The Renaissance Print*, 382n.38. On the three states, see Mazzariol and Pignatti, *La pianta prospettica*; Pignatti, 'La pianta di Venezia,' 10–11. On the absence of maps in Venetian inventories, see Federica Ambrosini, '"Descrittioni del mondo" nelle case Venete dei secoli XVI e

XVII,' 67–79; Woodward, *Maps as Prints*, 82–3. Early in the seventeenth century, the prints were recorded in the company of other city views in the inventories of Cardinal Francesco Maria del Monte in 1627 and Cardinal Francesco Barberini. But at the beginning of the sixteenth century, the map was unlikely to have been an item for a collector. Schulz, 'Jacopo de'Barbari's View,' 441, and 442fn.45.

75 These new values intensified after the League of Cambrai. Venality had resulted in a new generation of young patricians, who, already wealthy and untrained as merchants, rejected traditional values. The debate continued throughout the sixteenth century, as seen, for example, in the writing of Nicolò Zen, for whom commerce was one of the republic's 'original' values. Tafuri, *Venice and the Renaissance*, 1.

76 'Li Venetiani heranno molto piui inclinati ala terraferma, per essere piui delectevole et piazevole, cha al mare suo antiquo et cagione de ogni loro gloria, amplitudine et honore.' Priuli, *Diarii*, vol. IV, 49; Tenenti, 'Sense of Space,' 21.

77 'Li Padri Veneti et tuta la citade heranno tantto inclinati et destinati a questa terraferma, che piui non se poteva dire, et abandonava li viagij maritimi rispecto a questa terraferma; et questo procedeva perché, essendo li nobelli et citadini veneti inrichitti, volevanno triumfare et vivere et atendere a darssi apiacere et delectatione et verdure in la terraferma et altri spassi assai, abandonando le navigatione et viagij maritimi quali heranno piui fastidiosi et laboriossi: *et tamen* dal mare procedeva ogni bene.' Priuli, *Diarii*, vol. IV, 50. Tenenti's translation, 'Sense of Space,' 21–2.

78 'le excessive, et infruttuorse spexe.' ASV, Provveditori alle pompe, *Decreti* (1334–1689), 1495.

79 Ibid., 1514.

80 Domenico Morosini, *De bene instituta re publica*, ed. Claudio Vita-Finzi. Gaetano Cozzi, 'Domenico Morosini e il *De bene instituta re publica*,' 405–58, esp 415–16, 425.

81 Cozzi, 'Domenico Morosini,' 409. On parallels with Thomas More's *Utopia*, see 414–20.

82 Ibid., 435.

83 See Priuli, *Diarii*, vol. IV, 49–52. The Provveditore alle pompe targeted the Reggimenti, the colonial administration, with legislation in 1480 (reiterated in 1520, 1545, 1572, 1594, and 1595) to curtail display by prohibiting the appearance of servants in livery, and limiting numbers of horses, lavish decorations, and banquets. ASV, Provveditore alle pompe, *Capitolari* 1–11 1488–1683, 1v, 7v, 12r. Decrees were printed in Venice for circulation in its subject cities of Brescia (1593), Bergamo (1594, 1633), and Verona (1633).

84 Cozzi, 'Domenico Morosini,' 413–14; Mocenigo cites costs of the mainland:
'Notificandove che nel tempo nostro havemo diffalchado III miliona de
imprestidi, el qual debito dela camera fo creado per la guerra de Padoa,
Vicenza et Verona, et il nostro monte se atrova in VI milliona de ducati ... Et
questo è stado che ha fatto la guerra del Turcho, per modo che il mondo
dixe: Li Venetiani son signori di capitanii deli compagni et zurme de gallie.'
Renga de messer Thomado Mocenigo doxe alla Signoria, in *Bilanci generali*, ser. II,
vol. I pt. I, 94–7.

85 'Sichè, ritornando al proposito nostro, essendo perduta la terraferma, li
nobelli et citadini et populari veneti, dico li giovani, se meteranno sopra la
navigatione et li viagij et avadagneranno il perduto, *et ultra* il guadagno se
faranno valentissimi homeni et expertti in lo exercitio maritimo et in ogni
altra operatione, et forssi che 'l sarà de magior utillitade ala Republica Veneta cha le entrade dela terraferma.' Priuli, *Diarii*, vol. IV, 52. Tenenti's translation, 'Sense of Space,' 31.

86 The figure of Mercury could have been intepreted in different ways. His
authoritative position, heroic form, and symbolic identity as the god of trade
would have resecured long-standing republican values. He may also have
pointed to the growing ambivalence toward trade; as Jean-Christophe Agnew
has argued for late sixteenth-century England, Mercury signified the anxiety
of shifting market relations as he 'embodied the equivocal character of the
trade he was charged with protecting.' *Worlds Apart*, 57.

87 Niccolò Machiavelli's criticism of Venetian expansionism has often been
noted. See his references to Venice in his *Florentine Histories*, for example, VI:
26, 259–60. See Tenenti, 'Sense of Space,' 21; Muir, *Civic Ritual*, 46–7, 49.

88 Elisabeth Gleason, 'Reading between the Lines of Gasparo Contarini's Treatise on the Venetian State,' 255. For Savonarola, Venice offered the best form
of government: 'credo ... che la forma del governo de Venetiani sia molto
buona, et non vi paia vergona imparare da altri, perche quella forma che
hanno fudata loro da Dio: et poi che la presono, non e stata mai dissensione
civile intra loro.' Girolamo Savonarola, *Prediche ... sopra Aggeo Profeta*, 100.
Tafuri, *Venice and the Renaissance*, 199n.5. Guicciardini also saw Venice as a
model for emulation. Francesco Guiccardini, *The History of Italy*, trans. Sidney Alexander, 79.

89 'sono adunque i Geografi quelli, che vanno imitando (come ben dice Claudio Tolomeo) il dissegno di tutta la terra da noi conosciuto notando in piano,
overo in balle, i paesi, e la città, non con la propria forma loro, come si fa nel
dissegno, ma solamente con alcuni segnetti, ò punti tondi, o quadretti piccioli, onde più presto vanno imitando il dissegno, che dissegnino veramente il
sito loro. Et son differenti assai da Corografi, perche questi propriamente

dipingono, et dissegnino dal naturale la forma et la figura d'alcuni paesi, et
città particolari; come chi disegnasse il paese intorno a Roma, ò intorno a
Napoli. Oltra che i Corografi attendono piu alla qualità de'luoghi, rappre-
sentando le vere figure, et somiglianze loro; et i Geografi all'opposito attendono più alla quantità, descrivendo le misure, i siti, e la proportione delle
lontananze. Et i Corografi hanno bisogno del dissegno, et della pittura; ma
i Geografi non, potendo, essi con minute lettere, et segni dimostrare il sito,
et la figura di tutta la terra, come fanno.' Tommaso Garzoni, *La piazza universale di tutte le professioni del mondo, nuovamente formata*, 311–12. Garzoni's
explanation of chorography reflects the scientific organization of the disci-
plines in the sixteenth century. See Conley, *The Self-Made Map*, 13. Also see
David Woodward, *Maps as Prints in the Italian Renaissance*, 5–8.

90 Louis Marin, *Utopics: Spatial Play*, trans. Robert A. Vollrath, 99.

91 'Questo viso non e altro, che una potestà perspettiva, la qual apprende gli
oggetti visibili per sua proprietà singolare; appartenendosi all'occhio propriamente di vedere.' Garzoni, *Piazza universale*, 293.

92 Margaret L. King, *Venetian Humanism in an Age of Patrician Dominance*, 92;
also see Crouzet-Pavan, *'Sopra le acque salse,'* 139.

93 Marin, *Utopics*, 53, 71.

94 Ibid., 53.

95 See Jacques Lacan, *Four Fundamental Concepts*, 106.

96 The first two citations are De Cusa. The latter is Michel de Certeau, and his
emphasis. 'The Gaze: Nicholas of Cusa,' 14–15.

97 The woodcut might therefore be understood to represent a new place for
the Venetian subject within a symbolic order constituted by vision, by 'the
presence of others.' See Silverman on the relation between the 'presence of
others as such' and Lacan's concept of the gaze, what she describes as 'the
manifestation of the symbolic within the field of vision.' *Threshold*, 168. Also
see 133.

98 'Diciamo, dunque, che l'uomo in questo mondo è messo quasi in certo
teatro, nel quale siede Dio spettatore dell'azioni di lui: però, suo ufficio è di
ben imitare con le proprie le divine operazioni, e con tale imitazione cercare quanto più può di rassomigliarsi a Dio.' Paolo Paruta, *Opere politiche*, 1:
134. William Bouwsma's translation, *Venice and the Defense of Republican Liberty*, 208; also see 199–223.

99 Elisabeth Gleason, 'Reading between the Lines,' 257.

100 Ibid. 'Ma il sito di Vinegia piu tosto per un certo divino consiglio, che per
humana industria oltra la fede di tutti coloro, che non hanno visto quella
città.' Gasparo Contarini, *La Republica, e i magistrati di Vinegia*, IIIv. On utopian space and political institutions, see Marin, *Utopics*, 9.

101 See Machiavelli on 'republics ... imagined and seen,' *Florentine Histories*, 8: 29, 352; *The Prince*, 15: 90–1. On myth and allegory, see Marin, *Utopics*, 228–9.

102 Fra Paolino Veneto, *De mappa mundi*, c. 1321, cited in Patricia Fortini Brown, *Venice and Antiquity*, 55.

103 While the de'Barbari woodcut has elicited several interpretations, subsequent printed maps of Venice have more often been addressed by scholars in a catalogue format. See Schulz, 'The Printed Plans'; Cassini, *Piante*; Giuliana Mazzi, 'La cartografia per il Mito: Le immagini di Venezia nel Cinquecento,' in Lionello Puppi, ed., *Architettura e utopia nella Venezia del Cinquecento: Mostra, Venezia, Palazzo Ducale, Luglio–Ottobre 1980*, 50–68; Denis Cosgrove, 'The Myth and the Stones of Venice: An Historical Geography of a Symbolic Landscape'; Romanelli and Biadene, *Venezia piante e vedute*.

104 Giocondo Cassini sought to redress the print's status as a poor copy of de'Barbari's woodcut by pointing to the difference in angles adopted for the point of view. Where the earlier woodcut shifts from an almost perpendicular viewpoint over Giudecca toward an oblique angle for the distant landscape, Vavassore reversed the construction, using an oblique view in the foreground that becomes perpendicular as the distant point moves toward the islands of Murano to the north. The picture plane slopes toward the viewer, a process that explains why distant islands and the terraferma are not visible. This point of view enabled Vavassore to focus on the topographical details of the historical centre even more emphatically than de'Barbari. Cassini, *Piante*, 47. Puppi, ed. *Architettura e utopia*, cat. 2, 53–4. On Vavassore see Leo Bagrow, *Giovanni Andreas di Vavassore. A Venetian Cartographer of the 16th Century. A Desciptive List of His Maps*.

105 'come tu vedi qui dipintta nel mezo de uno maritimo lagumene ... Questa citta a populo i[n]finito et di tutte le parte del mondo per esercitar la marcantia vi concorrano.'

106 Pagan drew on Vavassore's print for the centre; however he also incorporated the islands, terraferma, and Lido following the precedent established by Bordone in his *Isolario*. Cassini, *Piante*, 53; Puppi, ed. *Architettura e utopia*, cat. 3 and 4, 54; on Pagan, see Leo Bagrow, *Matheo Pagano. A Venetian Cartographer of the 16th Century*. Benedetto Bordone, *Isolario di Benedetto Bordone*. On Bordone, see Lilian Armstrong, 'Benedetto Bordon, *Miniator*, and Cartography in Early Sixteenth-Century Venice.'

107 'narrare il sito, l'edificacion di tal luoco, la sua origine, gli habitanti, e la felicità del paese, e quando il luoco di cui si ragiona è incognito, allhora si estende in far più piano l'occhio, & la mente di chi guarda e legge.'

108 Pagan's text reads: 'Io adunque havendovi (come vedete) descritta Vinegia, ch'è lo splendore del mondo, non mi faticarò di voler dare particular noti-

zia di lei, essendo assai abastanza da per se notabile, ma solo per ischiarar questa carta, che vi tenete davanti esplicherà Vinegia.'

109 The smaller map was republished by Francesco da Salò sometime between 1562 and 1565, when he took over Pagan's *bottega* (Cassini, *Piante*, 53). On Pagan, see Leo Bagrow, *Matheo Pagano. A Venetian Cartographer of the 16th Century. A Descriptive List of His Maps.*

110 The dialogue begins with the Venetian asking: 'Ditemi, caro gentilhuomo, che vi pare di questa città?' The foreigner responds, after having praised the site and the buildings: 'Io ho veduto l'impossibile nell'impossibile ... tutte le parti minutamente di questa città in quella maniera che si dee considerar una sì gran cosa come è questa, era impossibile a farsi perfettamente; essendo adunque Venetia una impossibilità, viene anco ad esser posta nell'impossibile, essendo fondata nel mare, perch'ella è fuor dell'ordine di tutte l'altre città.' Francesco Sansovino [Anselmo Guisconi, pseud.], *Dialogo di tutte le cose notabili che sono in Venetia* [1556]. Cassini suggests that Sansovino may have been the author of the text that Pagan wrote in the textblock. *Piante*, 56n.1. According to Bonora, this publication was Sansovino's first foray into discussions of art. *Ricerche su Francesco Sansovino*, 186.

111 On the technological and aesthetic considerations of copperplate engraving, see Woodward, *Maps as Prints*, esp. 'Lecture I.'

112 On the basis of Forlani's output, Woodward dubs 1566 'the zenith of Venetian map engraving.' Ibid., 24. On Forlani, see David Woodward, *The Maps and Prints of Paolo Forlani: A Descriptive Bibliography*; Cassini, *Piante*, 58–61.

113 Cassini, *Piante*, 58.

114 'nondimeno, in parte habbiamo supplito con questa tavola, che qui è posta doue presa la chiesa, o altra cosa che si uole, con la lettera, o numero, quel numero, o lettera poi, si chercherà nella figura, & dove sarà, quello sarà il luogo cercato: & al conuerso, hauendo si la lettera o'l numero trouato nella figura, per la qui posta tauola si saprà che luogo egli è.' Leandro Alberti, *Isolario appartenenti alla Italia*. The map was included in the republication of Alberti's more famous *Descrittione di tutta Italia* (Venice, 1568) edited in Bologna in 1550 and published in Venice in 1553. See Cassini, *Piante*, 62 and n. 2.

115 The view of Venice is based on the Forlani view, with the legend and urban context more selective in their details, on account of the smaller size. See Cassini, *Piante*, 66–7. The map of Venice is accompanied with landscapes and engravings including Hoefnagel's view of the fire in the Ducal Palace. On the city plans in the *Civitates* see R.A. Skelton, 'Introduction,' in Georg Braun and Franz Hogenberg, *Civitates orbis terrarum 1572–1618*; Lucia Nuti,

Ritratti di città: Visione e memoria tra medioevo e settecento. R.A. Skelton has discussed the three types of views adopted for city maps: 'stereographic views' ('prospects' or profiles), depicting the subject as it presented itself to the eye of an observer at a point on the ground or not far above it; perspective or bird's-eye views, as seen obliquely from a more elevated point of vision; linear ground plans or 'plats' drawn from a theoretically vertical viewpoint; and 'map–views,' a combination of the latter two formats. The map of Venice was produced by combining the latter two modes, thereby demonstrating Braun's preference that 'towns should be drawn in such a manner that the viewer can look into all the roads and streets and see also all the buildings and open spaces.' Skelton, 'Introduction,' in Braun and Hogenberg, *Civitates orbis terrarum,* x–xi. Citing Braun, xi.

116 On the woodcut, see Michael Bury. *The Print in Italy, 1550–1620,* 183–4. Bury notes that the standards display the coat of arms of the Priuli. Since the face of the doge may resemble Girolamo Priuli (reigned 1556–9), and there was a copy of the print produced in 1561, it is likely the print was published at the end of the 1550s. *Print in Italy,* 184.

117 On the Alexandrine gifts, see Muir, *Civic Ritual,* 102–19.

118 The Contarini text was published in the vernacular in 1544. *La republica, e i magistrati di Vinegia ... nuovamente fatti volgari, etc.*

119 Gleason, 'Reading between the Lines,' 254, 256–7.

120 Ibid.

121 William Bouwsma, 'Venice and the Political Education of Europe,' in John Hale, ed., *Renaissance Venice,* 445–66. See J.G.A. Pocock's thesis on Contarini as a model for American republicanism, *The Machiavellian Moment: Florentine Political Thought and the Atlantic Republican Tradition.*

122 William Empson refers to two levels. *The Structure of Complex Words,* 346–7; Angus Fletcher, *Allegory: The Theory of a Symbolic Mode,* 70.

123 Woodward, *Maps as Prints,* 93–100.

124 See chapter 3.

125 Cassini, *Piante,* 74n.1.

126 The numbers of impressions pulled from prints is difficult to determine as most printers produced only a few impressions from a plate at a given time and plates also circulated between printers. Nevertheless, drawing on Tempesti and Zonca, Woodward provides an extremely useful discussion of the criteria for gauging the number of possible impressions, the speed with which these could be generated, and costs. He estimates the break-even point for a standard *reale* print to 'fall between about 110 and 220 impressions' while 'a sufficient margin of profit would probably have had to be in the range of 250 to 300 impressions.' *Maps as Prints,* 52; see 47–52. The sur-

face area of Franco's prints is about 1.68 times that of Woodward's *reale* (402–413 × 522 compared with 295 × 434). If it took twelve minutes to ink a *reale*, it would have taken at least twenty minutes to ink the larger plate, limiting the number of prints per day to thirty from Tempesti's fifty. Also see Landau and Parshall, *Renaissance Print*, 30–2.

127 Furio de Denaro, *Domenico Tempesti e i discorsi sopra l'intaglio ed ogni sorte d'intagliare in rame da lui provate e osservate dai più grand'huomini di tale professione.*

128 'questa Venetia intagliata, ampliata, agionta et abbellita assai più di quante per l'addietro ve ne siano alla vista universale uscite.'

129 'Dico adunque che chi vuole intendere come si governi una Rep. ò egli è Cittadino & membro di tal Rep. ò egli è forestiero. S'egli è membro di tal Rep. di cinque cose, sopra lequali si consulta, bisogna che sia perito. Delle facultà della Città, cioè quali siano le sue entrate & spese. Della guerra & pace ... Del mondo del difendere & guardare il paese, cioè che armi & quanto ricerchi tale difensione. Et per intender questo, è necessario sapere il sito di quello, s'egli è pianura, ò montagna, copioso ò povero di fiumi, propinquo à lontano dal mare. Di quelle cose, che si portano fuori, & di quelle, che si recano dentro, per saper qual siano quelle, che mancono, & quelli, che abondano. Et finalmente della introduttione delle leggi ... Considerando io adunque che voi non siete membro della nostra Città, tal che voi possiate per voi stesso havere inteso la sua amministratione, innazi alle predette cose vi narrero particularment il nostro governo: dopo questo seguitero l'ordine sopradetto, trattando di ciascuna cosa quanto sara necessario.' Donato Giannotti, *Libro de la republica de Vinitiani*, 10v, 11. Myron Gilmore's synopsis, 'Myth and Reality in Venetian Political Theory,' in J.R. Hale, ed., *Renaissance Venice*, 435.

130 Woodward, *Maps as Prints*, 82–3. Federica Ambrosini, 'Descrittioni del Mondo,' 67–79.

131 Examples include Sebastian Münster, *Cosmographia universalis*; Leandro Alberti, *Descrittione di tutta Italia*; Giulio Ballino, *De' disegni delle piu illustri città, & fortezze del mondo parte I; la quale ne contiene cinquanta: Con una breve historia delle origini, & accidenti loro, secondo l'ordine de'tempi.* Textual collections include Francesco Sansovino's *Ritratto delle più nobili et famose città d'Italia, etc.*; Pietro Bertelli, *Teatro delle città d'Italia* and *Teatro urbium italicarum.*

132 Bordone, *Isolario di Benedetto Bordone*; Giovan Francesco Camocio, *Isole famose porti, fortezze*; Tommaso Porcacchi, *L'isole piu famose del mondo*; Simon Pinargenti, *Isole che son da Venetia* (Venice: 1563); *Isole che son da Venetia nella Dalmatia, et per tutto l'Archipelago, fino a Costantinopoli, con le loro fortezze, e con*

le terre più notabili di Dalmatia. Giuseppe Rosaccio, *Viaggio da Venetia*; Münster, *Cosmographia universalis.* On *Isolari,* see Conley, *Self-Made Map,* chap. 5.

133 'percioche questa maravigliosa Città piantata in mezo all'acque salse, per gran providentia di Dio ha fra'l mare, et le lagune, ove è posta, una lingua di terra, chiamata Lito, che la difende dalle impetuose onde del mare: et essendo formato a guisa d'un'arco; si distende per spatio di xxxv. miglia; in modo che la Città, o è serrata da terra ferma, o da questo Lito difesa. È nondimeno questo lito aperto in cinque luoghi, per dare entrata a'navili grossi & piccoli, che di fuora vengono, da potersi ridurre in porto, et ancho accioche gli stagni, ove la Città è piantata, si mantengano pieni d'acqua.' Porcacchi, *L'isole piu famose,* 65–6. The books appeared in numerous editions following their appearance in Venice in 1572.

134 Helgerson, *Forms of Nationhood,* 132.

135 See Conley, *Self-Made Map,* 330n.8.

136 This rare folio is 380 × 540 mm. The same compendium was included by Giacomo Franco in *La città di Venetia ... Estratte dall'opere di G. N. Doglioni. Parte seconda.* Also see the Antonio Turini edition: Venice, 1614.

137 'La Città di Venetia, Con l'Origine, & governo di quella, Et i Dogi che visono stati, & tutte le cose notabili, che di tempo in tempo vi sono avvenute dal principio della sua edificatione fino à questi tempi, così accommodata.'

138 De Certeau, *Everyday Life,* 24. Woodward, *Maps as Prints,* 92. Conley, *Self-Made Map,* 334n.11. On charts and the interiorization of print, see Walter Ong, *Orality and Literacy,* 101.

139 'A'LETTORI PErche possa ciascuno, & speciamente i Nobili di questa Città (a cui tocca ben spesso di doverne discorrere nelle loro consulte) raccordarsi con poca fatica delle molte notabili imprese de'Vinitiani, hò io fatto la presente operina; nella quale v'arriccordo, che quei numeri della parte senistra delle linee, sono gli anni correnti di Christo, & ove in cambio di quelli si vede una linea, ha relatione all'anno sopraposto; che nel resto ogni cosa vi è chiara, & però non accade dirne altro. Iddio vi feliciti.'

140 Bonora discusses the practice of formulating and expressing opinions among Venetians and the related research that was required. She lists the kinds of information collected by Sansovino, which included government documents and, from his printing business, 'compendi storici, genealogie di famiglie illustri, raccolte di orazioni e di massime politiche, racconti di battaglie di autori antichi e moderni, descrizione dei costumi e della storia di altri popoli, trattati politici.' *Ricerche su Francesco Sansovino,* 147–8.

141 Anna Omodeo had the same impression. *Mostra di stampe popolari Venete del '500,* 37.

142 In Luca Contile, *Ragionamento sopra la proprietà della imprese.*

143 'Ecco ... il disegno della maravigliosa Città di Venetia in forma Sferica,

apunto vero ritratto del Mondo, la qual simiglianza è tanto dalla natura, & Arte fatta, simile a tutto l'Orbe della terra, che chi ben mira detto disegno, scuopre in un'alzare di ciglia il Polo Artico, & l'Antartico insieme. ove si vede anco il Levante, & Ponente, con tutte le altri parti ch'in esso Mondo concorrono, circondata parimenti dall'Acqua in maniera che ben pare il continente tutto circondato dal gran mar'Oceano. Qual è quel dunque si privo della cognitione di Cosmografia, che non sappia il mondo tutto primieramente esser partito in tre parti, cioè, Europa, Africa, & Asia; le qual parti tutte in un continente sono comprese, in maniera apunto, come è questa nobilissima Città; Sanno senza dubio i Geografi che fuori del nostro contenuto, è l'America. Si vede anco fuori del corpo contenuto di Venetia esser la Giudecca, in guisa che risembra il nuovo mondo; le Isole, & Penisole con li scogli, & secche, ogn'un che mirerà il disegno vedrà il tutto corrispondere alla vera similitudine del Mappamondo, come è detto; Potrei ancora dire che le contrade fossero tante in numero, quante sono le Provincie del mondo; mà perche haveva animo di far'un disegno maggiore di quello che è questo, & locar tutto sotto al suo Clima, & grado, sì in longhezza, come in larghezza, con la forma di tutta la machina mondiale.' *Habiti delle donne venetiane intagliate in rame nuovamente da Giacomo Franco*, dedication to Il Sig. Fabio Glisenti. On the privilege, see 292–3n.3.

144 'Era all'hora lo stato della Republica in apparente confidenza con tutti i Prencipi et con tutti si può dire in aperta amicitia et oltre ciò abondante di tutte le cose, le quali la fertilità del paese, l'industria degl'huomini et l'opportunità del sito suole apportare ne governi ben regolati ... Il commercio mercantile ... per ogni parte confluiva, tanto che si rendeva la città in traffico a qualunque altro luoco ... pur al presente si considerava forsi maggiore che in altri tempi si fusse stata.' Nicolò Contarini in Gaetano Cozzi, *Il Doge Nicolò Contarini. Ricerche sul patriziato veneziano agli inizi del Seicento*, 311–12; Domenico Sella's translation. 'Crisis and Transformation in Venetian Trade,' in *Crisis and Change in the Venetian Economy in the Sixteenth and Seventeenth Centuries*, ed. Brian Pullan, 88. Also see Alberto Tenenti, *Piracy and the Decline of Venice: 1580–1615*, trans. J. and B. Pullan.

145 Sella's translations, 'Crisis and Transformation,' 93, 94 from ASV S. Mr., reg. 141, 15 July 1602 and ASV Arte della Seta, busta 109/203, 8 August 1608.

146 Sella, 'Crisis and Transformation,' 88–96.

2 Costume and the Boundaries of Bodies

1 'Domenica mattina, che fu il seguente giorno, sua Maestà comparse poi in pubblico vestita tutta di pavonazzo, (ch'è il suo duolo) di saietta di Fiandra, con berretta in testa all'italiana col suo velo, et uno ferraiuolo lungo per

insino a'piedi, giuppone tagliato, calze, colletto di cuoio del medesimo con una gran ninfa di camicia molto ben acconcia, guanti profumati in mano, et in piedi scarpe e pianelle a usanza francese, e così è andata sempre pubblicamente mentre che ha dimorato qua. È giovine di 23 anni, di statura grande, di delicata persona, e di aspetto grave, stando con molta maestà, et ha un poco di barba nera.' Marsilio della Croce, in Davide Rampello, ed., *700 anni di costume nel Veneto: Documenti di vita civile dal XII al XVIII secolo*, 114.

2 For an example of earlier costume illustrations, see Albrecht Dürer, *Trachten-bilder ... aus der Albertina*. On interpreting appearances, see Maria Giuseppina Muzzarelli, *Gli inganni delle apparenze: Disciplina di vesti e ornamenti alla fine del medioevo.*

3 (1) Enea Vico, *Diversarum gentium aetatis habitus.* Vico, whose costume illustrations are usually identified as single sheets (1540–60), applied for a ten-year copyright to the Venetian senate in 1557 for 'li Libri della diversite degli habiti de diverse nationi del mondo.' BMV, IT VII 2500 (12077), Schedario di Horatio F. Brown, Privilegi Veneziani per la stampa, 1557 29 August (368). M.A. Ghering van Ierlant notes an edition of Vico's 1558 publication with twenty-eight engravings. *Mode in Prent (1550–1914).* There is also a record of an edition with seventy plates. The senate copyright indicates that Vico's publication was earlier than François Deserp's *Recueil de la diversité des habits qui sont de present en usaige tant es pays d'Europe, Asie, Affrique et Iles sauvaiges,* the collection usually referred to as the first costume book. Vico's engravings of seventy Spanish costumes and twenty-nine from other countries were used as sources for many subsequent costume illustrators. Giorgio Vasari refers to Vico's costumes in his brief discussion of printmaking: 'Disegnò anco Enea, a commune sodisfazione, et utile degli huomini, cinquanta abiti di diverse nazioni; cioè, come costumano di vestire in Italia, in Francia, in Ispagna, in Portogallo, in Inghilterra, in Fiandra, ed in altre parti del mondo, così gli huomini come le donne, e così i contadini, come i cittadini; il che fu cosa d'ingegno e bella e capricciosa.' *Le opere di Giorgio Vasari* [Facs. repr. of the 1906 ed. with the title: Le vite de' più eccellenti pittori ...], vol. V, 429. Although Vasari does not describe a book, the number of fifty suggests the illustrations circulated as a bound collection before Ferdinando Bertelli reproduced sixty of Vico's plates in 1563. (2) According to Olian, Donato Bertelli, *Le vere imagini et descritioni delle più nobilli città del mondo,* is a collection of city maps that incorporated all of the costumes published in 1563 by Ferdinando Bertelli. Jo Anne Olian, 'Sixteenth-Century Costume-Books,' 24. (3) Ferdinando Bertelli, *Omnium fere gentium nostrae aetatis habitus, nunquam ante hac aediti.* Ferdinando reproduced sixty

of Vico's costumes for this book. (4) Pietro Bertelli, *Diversaru[m] nationum habitus.* (5) Alessandro de Fabri, *Diversarum nationum ornatus.* (6) Cesare Vecellio, *De gli habiti antichi, et moderni di diverse parti del mondo.* (7) Vecellio, *Habiti antichi et moderni di tutto il mondo;* (8) Giacomo Franco, *Habiti d'huomeni et donne venetiane.* (9) Franco, *Habiti delle donne venetiane.* Franco requested a copyright for twenty years from the Senato Terra on 16 November 1591; however the *filza* includes Giacomo Franco among those supplicants who were not conceded privileges for 'delle habiti alla venetiana intagliato da lui.' ASV, Senato. *Terra,* 868; filza 121. Thus, Franco must have conceived of the series well before their publication in 1609, although probably not as early as 1570, as Anna Omodeo suggests, Catalogue ed. *Mostra Di Stampe Popolari Venete del '500,* 37. On 8 October 1609, he was granted a privilege for 'Habiti de huomeni, et Donne Venetiane, con la processione della S. N. et altri particolari, cioè tronfi, feste, et cerimonie publiche di questa città da lui intagliati, et fatti intagliar in Rame.' ASV, Senato. *Terra,* 77/1/8, Reg. 79, 95.

4 '[È] da infinita moltitudine di gente habitata, che vi concorre da varie nationi, anzi di tutto il mondo, ad essercitarvi la mercantia. Usanvisi tutti i linguaggi; & vestevisi in diverse maniere; havvisi d'ogni cose.' Giulio Ballino, *De' disegni delle piu illustri città, & fortezze del mondo parte I.*

5 'Percioche cominciando da gli habiti, indicativi dell'humore delle persone, noi vediamo che gran parte de gli Italiani, dimenticatisi di esser nati in Italia, & seguendo le fattioni oltramontane, hanno co pensieri mutato lo habito della persona, volendo parere quando Francesi, & quando Spagnuoli. Et certo con danno, & vergogna loro, & con manifesto segno della loro poca stabilità & fermezza, poi che non si è mantenuto mai, da quegli huomini che altre volte hanno signoreggiato l'altre nationi del mondo, un perpetuo & saldo tenore nelle cose loro. Sola questa città s'è conservata in generale meno corrotta fra tante, se bene in ogni tempo è stata, & è tuttavia rifugio de i forestieri, i quali sogliono introdurre in casa altrui l'usanze loro.' Francesco Sansovino, *Venetia città nobilissima,* 150v–151. The pagination of the edition is confused; the citation should be 146v–47.

6 Francesco Sansovino, *Delle cose notabili che sono in Venetia libri due. etc.,* 2–3v. Also see Thomas Coryate, *Coryats Crudities,* 258–9; Pietro Casola, *Canon Pietro Casola's Pilgrimage to Jerusalem in the Year 1494,* trans. M. Margaret Newett, 143; Stella Mary Newton, *The Dress of the Venetians. 1495–1525,* 9–11.

7 'Ma talhora quella licenza è cresciuta in tanto estremo grado, che a nostri Senatori è convenuto por freno a cosi sfrenate volontà con le leggi.' Sansovino, *Delle cose notabili,* 4r.

8 'dannate inventioni' in Giulio Bistort, *Il magistrato alle pompe nella repubblica di*

Venezia; studio storico, 149–50. Men's fashions were not excluded from such concerns, as evidenced by legislation prompted by war with the League of Cambrai. However, for the rest of the sixteenth century, it was the vicissitudes of women's dress that preoccupied the legislators. Provveditore alle Pompe. Capitolari 1–11 (1488–1683). Also on sumptuary laws: Maria Giuseppina Muzzarelli, *Gli inganni delle apparenze;* Alan Hunt, *Governance of the Consuming Passions: A History of Sumptuary Law;* Mary Margaret Newett, 'The Sumptuary Laws of Venice in the Fourteenth and Fifteenth Centuries,' in T.F. Tout and James Tait, eds, *Historical Essays First Published in 1902 in Commemoration of the Jubilee of the Owens College Manchester;* Pierogiovanni Mometto, 'Vizi privati, pubbliche virtù aspetti e problemi della questione del lusso nella Repubblica di Venezia (secolo XVI),' in Luigi Beringuer and Floriana Colao, eds, *Crimine, giustiza e società veneta in età moderna;* Brown, 'Behind the Walls,' esp. 319–29; Diane Owen Hughes, 'Sumptuary Law.'

9   The chronicler blames the 'voracious teeth' of luxury: '[I]l dente vorace'; 'doppo haver'avidamente abbracciato i vitii de forestieri … perchè sono rari coloro, i quali siano contenti della sorte, nelle quale son nati.' BMV, IT VII (9110); Misc. 72, 74, 79.

10 J.R. Hale, *Civilization of Europe in the Renaissance*, 20.

11 See 289n.131.

12 Karl Küp, 'Some Early Costume Books,' in *Costume, Gothic & Renaissance*, 3–9.

13 Abraham de Bruyn's *Omnium poene gentium imagines* consists of fifty folded oblong folio plates with 206 engraved figures. There are four to five full-page figures per sheet, each identified by a Latin caption. The series was printed by I. Rutus and published by Hadrian Damman, who wrote the introductory Latin text. This text was dropped and the number of costumes expanded in de Bruyn's *Omnium pene Europae*. The series has sixty-one oblong folio plates with 398 costumes. A single page of introductory text is printed in Latin, French, and German with the captions of the figures similarly translated. This publication also incorporated figures from de Bruyn's 1578 *Imperii ac sacerdotii ornatus* (Cologne). Many of de Bruyn's figures serve as sources for Jean-Jacques Boissard's engravings. *Habitus variarum orbis gentium.*

14 Sir Thomas Elyot, *The Book Named the Governor*, 37v.

15 The manuscript, now published in a facsimile, was linked to Milan by Fritz Saxl in his essay 'Costumes and Festivals of Milanese Society under Spanish Rule,' *Proceedings of the British Academy*, 400–56ff. Saxl's article is reprinted in the facsimile *A Tailor's Book*.

16 All twenty-eight figures of the sheet were copied by Alessandro Fabri in the third book of his costume series, which were published together in Padua in 1593. Although Fabri's prints are usually described as copies of Pietro Ber-

telli's costumes, none of these was reproduced by Pietro.

17 Kaja Silverman, *The Threshold of the Visible World*, 24; also see 36–7. Also see Jacques Lacan, 'The Mirror-Phase as Formative of the Function of the I,' in Slavoj Žižek, ed., *Mapping Ideology*, 93–9; Peter Dews, 'Adorno, Post-Structuralism and the Critique of Identity,' in Žižek, ed., *Mapping Ideology*, 48–9.

18 '[L]a demeurance n'est point terminée en l'estroicte closture d'une maison, d'une ville, ou d'un païs natal: mais luy est estendüe & descouverte par toutes les terres habitables & mers navigable.' 'Tous lesquelz selon leurs diverse especes, sont confinez, & limitez en particuliers elemens propres & naturels à eux ... Ce que faict un grand argument & tesmoignage que l'homme est le seul animant pour lequel tout le monde est faict, & qui par sa raison iuge & estime l'univers monde inferieur estre son Empire, son Royaume, sa citè, voire sa maison quand à la vie presente, le Ciel espere pour la future. D'ond le sage philosophe moral interrogué de quel païs il etoit, respondit estre Cosmopolite, c'est à dire citoyen du monde.' Nicolas de Nicolay, *Les quatre premiers livres des navigations et pérégrinations orientales*, preface.

19 Andrew Wheatcroft, *The Ottomans*, 39.

20 For example see the edition of Nicolay's *Les quatre premiers livres* that was prepared for Queen Elizabeth, and is now in the British Library, London.

21 On slaves and ethnicity see Iris Origo, who states that 'between 1414 and 1423 no less than 10,000 slaves were sold upon the Venetian market alone,' 'The Domestic Enemy: The Eastern Slaves in Tuscany in the Fourteenth and Fifteenth Centuries,' 329; Robert Smith, 'In Search of Carpaccio's African Gondolier'; see the images published in Hans-Joachim Kunst, *The African in European Art*. For further sources on images see Paul Kaplan, 'Veronese's Images of Foreigners,' in Massimo Gemin, ed., *Nuovi studi su Paolo Veronese*. Dennis Romano refers to Isabella d'Este's correspondence with a Venetian agent to obtain a 'little Moor' [moretta], 'as black as possible' [più negra che possibile]. *Housecraft and Statecraft: Domestic Service in Renaissance Venice, 1400–1600*, 119; Winthrop Jordan, *White over Black: American Attitudes toward the Negro 1550–1812*; Eldred Jones, *Othello's Countrymen: The African in English Renaissance Drama*.

22 For a summary of theories regarding the causes of skin colour, see Giuseppe Rosaccio, who eventually argues in favour of food: 'Onde, anche io confermando l'istessa ragione (per l'esperienza) dico ciò avvenire, della conformità de cibi, e perciò hanno i popoli Scrifini, Careli, Lappi, Piermi, & Biarmi, l'istessa sembianza, si come hanno parimente quelli della Verginia, Florida, Isole Canarie, Regno di Cogno, China, Maluche, & Isola del Giapon, con altre Isole ... Ma se noi vorremo rassigurar l'Italiano, ci trovaremo tanta

differenza, che non si potrà scorgere in lui regola universale di vera cognitione, come si farà nell'altre nationi' (48). *Il microcosmo*, 46–8. Peter Heylyn argued against this 'foolish supposition' when he reflected on the evidence posed by the New World: 'The inhabitants (though a great part of this Country lieth in the same paralell with *Ethiopia, Lybia,* and *Numidia*) are of a reasonable faire complexion, and very little (if at all) inclining to blacknesse. So that the extraordinary and continuall vicinity of the Sunne, is not as some imagine the operative cause of blacknese: though it may much further such a colour, as we see in our country lasses ... Others more wise in their owne conceit ... plainely conclude the generative feed of the *Africans* to bee blacke; but of the *Americans* to bee white; a foolish supposition, and convinced not only out of experience, but naturall Philosophie. So that wee must wholy ascribe it to Gods peculiar will and ordinance' (403). In Paolo Paruta's *Della perfettione della vita politica,* his interlocutor Michele Surian argues against climate as a cause of differences. *Opere politiche,* 1: 80–1; William Bouwsma, *Venice and the Defense of Republican Liberty,* 213.

23 *The New Shorter Oxford English Dictionary on Historical Principles,* 2458.

24 'Du peuple de Dieu issu d'une si bonne race & saincte semence des Patriarches, l'escriture impute la corruption, & depravation à la hantise & conversation avec les nations estrangeres. *Et commixti sunt inter gentes, & didicerunt opera eorum,* dit David, psal. 105. Et de vray, comme dit Platon livre 5. de legib. *Eum qui se improbis commiscuit, necesse est eadem pati. & agere quae tales agere & loqui inter se consueuerunt.* Comment sont auiourd'huy tous les pays & nations tant forlignees de leur candeur & sincerité premiere, sinon par un semblable meslange avec les estrangers? & nostre pays d'où vient il tant esloigné de sa premiere rondeur, que non seulement comme un Prothee il change tous les iours, se bigarre & metamorfose en ses habits, moeurs, langages, façons de faire; mais encor en ses ieux, plaisirs, voluptés, delices, vices, imite les nations plus dissolues? la response est preste: *Commixti sunt, & didicerunt opera corum.*' Jean de Glen, *Des habits,* np. but 1v.

25 See Origo's discussion on the appearance of slaves, 'The Domestic Enemy,' esp. 337. Wolfgang Neuber, 'The "Red Indian's" Body: The Physiognomy of the Indigenous American between Exoticism and Learned Culture in the Early Modern Period,' and Sonia V. Rose, ' "The Great Moctezuma," ' in Karl Enenkel et al., eds, *Modelling the Individual: Biography and Portrait in the Renaissance,* 109–32; Anthony Pagden, *European Encounters with the New World: From Renaissance to Romanticism.*

26 Hans Weigel and Jost Amman, *Habitus praecipuorum populorum.*

27 Theodor de Bry, *Admiranda narratio.*

28 The historical development of clothing – from Adam and Eve, to the Egyp-

tians, Romans, and moderns – is a common theme in costume books. See
the introductions in Hans Weigel, *Habitus praecipuorum populorum*; Vecellio,
De gli habiti (1590); de Glen, *Des habits, moeurs, ceremonies.*

29 In contrast to the ease with which missionaries converted inhabitants of the
New World, according to Cosimo Filiarchi, Muslims were tenacious followers
of their faith. *Trattato della gverra, et dell'vnione de'principi Christiani contra i
Turchi, & gli altri infedeli.* On predictions for the end of Mohammedanism,
when Muslims would be converted with the American Indians, see Marin
Sanuto, *Diari XXIII* coll. 154–5; Paolo Preto, *Venezia e i Turchi*, 71.

30 On the exactly reproducible statement see Williams M. Ivins, *Prints and
Visual Communication.*

31 Vecellio, *De gli habiti* (1590), 124v and 125v.

32 Coryat, *Coryats Crudities*, 261.

33 Casola, *Canon Pietro Casola's Pilgrimage*, 145.

34 The manuscript (Rome, Istituto Nazionale della Grafica, inv. no. F.N. 2818–
2833) is catalogue number 35 in Robert Scheller, *Exemplum: Model-Book Drawings and the Practice of Artistic Transmission in the Middle Ages (ca. 900–ca. 1470).*

35 'Plusiers savants personnages se sont employez à curieusement recercher &
descrire la situation des quatre principales parties du Monde, avec l'origine,
moeurs & conditions des peuples qui y sont: de sorte qu'ils ont donné con-
tentement singulier auz bon esprits & amateurs de science en ceste part. Res-
toit de representer au vray la forme & façons diverses de leurs vestements: ce
que i'ay tasché de faire le plus fidelement qu'il mea esté possible, ayant
recouvré par le moyen de quelques miens amis certaines figures rares & non
encores cognues par l'art de graveure ou d'Imprimerie.' De Bruyn, *Omnium
pene Europae*, 1581, preface.

36 Jacopo Ligozzi is another example of an artist who designed costume and scientific illustrations. With Medici patronage, he painted specimens of vegetation, fish, and birds in a technique characteristic of his slightly earlier
costume studies. See Gabinetto disegni e stampe degli Uffizi, *L'incisione
Bolognese nel secolo XVII.*

37 See David Landau and Peter Parshall on the status of botanical illustration as
'a kind of index or benchmark for the truthful imitation of nature in general.' *The Renaissance Print*, 245–59, esp. 256.

38 Ibid., 258.

39 Otto Brunfels, *Herbarum vivae eicones ad natura imitationem.*

40 Landau and Parshall, *Renaissance Print*, 252–3.

41 Leonhard Fuchs, *De historia stirpium commentarii insignes.*

42 Andrea Cesalpino, *De plantis libri XVI.* A.G. Morton, *History of Botanical Science*, 130, 132–41, 144–6.

43 See Juan Luis Vives's three books 'On Unmarried Young Women,' 'On Married Women,' and 'On Widows,' in *De institutione feminae Christianae* in C. Fantazzi and C. Matheeussen, eds, *Selected works of J.L. Vives*, vols. I (1996) and II (1998).

44 Vecellio, *Habiti antichi et moderni* (1598), 111.

45 Cited in Ian Maclean, *The Renaissance Notion of Woman*, 12. Also see Thomas Laqueur, *Making Sex: Body and Gender from the Greeks to Freud*.

46 'la formatione non è fatta dall'anima del padre, ò della madre, ma di un' altra terza che si trova, dentro al seme; e questa per esser vegetiva, e non più, non è capace d'imaginativa sino al tempo dovuto, da noi detto, ma solo segue i movimenti vegetabili, e naturali del temperamento, per ridurre al temperamento naturale gl'istromenti de'sensi, & non fa altro, se non conservar la sua specie.' Rosaccio, *Il microcosmo*, 46–7.

47 For example, see Giovanni Battista Della Porta, *Phytognomonica octo libris contenta*.

48 See Peter Parshall's discussion of the famous copyright case made against Christian Egenolff by Hans Weiditz in '*Imago contrafacta*: Images and Facts in the Northern Renaissance.'

49 See Boissard's address to his readers in *Habitus variarum orbis gentium*.

50 Landau and Parshall, *Renaissance Print*, 258.

51 BLL, Egerton 1215: Andrea Alciato, *Diverse imprese accommodate a diverse moralità*. This book was used as an album by Thobias Windt of Augsburg. It contains signatures dated from 1591–1604.

52 Leon Battista Alberti, *On Painting*, esp. 92–3 and 133–4fn.8.

53 On the frame and the locus of moral good, see Jacques Derrida on Immanuel Kant, *The Truth in Painting*, 114; Kant, *The Critique of Judgement*.

54 R.A. Skelton in Braun and Hogenberg, *Civitates*, xiii.

55 The only known copy of the engraving is at the Bibliothèque nationale in Paris. More influential was Magini's map of Italy, which was published in 1608, before Rosaccio's map was circulated by his son. The map by Magini, who had access to official maps, was more up-to-date than Rosaccio's. See Roberto Almagià, *Monumenta Italiae cartographica. Riproduzioni di carte generale e regionali d'Italia dal secolo XIV al XVII*.

56 See 289n.131.

57 *Dizionario della lingua italiana*, 9.

58 Ibid., 610.

59 J.C. Flugel, *The Psychology of Clothes*, pointed to the dramatic shift from the corset, with its elaborately profiled female breasts, to the emphasis on women's legs in flapper dresses in the early twentieth century.

60 Derrida, *Truth in Painting*, 114.

61 *Album amicorum habitibus mulierum omnium nationum Europae.*

62 The first extant album appeared in 1554, although one example has a signature that is dated 1548. Max Rosenheim, 'The Album Amicorum,' 252–3. Also see Hans Bots and Giel Van Gemert with Peter Rietbergen eds, *L'album amicorum de Cornelis de Glarges 1599–1683*, viii.

63 Rosenheim, 'The Album Amicorum,' 259.

64 In the seventeenth century, the Netherlands succeeded Germany in this regard and thus generated more albums including some that were owned by women; one of the earliest of these dates from 1595–8. M.A.E. Nickson, *Early Autograph Albums in the British Museum*, 20–1.

65 Melanchthon's *Loci communes theologici* was used in 1542 by the owner of earliest known album. Alciati's collection of emblems grew from 104 when first published in Augsburg in 1531 to 200 emblems by its 130th edition at the end of the century. The *Emblemata* was especially popular from 1557 to 1635; the emblems were sometimes used by signatories to embellish their comments. Nickson, *Early Autograph Albums*, 9n.1, 12, 13. Also see Rosenheim, 'The Album Amicorum,' 259.

66 Rosenheim, 'The Album Amicorum,' 253.

67 Bots, Van Gemert, and Rietbergen, eds, *L'album amicorum*, vii.

68 For example, see Sigmund Feyerabend, *Wapen und Stammbuch darinnen der Keys; Kunst- und Lehrbüchlein*. See Ilse O'Dell, 'Jost Amman and the Album Amicorum. Drawings after Prints in Autograph Albums,' 31–6.

69 Bots, Van Gemert, and Rietbergen, eds, *L'album amicorum*, vii, ix.

70 Ibid., xiii.

71 Ibid., xiv.

72 Ibid., viii, ix, xix. On misogyny in emblem books in general, and the feminist emblem book of Georgette de Montenay, see Sara F. Matthews Grieco, 'Georgette de Montenay: A Different Voice in Sixteenth-Century Emblematics.'

73 Bots, Van Gemert, and Rietbergen eds, *L'album amicorum*, xi.

74 Ibid.

75 See Nickson, *Early Autograph Albums*, 9–10.

76 Rosenheim, 'The Album Amicorum,' 258. Jean Jacques Boissard produced a book of emblems in 1593: *Emblematum liber. Ipsa Emblemata*. Published in Frankfurt am Main, his designs were engraved by Theador de Bry.

77 Bots et al., eds., *L'album amicorum*, xi.

78 Sigmund Feyerabend, *Stam- oder Gesellenbuch*, preface. Cited in O'Dell, 'Jost Amman and the Album Amicorum,' 31. Translation by Vera Kaden and Dr Kurt Ostberg.

79 BLL Egerton 1196, *Bibliorum utriusque testamenti icones.*

80 Margaret Rosenthal, 'Fashion and Identity in the Venetian Republic: Foreign

Travelers and Their Illustrated Costume Albums in the Late Sixteenth Century.'

81 Landau and Parshall, *Renaissance Print*, 259. Also see Parshall, '*Imago contrafacta*'; Claudia Swan, '*Ad vivum, near het leven*, from the Life: Defining a Mode of Representation.'

82 For earlier printed images of the dogaressa, see Boissard, *Habitus variarum orbis gentium*; de Bruyn, *Omnium poene Europae.*

83 'Io non trovo, che in tanti secoli, veruna delle Principesse passate habbia lasciatoci memoria dell'Habito suo. Credo nondimeno, che l'Habito loro fosse simile à quelli, de'quali s'è già fatto mentione, che usavano le Matrone antiche.' Vecellio, *De gli habiti* (1590), 80. In keeping with the historical thrust of this first edition, Vecellio lists the three last *dogaresse* and their husbands by name, highlighting the role of the dogaressa as the consort of the doge.

84 According to Ernesto Masi, the dogaressa was the 'simbolo femminile della virtù domestica.' Cited in Pompeo Molmenti, *La dogaressa di Venezia*, 9. On the *dogaresse*, see Holly Hurlburt's forthcoming book *Dogaresse of Venice, 1200–1500: Wives and Icons.*

85 Margaret F. Rosenthal, *The Honest Courtesan: Veronica Franco. Citizen and Writer in Sixteenth-Century Venice*, 2.

86 On politics, toleration, liberty, and licentiousness, see Willliam Bouwsma, 'Venice and the Political Education of Europe,' in John Hale, ed., *Renaissance Venice*, esp. 461. Also see Massimo Gemin, 'Le cortigiane di Venezia e i viaggiatori stranieri,' in Alfiero Bruno, ed., *Il gioco dell'amore*, 73, 79.

87 See the early seventeenth-century album of Moysis Walens. BLL Additional 18991.

88 Rosenheim traced more than fifty document illuminators and woodcutters in Nuremberg between 1550 and 1600, some of whose marks appear in the albums. 'The Album Amicorum,' 259. On the uses of models see R.W. Scheller, *A Survey of Medieval Model Books*; O'Dell, 'Jost Amman and the Album Amicorum.'

89 Codice Bottacin, Museo Bottacin 970 (1614). Ludovico Zorzi, 'Costumi e scene italiani: Il codice Bottacin di Padova,' in *Storia d'Italia. Volume secondo. Dalla caduta dell'Impero romano al secolo XVIII:* 2, n.p. but between 1466 and 1467.

90 Resemblances between many of these illustrations attest to the practice of copying after models and even the production of replicas of entire series by the same artist for sale to foreigners. Belkin was advised that 'the drawings were probably sold to European visitors without any caption ... These were added later after consulting with someone who was able to supply such infor-

mation.' Belkin, *Corpus Rubenianum*, 155–6n.6. Belkin publishes examples from collections in the L.A. Mayer Memorial (Jerusalem), the Veste collection in Coburg, the Castille illustrations (BN, Paris), and those of Lambert de Vos (Staatsbibliothek Brennen). In Venice, see the manuscript *Foggie diverse del vestire de'Turchi* BMV, IT IV 491 (5578).

91 Sigmundt Heldt (Helt, Held) the younger (1528–87, Nuremberg) names himself as the author in the foreword. The illustrations include numerous examples of religious attire, emperors, tournaments, German cities, and landscapes. The costumes present eleven Venetians; twenty-two Turks; fifty-seven Poles, Russians, Greeks, and Spanish Muslims; thirty Africans and North Americans; and seventeen examples from Spain. Nuremberg merits 101 illustrations and these include representations of trades and popular festivities. The codex concludes with sixty-seven views of peasant life. Theodore Hampe, in Christopher Weiditz, *Authentic Everyday Dress of the Renaissance.* Hampe notes that Feyerabend was a colleague of Heldt and praises the artist in Jost Amman's *Wapen und Stammbuch darinnen der Keys*; Berlin, Miscellaneous Institutions Staatliche Museen, *Katalog der Lipperheideschen Kostümbibliothek*, revised by Eva Nienholdt and Gretel Wagner-Neumann, 2 vols, Aa 1.1.

92 Weiditz, *Authentic Everyday Dress.* On illustrations of travel, see Giuliano Luchetta, 'Viaggiatori e racconti de viaggi nel cinquecento,' in *Storia della cultura Veneta: Dal primo quattrocento al Concilio di Trento II*, 435–9.

93 According to Hampe, both pictorial and literary examples were probably used as sources for the artists. In Weiditz, *Authentic Everyday Dress*, 10, 22–3.

94 The original has 154 cardboard-like pages, each about 150 mm in width and painted on one side with costumes from Spain, the Netherlands, Italy, France, Germany, England, Ireland, and Portugal. The cards were bound together and trimmed in the eighteenth century evidently in no particular order. Hampe attributes the paintings to Weiditz, a goldsmith, on the basis of their similarity to prints and the artist's visits to Spain in 1529 and to the Netherlands the following year. Further, his name accompanies a representation of the artist as a sea traveller seen on page 78 (plate I) of the facsimile (the order of the pictures in the facsimile is Hampe's). The painter's name was probably included by a professional scribe, who seems to have copied Weiditz's earlier notes onto the pages some twenty years later. Of particular interest is Hampe's assertion that the woodcut character of the paintings indicates the artist's intent to reproduce them in a book format.

Christopher Weiditz (ca. 1500–59), probably born in Strasbourg to the woodcarver Johann, was the younger brother of the draftsman and form-cutter Hans Weiditz. The woodcuts of the latter, with those of Israhel van Meck enem and Hans Burgkmair, would later be the chief sources for German attire in Ruben's costume book (Belkin, *Corpus Rubenianum*, 34). A sculptor and goldsmith, Christopher produced numerous portrait medals in Augsburg and then returned to Strasbourg in 1557, when he began to produce small folio woodcuts for a genealogy edition. These prints depict members of local elite families as types instead of portraits. Their profile format follows the conventions of portrait medals, a format that has also been compared to that used by Weiditz in his costume codex (Hampe, in Christopher Weiditz, *Authentic Everyday Dress of the Renaissance*, 17). He worked on another manuscript costume book ('Memmorjbuch der Klaytung vnnd der visirung zum Himel vun zum Fennlein,' 1542) with Paul Hector Mair, a blockcutter whose graphic style is similar to that of Weiditz.

Although there are no extant models for the costumes, the artist's use of pictorial and literary sources can be assumed on the basis of similarities to the Heldt manuscript (5–10, 23). Possible sources for the drawings include woodcuts of figures from the New World that were produced in light of the Vespucci letters that circulated in print from 1503. In Hampe's comparison of the Heldt illustrations with those of Weiditz, it is the latter that appears to be closer to the likely prototype and may in turn have provided sources for Heldt. Some figures are copied after Vico's engravings.

95 Rosenheim, 'The Album Amicorum,' 259–60.

96 Boureau is concerned with emblem books produced between 1580 and 1640. Alain Boureau, 'Books of Emblems on the Public State: *Côté jardin* and *côté cour*,' in Roger Chartier, ed., *The Culture of Print: Power and the Uses of Print in Early Modern Europe*, 266, and n. 17.

97 Ibid., 266.

98 BLL, Egerton 1201, Album amicorum of Hieronymi Holtzschuher from Nuremberg, 30.

99 See Angus Fletcher on the changing of personalities into allegories, *Allegory: The Theory of a Symbolic Mode*, 26–8.

100 On the 'doctrine of signatures,' see 207.

101 Hans Weigel and Jost Amman, *Habitus praecipuorum populorum*; Jost Amman, *Im Frauwenzimmer*; Jean-Baptiste Zangrius(?), *Album amicorum*; Franco, *Habiti delle donne venetiane*.

102 The etching is cat. no. 114 in Michael Bury, *The Print in Italy 1550–1620*, 166.

103 Zangrius, *Album amicorum*.

104 For full citation see 268n.6.

105 On the distinction between internal faith and external appearances, see John Martin, 'Spiritual Journeys and the Fashioning of Religious Identity in Renaissance Venice.' On the uses of dissimulation particularly with regard

to religious identity, see Perez Zagorin, *Ways of Lying: Dissimulation, Persecution, and Conformity in Early Modern Europe.*

106 With peace in March 1573 after the battle of Lepanto, there were growing numbers of Turkish businessmen in Venice. Preto, *Venezia e i Turchi,* 126–33. Concerns were raised over the presence of Turks throughout the city and complaints made that they were stealing and using Christian women. The Turks had themselves pressed for a Fondaco of their own, and with the increasing population of Muslims, the senate began to consider the idea. According to Preto, there was an *albergo* that responded to these needs by August 1579. Complaints that '*alloggiano rubbati et assassinati*' indicate the residence was as much for their own protection as for Christians (ibid., 130).

107 Randolph C. Head, 'Religious Boundaries and the Inquisition in Venice,' 202.

108 Ibid., 203.

109 Ibid., 178. Zagorin, *Ways of Lying,* esp. 13. On the Morescos, see 41n.5.

110 Head, 'Religious Boundaries,' 178, 175. Cases regarding Protestantism (58 per cent) far outnumbered those against Judaizing (2.7 per cent) in the years 1547–85 (ibid., 181). On the Inquisition in Venice, see John Martin, *Venice's Hidden Enemies: Italian Heretics in a Renaissance City.*

111 See Benjamin Ravid, 'From Yellow to Red: On the Distinguishing Head-Covering of the Jews of Venice,' 179, 187.

112 Ibid., 195, 187.

113 Brian Pullan, '"A Ship with Two Rudders": "Righetto Marrano" and the Inquisition in Venice.'

114 Head, 'Religious boundaries,' 190.

115 Ibid., 177.

116 Ibid., 194.

117 Ibid., 194; also see 194–5 and n. 58.

118 Ibid., 201–2.

119 In a trial discussed later in the chapter, Bartolomeo's testimony about his life as a Muslim had required some complicated explanations, including a substitute child for his circumcision. A *converso* would have been circumcised at birth before any forced or voluntary conversion to Christianity, and physical inspections were not always conclusive. In any event, more weight was placed on baptism. See Head, 'Religious Boundaries,' 192, 201. On the parallel between women's earrings and circumcision, see Diane Owen Hughes, 'Distinguishing Signs: Ear-Rings, Jews and Franciscan Rhetoric in the Italian Renaissance City,' 3–59, esp. 51.

120 The Inquisition trial is published in P.C. Ioly Zorattini, ed., *Processi del S*

Uffizio di Venezia contro Ebrei e Giudaizzanti (1548–1560), Storia dell'Ebraismo in Italia, Studi e Testi II, Sezione Veneta I. The Italian text and translation are in Head, 'Religious Boundaries,' 175.

121 Ibid., 176.

122 Sant'Ufficio, ASV, busta 91, Case 25, 1633.

123 The sign of the 'Hebrew' in this case was a red hat, following changes discussed by Ravid in 'From Yellow to Red.'

124 Head, 'Religious Boundaries,' 179.

125 Ibid., 183, 184.

126 Brian Pullan, '"The Inquisition and the Jews of Venice: The Case of Gaspare Ribeiro, 1580–81,' 215; Head, 'Religious Boundaries,' 187. On medieval trials and the Spanish Inquisition, see ibid., 183–7.

127 On the council and conduct books, see G. Pozzi, 'Occhi Bassi,' in Edgar Marsch and Giovanni Pozzi, eds, *Thematologie des Kleinen = Petits thèmes littéraires,* 162–205.

128 Linda Klinger and Julian Raby, 'Barbarossa and Sinan: A Portrait of Two Ottoman Corsairs from the Collection of Paolo Giovio,' in *Venezia e l'Oriente Vicino,* 47.

129 Charlotte Jirousek, 'More than Oriental Splendor: European and Ottoman Headgear, 1380–1580,' 25. Commenting on the exchange of clothes between heads of state, she notes the robes received by Queen Elizabeth from Murad III.

130 My thanks to Eric Dursteler for this information.

131 ASV, Collegio Ceremoniale II, 28–28v.

132 On the origins of dissimulation and religious persecution, see Zagorin, *Ways of Lying.* On conversions see Gino Benzoni , 'Il "farsi turco," ossia l'ombra del rinnegato,' in *Venezia e i Turchi: scontri e confronti di due civiltà,* 144–54.

133 The men were brought before the Inquisition in May 1631. ASV, Sant'Ufficio, busta 88, f. 303, May 1631, 22ff. Irregular pagination. Fra Giovanni depended on alms for support and Bartolomeo lived under a sottoportego, according to the domicile he provided the inquisitors.

134 A witness, a Neopolitan tailor, is brought forward early in the trial. Asked if he knew why he was being examined, he responds: 'm'imagino dover esser essaminato per quel frate dell'ordine di S. Ag[osti]no, spagnolo che si hà fatto turcho, et anco di un'altro soldato christiano pur spagnolo che si è fatto turcho, non sò il loro nome, il soldato può haver 30 anni inc[irc]a et è di statua [illegible] con poca barba negra, olivastro in faccia, et il frate può haver 18. ò 19. anni inc[irc]a per quanto mi mostra, et questo lo so, perche mardedì pross[im]o passato circa le 20. hore, in compagnia di un

Franc[esc]o, che hora è stato essaminato p[rim]a di me havendolo veduto
à uscire; et di un Dottore Napolitano, il quale è andato à Chiogga,
andassimo al casamento de turchi per intendere che cosa ha di un spagnolo
soldato che era stato in qua' compagnia in Milano et qui à Venetia; et
dimandano al Guardiano della casa, ci disse che il d[et]to spagnolo soldato
et anco il frate, vestiti da turchi con il turbante in testa erano stati condotti
da altri turchi sopra la gallera della mercantia; et che gli havevano tagliati li
capelli. del che restassimo molto maravigliati; massime havendo inteso che
il Frate ha professo et haveva ordini sacri. et habbiamo pensato che li
voglino condur in turchia per farli turchi.' N.p.

135 Giovanni Fecondo confesses that he was in fact a Christian. The following is
personal information about his family, baptism, and his plan to visit Rome
with another friar from whom he became separated: 'Et quì in Venetia son
andato cercando et domito sotto li porteghi per il gran bisogno. Et
finalm[en]te p[er] tentato dal demonio et sollecitato dalli turchi che si tro-
vano in Venetia, et particolarm[en]te da un Gio. Granatino chiamato Gio.
Lopes da Madrid, Il quale non no se si trovi ò sopra la galera della mercantia dove ero io, overo nel Ghetto cioè casa de Turchi, ne l'hò veduto da
lunedì pross[im]o passato in qua' à punto li'nella casa de Turchi, ove dalli
turchi è stato raso la testa, con mette li una beretta rossa, Et ivi in q[ues]ta
casa de Turchi sabbato passato istesso io deposi l'habito da Frate, et gli dissi
à quei turchi che io ero turco granatino, et che volevo andar in turchia à
ritrovare mio padre et mia madre, et essi mi rasero la testa, mi posero
questa crovata paonazza che hora hò indosso, et mi diedero questa baretta
verde, dicendoli anco che mi chiamavo Maometto. Et son restato in ghetto
la con li turchi da sabbato passato fino lunedi prossimo passato ove come
hò detto di sopra deposto l'habito da frate, in questo habito che mi vedete
fui condotto nella galera della mercantia, et fui da essi spesato, per esser
condotto in Constantinopoli, se bene veram[en]te co[me] mi volevo far
turco esteriorm[en]te ma non gia rinegar la fede col core. anzi mentre
ho tra turchi mentre loro dormivano mi segnavo et dicevo le mie or[azi]oni
[christ]iano.' 10.

   This is repeated during his sentencing: 'Che havessi apostato dal
q[uan]to convento et giunto à Venetia ivi mendicando et pratticando con
Turchi et lasciati indurre ad entrare nel loro Ghetto ò Casa, dove depon-
esti l'habito religioso, et ti fù rasa la testa, ti fu posto un crovata pavon-
azza et una beretta verde [rosso is crossed out] alla turchesca
maggiorm[en]te perche tra di loro havessi asserito d'esser turco Granatino, et chiamarti Maometto; si che fosti poi da loro condotto nella Galera della mercantia per esser à loro spese inviato à Constantinopoli, ove

(per quanto ne tuoi constituti giurati affermi) volevi con la bocca solam[en]te et non altram[en]te col core rinegare la q[ues]ta nostra fede Cat[toli]ca et viver, quanto all'esteriore, secondo la scelta turchesca; havendo in oltre à noi affermato di non havere mai col core negata la S[an]ta fede, anzi che ritrovandoti tra turchi, secretam[en]te ti segnavi con la croce et dicevi le or[azi]one [Christ]iane' (15). ASV, Sant' ufficio, busta 88, 303, May 1631.

136 Bartolomeo's initial testimony states: 'è vero che io hò detto di haver vissuto da [Crist]iano come per ceremonia nel modo che li altri Granatini vivevano ... hò detto la verità, che son turco Granatino, et voglio esser turco (ibid., 12–13). Later he recants: 'il timore di dio mi hà mosso il core per il quale hò fatto ricercare di esser essaminato perche Io hò peccato, et hò commesso li errori de quali son stato deposto ... cioè che ci ero disposto di andare in turchia et farmi turco, non però con il core, perche io son [Christ]iano, et sempre hò vissuto da Christiano ... Perciò stato giudicato vehementemente sospetto di heresia, cioe di haver creduto che sia lecito abbandonare la s[an]ta fede cat[toli]ca et ap[ostoli]ca Romana per abbracciare la setta maometana' (22).

137 Finding Fra Giovanni in prison, Giovanni Lopez turns himself in. His testimony includes the following: 'mi accuso di haver mangiato carne doi giorni di Venere nella casa de Turchi qui in Venetia. et questo non l'ho fatto per sprezzo, ma per il bisogno nel quale mi ritrovavo; per il quale bisogno ancora mi accuso di esser andato alla q[es]ta Casa de Turchi, alla quale mi son trattenuto 18. giorni , i quali turchi mi hanno rasa la metà della testa conforme al loro stile ... quale poi mi hò fatto tagliar da un Franc[esc]o Napolitano che è qui di fuori, ma non mi hanno mai dato altra veste da turco, sua hò sempre portato li mi à i stessi habiti che havevo ... Non mi hanno ricercato a farmi turco, ma desideravano di condur mi in Constantinopoli, perche io gli havevo detto che ho Granatino, et che mi chiamavo Usman ... Ne mai ho havuto dio' di apostatare la S[an]ta fede Christiana Cat[toli]ca et quel che hò fatto, l'ho fatto semplicem[en]te perche mi travavo in q[es]ta Città senza aiuto di sorte alcuna, et per sostentarmi, et son stato indotto di andar alli turchi' (ibid., 17).

138 'ha vestito in Palazzo un Villan con li suoi drappi rossi con una Romana e beretta tonda; poi diceva ecco qui il Rettor Falier ... io quando lo vidi habbi grandissimo dolor considerando l'atto brutto fatto contra un nobile.' ASV, Quarantia Criminale, busta 127, 16 June 1594, not paginated.

139 The Romana was associated with the *abito di semi-rappresentanza* worn by the Rettori particularly in the second half of the seventeenth century. In the sixteenth century, the term could be applied more generally to the costume of

Venetian nobles. Achille Vitali, *La moda a Venezia attraverso i secoli. Lessico ragionato*, 330–4.

140 'la veste era della forma che è quella che voi havette indosso, la quale era una pretina.' ASV, Quarantia Criminale, busta 127. A *pretina* was used frequently in the seventeenth century to refer to a closely fitting tunic similar to those worn by priests. Vitali, *La moda*, 316.

141 'non ti potevi tu immaginar che quelli drappi non si convenivano ad un contadino quale sei tu et che portandoli publicamente havesti datto ad'intendere divoler nell'habito immitar un Rettore et che perco ogn'uno sarebbe venuto con ammiratione a vederti.' ASV, Quarantia Criminale, busta 127, 1594.

142 'il giustificarsi di quanto è stato da me per zelo della publica dignità esposto ... il med.mo Contadino, da cui sappi la verità'; 'la mascherata fatta alla persona di uno Villano in veste rossa Romana d'ormisino, et beretta di Magistrato, per ordine d[e]l Il.mo. Bart.o Pesaro allora Vicerettore, perche nella piazza, et in altri luoghi publici esso Contadino si fingesse la persona all. Illmo Faliero già Rettore di Retimo, con sua irrisione e ludibrio é con poco rispetto di quel Ilmo Vicerettore.' Ibid. *Ormisino* refers to silk from Ormuz, an island in the Persian gulf. Vitale, *La moda*, 273.

143 On performatives, see John Langshaw Austin, *How to Do Things with Words*.

144 'Consiglio l'infrasento contadino il qual'e huomo di commune statura bruno in faccia con occhi rasi barba folta è longa di color grigia naso aquilino con un segneto negro appresso dalla parte sinistra et un'altro segno di cicatrice nel mezo d'esso naso per traverso dalla parte destra d'aspetto d'anni cinquanta sei inci[rc]a seben lui disse haverne sessanta vestito da Villano con braghesse sepezzate di tella bianca grossi colla tola camisa et senza altro giubone et un capello negro alla schiavona et stivali di corame negri.' Letter to the Doge dated 17 June 1594, ASV, Quarantia Criminale, busta 127.

145 Slavoj Žižek, *Enjoy Your Symptom: Jacques Lacan in Hollywood and Out*, 4.

146 For James Scott, it is the *public* outburst that threatens the status quo, the place where the vocalization transforms the private everyday forms of resistance into action. *Weapons of the Weak: Everyday Forms of Peasant Resistance*. Also see Žižek on the unspoken obscene rules, esp. 'Cynicism versus Irony,' in *The Invisible Remainder: An Essay On Schelling and Related Matters*, 203–7.

147 On the relation between unity, fragmentation and the imaginary see Jacques Lacan, 'Mirror-Phase,' in Žižek, ed., *Mapping Ideology*, 95; Silverman, *Threshold*, 49, 20–1. David Hillman and Carla Mazio, eds, *The Body in Parts:*

Fantasies of Corporeality in Early Modern Europe. On fragmentation, intersensoriality, and the *sensorium commune* of medieval philosophy, see Didier Anzieu, *The Skin Ego,* 103–4.

148 Lacan, 'Mirror-Phase.'

149 Lacan revises the mirror-phase theory to incorporate the mother who supports the infant's identification with the image. Also see Louis Althusser's theory of interpellation, 'Ideology and Ideological State Apparatuses,' in *Cultural Theory and Popular Culture: A Reader.*

150 Jaques Lacan, *The Four Fundamental Concepts of Psycho-Analysis,* 106.

151 Lacan's emphasis, ibid., 268.

152 Lacan's emphasis, ibid., 107. Silverman, *Threshold,* 196.

153 Silverman, *Threshold,* 196, 202. Silverman stresses the difficulty of this process, pointing out that Lacan's account of the child's jubilation – the subject's sense of 'altogetherness' – depends upon the double experience of integrating the image with its bodily ego. Ibid., 17.

154 Ibid., 13, 18, 19.

155 Lacan, *Four Fundamental Concepts,* 268.

156 Anzieu, *Skin Ego,* esp. 31–2, 105.

157 Silverman, *Threshold,* 12.

158 Ibid., 16.

159 Anzieu, *Skin Ego,* 3, 4. On the subject's emergence into object-relations, see 64–5.

160 Ibid., 97. The unifying envelope, or 'sac,' the protective barrier of the 'screen' and the 'sieve,' which filters and records exchanges with the world, all emphasize the ego's corporeity. The latter is a function of the skin, 'which makes representation possible.'

161 Ibid., *Skin Ego,* 83, 85.

162 Silverman is referring to 'the *'moi'* or 'belong-to-me' aspect of the ego. *Threshold,* 10.

163 The body, through its relation to other objects in the world, is continually constituted through touch, a model that accounts for the ego's sense of 'both "sameness" and "otherness." ' For Silverman, 'sameness' can be explained through proprioceptivity: 'the body's sensation of occupying a point in space, and with the terms under which it does so. It thus involves a nonvisual mapping of the body's form.' *Threshold,* 16.

164 Anzieu, *Skin Ego,* 31. In addition to external imagery, the tactile experiences of clothing also press against the surface of the body, what Jean Laplanche describes as 'an identification with a form conceived of as a limit, or a sack: a sack of skin.' Silverman, *Threshold,* 11; Jean Laplanche, *Life and Death in Psychoanalysis.*

165 Paul Schilder, *The Image and Appearance of the Human Body: Studies in the Constructive Energies of the Psyche*, 126; Silverman, *Threshold*, 13.
166 See Anzieu, *Skin Ego*, 103.
167 Fynes Moryson, *An Itinerary Containing His Ten Years of Travel*, 4: 220. Patricia H. Labalme, 'Venetian Women on Women: Three Early Modern Feminists,' 106.
168 Laplanche, *Life and Death*, 81–2; Silverman, *Threshold*, 12.
169 See Anzieu, *Skin Ego*, 91. Silverman, *Threshold*, 97.

3 Allegory, Order, and the Singular Event

1 David Rosand, '*Venezia figurata*,' in Rosand, ed., *Interpretazioni Veneziane. Studi di storia dell'arte in onore di Michelangelo Muraro*, 177; *Myths of Venice: The Figuration of a State*, 26–46, 97, 100–8, 114–17, 130, 138, 147.
2 Deborah Howard comments on the assonance between Venus with Venice. 'Venice as a Dolphin: Further Investigations into Jacopo de'Barbari's View,' *Artibus et historiae* 35 (1997): 106.
3 See 282n.71.
4 'Questa è d'ogni alto ben nido fecondo/Venetia: e tal che chi lei vede stima/Veder raccolto in breve spatio il mondo.'
5 On the painting and Grimani patronage see Michel Hochmann, 'Le mécénat de Marin Grimani.'
6 On the architecture and its meanings see Sansovino, *Venetia città nobilissima*, 104v–119v. On the importance of these sites for the sixteenth-century project of *renovatio urbis*, see Manfredo Tafuri, *Venice and the Renaissance*, 164. Also see Tafuri, '"Renovatio urbis Venetiarum"': Il problema storiografico,' in '*Renovato Urbis': Venezia nell'età di Andrea Gritti (1523–1538)*, 9–55.
7 See page 32.
8 See Edward Muir and Ron Weissman, 'Social and Symbolic Places in Renaissance Venice and Florence,' in John A. Agnew, ed., *The Power of Place. Bringing Together Geographical and Sociological Imaginations*, 81–104, esp. 91. Dennis Romano, 'Gender and the Urban Geography of Renaissance Venice.' On the mobility of women in the city, see Monica Chojnacka, *Working Women of Early Modern Venice*.
9 See Pat Simons, 'Women in Frames: The Gaze, the Eye, the Profile in Renaissance Portraiture.' On the subject's identification with imaginary, symbolic, and structural forms, including place, see Kaja Silverman, *The Threshold of the Visible World*, 70.
10 Richard Mackenney, *Tradesmen and Traders: The World of the Guilds in Venice and Europe, c.1250–c.1650*, 135.

11 On Venetian Renaissance ceremonial, see Matteo Casini: *I gesti del principe. La festa politica a Firenze e Venezia in età rinascimentale*, '*Triumphi* in Venice in the Long Renaissance'; '"Dux habet formam regis"; Morte e intronizzazione del principe a Venezia e Firenze nel cinquecento.' See also Patricia Fortini Brown, 'Measured Friendship, Calculated Pomp: The Ceremonial Welcomes of the Venetian Republic,' in Barbara Wisch and Susan Scott Munshower, eds, *All the World's a Stage. Art and Pageantry in the Renaissance and Baroque. Part 1*; Adrian Giurgea, 'Theatre of the Flesh: The Carnival of Venice and the Theatre of the World'; Giustina Renier Michiel, *Origine delle feste veneziane*, 1829; Edward Muir, 'Images of Power: Art and Pageantry in Renaissance Venice' and *Civic Ritual in Renaissance Venice*; Pompeo Molmenti, *La storia di Venezia nella vita privata dalle origini alla caduta della repubblica*; Biance Tamassia Mazzarotto, *Le feste veneziane: i giochi popolari, le cerimonie religiose e di governo*; Lina Urban: *Processioni e feste dogali: 'Venetia est mundus'*; 'Apparati scenografica nelle feste veneziane cinquecentesche'; 'La festa della Sensa nelle arti e nell'iconografia'; 'Teatri e "Teatri del Mondo" nella Venezia del cinquecento'; 'Feste ufficiali e trattenimenti privati,' *Storia della cultura Veneta. Il seicento*. On the routing of ceremonies: Louis Marin, 'Notes on a Semiotic Approach to *Parade, Cortege*, and *Procession*,' in *Time Out of Time: Essays on the Festival*, 220–8.
12 Muir, *Civic Ritual*, 5.
13 Ibid.
14 Casini, 'Dux habet formam regis,' 295.
15 Patricia Fortini Brown, *Venetian Narrative Painting in the Age of Carpaccio*, 172.
16 Scholars have generally emphasized either the long-term changes of these formal structures or the short-term political contingencies of the specific event. For example, Åsa Boholm's anthropological approach led her to express frustration with Sanuto's emphasis on the particulars of Venetian ritual. *The Doge of Venice: The Symbolism of State Power in the Renaissance*, 246. Although Casini refers to a variety of anthropological theorists, he focuses on the political contingencies of gestures, changes in order, and factions. See esp. *I gesti*.
17 Muir, *Civic Ritual*, 6–7; Casini, '*Triumphi*,' 35, 38.
18 Casini, 'Dux habet formam regis,' 289.
19 Mackenny on Muir's thesis. *Tradesmen and Traders*, 133; Edward Muir, 'The Ritual of Rulership in 16th-Century Venice: A Study in the Construction of Myth and Ideology,' also see Casini, 'Dux habet formam regis,' 295. The growing division between the aristocratic and popular elements of festivals has been attributed to the new political factions of the *giovani* and *vecchi* (youths and elders). The *calzaioli*, patrician youth groups responsible for

pageantry in the early part of the century, would have become senators in the latter decades, suggesting a continuity of control over pageantry by specific individuals. Casini, 'Dux habet formam regis,' 296–7.

20 Fredric Jameson, *The Political Unconscious: Narrative as a Socially Symbolic Act*, 29–30.

21 On the visit see ASV Collegio Ceremoniale, I: 43; *Ragguaglio dell'entrata di Henrico III*; Rocco Benedetti, *Le feste et trionfi fatti dalla Sereniss. Signoria di Venetia nella Felice Venuta di Henrico III*; Sansovino, *Venetia città nobilissima*, 161v–67v; Guglielmo Berchet, 'Documenti,' *Archivio Veneto* 13 (1876): 51–2; Pier de Nolhac and Angelo Solerti, *Il viaggio in Italia di Enrico III*. Secondary sources include: P.L. Fantelli, 'L'ingresso di Henrico III a Venezia di Andrea Vicentino,' 95–9; Lionello Puppi, ed., *Architettura e utopia nella Venezia del cinquecento*, 160–2; Lina Urban, *Processioni e feste dogali*, 174–6; Egon Verheyen, 'The Triumphal Arch on the Lido: On the Reliability of Eyewitness Accounts,' in Karl-Ludwig Selig and Elizabeth Sears, eds, *The Verbal and the Visual*, 215; Wolfgang Wolters, 'Le architetture erette al Lido per l'ingresso di Enrico III a Venezia nel 1574,' and 'Visite di stato' in Wolters, ed., *Storia e politica nei dipinti di Palazzo Ducale*, 216–22.

22 On relations with the French and the rapidity with which the Venetian patriciate forgot the massacres of the Huguenots, see Berchet, 'Documenti,' 51–2. On the political question of Spanish or French precedence with the ambassadors during the ceremonies, see 62–4, 104–5.

23 Wolters, *Storia e politica*, 218.

24 Verheyen, 'The Triumphal Arch,' 213. See his chronology of the five descriptions printed in 1574 (214n.4). The king's dire financial needs were another issue; if these had been revealed (including payments from Paris and loans from the Venetians), his prestige would have been severely limited. On the publicity see de Nolhac and Solerti, *Il viaggio in Italia di Enrico III*.

25 Instead of the Corpus Christi feast, they participated in the *inventio* of San Marco, which the state delayed for four days. Urban, *Processioni e feste dogali*, 170–3.

26 Carleton, in David Chambers and Brian Pullen with Janet Fletcher, *Venice: A Documentary History, 1450–1630*, 27.

27 Ibid., 28–9.

28 Roberto Cessi summarizes: 'La baldoria, l'allegria, la festività, il lusso, dilaganti nonostante la rigida repressione, non erano simboli di floridezza e di sana vigoria; piuttosto mascheravano in un alone di splendore e di falsa gaiezza sintomi di corruzione e di decadenza.' *Storia della repubblica di Venezia*, 2: 136.

29 P. Brown, *Venetian Narrative Painting*, 171.

30 Walter Benjamin, 'The Work of Art in the Age of Mechanical Reproduction,' in Hannah Arendt, ed., *Essays and Reflections*, 221.

31 Sergio Bettini, *Venezia*, 31; Giurgea's translation, 'Theatre of the Flesh,' 159.

32 Sources include: *Ultimi avisi di Venetia*; Rocco Benedetti, *Ragguaglio delle allegrezze*; Onorato Caetani and Gerolamo Diedo, *La battaglia di Lepanto (1571)*; Paolo Paruta, *The History of Venice ... The Wars of Cyprus*, 6–127.

   For a variety of essays, see Gino Benzoni, ed., *Il Mediterraneo nella seconda metà del '500 alla luce di Lepanto*. For bibliography, see Maddalena Redolfi, ed., *Venezia e la difesa del Levante da Lepanto a Candia 1570–1670*. Also see Iain Fenlon's forthcoming book. On Turks in Venice, see Paolo Preto, *Venezia e i Turchi*. On the Turkish position, see Halil Inalcik, 'Lepanto in the Ottoman Documents,' in Gino Benzoni, ed., *Il Mediterraneo nella seconda metà del '500 alla luce di Lepanto*; Halil Inalcik, *The Ottoman Empire. The Classical Age 1300–1600*. On relations with the Ottomans before Lepanto, see Marie F. Viallon, *Venise et la Porte Ottomane (1453–1566)*.

33 Bragadin's skin remained in Constantinople until 1596, when the relic was translated back to Venice and housed in SS Giovanni e Paolo. For details see *Relatione di tutto il successo di Famagosta*. Also see the grisaille painting of the flaying of Bragadin in the ceiling of the Sala del Gran Consiglio.

34 *[ ] Et ultima disperatione di Selim Gran Turco per la perdita della sua Armata* (Venice: [1575?]).

35 Cyprus was only the most recent Venetian possession lost to the Porte. The island had been added to the Stato da Mar in 1479. On the economic shift to the mainland see pages 44–7.

36 Braudel, 'Bilan d'une bataille,' in Benzoni, ed., *Il Mediterraneo*, 118.

37 According to Braudel, 60,000 out of 100,000 were killed or wounded. Ibid., 116.

38 *L'anno felicissimo. M.D. LXXI. Il Settimo d'Ottobre; Il bellissimo e sontuoso trionfo fatto nella magnifica città di Venetia nella publicatione della Lega; Canzone fatta alla serenissima republica venetiana; Capitolo a Selin imperator de Turchi; Nuova canzone a Selin imperator de Turchi in lingua venetiana; Ordine, e dechiaratione di tutta la Mascherata; Relatione di tutto il successo di Famagosta; [ ] Et ultima disperatione de Selim; Ultimi avisi di Venetia. Narratione della guerra principiata contra il gran Turco.* Also see Maddalena Redolfi, ed., *Venezia e la difesa del Levante da Lepanto a Candia*, 32–9.

39 On visual representations produced in view of the battle see Iain Fenlon, 'Lepanto: The Arts of Celebration in Renaissance Venice,' 201–36; Ernst Gombrich, 'Celebrations in Venice of the Holy League and the Victory of Lepanto'; Wolfgang Wolters, 'Il Trionfo di Lepanto (1571),' in *Storia e politica*, 207–15. For a summary and bibliography, see Stefania Mason Rinaldi, '*Le*

virtù della repubblica e le gesta dei capitani. Dipinti votivi, ritratti, pietà,' in Redolfi ed., *Venezia e la difesa del Levante*, 13–18.

40 For example: 'Mandovi ancora una altra carta stampatasi qui della rotta de Turchi, che a me par meglio della altra, mandatavi piu settimane sono. Sono stato con il Danese (Danese Cattaneo), et si è dato ordine di farvi ritrarre et colorire le galee sottili et le grosse da poppa, da prua et per fianco con le palvesate et con altre appartenenze; et subito che si haranno, vi si manderanno, siche habbiate patientia, tanto che si faccino, et intanto valetevi delle carte mandatevi.' Letter from Cosimo Bartoli in Venice to Vasari in Rome 12 March 1571. Giorgio Vasari, *Der Literarische Nachlass Giorgio Vasaris*, 656; also see 632, 661, 662–3.

41 See Preto, *Venezia e i Turchi*, 96; also 96–100.

42 Bernardo Navagero explains the problem in some detail: 'E prima che io dica altro dirò, che volesse Dio che in un maneggio di tanta importanza a vostra serenità quanto è quello di Costantinopoli, potessero li ministri di questo illustrissimo dominio usar la loro medesima lingua per interprete de'loro concetti, e che potessero intendere quello che vien loro risposto senza alcun intermezzo, perchè certo le cose procederebbero più direttamente. Dirà, per esempio, un'ambasciatore o bailo di vostra serenità, parole d'efficacia e piene di dignità, e il dragomanno è poi in libertà di riferire quanto gli piace. Risponderà il pascià qualche volta parole sopra le quali si potrebbe far gran fondamento, o in una parte, o nell'altra; le quali riferite, o non sono quelle medesime, o se pur s'accostano, perdono il vigore e la forza. E però in tante difficoltà quante sono in negoziare a quella Porta, reputo che questa sia una delle principalissime ed importanti, ed alla quale difficilmente trovo rimedio; perché non potendo saper li baili e li ambasciatori la lingua turca, è necessario che si riportino a quanto loro è riferito.' Venice, Legislative Bodies, *Relazioni degli ambasciatori veneti, series 3, Relazioni dagli stati Ottomani*, 1: 102–3. On the *dragomanni* (interpreters) see Carla Coco and Flora Manzonetto, *Baili veneziani alla sublime porta*, 105–9.

43 Venice, Legislative Bodies, *Relazioni degli ambasciatori veneti*, 2: 418. Coco and Manzonetto, *Baili veneziani*, 109. Ibid.,105.

44 'Les uns parce qu'ils sont bannis des îsles de Votre Seigneurie, les autres en raison des salaires élevés qui leur sont offerts, s'en vont chassés par la faim, ou pour gagner en quatre mois sur les galères du Grand Turc ce qui'ils gagnent en une année entière sur les galères de Votre Seigneurie.' Marcantonio Donini is cited in Philippe Braunstein and Robert Delort, *Venise. Portrait historique d'une cité*, 113; Mackenny, *Tradesmen and Traders*, 219.

45 'abiura,' 'fuga,' 'rinnegazione,' and 'tradimento.' Preto, *Venezia e i Turchi*,

176. It is possible that these examples – ubiquitous in senate deliberations, reports from ambassadors and governors, and cases in the Inquisition office – were overstated, indicating instead, as Preto asks 'solo tiepidezza religiosa or temporaneo opportunismo?' (176).

46 See Steve Ortega, 'Ottoman Muslims in the Venetian Republic from 1573 to 1645: Contacts, Connections and Restrictions'; Paul Kaplan, 'Veronese and the Inquisition: The Geopolitical Context,' in Elizabeth Childs, ed., *Suspended License: Essays in the History of Censorship and the Visual Arts*; Brian Pullan, *The Jews of Europe and the Inquisition of Venice, 1550–1670*; Randolph C. Head, 'Religious Boundaries and the Inquisition in Venice: Trials of Jews and Judaizers, 1548–1580.'

47 Preto, *Venezia e i Turchi*, 154–5.

48 'ingannare molte particolari persone idiote' Matteo Zane (1594), Venice, Legislative Bodies, *Relazioni degli ambasciatori veneti*, 3: 405. Preto, *Venezia e i Turchi*, 154.

49 Inalcik, *The Ottoman Empire*, 6.

50 'di grande ignominia et vergogna alo Imperio Venetto ... li Turchi sonno valenthomeni, e li Christiani sonno putane.' Girolamo Priuli, *I diarii. (1494–1512)*, tome 24, part 3, vol. IV, 394–5. Preto, *Venezia e i Turchi*, 21.

51 'Il malcontento dei suditi, le divisione interne, l'avarizia, l'effeminatezza, la corruzione nella vita privata e pubblica.' Ibid., 63. Lorenzo Bernardo called the Sultan 'un Sardanapalo allevato nelli serragli fra buffoni, nani e muti.' Venice, Legislative Bodies, *Relazioni degli ambasciatori veneti*, 2: 368–73. Preto, *Venezia e i Turchi*, 66.

52 The army was 'debole, disabitato e rovinato in gran parte,' with soldiers 'sfidati dall'oziosa e viziosa vita.' Venice, Legislative Bodies, *Relazioni degli ambasciatori veneti*, 1: 280–1, 307–14; Preto, *Venezia e i Turchi*, 63–4.

53 'bestemmiare, bere, fumare come un turco.' Ibid., 117.

54 'A questo cosi fatto Re, morto come s'è detto, successe Selim huomo tutto dato alle voluttà, corruttor della sua legge, senza fede, mancator della sua parola, & tutto il contrario di quel ch'era suo padre, onde non senza ragione si crede da Turchi medesimi ch'esso non sia figliuolo di Seleiman, ma d'uno hebreo. Percioche essi dicono, che non potendo la Rossa tanto amata da Seleiman haver figliuoli con lui, fingendo d'esser gravida, tolse un bambino d'una sua amica hebrea, & sopponendolo lo piantò per figliuolo al marito. Ma non molti anni dopo ella ne fece de gli altri, i quali tutti morirono, restando successore a tanto stato il predetto Selim.' Francesco Sansovino, *Gl'annali Turcheschi overo vite de Principi della casa Othomana*, 222–3.

55 'All'incontro quale alterezza, qual fasto, qual maggior superbia si può rappresentare a'nostri occhi di quella del Turco?' Sansovino, *Informatione ... a soldati christiani*, n.p.

56 Sansovino, *Lettera overo discorso sopra le predittioni fatte in diversi tempi da diverse persone.*

57 On Sansovino's views of the Ottomans, see Elena Bonora, *Ricerche su Francesco Sansovino: imprenditore, librario e letterato,* esp. 125–37.

58 'Huomini d'ossa & di carne come voi.' Sansovino, *Informatione ... a soldati christiani,* unpaginated.

59 'Questi cosi fatti Azamoglan, rozzi, & villani, sono per lo più gente cattiva & bestiale: & per ordinario odiano a morete i Christiani, a'quali cercano di fare ogni dispiacere & insulto: ma qual maraviglia è, poi ch'esse non riconoscono, ne anco padre ne madre, come veramente barbari & contadin, & usati da piccoli con gente strana & che non hanno altro oggetto che il Signor loro, il quale adorano sopra tutte le cose del mondo?' Ibid.

60 'Ammazzerebbe i nobili & segnalati capi de christiani, come nemico mortale dell'alte prosapie de gli huomini chiari & di conto,' Ibid.

61 On Ottoman social organization, see Halil Inalcik and Donald Quataert, eds, *An Economic and Social History of the Ottoman Empire 1300–1914;* Inalcik, *The Ottoman Empire;* Gülru Necipoğlu, *Architecture, Ceremonial, and Power: The Topkapi Palace in the Fifteenth and Sixteenth Centuries,* 252–6.

62 See Braudel 'Bilan d'une bataille,' in Benzoni, ed., *Il Mediterraneo,* 115–16.

63 On the 1526 law 'requiring registration of all marriages,' see Stanley Chojnacki, 'Marriage Regulation in Venice, 1429–1535,' in S. Chojnacki, *Women and Men in Renaissance Venice: Twelve Essays on Patrician Society.*

64 The last phrase is a paraphrase of Bonora's words, *Ricerche,* 107. On Ottoman–Venetian relations, see Peter Sebastian, 'Ottoman Government Officials and Their Relations with the Republic of Venice in the Early Sixteenth Century,' in Colin Heywood and Colin Imber, eds, *Studies in Ottoman History in Honour of Professor V.L. Ménage,* esp. 332–5.

65 On the secret negotiations, see Braudel, 'Bilan d'une bataille,' 115. According to Sanuto, during the League of Cambrai, the Venetians considered seeking an allegiance with the Ottomans. Preto, *Venezia e i Turchi,* 25.

66 ASV, Collegio, *Cerimoniale* I, 39, 40.

67 Ibid.

68 An anonymous chronicler described the procession but did not indicate which group was responsible for the *apparati. Il bellissimo et sontuoso trionfo fatto nella magnifica città di Venetia nella publicatione della lega.* See Gombrich, 'Celebrations in Venice.'

69 Predictions of the end of Mohammedanism were coupled with the desire for the conversion of the American Indians. Popular sentiment was fuelled by figures such as Paolo Angelo, a priest from Albania, who wrote of Turks and Protestants as 'i nemici più pericoloso e imminenti di una Cristianità sfibrata dalla corruzione morale.' Preto, *Venezia e i Turchi,* 71. One particularly ven-

omous attack, published in 1572, described the Turks as 'porchi' because Muslim laws, as M. Cosimo Filiarchi asserted, were the laws of pigs. Combining myths from the New World with familiar stereotypes, he cited four causes for a just war, including practices of sodomy and cannibalism that he attributed to the infidels' inversion of 'natural laws.' See M. Cosimo Filiarchi, *Trattato della gverra, et dell'vnione de'principi Christiani contra i Turchi, & gli altre infedeli*, 76, 78. On the tradition of the Turks as the antichrist, see Preto, *Venezia e i Turchi*, 68–9n.3.

70 Gombrich's translation, 'Celebrations in Venice,' 62–3.

71 Preto, *Venezia e i Turchi*, 75, 76. Bataillon, 'Mythe et connaissance de la Turquie en Occident au milieu du XVIe siècle,' in Agostino Pertusi, ed., *Venezia e l'Oriente fra tardo Medioevo e Rinascimento*, 452–3, 457–69. Jean Deny, 'Les pseudo-prophéties concernant les Turcs au XVIe siècle.'

72 The League was concluded on 20 May. ASV, Collegio, *Cerimoniale* II, 28–28v. On the victory, see *Ordine di far processione per la vittoria havuta contra Turchi et che si vadi ogn'anno a 7'Ottobre a S.ta Giustina* 19 October 1571, ASV, Collegio, *Cerimoniale* II, 40. On the return of Onfrè Giustiniano's galley with news of the victory, see ASV, Collegio, *Cerimoniale* II, 28–28v.

73 Braudel, 'Bilan d'une bataille,' in Benzoni, ed., *Il Mediterraneo*, 119. On the contrast between long periods of peace and then moments of explosive violent engagement, see Preto, *Venezia e i Turchi*, 53.

74 John Hale, 'The Venetian Army,' 175; Carlo Dionisotti, 'Lepanto nella cultura Italiana del tempo,' 132–4; Braudel, 'Bilan d'une bataille,' 115–16, all in Benzoni, ed., *Il Mediterraneo*.

75 Angus Fletcher, *Allegory: The Theory of a Symbolic Mode*.

76 On the painting, c. 1593, see Stefania Mason Rinaldi, *Palma il Giovane, l'opera completa*, cat. 535, 142; Staale Sinding-Larsen, *Christ in the Council Hall: Studies in the Religious Iconography of the Venetian Republic*, 24–7. Wolters, *Storia e politica nei dipinti di Palazzo Ducale*, 204–6.

77 See Barbara Johnson, *In the Wake of Deconstruction*, 59.

78 The painting – dated from 1571 to as late as 1578 – may have been the central part of a larger work painted for S Pietro Martire on Murano. On the painting see Ettore Merkel, 'Allegoria della vittoria di Lepanto,' in *Paolo Veronese restauri: [mostra] 1 giugno–30 settembre [1988]*; Terisio Pignatti and Filippo Pedrocco, *Veronese*, 1: 186, 277–9; 2: 313; Pignatti, *Veronese*, 1: cat. 166, 133; Maddalena Redolfi ed., *Venezia e la difesa*, cat. 15, 29–30.

79 Francesco Camocio, Antoine Lafréry, Bolognini Zalterii, Paolo Forlani, among others, produced printed views of land battles and the Ottoman army. For example, see Lafrery's *Ordine con il quale l'escercito Turchesco suole presentarsi in campagna*, Rome, 1566 (Newberry Library, Novacco 2F 48).

80 'AVERTIMENTO Inanzi l'Armata Christiana vano il giorno otto galere per disco-
prire, et havendo notitia dell Armata dell Inimico devono subito tornare
nelle loro Squadre.' Royal Geographical Society, London, Lafreri Atlas
(Tooley, 611), 78.

81 On theoretical geography see Barbara Belyea, 'Images of Power: Derrida/
Foucault/Harley.'

82 'In questo modo si presuppone vi da venire l'Armata del Turco.' Royal Geographical Society, London, Lafreri Atlas (Tooley, 611), 78.

83 'il giorno della bataglia, che fu alli VII d'Ottobre, 1571, il giorno di S.ta. Jus-
tina alle 17 hore'; 'Il primo tirò fece le galere più grosse.'

84 See Norman Bryson, 'The Gaze and the Glance,' in *Vision and Painting: The
Logic of the Gaze.*

85 Royal Geographical Society, London, Lafreri Atlas (Tooley, 611), 100.

86 'Curiosi Lettori/Non vi maravigliate, se questa nostra carta non si puó distin-
tamente/conoscere, come se fusse una cosa ferma, et stabile; perche inanti
che fusse/finita la stupendissima battaglia, furono fatte infinite mutationi, di
tal modo,/ che stetero li combattenti de l'una, et l'altra parte attaccati insieme demos/trando ognuno la sua virtú.'

87 One particularly interesting map, in the British Library, signed Marij Tigrino
and printed in Rome by Michele Tramezzino in 1572, deals with this representational dilemma by abandoning a single field in favour of a variety of
views and explanatory cartouches. To organize the large folio sheet, the
designer has deployed a series of perspectives including a map of Europe, a
map of the gulf, the formations in anticipation of the battle, the first shot,
and independent costumed figures. The centre has been reserved for a confused mélange of vessels, ensigns, bodies, and toponyms.

88 Giovanni Francesco Camocio, who specialized in maps of military contests,
including Lepanto, also published a list of names: *L' ordine delle galere et le
insegne loro con li fano, nomi cognomi delli magnifici, & generosi patroni di esse.*

89 See James S. Grubb, 'Memory and Identity: Why Venetians Didn't Keep *ricordanze*,' 375–87, esp. 379–80.

90 On the votive paintings of the doges, see Wolfgang Wolters, *Storia e Politica*,
93–135; for Veronese's painting of Venier, 125–8. As Sinding-Larsen pointed
out, Sansovino describes the *modello* instead of the finished painting in his
1581 *Venetia città nobilissima.* The painting is thus conventionally dated to
between 1581 and 1582 and thereby also seen to follow Girolamo Bardi's
scheme for the decorations of the Palazzo Ducale. However Pignatti and
Pedrocco, following Valcanover, and on the basis of style and the 1983 resto-
ration, date the work to the end of the 1570s. *Veronese: Catalogo completo*, 238.
Pignatti, *Veronese*, 1: 85; cat. 283: 155–6; Pignatti and Pedrocco, *Veronese*, 2:

310, cat. 261, 373–4. Sinding-Larsen, *Christ in the Council Hall*, 95–8. On the *modello* see Richard Cocke, *Veronese's Drawings: A Catalogue Raisonnée*, Stefania Mason Rinaldi, 'Le virtù della repubblica e le gesta dei capitani dipinti votivi, ritratti, pietà,' in Maddalena Redolfi ed., *Venezia e la difesa*, 13–18, esp. 14. Despite the changes in the finished work, Cocke maintains the painting retains both its public and private dimension. Instead of mitigating the individual success of Venier, he sees the change as resulting in a more prominent division of space between the earthly and terrestrial. *Veronese's Drawings*, 207, cat. B7.

91 The drawing (300 × 407 mm.) is in British Museum, Prints and Drawings, inv. 1861–8–10–4.

92 On Barbarigo, see G.A. Quarti, 'La morte di Agostino Barbarigo nella battaglia di Lepanto,' *Crociata Anno IV* 15, no. 5 (September/October 1937), 169–77.

93 'Maravigliosa cosa e memorabile per tutti i secoli fu bene vedere il Veniero, tutto canuto e nalla estrema sua vecchiezza soldato novello, avanzar nel fatto d'arme i giovani, ché, come il serpente alla primavera uscito di tenebre, lasciata la vecchia spoglia, della nuova e splendente scorza altiero, sentendosi ringiovenito e più che mai robusto, col fuoco deli occhi e col vibrar della lingua, dovunque va, ad ogni animale terro e morte apporta, così il Veniero, lucente di chiaro acciar che il capo li arma e il busto, come se nella patria avesse con la toga la vecchiezza deposta e vestendosi il corsaletto s'avesse di nuovi, giovani e gagliardi membri vestito, con ruina e morte de'nemici fece nell'armi prove onoratissime.' Emilio Maria Manolesso is cited in Dionisotti, 'Lepanto nella cultura italiana del tempo,' in Benzoni, ed., *Il Mediterraneo*, 135.

Venier, who had no military experience, replaced Girolamo Zane, who was seventy-six at the time of his trial. Criticism of Zane's management and lack of discipline (particularly concern over sodomy and blasphemy) led to his recall and subsequent trial. Venier, by contrast, was characterized as restoring discipline. Ugo Tucci, 'Il processo a Girolamo Zane Mancato Difensore di Cipro,' in Benzoni, *Il Mediterraneo*, 409–33.

94 Stefania Mason Rinaldi questions Sinding-Larsen's interpretation of the Mocenigo portrait as a celebration of the peace he negotiated with the Turks. 'Le virtù della repubblica,' in Redolfi ed., *Venezia e la difesa*, 14. The lion presenting the text *pax* is repeated in several Lepanto woodcuts before the peace was signed. Moreover, as is often pointed out, the peace was not only economically but also politically costly since the Venetians were seen to be traitors to Christianity.

95 As Sinding-Larsen pointed out, Sansovino's 1581 description follows

Veronese's *modello* rather than the painting, suggesting that the latter was not placed above the tribune until the 1580s. See Sinding-Larsen, *Christ in the Council Hall*, 95–8, and his earlier 'The Changes in the Iconography and Composition of Veronese's Allegory of the Battle of Lepanto in the Doge's Palace'; Mason Rinaldi, 'Le virtù della repubblica,' in Redolfi, ed., *Venezia e la difesa*, 18fn.12.

96 Mason Rinaldi comments on the increasingly universal tone after 1577 in the Scrutinio and Sala del Maggior Consiglio: 'le virtù di Venezia, del suo governo e dei singoli cittadini che ne sono sostegno.' 'Le virtù della repubblica,' in Redolfi, ed., *Venezia e la difesa*, 14. Also see William Bouwsma's parallel between Paolo Paruta's interest in history and Girolamo Bardi's plans for the redecoration of the Palazzo Ducale, published in 1587. *Venice and the Defense of Republican Liberty: Renaissance Values in the Age of the Counter Reformation*, 223.

97 Girolamo Bardi, *Dichiarazione di tutte le historie che si contengono nei quadri posti nuovamente nella Sala dello Scrutinio e del Gran Consiglio nel Palazzo Ducale della Serenissima Repubblica di Venezia*.

98 'Barbarigo raggionando me referite che i dicevano che noi non volevimo combater ma che fenzevimo.' Rawdon Brown, *Notice of, and Extracts from The Report presented to the Doge and Senate of Venice, by Sebastian Venier, Captain General of the fleet of the Republic at Lepanto, on his return from service, On 29th of December, 1572*, 16.

99 'li mostrai ... in qual pericolo si trovavano, et quanto bisognava, che mettessimo tutte le nostre forze per difenderci noi nostre mogli, figliuoli, et beni da un nimico, che non admette conti, ne cavallieri, ne gentilhuomini, ma solo mercanti, et popoli, che facciano buoni li suoi datii, et seguito alla sua corte: admette villani, che lavorano la terra, togliendo all'uno, et all'altro, li beni et figliuoli, et vergognadoli le donne secondo l'appetito loro.' Pompeo Molmenti, *Sebastiano Veniero e la battaglia di Lepanto*, 284. Preto, *Venezia e i Turchi*, 167.

100 Gleason, 'Reading between the Lines,' 257. Gasparo Contarini, *La republica, e i magistrati di Vinegia ... nuovamente fatti volgari, etc.*

101 'una virtù di maggiori.' Paolo Paruta, *Opere politiche*, 1: 315. Preto, *Venezia e i Turchi*, 167–8.

102 Members of the Holy League are identified by name in another engraving but they are pictured together. Giacomo Franco, *Habiti d'huomeni et donne venetiane*.

103 On Tintoretto's portrait (Vienna, Kunsthistorisches Museum), see *Jacopo Tintoretto ritratti*, cat. 33, 144; on Tintoretto's portraits of Venier, see Rossi, *Jacopo Tintoretto: I ritratti*, Venice: 1974, 151–2.

104 The term is from Judith Butler, 'Performative Acts and Gender Constitution: An Essay in Phenomenology and Feminist Theory,' in Sue-Ellen Case, ed., *Performing Feminisms: Feminist Critical Theory and Theatre*, 270–82.

105 Vives continues: 'because every time she issues forth into public she undergoes what we might almost call a fatal judgment of her beauty, modesty, prudence, propreity and integrity, since there is nothing more fragile or more vulnerable that the reputation and good name of women, so that it may well seem to hang by a cobweb.' Juan Luis Vives, *De institutione feminae christianae*, in C. Fantazzi and C. Matheeussen, eds, *Selected works of J.L. Vives*, 1: 127.

106 Ibid.

107 Ibid., 2: 112.

108 Georgina Masson's translation, *Courtesans of the Italian Renaissance*, 152.

109 Vecellio, *De gli habiti*, 138.

110 For example, legislation in 1539 states: 'Che le meretrice che stanno sopra le strade publiche, debbano andar ad habitar personalmente alli lochi publici sotto pena d'esser frustato ... Che le meretrice, ovvero cortesane, non possino andar habitar all'Incontro delli chiese. Che le disse non possino andar nelle chiese le fete principal et andando l'altri girorni, non possino andar a Intenochiarsi ne sentar nel loco, dove sono le Zentildone et citadine ma contane ma lontano da loro.' ASV, Provveditore alla Sanità 5, 1539. See also ASV, Provveditore alle Pompe, *Capitolari* 1–11 (1488–1683). G. Bistort, *Il magistrato alle pompe nella repubblica di Venezia; studio storico*, 55–65, esp. 65. Also see Guido Ruggiero, *Boundaries of Eros: Sex Crimes and Sexuality in Renaissance Venice*, 35–6, 49; L. Menetto and G. Zennaro, eds, *Storia del malcostume a Venezia nei secoli XVI–XVII*, 45–64; Giovanni Scarabello, 'Devianza sessuale ed interventi di giustizia a Venezia nella prima metà del XVI secolo,' in Neri Pozza, ed., *Tiziano e Venezia: Convegno Internazionale di Studi, Venezia, 1976*, 83; Margaret Rosenthal, *The Honest Courtesan: Veronica Franco. Citizen and Writer in Sixteenth-Century Venice*, 27.

111 According to Sir Henry Wotten, the English ambassador to Venice, the 1617 festival of the Ascension 'hath this year been celebrated here with a very poor show of *gondole*, by reason of a decree in Senate against the courtesans, that none of them shall be rowed *con due remi*; a decree made at the suit of all the gentlewomen, who before were indistinguishable abroad from those baggaes.' In Logan Smith, *The Life and Letters of Sir Henry Wotton*, 2: 114; Muir, *Civic Ritual*, 133n.76.

112 'Che alcuna nobile, cittadina, putta, o, altra, che per anno uno continuo havesse habitato in questa città, eccettuata la Dogaressa figlie, e more di sua

serenità habitante in Dogado, non possino portar, ne usar cosi in cassa, come fuori, ne in alcuna terra del dominio nostro, come persona publica, o, privata, se non vestimenti schietti di un solo color cio é velado, raso, damasco, ormesin, et simil altre cose di seda et bavesse, che siano tessute di un solo color, eccettuati li ormesini ganzanti, et li brocadelli, sopra li quali vestimenti non vi possi esser alcuna cosa, ma il vestir in ogni uso della persona sua sia schiettissime senza alcuna sorte di lavoriero.' ASV, Provveditore alle Pompe, *Capitolari* 1–11 (1488–1683), 1562, 1v. 'Le meretrice non possino portar ori, ne arzenti di sorte alcuna ne alcuna sorte di zoglie et dire imaginar si possi, cusi buone come false, ne vestimenti di seda di sorte alcuna, ne in casa, ne fuori di casa.' Ibid., 1574, 19. 'sono cusi ardite et insolenti le meretrice habitante in questa Città ... le Meretrice che sarano una volta condenate per l'atto dell pompe, se serano cusi temerarie et di tanta audatia che ardiscano contra far anchora ad alcun ordine ò leggie del predetto officio.' Ibid., 11 July 1579, 25.

113 Margaret Rosenthal, *Honest Courtesan*, 2, 19–20. On politics, liberty, and licentiousness, see William Bouwsma, *Venice and the Defense*, 461. Also see Massimo Gemin, 'Le cortigiane di Venezia e i Viaggiatori Stranieri,' in Doretta Davanzo Poli, *Le cortigiane di Venezia dal Trecento al Settecento: Catalogo della mostra: Venezia, Casinò municipale Ca' Vendramin Calergi, 2 febbraio–16 aprile 1990*, 73, 79.

114 On the 1597 coronation, see ASV, Collegio, *Cerimoniale* II, 9; BMV, IT VII 2540 (8838), 238. Giovanni Rota, *Lettera nella quale si descrive l'ingresso nel Palazzo Ducale della serenissima Morosina Morosini Grimani prencipessa di Vinetia*; Dario Tutio, *Ordine et modo tenuto nell'incoronatione della Serenissima Moresina Grimani Dogaressa di Venetia*; Agostino Michele, *Oratione di Agostino Michele nella coronatione della Serenissima Prencipessa di Vinegia Moresina Grimani*; Giovanni Nicolò Doglioni [Leonico Goldioni, pseud.], *Le cose maravigliose et notabili della città di Venetia*, 66–82; Sansovino-Stringa, *Venetia città nobilissima*, 280–94, 431–2; Giovanni Palazzi, *La virtu in giocco overo dame patritie di Venetia famose per nascita, per lettere, per armi, per costumi*, 111–16; G.M. Piave, 'Feste fatte in Venetia pella incoronatione della Serenissima Dogaressa Morosina Morosini Grimani,' in *Emporio artistico-letterario ossia raccolta di amene lettere, novità. II* (1847): 9–13, 49–52.

Modern accounts include Maximilian Tondro, 'Memory and Tradition: The Ephemeral Architecture of the Dogaresse of Venice in 1557 and 1597'; Lina Urban, *Processioni e feste dogali*, 205–15; Pompeo Molmenti, *La dogaressa di Venezia*, 287–305; Edgcumbe Staley's lively, if sometimes inaccurate, discussion, *The Dogaressas of Venice*, 282–8; Muir, *Civic Ritual*, 293–6; Giovanni Scarabello, 'Le dogaresse,' in Gino Benzoni, ed., *I dogi*, 176; Andrea da

Mosto, *I dogi di Venezia nella vita pubblica e privata*, 315–22; Claudio Rendina, *I dogi: Storia e segreti*, 327–8.

On the *dogaresse*, see Åsa Boholm, 'The Coronation of Female Death: The Dogaressas of Venice'; Holly Hurlburt's forthcoming *Icons and Wives: The Dogaresse of Venice, 1300–1500.*

115 The dress was described in the ceremonial register: 'Il vestire di sua Serta era una sotto veste con le maniche strette di panno d'oro, et sopra quella un manto di sopariccio d'oro. Et havea coperto il capo d'un velo bianco, che gli scorreva fin sopra le spalle, et di sopra una bereta dello istesso sopariccio d'oro all'usanza ducale, mà col corno alquanto più piccolo. Et in piedi tenea Zoccoli di panno d'oro.' ASV, Collegio, *Cerimoniale* II, 9.

116 According to Tutio, the *Venetia* float was fashioned in the guise of an antique *carro* drawn by two large sea horses under the guidance of Neptune and the God of the Adriatic. A tableau vivant presented a triumphant and regal Venice in the process of crowning kneeling figures dressed as the doge and dogaressa. They were accompanied by Justice, Religion, Faith, and Prudence. Tutio, *Ordine et modo tenuto*, 10.

117 Hurlburt discusses this transformation in her forthcoming *Icons and Wives.*

118 On one of the pediments of the floating *teatro*, St Mark was painted in the act of crowning the couple, 'comme pour montrer qu'il les avait lui-même choisis pour régner sure les mers.' Michel Hochmann, 'Le mécénat de Marin Grimani,' 42.

119 Morosina provided for the dwarfs in her will. On the will see Da Mosto, *Dogi*, 317–22. On dwarfs and court culture, see the remarks of Lauro Martines, *Power and Imagination*, 231, 309–10. On ceremony and aristocratic family display, see Muir, 'Images of Power,' 48; *Civic Ritutal*, 294–5.

120 The chronicler of the *pugni* is cited by Robert C. Davis, *The War of the Fists: Popular Culture and Public Violence*, 209n.44.

121 For example, see Agostino Michele, *Oratione*, Alati Alessandro, cited by Molmenti, *Dogaressa*, 287–8. Also see Jonathan Shiff, *Venetian State Theater and the Games of Siena. 1595–1605. The Grimani Banquet Plays*, esp. 139.

122 The event was prohibited by the senate on 10 January 1645, amid growing concern over elaborate clothes and changing styles. Molmenti cites the considerations with which the decree began: 'Conviene nel proprio sostenimento de la publica grandezza prefiggere anco quegli ordini, che niente offuscando il lustro e il decoro ne le cerimonie de le Dogaresse sian per togliere l'obbligatione d'eccessivi dispendii, aggravanti in particolare l'Arti, e i popoli ad altri pesi obligati.' The decision stated: 'in ogni tempo a venire sia prohibito il farsi l'incoronatione de le Dogaresse come attione non necessaria et poco aggiustata a la moderation del Governo.' Cited by

Molmenti, *Dogaressa*, 319–20. The entry of the dogaressa could continue in a curtailed fashion – preferably without the Benediction in S Marco – but the procession and use of the Bucintoro were banned.

123 Rota, *Lettera*; Muir, *Civic Ritual*, 294. On the new limited role of the doge and dogaressa, as redefined in the *promissione* of 1252, see Staley, *Dogaressas of Venice*, 98; Tondro, 'Memory and Tradition,' 24–30.

124 Morosina Morosini was one of four *dogaresse* in the sixteenth century. Between 1486 and the coronation of Zilia Dandolo Priuli in 1557, the wife of Lorenzo Priuli (1556–9), no wife survived to accompany her husband to the Palazzo Ducale. War with the Turks precluded any coronation ceremony for Loredana Marcello, the wife of Alvise Mocenigo (1570–7). See Casini, 'Dux habet formam regis,' 290–303; Molmenti, *dogaressa*, 278–79; Scarabello, 'Le dogaresse,' in Benzoni, ed., *I dogi*, 176. Because Sebastiano Venier died within a year of taking office, there had not yet been a procession to the Palazzo Ducale for his wife. This was the reason, in part, according to one chronicle, why she was given a pension, the service of four maids, and a gondola after Venier's death. BMV, IT VII 811 (7299), 1578, 2.

125 Rota, *Lettera*, n.p.

126 Tutio, *Ordine et modo tenuto*, 14; Rota, *Lettera*, n.p.; Muir, *Civic Ritual*, 294n.124.

127 Tutio, *Ordine et modo tenuto*, 14.

128 Rota, *Lettera*, n.p.

129 'non di bianco, ma di altro colore, come di verde, di rosa secca, e di pavonazzo, secondo più pareva loro convenir all' età sua.' Sansovino-Stringa, *Venetia città nobilissima*, 282.

130 Tutio, *Ordine et modo tenuto*, 13.

131 See Sansovino-Stringa, *Venetia città nobilissima*, 283. On Archangela Tarabotti's defence of *zoccoli*, which 'suitably elevate the female as a miracle of nature,' see Patricia H. Labalme, 'Venetian Women on Women: Three Early Modern Feminists,' 101.

132 Bistort, *Magistrato alle pompe*, 34.

133 'rilucendo quelle donne tutte come specchi per tante pretiose pietre che havevano attorno.' Pietro Marcello is describing the women during the entry of the Queen of Poland. *Vite de' prencipi di Vinegia*, 370; Bistort, *Magistrato alle pompe*, 36.

134 Marin Grimani commissioned a vast number of paintings, particularly portraits, for his family palace at S Luca. Two of these, identified as his consort and himself, were painted by Jacopo Tintoretto in 1578 and displayed in the entrance. Hochmann, 'Le mécénat de Marin Grimani,' 50n.22. On Leandro's portraits, see Puppi, ed., *Architettura e utopia*, cat. 398, 247–8.

135 According to Wolfgang Wolters, the choice of subject matter, almost two decades after the visit, was prompted by need of French support. *Storia e politica*, 216.

136 Hochmann, 'Le mécénat de Marin Grimani,' 48–9.

137 See Fortini Brown, 'Measured Friendship'; Casini, *I gesti del principe*, 38n.79.

138 On Venetian liberty, see 282n.71.

139 While the gestures and costumes of the key protagonists were copied from Palma Giovane's *Arrival of Henry III at Palazzo Foscari*, a number of group portraits of the arrival were commissioned by participants, and others were copied later by Vicentino. See Wolters, *Storia e politica*, 218 and n.1.

140 Wolters, 'Le architetture erette al Lido.'

141 Manfredo Tafuri, *'Renovato Urbis': Venezia nell'età di Andrea Gritti* (1523–1538).

142 Sansovino refers to the Logetta as a 'ridotto de nobili' in his description. *Venetia città nobilissima*, 111–12.

143 'ritrovo della nobiltà.' Wolters, 'Le architetture erette al Lido,'

144 'andarono in trionfo secondo il consueto fino a pie del campanile vicino alla loggetta, nella quale erano gli ambasciadori dell'Imperatore, del Duca di Savoia, & del Duca di Urbino.' Sansovino, *Venetia città nobilissima*, 154–54v. Wolters, 'Le architetture erette al Lido,' 288.

145 On the decorations and inscriptions that encrusted the arch, see Tutio, *Ordine et modo tenuto*, 11–13; Sansovino-Stringa, *Venetia città nobilissima*, 281–2; Rota, *Lettera*. Tondro, 'Memory and Tradition.'

146 Michel Hochmann, 'Le mécénat de Marin Grimani,' 45.

147 See pages 58–9.

148 On analogies between the patriarchal family and the state, see Daniela Frigo, 'Dal Caos all'Ordine,' in Marina Zancan, *Nel cerchio della luna*, 57–93. On domestic economics and political theory in Giovanni Caldiera, see Margaret L. King, 'Personal, Domestic, and Republican Values in the Moral Philosophy of Giovanni Caldiera,' esp. 552–7.

149 Casini, 'Dux habet formam regis,' 297.

150 'che il non sentirsi strepito alcuno.' Tutio, *Ordine et modo tenuto*, 18.

151 Coats of arms and human figures were cartographic traditions used to identify control over geographic space. For example, see the printed map of *Lotharingia* from the 1513 Strasbourg edition of Ptolemy's *Geography* in which arms mark specific dominions on the map as well as decorate the frame. A striking example of the use of figures to represent rulers can be seen in the six manuscript navigational charts produced in 1594 by Juan Oliva in Messina and now in the Newberry Library.

152 Cassini notes the Vecellian character of the cartouche in the first state of the map. Giocondo Cassini, *Piante e vedute prospettiche di Venezia (1479–1855)*, 74n.1.

153 'Et questo è l'Habito usato non solamente dalla nobiltà, ma da' Cittadini, et da chiunque si compiace di portarlo, come fanno quasi tutti i Medici, gli Avvocati, et Mercanti, i quali tutti se ne vestono volentieri, poiche essendo Habito proprio della nobiltà, porta seco ne gli altri anchora gran riputatione.' Vecellio, *De gli habiti*, 106. The costume of the young man resembles Vecellio's *Scudieri del doge* (115).

154 Staley posits a relation between this 'Marriage of the Adriatic' and the origins of the dogaressa's coronation pageant. *Dogaressas of Venice*, 134.

155 The ring, or *vera*, was the most significant of those gifts received, according to legend, from Alexander III in thanks for protection from the republic in the twelfth century. On the Sensa, see Åsa Boholm, *Doge of Venice*, 238. Muir, *Civic Ritual*, 112–21; Lina Urban, 'La festa della Sensa,' esp. 315.

156 On the difference between the Sensa and carnival, with its potential for inversion, see Muir, *Civic Ritual*, 132; also see 118–33.

157 Casini, '*Triumphi*,' 31n.44.

158 Tutio, *Ordine et modo tenuto*, 5–6. On the architecture see, Tondro, 'Memory and Tradition.'

159 Tutio, *Ordine et modo tenuto*, 5–6; Rota, *Lettera*. Sansovino-Stringa, *Venetia città nobilissima*, 431–2. On the tradition of floating *teatri del mondo* including the one designed by G.A. Rusconi for the Compagnia della Calza degli Accesi in 1564, see Lina Urban, 'Teatri e "Teatri del Mondo" nella Venezia del Cinquecento,' 142–4; Puppi, *Architettura e utopia*, 162–4; Denis Cosgrove, *The Palladian Landscape: Geographical Change and Its Cultural Representations in Sixteenth-Century Italy*, 233, 241–2.

160 See 284–5n.89.

161 'I Cosmografi siano quelli ... descrivono le nature, et proprietà de'paesi, et delle cose, che in essi sono, i costumi, i popoli, le cose notabile accadute di tempo in tempo.' Garzoni, *Piazza universale*, 313.

162 'l'ordine che fu tenuto nell'acompagnar la Serenissima Prencipessa di Venetia Moresina Moresini Grimani, MDXCVII, 4 Maggio.'

163 See Stanley Chojnacki, 'Subaltern Patriarchs: Patrician Bachelors in Renaissance Venice,' in Clare Lees, ed., *Medieval Masculinities: Regarding Men in the Middle Ages*, 73–90.

164 Virginia Cox, 'The Single Self: Feminist Thought and the Marriage Market in Early Modern Venice,' 546. The latter term is Cox's (see 540–7).

165 Cox cites Patriarch Giovanni Tiepolo's 1629 letter to the doge. Ibid., 540.

166 Ibid., 542–3. On conventual legislation see L. Menetto and G. Zennaro, eds, *Storia del malcostume,* 145–87.
167 Cox, 'Single Self,' 534.
168 Ibid., 529.
169 Chojnacki, 'Subaltern Patriarchs,' esp. 78–9.
170 Cox, 'Single Self,' 543.
171 See Patricia Allerston, 'Reconstructing the Second-Hand Clothes Trade in Sixteenth and Seventeenth-Century Venice.' On masquerading and cross-dressing, see Muir, *Civic Ritual,*166, 175, 175n.118, and 177.
172 'Perche gli Habiti donneschi sono molto soggetti alla mutatione, et variabili più che le forme della Luna: non è possibile in una sola descrittione metter tutto quello, che se ne può dire.' Vecellio, *De gli habiti,* 140–1.
173 'et porta seco diversità d'ornamento ... non hai mai fine, e mai si fornisce d'imparare quanto alla forma de gli abiti, i quali alla giornata si variano tanto che i sartori ne sanno meno in lor vecchiezza, che sul principio che aprono bottega. Però gli è necessario un gran giudicio a voler contentare. Et sodisfare a tutte ... e donne sopra tutto, che ogni giorno mutano usanza e modo di vestire.' Garzoni, *Piazza universale,* 819.
174 Diane Owen Hughes, 'Sumptuary Law and Social Relations in Renaissance Italy,' in John Bossy, ed., *Disputes and Settlements. Law and Human Relations in the West,* 90.
175 On sumptuary laws, see 293–4n.8.
176 Bistort, *Magistrato alle pompe,* 125.
177 See Junkerman, '*Bellissima donna,*' 214, 218.
178 Bistort, *Magistrato alle pompe,* 116.
179 Francesco Barbaro, *On Wifely Duties,* in Kohl et al., eds, *The Earthly Republic: Italian Humanists on Government and Society,* 206.
180 Barbaro, *On Wifely Duties,* 208. For Vives's variation on Plutarch's story concerning the shoes of Egyptian women, see *De Institutione,* 1: chap. 8, 91; see 75–91.
181 Vecellio explains how costume is used to distinguish the wives of officials. For example, in his discussion of the wives of the governors of Venetian mainland cities, he states, 'Le mogli di quei Gentil'huomini, che sono mandati al governo di qualche Città, fortiscono il nome stesso de'mariti, et sono chiamate Podestaresse, Capitane, et simili. Onde quel nome straordinario si tira anchora dietro qualche polita foggia di vestire secondo il decoro. Et perciò queste vanno molto sontuose, et con habiti conformi a'titoli, et a'gradi.' Vecellio, *De gli habiti,* 135.
182 De Luca is cited by Diane Owen Hughes, 'Representing the Family: Portraits and Purposes in Early Modern Italy,' 30.

183 Luther is cited in Ian Maclean, *Renaissance Notion*, 10.

184 Maclean, *Renaissance Notion*, 12.

185 Giovanni Caldiera is cited in Margaret L. King, 'Personal, Domestic, and Republican Values in the Moral Philosophy of Giovanni Caldiera,' 566.

186 On the concept of the cosmos, status, and 'sartorial emblems of position,' see Fletcher, *Allegory*, 109–10, 118–19.

187 See Scarabello, 'Le dogaresse,' in Benzoni, ed., *I Dogi*, 172.

188 'questa Venetia intagliata, ampliata, agionta et abbellita assai più di quante per l'addietro ve ne siano alla vista universale uscite.'

189 See chapter 2.

190 Vives, *De Institutione*, 2: 117. On the ideology of movement see Sharon Fermor, 'Movement and Gender in Sixteenth-Century Italian Painting,' in Kathleen Adler and Marcia Pointon, eds, *The Body Imaged: The Human Form and Visual Culture Since the Renaissance*, 137.

191 Vives, *De Institutione* 2: 123.

192 Barbaro, *On Wifely Duties*, 205. See Vives on the Virgin Mary as an exemplar who 'uttered not a word' to the Magi and 'at the cross ... was entirely speechless ... because she had learned not to speak in public.' *De Institutione*, 2: 141.

193 'Con tutto ciò hanno le donne d'hoggidì tanto imperio sopra gli huomini che possono gloriarsi che stando ritirate in casa, governano le Città, e le cose publiche à lor voglia.' Stefano Guazzo, *La civil conversazione*.

194 See Alasdair Macintyre's concept of the character. *After Virtue: A Study in Moral Theory*, 27–31. See below 328n.3.

195 On the conflict between Grimani and Donà over the new Procuratie, and Donà's related opposition to ostentation, luxury, and ties with Rome, see Manfredo Tafuri, *Venice and the Renaissance*, chap. 7. See above 271nn.39, 40.

196 Casini, 'Dux habet formam regis,' 302–3.

197 'Il Doge spinto dalla moglie aveva fatto domanda per l'incoronazione e l'ottenne malgrado la opposizione dei più vecchi senatori. Non venne però ammesso che fosse tenuta anche una giostra.' Da Mosto, *Dogi*, 315–16. Tondro questions the idea that the coronation was delayed for political reasons on the basis that 'a clause in doge Grimani's promissione required him to stage the ceremonial entry of his wife within a year of his election, which indicated the patriciate's support for this ceremony.' 'Memory and Tradition,' 65.

198 Thomas Coryat discusses the 'indulgence' of Venetians for prostitutes, whom he compares to all those Venetian women 'coope[d] up,' by their husbands: 'For they thinke that the chastity of their wives would be sooner

assaulted, and so consequently they should be *capricornified* were it not for these places of evacuation.' Coryat, *Coryat's Crudities*, 265.

199 Giovanni Michele Bruto, *La institvtione di vna fancivlla nata noblimente. L'institvtion d'vne fille de noble maison*, trans. [by J. Bellere], 26a–28a. Ruth Kelso, *Doctrine for the Lady of the Renaissance*, 61.

4 Reproducing the Individual: Likeness and History in Printed Portrait Books

1 Vecellio also uses Venier as the model for his doge, but he also refers to his successor Nicolò dà Ponte. *De gli habiti*, 78.

2 'Io ho cavato questo da un ritratto del Principe Veniero, dipinto in quell'Habito, ch'egli portò, quando fu creato Generale della Republ. Venetiana nell'ultima guerra, che ella hebbe con Selino gran Turco.' Ibid., 103. On Venier as an ideal type, see Pompeo Molmenti, *Sebastiano Veniero e la battaglia di Lepanto*, 123–4. Also see *Sebastiano Veniero dopo la battaglia di Lepanto*.

3 Of interest here is Alasdair MacIntyre's concept of 'characters,' which he defines as the ways in which social roles are limited by a culture's expectations of how those roles are performed. Social roles may be constructed by institutions, but a *character* is something that provides a culture with its moral ideals. As MacIntyre explains, 'social type and psychological type are required to coincide. The *character* morally legitimates a mode of social existence.' A society's moral philosophies can be expressed through the actions of individuals and social roles, but also symbolically, through art. Where an image defines the expectations of the role, that character is embodied by an individual, as in this case with Venier. It is the gap between the role and how it is performed – the disagreement between them – that can be seen to define the self. Alasdair Macintyre, *After Virtue: A Study in Moral Theory*, 29, 27–31.

4 Giovanni Pietro Contarini, *Historia delle cose successe dal principio della guerra mossa da Selim ottomano a' Venetiani, fino al du della gran giornata vittoriosa contra Turchi*, 54.

5 For example, see Pietro Bertelli, *Effigie naturali de li Serenessimi Principi di Venetia; Vite degl'imperatori de'Turchi con le loro effiggie intalgiate* [*sic*]; *Effigie de sommi Pontefici dalla sedia d'Avignone ritornati a Roma fino a questi tempi* (1611); Jean Jacques Boissard, *Vitae et icones svltanorvm Tvrcicorvm*; Giacomo Franco, *Effiggie naturali dei maggior Prencipi et piu valorosi capitani*.

6 See Adrian W.B. Randolph, 'Introduction: The Authority of Likeness,' 1–5, and other essays in *Word & Image* 19, nos. 1 & 2 (January–June 2003). On

portrait books, see Milan Pelc, *Illustrium imagines: Das Porträtbuch der Renaissance*; Cecil Clough, 'Italian Renaissance Portraiture and Printed Portrait-Books,' in Dennis E. Rhodes and Denis V. Reidy, eds, *The Italian Book: Studies Presented to Dennis E. Rhodes*; Eugene Dwyer, 'Marco Mantova Benevides e i rittratti di giureconsulti illustri'; 'André Thevet and Fulvio Orsini: The Beginnings of the Modern Tradition of Classical Portrait Iconography in France.'

7 Gülru Necipoğlu, 'Süleyman the Magnificent and the Representation of Power in the Context of Ottoman–Hapsburg–Papal Rivalry.'

8 David Woodward's translation, *Maps as Prints in the Italian Renaissance*, 93.

9 See Susan Stewart, *On Longing: Narratives of the Miniature, the Gigantic, the Souvenir, the Collection*, 125.

10 Isabella Palumbo-Fossati cites an inventory of Elena Polo's dowry, which records two portraits for 'di buona memoria.' ASV, *Notario F. Mondo*, reg. 8305, f. 103v (6 February 1567). 'Ritratti in piedi' were recorded in the 'portego' of the merchants Zuanfrancesco Calderini, Nicolò Franceschi, and Gerolamo Tasca. ASV, *Cancelleria inferiore*, Miscellanea notai diversi, *Inventari*, busta 42 (10 February 1577); Isabella Palumbo-Fossati, 'L'interno della casa dell'artigianato e dell'artista nella Venezia del cinquecento,' 145, and nos. 64 and 65. I am grateful to Patricia Fortini Brown for referring me to this study.

11 Federica Ambrosini, '"Descrittioni del mondo" nelle case Venete dei secoli XVI e XVII,' 67, 70. Woodward, *Maps as Prints*, 76. Palumbo-Fossati, 'L'interno della casa,' 146–8; on interiors, see Patricia Fortini Brown, 'Behind the Walls: The Material Culture of Venetian Elites,' in John Martin and Dennis Romano, eds, *Venice Reconsidered: The History and Civilization of an Italian City-State 1297–1797*, 310.

12 Federica Ambrosini, 'Descrittioni del mondo,' 132.

13 Ibid., 149.

14 Venetian mirrors were sought after by rulers and officials of the courts, since courtiers could emulate the poses and gestures of their princes. Sabine Melchior-Bonnet, *The Mirror: A History*, chap. 1, esp. 25–9.

15 Consignments of Venetian mirrors recorded in Wilfrid Brulez's study of Flemish merchants between 1569 and 1596 include: England (26 August 1569, no. 3), ten mirrors to Spain (18 August 1580, no. 22), three containers to Flemish merchants in Cádiz and Seville (15 May 1589, no. 223); mirrors of different types, valued at one hundred ducats, were shipped to Lisbon (8 June 1592, no. 337), and a case was sent to Amsterdam (16 June 1595, no. 602). English merchants were charged with 'deux caisses contenant 135 1/2 douzaines de mirroirs aux encadrements décorés' for London (14 October 1596, no. 687). *Marchands Flamands à Venise I (1568–1605)*.

16 Ibid., 630–3.

17 Ibid., 632. For Vrin's consignments of mirrors, see nos. 602, 669, 676, 713.

18 Palumbo-Fossati, 'L'interno della casa,' 145.

19 See 274n.61.

20 John Martin, 'Inventing Sincerity, Refashioning Prudence: The Discovery of the Individual in Renaissance Europe.'

21 See 280n.62, 284–5n.89.

22 Francesco Sansovino, *Delle cose notabili che sono in Venetia libri due. etc.*, dedication.

23 'effigie al naturale' and 'ritratto della città meravigliosa di Venetia.'

24 'Saranno in questo Quarto Libro i ritratti di quegli Orsini, che per l'honorata virtù loro sono stati famosi in diversi tempi: Conciosia che essendo io desideroso di non pretermettere parte alcuna che sia necessaria, o ch'io possa imaginarmi che torni bene a questa materia, ho giudicato, ch'il mio pensiero sia per apportar non poco utile & diletto a tutti coloro che leggeranno le cose presenti. Perchè gli huomini molte volte son curiosi di riconoscer nell'effigie quelle virtù, le quali essi hanno sentito celebrare, & esaltar ne grandi, dalla fama del mondo vivente, & dagli scrittori, atteso che non meno si trahe profitto dalla presenza delle persone eccellenti per valore, che dalla memoria de lor fatti honorati: onde si come a chi studiosamente ricerca le Historie è necessaria la cognitione della Cosmografia, per rispetto de luoghi, dove avennero le cose scritte, così conferisce molto alla medesima Historia, lo haver sotto gli occhi le imagini di coloro de'quali si leggono le pruove segnalate & illustri. Percioche vedendosi spesse volte che l'opere non corrispondono ai volti, & che talhora sotto bellissimi visi, si cuoprono scelerati & horrendi pensieri; il Lettore, salendo quasi come per gradi alla maraviglia, si riduce da quella, a contemplare i miracoli della natura che ella sà fare intorno alle somiglie dell'huomo. Et trovando le forze dell'animo nostro implicate insieme con la fattura del viso, in quella maniera che è congiunto insieme l'odorato, il gusto, & il colore con la fattura d'un frutto, fa le più volte dal viso indubitato giudicio de cuori humani. Ora in queste imagini di huomini così chiari, habbiamo da notare, che nella gente Orsina si vede grandezza & maestà nel sembiate & nel volto, perchè essendo pieni di spirito & di vigor militare, con le fronte aperte, & con le bocche per la maggior parte assai grandi, significative di huomini di molta eloquenza, & con aspetti veramente reali, possiamo chiaramente credere (quando non si havesse altra cognitione dell'origine loro) che essi siano senza alcun dubbio discesi d'altissimo, & nobil sangue, se dalla faccia (che è vera dimostratrice degli animi nostri) si dee far coniettura della grandezza de'generosi, et alti pensieri.' Francesco Sansovino, 'Degli huomini illustri di Casa Orsina,' *L'historia*

di Casa Orsina, Libro Quarto, 63; Clough, 'Italian Renaissance Portraiture,' 184.

25 'Questo volto cosi asciutto, & di color macilente, dimostrativo di qualità di huomo nervoso, & per natura agile & forte, è il vero ritratto del Signor Camillo Orsino, figliuolo del precedente signor Paolo, il quale allevatosi ne gli studi honorati della militar disciplina sotto Nicola Orsino, Bartolomeo da Liviano, et Gian Iacomo Trìulci, gli trapassò di gran lunga d'autorità, di prudenza, & de fede.' Sansovino, *L'historia di Casa Orsina*, Libro 3, 81. For further examples see his biographies of Giordano Orsino (85v) and Nicola Orsino Conte di Pitigliano (74).

26 Clough, 'Italian Renaissance Portraiture,' 185. Blank spaces in André Thevet's *Les vrais pourtraits et vies des hommes illustres* were interpreted by Rouben C. Cholakian as evidence of the geographer's scrupulous concern with accuracy. However, as Eugene Dwyer has demonstrated, this was part of the fiction of authenticity woven by Thevet. See 'André Thevet and Fulvio Orsini: The Beginnings of the Modern Tradition of Classical Portrait Iconography in France,' 467–80, esp. 472.

27 See page 135.

28 Ennio Concina, *A History of Venetian Architecture*, 184.

29 The album may have served as a companion to biographies printed earlier in Padua. Clough, 'Italian Renaissance Portraiture,' 185. On Benevides's collections see Eugene Dwyer, 'Marco Mantova Benevides,' 59–71.

30 Clough, 'Italian Renaissance Portraiture,' 186. See Pelc for earlier examples. *Illustrium imagines.*

31 Clough, 'Italian Renaissance Portraiture,' 186, 188, 189. On portraits of cardinals and popes see Michael Bury, *The Print in Italy, 1550–1620.*

32 *Dizionario enciclopedico Bolaffi dei pittori e degli incisori italiani dall' XI al XX secolo*, 5: 149.

33 Ferdinando, the originator of the Bertelli 'dynasty,' worked in Padua, Venice, and Rome. Donato Bertelli, perhaps Ferdinando's brother, was active in Venice at the sign of San Marco from 1558 to 1592. He was known for portraits and maps. Andrea Bertelli continued at the bookstore from 1594 to 1601. Francesco, possibly Pietro's father, was active in Venice and Padua from as early as 1572 to 1594. Another younger Francesco, perhaps Pietro's son, continued his father's business in Padua, publishing *Il carnevale, Italiano mascherato* in 1642. Luca Bertelli, likely a brother of either Pietro or the elder Francesco, was active in Venice from 1560 to 82 and, in the second half of the sixteenth century, in Rome, where Orazio and Giovanni also worked. Luca was also active in Padua between 1563 and 1594. See Paolo Bellini, 'Stampatori e mercanti di stampe in Italia nei secoli XVI e XVII'; Bury, *The*

Print in Italy, 221–2; Gert Jan van der Sman, 'Print Publishing in Venice in the Second Half of the Sixteenth Century.'

34 For bibliography, see Milan Pelc, *Illustrium imagines.*

35 On Giovio's collection see Linda Alice Klinger, 'The Portrait Collection of Paolo Giovio.' Klinger suggests that the collection of portraits was not only in the Villa but also in his townhouses (72).

36 Klinger, 'Paolo Giovio,' 28–9.

37 Clough, 'Italian Renaissance Portraiture,'199. Paolo Giovio, *Elogia veris clarorum virorum imaginibus apposita quae in Musaeo Ioviano Comi spectantur; Elogia virorum bellica virtute illustrium veris imaginibus supposita quae apud Musaeum spectantur.* Klinger questions the assumption that the display of the portraits in the museum conformed to the four categories into which Giovio organized the biographies in his 1546 publication: 'men distinguished by their "productive genius," now deceased; those still living; artists and faceti; and lastly, popes, kings, and generals.' 'Paolo Giovio,' 72.

38 Ibid., 79. Paolo Giovio, *Elogia virorum bellica virtute; Elogia virorum literis illustrium; Musei ioviani imagines;* Nicolas Reusner, *Icones sive imagines viuae, literis clarorum virorum.*

39 Klinger, 'Paolo Giovio,' chap. 3.

40 Ibid., 195–212.

41 Giovanni Bonifacio, *L'arte de cenni,* preface.

42 'I concetti de gli animi nostri in quattro maniere si possono esprimere; con i cenni, co'l parlare, con lo scrivere, e con i simboli. Del parlare, e dello scrivere molti valent'huomini hanno accuratamente trattato, & insegnato come in tutte le favelle potiamo rettamente, & ornatamente con la lingua, e con la penna farci intendere. De'simboli, con i quali l'huomo, celando i suoi pensieri al volgo, quelli eruditamente e misteriosamente scuopre à gli intendenti, è stato da alcuni scritto: il che come cosa naturale in tutte le età essere avenuto, chiaramente si vede, benche diversamente secondo le qualità delle nationi, e proprietà de'costumi loro.' Ibid., 3.

43 'E tanto più tralasciando questa inestricabil confusione di parlari, dobbiamo abbracciar questa cognition de'cenni, con la quale si forma una immutabil favella, che naturalmente è da tutte le genti egualmente intesa. Ilche massimamente si scorge nella pittura, il cui artificio versando in rappresentar i gesti, & i moti, e per conseguenza gli affetti de gli huomini, è perciò da tutte le genti con diletto egualmente intesa: onde l'opere de'nostri pittori non sono meno stimate, & havute care da gli Asiatici, da gli Africani, e da gli Antipodi istessi, di quello che siano da noi medesimi.' Ibid., 12.

44 On Della Porta, see Luisa Muraro, *Giambattista Della Porta mago e scienziato: In appendice l'indice della Taumatologia;* Louise George Clubb, *Giambattista della*

Porta, Dramatist. On physiognomy see Patrizia Magli, *Il volto e l'anima: Fisio-gnomica e passioni*; Ulrich Reisser, *Physiognomik und Ausdruckstheorie der Renais-sance*; Lucia Rodler, *I silenzi mimici del volto.* On portraits and physiognomy, see Flavio Caroli, *L'arte dalla psicologia alla psicanalisi; Storia della fisiognomica: Arte e psicologia da Leonardo a Freud.*

45 Both Della Porta and Paolo Giovio drew on images that were widely diffused, making it difficult to be certain of the source. Francis Haskell notes that identifying sources for Della Porta's illustrations is complicated by the extent to which he altered the faces to make them resemble the animals. *History and Its Images: Art and the Interpretation of the Past*, 63. On Stimmer's own licence with Giovio's paintings, see Klinger, 'Paolo Giovio,' catalogue no. 136.

46 'Fu il Poliziano di costume censurabili. Né ebbe aspetto gradevole, per quel suo naso spropositato e l'occhio losco che davano al viso un'aria assai poco benevola. Di natura accorto e sottile, ma pieno d'invidia malcelata, da un lato si faceva continuamente beffe delle opere altrui; dall'altro non poteva sopportare che nessuno, per quanto mosso da buone ragione, osasse criti-care le sue.' Paolo Giovio, *Ritrattti degli uomini illustri*, 119.

47 'Lettor, hai qui il gran naso del Rinosceronte, dal cui mezzo nasce un corno, con la viva effigie di Angelo Poliziano.' Unless noted otherwise, all citations are from the 1988 edition: Della Porta, *Della fisonomia dell'uomo*, book II, chap. 7, 159.

48 In an illustration for the chin, for example, Della Porta compares the pro-files of three men. The radically different proportions of their facial features are highlighted by horizontal lines and the caption 'Rapportiamo nella pre-sente tavoletta varie sorti di barbe, acciò quello che diciamo in lettere lo si veggia con gli occchi.' Della Porta, *Della fisonomia*, book II, chap. 20.

49 Luisa Muraro, *Giambattista Della Porta*, 62.

50 For example: 'Filone e Trogo toglievano anco i segni dalle piante; perché, essendo la virtù vegetativa commune a tutti i viventi, toglievano i segni della vita lunga dalle piante, dicendo così: chi ha i capelli lunghi e fermi, sono di lunga vita, perché le piante che han lunga vita non lasciano mai le frondi, come il Pino, Cipressi e altri.' Della Porta, *Della fisonomia*, book I, chap. V, 33. On signs in animals see chap. 3, 24–7. On the analogies between flora and fauna, see Della Porta's *Phytognomonica octo libris contenta*. His manu-script on chiromancy was only published in 1677; Pompeo Sarnelli's transla-tion, *Della Chirofisonomia*, is published in a critical edition with the Latin manuscript: Oreste Trabucco, ed. *De ea naturalis physiognomioniae parte quae ad manuum lineas spectat libri duo.* Clubb, *Giambattista della Porta, Dramatist*, 24–5.

51 'È dunque una scienza che impara de' segni che sono fissi nel corpo, et acci-

denti che trasmutano i segni, investigar i costumi naturali dell'animo ... Il nome della Fisonomia ... quasi volesse dir legge o regola di Natura; cioè, per certa regola, norma et ordine di Natura si consosce da tal forma di corpo tal passione dell'anima.' Della Porta, *Della fisonomia*, book I, chap. 30, 108.

52 'Nella tavola di sotto sono i ritratti di Messalina e Faustina Auguste, cavati dalle medaglie di bronzo et argento, e statue loro, dal Museo del Signor Gio. Vincenzo della Porta, mia fratello.' Della Porta, *Della fisonomia*, book VI, chap. 21, 558–9. On the medallions and busts collected by Della Porta's uncle and his brother, see Haskell, *History and Its Images*, 61–3.

53 'Ma or tratteremo di due donne Auguste infamissime, e prima di Messalina. Ella era molto irsuta di peli, come stimo, ché essendo ben fornita di capelli e di ciglia, si può giudicar che così fosse nelle parti coperte; la tempia ancor pelose, che quasi tutta la fronte ancora occupano. Era di faccia e di collo delicato e sottile; et il collo, quasi saggio che tali fussero le gambe e le braccia, che seguon sempre la medesima proporzione; l'occhio grasso e lascivo e cavo, la barba quasi rivolta al naso, la bocca che giace nel cavo; e par che le mascelle si contraggano nel volto allegro. Era di capelli biondi, come scrive Giovenale. Fu esempio di libidine, e superò tutte le donne Romane del suo tempo. Si fe' fare una stanza in Palazzo da meretrice, contendendo con le altre publiche meretrici per riportarne in quello esercizio trionfo e palma. Così costringeva le altre matrone Romane a far com'ella faceva; anzi le facea forzare nel suo palazzo insino alla presenzia de' mariti, e queste sole persone ricevevano da lei onori e magistrati. Sotto nome di Licisca meretrice, entrava la mattina, e stando tutt'il giorno nell'esercizio, era la sera ultima a partirsi, stanca, ma non ancor sazia di libidine; e cercava di più il prezzo dell'opra. Queste et altre disoneste sue opre sono scritte da Svetonio e da Dione.' Della Porta, *Della fisonomia*, book VI, chap. 21, 558–9.

54 'Fu Faustina ancor piena di capelli, magra, e simile di fattezze e di costumi; che veniva ancora a giacersi con i gladiatori, et altre persone basse; di che ne son piene tutte l'istorie.' Ibid., book VI, chap. 21, 559. See Haskell, *History and Its Images*, 64. Like Della Porta, Paolo Giovio believed that a text was more trustworthy than an image. Klinger, 'Paolo Giovio,' 'Introduction,' esp. 39, 43.

55 Haskell, *History and Its Images*, 67.

56 Della Porta, *Della fisonomia*, book I, chap. 31, 109–10.

57 'Delle già dette varietà di fronti se ne elegge la mezzana, dove si descrive la miglior qualità delle fronti. La fronte quadrata, e per la proporzion della faccia mediocre, dimostra uomo magnanimo, e ciò perché s'assomiglia alla fronte del Leone.' Ibid., book II, chap. 7, 132–3.

58 'Qui sotto si proponne la fronte umana di forma quadrata simile a quella del

Leone con esatta descrizion, acciò non t'inganni nella similitudine.' Ibid., book II, chap. 7, 133.

59 The caption for the 'Naso schiacciato' states: 'Qui sotto si dipinge il naso del Leone, e mirando all'incontro vedrai quello dell'uomo, acciò possi trarre comparazione.' Ibid., book II, chap. 7, 168; 'Ecco di nuovo l'imagine del Leone, nella quale ha lo labbro inferiore delicato, per poterlo rassomigliare all'uomo,' book II, chap. 12, 193.

60 Michel Foucault, *The Order of Things. An Archaeology of the Human Sciences*, part one, 3–77.

61 The meaning of rascism today, according to the on-line *Oxford English Dictionary*, is 'The theory that distinctive human characteristics and abilities are determined by race.'

62 See Adriana Boscaro for a complete list of the printed primary sources, *Sixteenth Century European Printed Works on the First Japanese Mission to Europe. A Descriptive Bibliography*; Beniamino Gutierrez, *La prima ambascieria giapponese in Italia*; Luís Froís, *La première ambassade du Japon en Europe. 1582–1592, Première partie le traité du Père Frois*; Alexandro Valignano, *Il cerimoniale per i missionari del Giappone*. For further documents and sources see Guglielmo Berchet, *Le antiche ambasciate giapponesi in Italia*; Guglielmo Berchet, 'Documenti del saggio storico sulle antiche ambasciate giapponesi in Italia.' BMV, IT VII 811 (7299), 1585.

63 Secondary sources on the embassy and the Jesuits in Japan include J.F. Moran, *The Japanese and the Jesuits: Alessandro Valignano in Sixteenth-Century Japan*; Adriana Boscaro, 'Giapponesi a Venezia nel 1585,' in Lionello Lanciotti, ed., *Venezia e l'Oriente*, 409–29ff.; 'La visita a Venezia della prima ambasceria giapponese in Europa,' *Il Giappone, anno V.*; Enrico Fasana and Giuseppe Sorge, *Civiltà indiana ed impatto Europeo nei secoli XVI–XVIII: L'apporto dei viaggiatori e missionari italiani*; Yasunori Gunji, *Dall'isola del Giapan: La prima ambasceria giapponese in occidente*; Giuseppe Sorge, *Il Cristianesimo in Giappone e il de missione*; Judith Brown, 'Courtiers and Christians: The First Japanese Emissaries to Europe'; C.R. Boxer, *The Christian Century in Japan, 1549–1650*.

'Portano due veste longhe quella di sopra senza maniche, quella di sotto con maniche sopra spalla, e sopra petto ha guisa di pacienza fin'alla cintura, come portano i Certosini in cella, o di S Francesco di Paula ma senza capuzzo, tutte di seta biancha come ormesino sottile, ricamate di varii colori, a foiami e linee, con diverse figure di uccelli e altri animali, e gioie all'Arabesca, capello di feltro berettino con traccia d'oro alla Spagnola, camiscia col collare crespo pur alla Spagnola, cintura di seta con l'arme attaccate, faccia veneranda, di colore Affricano, picola statura, anni 18. in circa.' *Avisi venuti novamente da Roma delli 23. di Marzo 1585.* On the illustration, see Boscaro, *Sixteenth Century European Printed Works*, nos. 20, 20 bis, and 34, pages 42–5, 74–5. The translation is Adriana Boscaro's, in *Sixteenth Century European Printed Works*, 44.

64 Abraham de Bruyn, *Imperii ac sacerdotii ornatus. Diversarum item gentium peculiaris vestitus.*

65 'La differenza è poca fra di loro.' *Compendio storico delle cose più notabili di Milano ed in paricolare della famiglia Monti* in the Biblioteca Ambrosiana di Milano, ms. P., 248–51. See Gutierrez, *La prima ambascieria*, 68. The portraits are published in Brown, 'Courtiers and Christians,' 879–84. The same portraits appear on a broadsheet that was printed in Augsburg in 1586, and here too, any differences between the Jesuit who accompanied them, Padre Mesquita, and the Japanese can be attributed to the age of the youths. See Boscaro, 'Giapponesi a Venezia nel 1585,' fig. 49.

66 J. Brown, 'Courtiers and Christians,' 878.

67 'The people are all white, and very cultivated, and even the common people and the peasants are well brought up and marvellously polite among themselves, so that it seems as if they had all been brought up at court.' Alessandro Valignano, *Sumario de las cosas de Japón*, 5.

68 Brown 'Courtiers and Christians,' 885.

69 See Jonathan Crary; *Techniques of the Observer: On Vision and Modernity in the Nineteenth Century*; Kaja Silverman, *The Threshold of the Visible World.* On matter before meaning see Whitney Davis, *Replications: Archaeology, Art History, Psychoanalysis.*

70 See Valignano, *Cerimoniale.* As the representative of the Father General, the Visitor is the highest position in the Society of Jesus. On Valignano see Moran, *The Japanese and the Jesuits*, 20–8.

71 Jesuit success in Asia depended upon their being the sole beneficiary of funding received through Portuguese trade. The success of Philip II's new status as king of both Spain and Portugal required the continued monopoly of religious power in Asia by the Portuguese and their linked economic pursuits. Thus, the Jesuits pressed Philip to maintain their monopoly, and this in turn helped Philip's relations with the Church. For the latter, faced with the loss of much of northern Europe, the embassy offered a chance to display the global successes of Catholicism. Brown, 'Courtiers and Christians,' 887–8. Also see Moran, *The Japanese and the Jesuits*, and Sorge, who discusses hostilities in Asia over trade by the Dutch Protestants. *Il Cristianesimo*, 29.

72 Gregory died in April 1585 when the Japanese were in Italy. Sixtus V expanded funding to the Jesuits but also opened the door to Franciscan competition. See Sorge, *Il Cristianesimo*, 19–20.

73 Brown, 'Courtiers and Christians,' 894.

74 Gio. Nicolò Doglioni in Berchet 'Documenti del saggio storico,' 124. Doglioni's firsthand account was published by Stringa in his edition of Sansovino's *Venetia città nobilissima* and reproduced in Berchet, 'Documenti del saggio storico,' 123–38. It certainly impressed the Japanese, for whom the procession at San Marco was the most memorable experience of their visit. Sorge, *Cristianesimo in Giappone*, 84. Also on the visit, see ASV, Collegio, *Cerimoniale* I, 104–5; Boscaro, 'La visita a Venezia.' Lina Urban, 'Feste ufficiali e trattenimenti privati,' *Storia della cultura Veneta. Il seicento.*

75 Additional Manuscript 9852, Missionary conferences of 1580–91. Father Valignano's 'Sumarios' of 1580 and 1583, 22–5. Excerpted in Boxer, *The Christian Century*, 74–6.

76 In Francis Xavier's letter to the Jesuits at Goa, 5 November 1549. Excerpted and translated in Boxer, *The Christian Century*, Appendix 1, 401. Josef Franz Schütte, *Valignano's Mission Principles for Japan*, vol. 1, part 1: 131. On the class–race issue, see Moran, *The Japanese and the Jesuits*, 95–114.

77 Boxer, *The Christian Century*, 80.

78 Schütte, *Valignano's Mission Principles*, part 1, 131.

79 Boxer, *The Christian Century*, 81. J. Brown 'Courtiers and Christians,' 885 and note 32.

80 Boxer, *The Christian Century*, 78.

81 Valignano, *Cerimoniale*, 21, 24. Boscaro, 'La visita a Venezia,' 19.

82 Valigniano's 'resolutions' – what the Jesuits needed to adopt – were published in January 1582. These were *'pulizia,' 'forme di cortesia,' 'dignità,'* and *'dell'amore dei Giapponesi.' Cerimoniale*, 32–5. Also see chapter one, 152: sections 37 and 38. Gunji, *Dall'isola del Giapan*, 124.

83 Valignano, Letter of dedication, *Libro primero del principio y progresso de la religíon christiana en Jappón y de la especial providencia de que Nuestro Señor usa con aquella nueva iglesia* (unpublished), British Library, Additional Manuscript 9857. Excerpted and translated in Moran, *The Japanese and the Jesuits*, 29.

84 A summary of the foreignness Valignano perceived is found in one of his 'Sumarios.' Additional Manuscript 9852, Missionary conferences of 1580–91. Father Valignano's 'Sumarios' of 1580 and 1583, 22–5. Exerpted and translated by Boxer, *The Christian Century*, 77. Much about the Japanese was admired; however, the Jesuits cite pratices of pederasty, abortion, usury, idolatry, selling their own people as slaves, and bellicosity. See Moran, *The Japanese and the Jesuits*, 95–114. Valignano, Additional Manuscript 9852, Missionary conferences of 1580–91. Father Valignano's 'Sumarios' of 1580 and 1583, 22–5. Excerpted and translated in Boxer, *The Christian Century*, 74–6.

85 'Ciononostante trascorsi interamente il primo anno muto come una statua ...
Ed ora, al terzo anno, sono in grado di comprendere come bisogna guidare
il Giappone.' 'Per più di un anno mi diedi da fare unicamente per penetrare
i loro usi e costume.' Letter to the Father General from Bungo, 7 October
1581; Schütte's translation from the Spanish original. Valignano, *Cerimoniale*,
19. Contact between Europe and the Japanese began in 1543 with the Portuguese, and in 1549 missionaries arrived and commercial links were established. Valignano had been in Asia since 1574.

86 'Più degli altri popoli della terra, i Giapponese osservano un esatto e circo-
stanziato cerimoniale nel vestire, nel mangiare, nei rapporti col personale di
servizio, nell'ordinamento della casa, nell'accogliere gli ospiti, e in tutte le
singole manifestazioni, secondo le persone e i gradi sociali.' Valignano, *Cerimoniale*, 28. Valignano devised a cultural exam for the Europeans, worked to
establish a seminary, and even made plans for mission architecture that
would reflect the local environment.

87 '*non* si dovevano cioè, imitare in *tutte* le loro cerimonie i Bonzi che si esauri-
vano in queste manifestazioni esteriori. Noi invece cerchiamo la salvezza
delle anime e la virtù interre.' Ibid., 25–6.

88 Valignano, *Cerimoniale*, 131.

89 Sorge, *Cristianesimo*, 11.

90 This first mission was initiated in the Tensho period (1573–92). Date Masa-
mune initiated a second trip that arrived in Rome in 1615 and returned to
Japan in 1620. On the 'missione de era Keicho- (1596–1615)' or 'missione di
Hasekura Tsunenaga,' see Sorge, *Cristianesimo*; Fasana and Sorge, *Civiltà indiana*.

91 Valignano, 'Les instructions du Père Valignano pour l'ambassade japonaise
en Europe,' in J.A. Abranches, J.A. Pinto, and Henri Bernard, eds, *Monumenta Nipponica*, 395–8. Moran's translation, *The Japanese and the Jesuits*, 8–9.

92 Venetians were reluctant to entertain the embassy because the youths were
'merely relatives of feudal lords.' Brown, 'Courtiers and Christians,' 889.
Franciscans similarly criticized the Jesuits for misleading Europeans about
the status of the ambassadors, which prompted an *Apología* from Valignano.
Moran, *The Japanese and the Jesuits*, 15.

93 Moran, *The Japanese and the Jesuits*, 10–11.

94 Gualtieri, *Relationi della venuta*, 89. *Relatione del viaggio*. Berchet, *Antiche
ambasciate*. Brown, 'Courtiers and Christians,' 876.

95 'Vestono di panni di seta molto leggieri come il Taffettà, ò Ormesino, tessuto
di varii colori bellissimi con diverse sorti di fiori, uccelli, & altri animali del
Giappone, portano mezzi stivaletti ò Borzachini di certa pelle tanto sottile e
pastosa che starebbono in un pugno, sono colorati, & lustri che paiono di

seta, tutti d'un pezzo con una sola apertura che allaciano con cordele. Il piede di quelli stivaletti e à guisa di quei guanti che hanno il ditto grosso separato, e gl'altri uniti, le scarpe sono come quelle de cappuccini, senza calcagno, acute in ponta: per tomora hanno un sol cordone che cuopre appena la ponta delle dita, di maniera che à quelli che hanno l'uso, pare impossibile il caminare con quelle, portano una veste longa di seta quale cacciano nelli calzoni fatti alla marinaresca, lunghi sino al tallone, & uniti in modo sino al fine che paiono una veste & questi talmente stringono con le veste sopra i galloni che pare tutto un solvestimento, portano oltre di ciò una banda di seta ben larga su la spalla destra e sotto il braccio sinistro, al modo de nostri soldati.' *Relatione del viaggo*, 7v.

96 'gli *hakama* vengono descritti come calzoni alla marinara, il *kataginu* come un amitto sacerdotale, un indumento monastico ... o una tracolla militare; i *tabi* e gli *zori* vengono paragonati rispettivamente a stivaletti e a sandali.' Gunji, *Dall'isola del Giapan*, 138.

97 The Venetian ambassador's description is similar: 'Vestono un'habito alla marinaresca, con braghesse longhe fino alli piedi, senza dulimano ò altro habito longo di sopra, cinti con una mezza scimitarra al lato destro, un martello colla ponta di ferro, et un cappello in testa alla spagnola con penne, et le camiscie con ninfe.' ASV Senato dispacci ambasciatori. Roma ordinaria, f.19, c. 38 r.

98 'Si sono vestirsi con vesti lunghe romane, con passamani d'oro all'intorno, et pajono hora tanti dottori bolognesi.' The letter from Priuli in Rome to the Doge, dated 6 April 1585, is in Berchet, 'Documenti del saggio storico,' 157.

99 'Poco dopo l'arrivo mandò molte pezze di Drappi di Seta, accoiche scegliessero quelli che piu loro piacevano per vestirsi all'Italiana, e li ha fatto fare sin hora doi vestiti per uno, e dato ordine per altri.' *Relatione del viaggo*, 6v–7.

100 'quel medesimo loro stranissimo abito giapponese in che comparvero, non serviva tanto alla curiosità come alla divozione, parendo in esso, quali veramente erano, gente venuta d'un altro mondo.' Berchet, 'Documenti del saggio storico,' 137–8.

101 'In quanto al corpo, sono di statura piccioletta, di colore olivastro, hanno gl'occhi piccioli, le palpebre grosse, il naso alquanto largo nel fine, ma d'aspetto ingenuo è signorile, & che non ha niente del barbaro.' He continues with their behaviour: 'Nelle maniere sono civili, cortesi, e modesti, fra di loro si portano molto rispetto, servando sempre nell'andare il medesimo ordine.' *Relatione del viaggo*, 7.

102 'questi Giamponesi sono di statura mediocre, pallidi di faccia, con nasi

larghi e labbri grossi a guisa di saracini e tutti sono d'una efigie tanto somiglianti che dificilmente si conosce luno da laltro et mostra esser giente di buona creanza.' Cited in Gunji, *Dall'isola del Giapan*, 139.

103 'Questi signori Giapponesi tutti quattro sono giovani che il maggior non passa 20 anni, hanno le faccie poco differenti l'una dall'altra, sì come s'intende che sono quasi tutti di quel paese, di carne alquanto bruna.' ASV, Collegio Cerimoniale I, 104–5; Berchet 'Documenti del saggio storico,' 174.

104 Priuli, the Venetian ambassador refers twice to their faces: 'Sono questi giovani di età di 18, in 20 anni, di statura mediocre, et di colore olivastro ... Hanno tutti brutta ciera et brutto colore di carne, come ho detto sopra.' ASV Senato dispacci ambasciatori. Roma ordinaria, f. 19, c. 38r.

105 According to Gualtieri, 'la carnagione, se ben dicono che nel Giapone suole essere bianca, e è verisimile per li grandi freddi, che vi fanno, pure in questi per lunghezza e disagi del viaggio, s'è colorita in modo, che più tosto tira all'olivastro.' *Relationi della venuta*, 157; Brown's translation, 'Courtiers and Christians,' 885.

106 Valignano, *Ceremoniale*, esp. 32 , 130.

107 *Capitolo a Selin imperator de Turchi: Delle feste et allegresse ch'ei faceva in Costantinopoli ... della presa del'Isola di Cipro.*

108 *[ ] Et ultima desperatione de Selim Gran Turco per la perdita della sua Armata.*

109 *Relatione di tutto il successo di Famagosta.*

110 Fernand Braudel, 'Bilan d'une bataille,' in Gino Benzoni, ed., *Il Mediterraneo*, 116.

111 Paolo Sarpi writes 'Sancte Turca, libera nos' in a letter to Jérôme Groslet de L'Isle, 28 April 1609, adding later, on 28 March 1617, 'sono meno cattivi che spagnoli.' in D. Busnelli, ed., *Lettere ai protestanti*, I: 78. Paolo Preto, *Venezia e i Turchi*, 314–15.

112 Necipoğlu, 'Süleymân the Magnificent,' 407; Julian Raby, *Venice, Dürer and the Oriental Mode*, 25.

113 Necipoğlu, 'Süleymân the Magnificent,' 407; Lisa Jardine and Jerry Brotton, *Global Interests: Renaissance Art between East and West*, esp. 42. On local criticism of the use of western architects for Mehmed's palace, see Gülru Necipoğlu, *Architecture, Ceremonial, and Power. The Topkapi Palace in the Fifteenth and Sixteenth Centuries*, 250. Also see Michael Rogers, 'The Arts under Süleymân the Magnificent,' in Halil Inalcik and Cemal Kafadar, eds, *Süleymân the Second and His Time*.

114 The difficulties of maintaining two fronts had the effect of limiting Süleymân's campaigns against Iran. See Rhoads Murphey, 'Süleymân's Eastern Policy,' in Inalcik and Kafadar, eds, *Süleymân the Second and His Time*, 229–48. Necipoğlu, 'Süleyman the Magnificent,' 424–5.

115 Elena Bonora, *Ricerche su Francesco Sansovino imprenditore librario e letterato*, 113.

116 Some examples include Luigi Bassano, *Costumi et i modi particolari della vita de'Turchi*; Antonio Menavino, *Trattato de costumi et vita de Turchi*; M. Cosimo Filiarchi, *Trattato della guerra, et dell'unione de'principi Christiani contra i Turchi & gli altri infédeli*; Giovanni Francesco Loredano, *La Turca. Comedia*; Giuseppe Rosaccio, *Viaggio da Venetia*.

117 Gigliotti's portrait book was also published by Filippo Thomassino and Giovanni Turpino in Rome in 1600.

118 The dedication begins: 'L'imperio del Signor Turco è pervenuto à di nostri à tanta grandezza, che le sue forze sono riputate incomparabili, & quasi ad un certo modo invincibili.'

119 Rolf Kultzen and Peter Eikemeier, *Venezianische Gemaelde des 15. und 16. Jahrhunderts*, 236–9, plates, 118–31.

120 For a summary of Ottoman–European relations see Paolo Preto, 'The Papacy, Venice and the Ottoman Empire,' in Inalcik and Kafadar, eds, *Süleymân the Second and His Time*, 195–202.

121 According to Cemal Kafadar, the prevailing view of modern scholars that Ottoman Turks found commerce distasteful has been overstated. Instead of a reduction in Ottoman mercantile activity, the opposite occurred in Venice, where traders were even protected by Islamic law. 'A Death in Venice (1575): Anatolian Muslim Merchants Trading in the Serenissima,' in Raiyyet Rüsûmu, ed., 'Essays Presented to Halil Inalcik on His Seventieth Birthday by His Colleagues and Students.'

122 Concerns were raised over the dispersion of Turks throughout Venice and there were complaints that they were stealing and using Christian women. The Turks had themselves pressed for a Fondaco of their own, in part for their protection from attacks, and with the increasing population of Muslims, the senate began to consider the idea. According to Preto, there was an albergo that responded to these needs by August 1579. Preto, *Venezia e i Turchi*, 129–31. On Turks in Venice see Steven Ortega, 'Ottoman Muslims in the Venetian Republic from 1573 to 1645: Contacts, Connections and Restrictions.' On Venetians in Constantinople, see Eric Dursteler, 'Identity and Coexistence in the Early Modern Mediterranean: The Venetian Nation in Constantinople.' Also see *Venezia e i Turchi: Scontri e confronti di due civiltà*.

123 'doi quadreti con Turcho e Turcha,' ASV, *Notario G. Bianchini*, reg. 479, f. 54 (1581, 29 October); Palumbo-Fossati, 'L'interno della casa,' 132n.45.

124 Palumbo-Fossati 'L'interno della casa,' 130. For example, see the will of Carlo Helman, who became a citizen of Venice. Brulez, *Marchands Flamands*, 656.

125 Palumbo-Fossati, 144–5.

126 See chapter 2.

127 *Trattatello in Francese antico colla versione Italiana.*

128 Linda Klinger and Julian Raby, 'Barbarossa and Sinan: A Portrait of Two Ottoman Corsairs from the Collection of Paolo Giovio,' in *Venezia e l'Oriente Vicino,* 49. Klinger, 'Paolo Giovio,' 67.

129 Paolo Giovio's *Elogia,* or brief lives, were first published in Venice in 1545 without portraits; likewise, his military heroes were not accompanied by images when published in Florence 1551. A manuscript with miniature portraits sent to France later appeared in print, and after his death, his *Elogia* were published with some portraits. On Giovio, see T.C. Price Zimmerman, *Paolo Giovio: The Historian and the Crisis of Sixteenth-Century Italy.*

130 'Ho raccolto & intagliate l'effigie più naturali che si sono potute havere de i maggior Prencipi & de i più celebri Capitani della nostra età, & quelle, che vi mancano, si procurano anco di havere più vere che si può, per aggiungerle quanto prima. Io, havendo in consideratione la cospicua & gloriosa nobiltà de i Prencipi qui ritratti, & insieme le celebrate & famose virtù de gli altri, non ho creduto di poter dedicar ad altri più degnamente cosi fatta raccolta, che à V. E. la quale, havendo in se stessa congionta illustrezza antichissima di nobiltà, con meriti segnalati & con splendore immortale di propria virtù, giustamente può servire appunto di scorta à cosi gloriosa serie d'Heroi, & condurli in vista & in consideratione del Mondo.' Franco, *Effiggie naturali,* dedication.

131 Giovanni Gaetano Bottari documents many such letters. For example, see no. 42 from Pietro Aretino to Paolo Giovio in 1545 regarding the portrait of the Venetian Daniele Barbaro: 'cotanto sicuramente entro a dirvi che il ritratto del chiaro Barbaro Daniello è in foggia vivo ne'colori che l'hanno tolto dal vero, ch'essendo egli, ed il suo esempio insieme, l'arte che si crede diventata la natura, e la natura che si pensa conversa nell'arte, riducono in uno e l'essere e'l parere ... appare sì bene l'aurea nobilità dell'illustrare petto del laudato giovane, che mentre il guardo altrui si affigge in lei, sino all'egregio del pensiero, sino al generoso della mente, sino al candido dell'anima, se gli scorge nel reale spazio della serena fronte ... sì per miracolo della man di quello, da cui nasce l'effigie, sarà dalla prestanza del vostro sacro giudicio istimato, tra le immagini molte che di ogni famoso avete, una delle più riguardate.' *Raccolta di lettere sulla pittura, scultura ed architettura scritte da' più celebri personaggi dei secoli XV, XVI e XVII,* 3: 128–9.

132 For example, compare the range documented by Clough, 'Italian Renaissance Portraiture.' As Klinger notes, Paolo Giovio uses the term *verae effigies* interchangeably with *verae imagines* in the two *Elogia,* but for the Ottoman images, the term is *vera simulacra.* 'Paolo Giovio,' 58, 185, fns. 6 and 7.

133 Marcucci, *Vite et effigie di tutti li pontifici romani con le loro armi.* In his dedication to the patron, Cardinal Scipione Borghese, he describes the popes: 'raccolte compendiosamente, & con le loro effigie, quanto più si può, al naturale rappresentate,' adding in his address to the readers that they are based on 'medaglie, e dalle Pitture, con la maggior diligenza, che si sia potuto.'

134 See Clough's comments on Philippe Galle's album *Virorum doctorum de disciplinis benemerentium XLIIII imagines,* published in Antwerp in 1572. 'Italian Renaissance Portraiture,' 192. Dwyer makes the point that Thevet concealed his use of sources by claiming that he had found the portraits close to the sitter's native city. Dwyer concludes 'Thevet never freed himself of the geographer's habit of locating authority in the observer rather than in the artifacts themselves.' 'Thevet and Orisini,' 474, 480. Klinger makes a similar observation about Paolo Giovio, 'Paolo Giovio,' 171–6.

135 David Landau and Peter Parshall, *The Renaissance Print,* 259. Also see Peter Parshall, '*Imago contrafacta*: Images and Facts in the Northern Renaissance.'

136 Clough, 'Italian Renaissance Portraiture,' 194.

137 Ibid. According to Klinger, this interest in copying the collection occurred even before Stimmer's woodcuts were published. 'Paolo Giovio,' 79.

138 Rosanna Pavoni, 'Paolo Giovio, et son Musée de Portraits à propos d'une exposition,' 114. Klinger, 'Paolo Giovio,' 9.

139 Pavoni, 'Paolo Giovio,' 114.

140 Seyyid Lokman commented on the difficulty of obtaining images of the sultans when he produced his album of panegyrics with portraits by Nakkas Osman in 1573. Nurhan Atasoy, 'The Birth of Costume Books and the Generci Mehmed Album,' in *Fenerci Mehmed, Osmanli kiyafetleri: Fenerci Mehmed Albümü,* 22–3. The grand vizier, Sokullu Mehmed Pasha, who was included among those portrayed, assisted in the acquisitions of models from Europe. As in the west, the portraits and the biographies of the men were reconstructed on the basis of research 'to ensure,' as Atasoy explains, 'that the portraits were true to life' (23). Earlier, the sultans had retained Muslim and Western artists to make their own images. Necipoğlu, *Architecture, Ceremonial, and Power,* 252.

141 Esin Atil, 'The Image of Süleymân,' in Inalcik and Kafadar, eds, *Süleymân the Second and His Time,* 334, 333.

142 Ibid., 334.

143 Clough cites a study of the portrait of Pope Nicholas IV that shows 'with one possible exception all these portraits can be traced to Cavaliere's engraving published in 1580.' Clough, 'Italian Renaissance Portraiture,' 194.

144 Carlo Pasero, 'Giacomo Franco, editore, incisore e calcografo nei secoli XVI e XVII,' 335. Franco was not always consistent about his signature, as Emmanuele Cicogna complained. *Delle inscrizioni Veneziane raccolte ed illustrate*, 5: 431–2.

145 Artists who engraved their own designs, and many of those who engraved prints after paintings by others, were usually members of the Arte dei Depentori, the painters' guild. By contrast, popular printmakers like Giacomo Franco were enrolled in the Arte dei Stampatori e Librari, the guild of printers and booksellers.

146 Hans Belting's emphasis in *Likeness and Presence: A History of the Image before the Era of Art*, 459.

147 On the origins of dissimulation and religious persecution, see Perez Zagorin, *Ways of Lying: Dissimulation, Persecution, and Conformity in Early Modern Europe*, 162–205.

148 Giovanni Battista della Porta, *La turca comedia nuova*. See Clubb, *Giambattista della Porta*, 172–85, who notes della Porta's presence in Venice in 1580, 1592, and perhaps in 1601.

149 For example, Argento explains to Gerofilo that he had to marry rich because his parents were poor, and that the woman was ugly: 'Ger. Forse non era bella/ Arg. Dico peggio/ Ger. Brutta, archibrutta?/ Arg. Peggio/ Ger. Fastidiosa, ritrosa, mal conditionata/ Arg. Peggio/Ger. Ma, che cosa si puol trovar peggio?/ Arg. Non si può dir tanto peggio, Peggio, che non sia mille volte più. Ella haveva una fisochionomia più tosto di Vacca, che di Donna, ma era asciutta, che pareva il ritratto della peste, e della carestia, gli occhi guerci, spaventosi, usciti fuori, che mirando te, pareva, che mirasse altrove, il naso tanto lungo, che volendo uscir fuori, la punta era già in Piazza, e la persona ancora in casa. Il Mostaccio di babuino, la carne dura, & nera come storno.' Della Porta, *La turca*, 13 r.

150 Clarice states: 'Voi pur attendete à stringermi, & annodarmi, hor chi più mi potrebbe far un Turco? O forse vestendo l'habito Turchesco, havete appreso i costumi Turcheschi.' Ibid., 41r.

151 'Ero. Ho disperso Eugenio nella oscurità della notte, e dubito, che non si vogliano burlar di me, che haranno tolte, & rubbate le Donne, e stieno in salvo, e mi vogliano dar una compita allegrezza, Ma eccolo, che vien ridendo, non tel dissi io?/ Der. Lo spaventerò prima con li gridi, poi lo farem nostro, Brè, brè, brè, fermati, che sei mio./ Ero. Ah, ah, ah, come gentilmente fingi il Turco, se non havessi con questi occhi visto travestirti, ti giudicarei Turco verissimo, così tu hai il gesto, e'l portamento./ Der. Conoscerai bene se son Turco, o travestito./ Ero. Oh come attacchi ben le

mani, o che compagni, e come fan bene l'arte loro, se fussero di razza Turchesca, non la farebbon più verisimile, e non si può far meglio, il fatto riuscirà assai bene.' Ibid., 45v.

152 'Il desiderio di esser con voi, e l'habito di Turco mi hanno ingannata, appena il vidi, che subito venni, conobbi le vesti del mio Signore, non la persona.' Ibid., 46v.

153 Clubb, *Giambattista della Porta*, 175.

154 Eugenio Albéri, *Relazioni degli ambasciatori veneti al senato. Serie III: I Turchi*: 'avaro come tutti gli altri turchi' (vol. 1, 70) and 'è di natura molto avaro come sono universalmente tuti Turchi.' Ragazzoni, a secretary, presented his report to the Senate on 16 August 1971. Vol. 2, 81.

155 G. Boerio, *Dizionario del dialetto veneziano*, 1: 544. On the range of meanings of the word 'Turco' see Preto, *Venezia e i Turchi*, 116–19.

156 'Gli Arabi sono latroni, d'animo doppi, fraudolenti, d'animo servile, instabili, desiosi di gaudagno...Gli Africani lussuriosi, mancatori di fede e temerarii ... gl'Italiani splendidi, di regal nobiltà; i Francesi pazzii et inconsiderati.' Della Porta, *Della fisonomia*, book 1, chap. 16, 68. Della Porta summarizes how Hippocrates, Aristotle, Ptolemy, and Plato attributed group identity to geographical location. The cold north makes the inhabitants white, audacious, quick to give advice, wild, and extravagant. By contrast, heat in equatorial climes causes black skin and cruel natures. Temperate zones produce scientists and merchants. See 67–70.

157 'Catilana ebbe un simil naso, e fu ambizioso, avaro, rapace.' Ibid., book 2, chap. 7, 162.

158 'Maometto secondo Re de'Turchi fu di naso adunco e rilevato, che quasi giongeva al labro di sovra; e fu di grande animo.' Ibid., 164.

159 'Selimo figlio di Baiazete fu di naso arcato, e liberalissimo, emulo del grande Alessandro. Solimano ancora, figlio di Selimo, fu di naso adunco, guerriero e splendido.' Ibid.

160 Klinger and Raby, 'Barbarossa and Sinan.'

161 'Havea la faccia gialduccia, gl'occhi grifagni, le ciglia arcate, & il naso si adunco, che pareva che la punta gli toccasse le labbra ... Fu notabilmente crudele cosi in guerra come in Pace, poiche per ogni picciola cagione faceva ammazzare quei giovanetti del Serraglio, ch'esso amava lascivamente.' Bertelli, *Vite degl'imperatori*, 31.

162 Haskell, *History and Its Images.* 67

163 Lina Bolzoni, *The Gallery of Memory: Literary and Iconographic Models in the Age of the Printing Press*, xxiii.

164 'Né hebbi minor pensiero a visitare tutte le carceri publiche, dove sempre è

racchiusa gran moltitudine de' facinorosi ladri, parricidi, assassini di strada e d'altri uomini di simile fattezza, per vedere diligentemente le loro mani; doppo, contemplando i piedi e le mani de gli animali, conferii le loro figure con quelle de gli huomini, non senza naturali ragioni, e con l'istesso metodo del quale mi sono servito nella *Fisonomia*.' *Della Chirofisonomia*, in *De ea naturalis physiognomioniae*, 92. His account of making wax figures from plaster casts of criminals begins on 91. The complete passage is cited and translated by Clubb, *Giambattista della Porta*, 40–1.

165 Giovanni Battista della Porta, *Della fisonomia dell'huomo*, 'Proemio,' n.p.

166 'Apresso è ben d'avvertire che non da un segno solo, né ancora da due, l'uomo deve con sicurezza far subito giudizio della verità; ma dai più e maggiori; e poi da quelli tutti che più convengono insieme si deve tôr il giudizio.' Della Porta, *Della fisonomia*, 106.

167 'E propria ancor questa arte de Poeti, e di pittori. i quali introducendo ne i loro Poemi, e pitture persone di varii costumi, e descrivendo le fattezze, ce le diano convenevoli ... Potrà ancora questa scienza non solo dal conoscere gl'altrui costume esser giovevole, ma de suoi proprii, acciò che noi stessi di noi medesimi diventiamo Fisonomi. Habbiam letto appresso gl'antichi Socrate Filosofo haver usato lo specchio per la buona institution de costumi, ilche fù ancora accettato da Seneca, che l'huomo possa specchiar se stesso, perche conoscendo le nostre imperfettioni ricorriamo al consiglio, & all'emenda.' Della Porta, *Della fisonomia* (1610), 'Proemio,' n.p.

168 Della Porta, *Della fisonomia*, 108. Della Porta was also experimenting with mirrors, which he discusses in several publications including *De refractione, optices parte* (1593).

169 Richard Trexler, 'Introduction,' in Trexler, ed., *Persons in Groups*, 16. Ronald Weissman, 'The Importance of Being Ambiguous: Social Relations, Individualism, and Identity in Renaissance Florence,' in Zimmerman and Weissman, eds, *Urban Life in the Renaissance*.

170 'Mi è piaciuto di mettere il Signor Paolo Giordano fra l'imagini de passati huomini illustri di Casa Orsina, accioche si come da lui sono cominciate non pur le mie presenti fatiche, ma si seguiranno ancora le future in questa gravissima & lunghissima impresa sotto il suo feliciss. auspicio, cosi ancora finiscano in lui. Percioche questo Principe singulare, di bella, grande, & ben formata statura, & con volto come si vede, fra il piacevole & il grave, & con aspetto benigno & dimostrativo delle doti eccellenti del suo cuor generoso, empiendo l'altrui vista di grato diletto, & accompagnando con affabil maniera le qualità sue notabili & chiare, s'aquista intera lode di incomparabil cortesia con ogniuno.' Sansovino, *L'historia di Casa Orsina*, 91.

171 Linda Aleci suggests such an experience for Paolo Giovio inside his museum. 'Images of Identity: Italian Portrait Collections of the Fifteenth and Sixteenth Centuries' in Nicholas Mann and Luke Syson, eds, *The Image of the Individual: Portraits in the Renaissance*, 79.

172 John Hale, 'The Discovery of Europe,' *The Civilization of Europe in the Renaissance*, 3–50.

173 Si può per tanto dire, che l'Europa a'nostri giorni comprenda tutta quella parte del Mondo, nella quale è conosciuta la fede di Christo, et qualche parte del paese del Turco. Cesare Vecellio, *De gli habiti antichi*, 3r; *Habiti antichi et moderni di tutto il mondo*.

174 John Hale, 'Printing and Military Culture of Renaissance Venice,' 61; John Hale, *The Civilization of Europe*, 39–42; *Venezia e i turchi*, 154–5.

175 See James S. Grubb, 'Memory and Identity: Why Venetians Didn't Keep *ricordanze*,' 375–87, esp. 379–80.

176 Silverman, *Threshold*, 21. According to Freud, aggression is 'the libidinal complement to the egoism of the instinct of self-preservation.' 'Introduction to Narcissism,' *The Basic Writings of Sigmund Freud*, , 73–4; Also see Jacques Lacan, *The Four Fundamental Concepts of Psycho-Analysis*, 193–4.

177 Silverman, *Threshold*, 23, 60. As images of military prowess these images may be understood as projections of Venetian lack, the 'unwanted exteriority' in Silverman's terms, that 'promotes aggressivity; located at a stubborn distance from the figure standing in front of it, the idealizing representation becomes a threatening rival which must be destroyed' (60; also see 67–8; 206).

178 On Ottavio Leone, see Giovanni Baglione, *Le vite de'pittori, scultori, et architetti*, fascimile , 321–2 [223–4]. On the drawing and prints and the status of the artist, see Susan Barnes, 'The *Uomini Illustri*, Humanist Culture and the Development of a Portrait Tradition in Early Seventeenth-Century Italy,' in Susan Barnes and Walter Melion, eds, *Cultural Differentiation and Cultural Identity in the Visual Arts*. Studies in the History of Art 27, 81–92. On the technique *alla macchia* and Leone's naturalistic portrait style, see John T. Spike, 'Ottavio Leoni's Portraits *alla macchia*,' in *Baroque Portraiture in Italy*, 12–19. On Leone's portraits and idealism, see Hanno-Walter Kruft, 'Ein Album mit Porträtzeichnungen. Ottavio Leonis.'

179 Baglione, *Le vite de'pittori*, 144; Spike, 'Ottavio Leoni's Portraits,' 12. Baglione explains the technique in his life of the father, and also attributes the skill to Ottavio in his biography (321).

180 Spike, 'Ottavio Leoni's Portraits,' 14.

181 Ibid. Barnes, 'Uomini illustri,' 84.

182 Barnes suggests Leoni's planned scenes may be compared with Giovanni

Battista Marino's *Galeria* published in Venice in 1619. Barnes, 'Uomini illustri,' 87.

183 Spike notes that the sole exception was Leoni's father, then deceased. 'Naturalism,' 14.

184 Barnes, 'Uomini illustri,' 86.

185 *The New Shorter Oxford English Dictionary* (Oxford: Clarendon Press, 1993), 1304. See John Martin, 'Inventing Sincerity.'

Conclusion

1 'Quattro libri delle Città del Mondo de Georgio Brun.' Wilfrid Brulez, *Marchands Flamands à Venise I (1568–1605)*, 642.

2 See Tom Conley, *Self-Made Map*, esp. 12.

3 G. Mazzariol and T. Pignatti, *La pianta prospettica*. On the self as a product of geographic consciousness and also a producer of this space, see Conley, *Self-Made Map*, esp. 2, 20–1.

4 L.C. Matthew, 'The Painter's Presence: Signatures in Venetian Renaissance Pictures.'

5 Carlo Pasero, 'Giacomo Franco, editore, incisore e calcografo nei secoli XVI e XVII,' 335. Franco was not very consistent about his signature, as Emmanuele Cicogna noted, *Delle inscrizioni Veneziane raccolte ed illustrate*, 5: 431–2.

6 Max Rosenheim, 'The Album Amicorum,' 261.

7 By 1580, if not earlier, a dictionary was available in Venice to translate among Italian, Greek, Turkish, and German. E. Teza, *Vocabulario nuovo con il quale da se stessi, si può benissimo imparare diversi linguaggi, cioè, italiano e greco, italiano e turco, et italiano e todesco, E di nuovo con somma diligentia, ricoretto*. Paolo Preto, *Venezia e i Turchi*, 99.

8 Theodor de Bry and Johann Israel de Bry, *Alphabeta et characteres, iam indè à creato mundo ad nostra usq; tempora; apud omnes nationes, usurpatj … in aere efficti*.

9 Jean-Baptiste(?) Zangrius, *Album amicorum*.

10 Giovanni Baglione, *Le vite de'pittori, scultori, et architetti*, 321–2 [223–4].

11 This is a paraphrase of Sabine Melchior-Bonnet's account. Of particular interest is her comparison between the convex mirror, with its myriad reflections of the world around the viewer (analogous with the Renaissance microcosm/macrocosm) and the plane mirror with its partial view (the perspective of the individual). *The Mirror: A History*, 130–1.

12 On Descartes and his suspiciousness of sight, see Lyle Massey, 'Anamorphosis through Descartes or Perspective Gone Awry.'

13 *The New Shorter Oxford English Dictionary* (Oxford: Clarendon Press, 1993), 1304.

14 Erwin Panofsky, *Perspective as Symbolic Form*. On Panofsky, see Elkins, *Poetics of Perspective*, chap. 5. Donald Preziosi, *Rethinking Art History*, 111–21.

15 As Christopher Wood points out, there is a certain incompatibility between something that 'describe[s] the world according to a rational and repeatable procedure' and is also a reflection of its context. Wood in Panofsky, *Perspective*, 13.

16 Ibid., 13.

17 Ibid., 67–8. Panofsky cites Ernst Cassirer, for whom 'the spiritual meaning is attached to a concrete, material sign and intrinsically given to this sign' (40–1). Cassirer's concept was based on Kant's distinction between objectivity and subjectivity, a process through which subjective and sensate perceptions of forms, when shared by a community, were shown to be objective, even universal. Cassirer, as Michael Podro explains, associated the objective with the mind, and the subjective, by contrast, with external sense perceptions. *The Critical Historians of Art*, 182. As a symbolic form, as in Kant's *Critique of Judgement*, the art object – here perspective – bridges the divide between the mind and the senses. As a mode of representing the world, perspective seems to Panfosky to facilitate identification with that world by the 'carrying over of artistic objectivity into the domain of the phenomenal.' Panofsky, *Perspective*, 72. Through the 'objectification of the subjective,' perspective translated the subject's singular experience into the modern and rational space of critical philosophy, or art into science. Panofsky, *Perspective*, 65. As Wood notes, the essay seems to collapse Panfosky's distinction between artistic perception and cognition. In Panofsky, *Perspective*, 13. Also see Immanuel Kant, *The Critique of Judgement*, esp. part 1, 55, 63, 67; Podro, *Critical Historians*, 188–9.

18 Hubert Damisch, *The Origin of Perspective*. For critiques of Damisch, see Whitney Davis, '"Virtually Straight," Review of *The Origin of Perspective* by Hubert Damisch'; Christopher Wood, 'Review of *The Origin of Perspective* by Hubert Damisch,' esp. 248–9.

19 On proof and origins, see Elkins, *Poetics of Perspective*, 11.

20 Jacques Lacan, *The Four Fundamental Concepts of Psycho-Analysis*, 86–9; Jacques Lacan, 'The Mirror-Phase as Formative of the Function of the I,' in Slavoj Žižek ed., *Mapping Ideology*.

21 See Lacan's critique of Descartes. *Four Fundamental Concepts*, 80. Elkins points to an earlier critique by Nietzsche, who saw that 'emphasizing individual views involves the false inference that there is an ego, "looking out" at things – a critique that is widely attributed to Lacan. 'A kind of perspective in see-

ing,' Nietzsche thought, was mistakenly made 'the cause of seeing,' resulting in 'the invention of the "subject," the "I."' Elkins citing Nietzsche, *Poetics of Perspective*, 39.

22 Lacan, *Four Fundamental Concepts*, 215.

23 Kaja Silverman, *Threshold of the Visible World*, 92.

24 Nicholas Cusa, *Nicholas of Cusa's Dialectical Mysticism: Text, Translation, and Interpretive Study of* De Visione Dei, 110–17.

25 David Harvey, *The Condition of Postmodernity: An Enquiry into the Origins of Cultural Change*, 246, also see 246–50.

26 See Judith Butler, 'Performative Acts and Gender Constitution: An Essay in Phenomenology and Feminist Theory,' in Sue-Ellen Case ed., *Performing Feminisms: Feminist Critical Theory and Theatre*, 270–82.

27 See Butler on Jacquelyn Rose's argument in *Sexuality and the Field of Vision*, 'Performativity's Social Magic,' in Theodore Schatzki and Wolfgang Natter, *The Social and Political Body*, 44.

Bibliography

Manuscript Sources

Venice, Archivio di Stato (ASV)

Collegio, *Cerimoniale.* Registri I–III.
Giustizia Vecchia, *Costituti,* no. 49
Provveditore alle Pompe,
    Capitolari 1–11 (1488–1683)
    Decreti (1334–1689)
Provveditore alla Sanità, *Decreti al Senato,* 5, 1486–1612
Quarantia Criminale, busta 127, 1594
Sant'Ufficio, Busta 88, 1631
Sant'Ufficio, Busta 91, 1633
Senato dispacci ambasciatori. Roma ordinaria, f. 19
Senato, *Privilegi,* 1374–1495, 1563–93
Senato, *Terra,* 1580–1616

Venice, Biblioteca Nazionale Marciana (BMV)

IT IV 491 (5578) Foggie diverse del vestire de'Turchi
IT 210 (8188)
IT VII 537 (8311)
IT VII 811 (7299), 1578–85
IT VII 1640 (7983)
IT VII 1891 (9110) Misc
IT VII 2540 (8838)
IT VII 2540 (12432)

IT VII 2500 (12077) Schedario di Horatio F. Brown.
Privilegi Veneziani per la stampa, 1529–97.

Venice, Biblioteca del Museo Civico Correr (MCV)

Biblioteca del Museo Correr, ms. classe IV 119, Mariegola degli stampatori e
  librai, ms. membranaceo e cartaceo, cc 454, sec. XV–XIX (anni 1573–1574,
  addizioni 1574–1857).
Melvazzi 110

Padua, Museo Bottacin

Codice Bottacin, MB 970 (1614)

Milan, Biblioteca Ambrosiana

Compendio storico delle cose più notabili di Milano ed in paricolare della famiglia Monti
  in the di Milano. Ms. P., 248–51.

London, British Library (BLL)

Additional Manuscript 9857. Alessandro Valignano, *Libro primero del principio y
  progresso de la religíon christiana en Jappón y de la especial providencia de que Nuestro
  Señor usa con aquella nueva iglesia.* (unpublished) (1601).
Additional Manuscript 9852. Missionary conferences of 1580–91. Alessandro
  Valignano, 'Sumarios,' 1580, 1583.
Egerton 1215, Andrea Alciato, *Diverse imprese accommodate a diverse moralità.* Lyon:
  Gulielmo Rouillio, 1564+.
Egerton 1186, Album of Honae et Petri Portner (1567–1608).
Egerton 1196, *Bibliorum utriusque Testamenti icones, summo artificio expressae, histo-
  rias sacras ad vivum exhibentes, & oculis summa cum gratia repraesentantes.* Frank-
  furt am Main: Sigismund Feyerabend, (1571+).
Egerton 1191, Album of Sigm Ortelli (1573–9).
Egerton 1192, Album of P. Behaim Pat. Norim (1574–80) C.16. 1574–90.
Egerton 1196, Album of Carolus Scheurl (1579–90).
Egerton 1199, Album of Seb. Zehii vel Zach. Augustani (1581–1600).
Egerton 1201, Album of Hieronymi Holtzschuher from Nuremberg (1584–1608).
Egerton 1204, Album of Benedictus Carpzor of Brandenburg (1585–9).
Egerton I.216, *Stam- oder Gesellenbuch.* Frankfurt at Main: Feyerabend, 1583.
Additional 15699, Stammbuch of Alex Faber (1574–90).

Additional 17028, Stammbuch of H.H. Pilgram (1612–15).
Additional 18991, Album of Moysis Walens (1605–15).
Additional 19478, Album of Joh-Sigismund Von Bernstein (1613–17).

London, Royal Geographical Society

Lafreri Atlas, Tooley, 611

Anonymous Published Sources

L'Anno felicissimo. M.D. LXXI. Il Settimo d'Ottobre. Venice, 1571.
Avisi venuti novamente da Roma delli 23 di Marzo 1585 dell'entrata nel publico Concis-toro de due Ambasciatori mandati da tre Re potenti del Giapone. Bologna: Alessandro Benacci, 1585.
Il bellissimo e sontuoso trionfo fatto nella magnifica città di Venetia nella publicatione della lega ... et appresso alcuni avisi di Famagosta, e di Candia. Brescia, 1571.
Breve ragguaglio dell'isola del Giapone hauuto con venuta a Roma delli legati di quel regno. Rome: Bartholomeo Bonfadino & Tito Diani, 1585.
Canzone fatta alla serenissima republica venetiana. Sopra la presente guerra, con il vaticino della vittoria. Venice: [Domenico Farri], [not before 1571].
Capitolo a Selin imperator de Turchi; Delle feste et allegresse ch'ei faceva in Costantinopoli ... della presa dell'Isola di Cipro. Venice[?], 1580[?].
Cronica breve de i fatti illustri de' re di Francia. Venice: Giunti, 1588.
Emblematum liber. Ipsa Emblemata. Frankfurt am Main, 1593.
Nuova canzone a Selin imperator de turchi in lingua venetiana. Venice: [Domenico Farri], 1572.
Ordine di far processione per la vittoria havuta contra Turchi et che si vadi ogn'anno a 7'ottobre a S.ta Giustina. 1571.
Ordine, e dechiaratione di tutta la Mascherata, fatta nella città di Veneta la Domenica di Carnevale, 1571 per la ... Vittoria contra Turchi. Venice: Giorgio Angelieri, 1572.
Prosapia vel genealogia imperatorum turcicorum. Das ist: Ein kurtzer summarischer ausszug aller türckischen kayser ... Straubing: A. Sommer, 1597.
Ragguaglio dell'entrata di Henrico III. Re di Francia et di Polonia nella citta di Venetia, Et delli superbissime apparati, & cerimonie fatte da quella Republica nell'incontrare, ricervere, & honorare Sua Maestà. Rome: Heirs of Antonio Blado Stampatori Camerali, 1574.
Recueil des effigies des roys de France. Paris, 1567.
Relatione di tutto il successo di Famagosta. Dove s'intende minutissimamente tutte le scaramuccie, batterie, mine, & assalti dati ad essa Fortezza. Et ancora i nomi de i

Capitani, & numero delle Genti morte, cosi de Christiani, come de Turchi. Et medesi-mamente di quelli, che sono restati prigioni. Venice: G. Angehiri, 1572.

Relatione del viaggio et arrivo in Europa, & Roma de principi giapponesi. Venice: Paolo Meietto, 1585.

A Tailor's Book [Facsimile of the manuscript in the Fondazione Querini Stampa-lia with essays by Alessandra Mottola Molfino et. al.]. Turin: Gruppo GFT and Modena: Edizioni Panini, 1987.

Ultimi avisi di Venetia. Narratione della guerra principiata contra il gran Turco. Viterbo, 1570.

[ ] Et ultima disperatione de Selim Gran Turco per la perdita della sua Armata. Venice, [1575?].

Primary Sources by Author

Alberti, F. Leandro. *Descrittione di tutta Italia.* Venice: Salicato, 1588; edited in Bologna in 1550 and published in Venice in 1553.

Alberti, Leon Battista. *On Painting.* New Haven: Yale University Press, 1966.

Alcega, Juan de. *Tailor's Pattern Book 1589. Facsimile.* Translated by Jean Pain and Cecilia Bainton. Carlton, Bedford: Ruth Bean, 1979.

Amelot de la Houssaye, Abraham Nicolas. *The History of the Government of Venice.* London: H.C. for John Starkey, 1677.

Amman, Jost. *Im Frauwenzimmer Wirt vermeldt von allerley schönen Kleidungen unnd Trachten der Weiber, hohes und niders Stands, wie man fast an allen Orten geschmückt unnd gezieret ist, Als Teutsche, Welsche, Frantzösische, Engelländische, Niderländische, Böhemische, Ungerische, und alle anstossende Länder.* Frankfurt: Feyerabend, 1586.

Amman, Jost, and Hans Sachs. *The Book of Trades.* New York: Dover, 1973.

Apian, Peter (Apianus, Petrus). *Cosmographia ... per Gemmam Frisium ... ab omni-bus vindicata mendis.* Antwerp: Gregorio Bontio, 1550.

Baglione, Giovanni. *Le vite de'pittori, scultori, et architetti. Fascimile.* Vatican City: Biblioteca Apostolica Vaticana, 1995.

Ballino, Giulio. *De' disegni delle piu illustri città, & fortezze del mondo parte I; la quale ne contiene cinquanta: Con una breve historia delle origini, & accidenti loro, secondo l'ordine de'tempi.* Venice: Bolognino Zaltieri, 1569.

Barbaro, Francesco. *On Wifely Duties.* In *The Earthly Republic: Italian Humanists on Government and Society.* Edited [and translated by] Benjamin G. Kohl and Ronald G. Witt with Elizabeth B. Welles. Philadelphia: University of Pennsylva-nia Press, 1978.

Bardi, Girolamo. *Dichiarazione di tutte le historie che si contengono nei quadri posti nuovamente nella Sala dello Scrutinio e del Gran Consiglio nel Palazzo Ducale della*

Serenissima Repubblica di Venezia. Venice: Salicato, 1602.

Bassano, Luigi. *Costumi et i modi particolari della vita de'Turchi.* Monaco di Baviera: Casa Editrice Max Hueber, 1963.

Benedetti, Rocco. *Ragguaglio delle allegrezze, solennità, e feste, fatte in Venetia per la felice vittoria, Al Clariss. Sig. Girolamo Diedo digniss. Consigliere di Corfu.* Venice: G. Perchaccino, 1571.

– *Le feste et trionfi fatti dalla Sereniss. Signoria di Venetia nella felice venuta di Henrico III. Christianiss. re di Francia et di Polonia.* Venice: Alla libreria della stella, 1574.

Benavides, Marco Mantova. *Illustrium iureconsultorum imagines quae inveniri potuerunt ad vivam effigiem expressæ.* Rome: Antoine Lafréry, 1566.

Berlin. Miscellaneous Institutions Staatliche Museen. *Katalog der Lipperheideschen Kostümbibliothek.* Revised by Eva Nienholdt and Gretel Wagner-Neumann. 2 vols. Berlin: Verlag Gebr. Mann, 1965.

Donato Bertelli. *Le vere imagini et descritioni delle più nobilli città del mondo.* Venice, 1578.

Bertelli, Ferdinando. *Omnium fere gentium nostrae aetatis habitus, nunquam ante hac aediti.* Venice: Ferdinando Bertelli, 1563.

Bertelli, Pietro. *Diversarum nationum habitus, centum, & quattuor iconibus in aere incisis diligenter expressi, item ordines duo processionum.* Padua: Pietro Bertelli and Alcia Alciato, 1589–96.

– *Effigie naturali de li Serenessimi Principi di Venetia.* Venice? 1600?

– *Effigie de sommi Pontefici dalla sedia d'Avignone ritornati a Roma fino a questi tempi,* 1611.

– *Teatro delle città d'Italia, con le sue figure intagliate in rame, & descrittioni di esse. Nuovamente tradotto di Latino in Toscano, & accresciuto sì di figure, come di dichiarationi.* Vicenza: D. Amadio, 1616.

– *Teatro urbium italicarum, collectore P. Bertellio, etc.* Venice: P. Bertellium, 1599.

– *Vite degl'imperatori de'Turchi con le loro effiggie intalgiate [sic] in rame e datte in luce da P. Bertelli, 1599.* Vicenza: G. Greco, 1599.

Blessi, Manoli. *Manoli Blessi nella rotta dell'armata de Sultan Selin, ultimo re de Turchi.* Venice? 1572?

Boissard, Jean Jacques. *Emblematum liber. Ipsa Emblemata.* Frankfurt am Main, 1593.

– *Habitus variarum orbis gentium. Habitz de nations estranges. Trachten mancherley Völcker des Erdskreysz.* Mechlin, 1581.

– *Vitæ et icones sultanorum Turcicorum, principum Persarum, aliorumque illustrium heroum heroinarumque ab Osmane usque ad Mahometem II. Frankfurt am main:* Theador de Bry, 1596.

Bonifacio, Giovanni. *L'arte de'cenni con la quale formandosi favella visible, si tratta della muta eloquenza, che non è altro che un facondo silentio. Divisa in due parti. Nella prima si tratta de i cenni, che da noi con le membra del nostro corpo sono fatti …*

Nella seconda si dimostra come di questa cognitione tutte l'arti liberali, e mecaniche si prevagliano. Vicenza: Francesco Grossi, 1616.

Bordone, Benedetto. *Isolario di Benedetto Bordone.* Venice: Nicolo d'Aristotile, detto Zoppino, 1534.

Boschini, Marco. *Le minere della pittura veneziana.* Venice: F. Nicolini, 1664.

Bosse, Abraham. *La maniere universelle de M. Desargues pour pratiquer la prospective par pétit-pied, comme le géometral.* Paris: De l'Imprimerie de Pierre Des-Hayes, 1648.

Bots, Hans, and Giel Van Gemert, with Peter Rietbergen, eds. *L'album amicorum de Cornelis de Glarges 1599–1683.* Amsterdam: Holland University Press, 1975.

Braun, Georg and Hogenberg, Franz. *Civitates orbis terrarum 1572–1618.* Amsterdam: Theatrum Orbus Terrarum Ltd., 1965.

Brunfels, Otto. *Herbarum vivæ eicones ad nature imitationem.* Argentorati: Joannem Schottum, 1530.

Bruto, Giovanni Michele. *La institutione di una fanciulla nata noblimente. L'institution d'une fille de noble maison.* [Translated by J. Bellere.] Antwerp: Plantain, 1555.

Bruyn, Abraham de. *Imperii ac sacerdotii ornatus. Diversarum item gentium peculiaris vestitus.* Cologne: J. Rutz, 1578.

– *Omnium pene Europae, Asiae, Aphricae atque Americae gentium habitus, elegantissime aeri incisi: quibus accedunt Romani pontificis, Cardinalium, Episcoporum, una cum omnium ordinum monachorum et religiosorum habitus.* Antwerp: M. Colyn, 1581.

– *Omnium poene gentium imagines, ubi oris totiusque corporis et vestium habitus, in ordinis cuinscunque ac loci hominibus diligentissimé exprimuntur.* [Cologne]: I. Rutus, 1577.

– [Twelve plates of animals and insects, with descriptions in Latin verse. Engraved by A. de Bruyn.] Antwerp? 1583?

Bry, Theodor de. *Admiranda narratio ... de commodis et incolarum ritibus Virginiae, nuper admodum ab Anglis, qui à Dn. Richardo Greinuile ... in coloniam anno M.D.LXXXV. deducti sunt inventae, sumtus faciente Dn. Waltero Raleigh ... Anglico scripta sermone à Thoma Hariot ... nunc autem primum Latio donata à C.C.A.* Frankfurt: J. Wecheli, 1590.

Bry, Theodor de, and Johann Israel de Bry. *Alphabeta et characteres, iam indè à creato mundo ad nostra usq; tempora; apud omnes nationes, usurpatj ... in aere efficti.* Frankfurt, 1596.

Caetani, Onorato, and Gerolamo Diedo. *La battaglia di Lepanto (1571).* Palermo: Sellerio editore, 1995.

Camocio, Giovan Francesco. *Isole famose porti, fortezze, e terre maritime ...* Venice: Libraria del segno di S Marco [Ferdinando Bertelli], 1575.

— *L'ordine delle galere et le insegne loro con li fano, nomi cognomi delli magnifici, & generosi patroni di esse, che si ritrovorno nella armata della santissima lega, al tempo della vittoriosa & miracolosa impresa ottenuta, & fatta con lo aiuto divino. Contra la orgoliosa, et superbaarmata turchescha.* Venice: Camocio, 1571.

Casola, Pietro. *Canon Pietro Casola's Pilgrimage to Jerusalem in the Year 1494.* Historical Series, no. 5. Translated by M. Margaret Newett. Manchester: University of Manchester, 1907.

Castiglione, Baldesar. *The Book of the Courtier.* Translated by Charles Singleton. New York: Doubleday, 1959.

Çelebi, Evliya. *The Intimate Life of an Ottoman Statesman: Melek Ahmed Pasha (1588–1662): As Portrayed in Evliya Çelebi's Book of Travels.* Translated and commentary by Rhoads Murphey. Albany: State University of New York Press, 1991.

Cesalpino, Andrea. *De plantis libri XVI.* Florence: Georgium Marescottum, 1583.

Colombina, Gasparo. *Discorso sopra il modo di disegnare, dipingere, & spiegare secondo l'una, & l'altr'arte gli affetti principali, si naturali, come accidentali nell'huomo, secondo i precetti della fisonomia.* Padua: Giovanni Temini, [16??].

Commandino, Federico. *Federici Commandini Urbinatis in planisphaerium Ptolemaei commentarius* (Venice: Aldus, 1558)

Contarini, Gasparo. *La Republica, e i magistrati di Vinegia ... nuovamente fatti volgari, etc.* Translated by E. Anditimi. Venice: Girolamo Scotto, 1544.

Contarini, Giovanni Pietro. *Historia delle cose successe dal principio della guerra mossa da Selim ottomano a' Venetiani, fino al dì della gran giornata vittoriosa contra Turchi.* Venice: Francesco Rampazetto, 1572.

Coryat, Thomas. *Coryats Crudities Hastily gobled up in five Moneths travells in France, Savoy, Italy, Rhetia commonly called the Grisons country, Helvetia aliàs Switzerland, some parts of high Germany, and the Netherlands; newly digested in the hungry aire of Odcombe in the county of Somerset, & now dispersed to the nourishment of the travelling members of this kingdome.* London: William Stansby, 1611.

Cusa, Nicholas. *Nicholas of Cusa's Dialectical Mysticism: Text, Translation, and Interpretive Study of* De Visione Dei. Translated by Jaspar Hopkins. Minneapolis: The Arthur J. Banning Press, 1985.

Cusa, Nicholas. *Nicholas of Cusa: Metaphysical Speculations: Six Latin Texts.* Translated by Jaspar Hopkins. Minneapolis: Arthur J. Banning Press, 1998.

Della Casa, Giovanni. *Galateo ovvero de'costumi.* Edited by Carlo Cordié. Milan: Riccardo Ricciardi Editore, 1993.

Della Porta. *See* Porta, Giovanni Battista della.

Deserps, François. *Recueil de la diuersité des habits qui sont de present en vsaige tant es pays d'Europe, Asie, Affrique et Illes sauvages, le tout fait apres le naturel.* Paris: Richard Breton, 1562.

Doglioni, Giovanni Nicolò [Leonico Goldioni, pseud.]. *Le cose maravigliose et notabili della città di Venetia.* [F. Sansovino, *Delle cose notabili che sono in Venetia. Riformate, accommodate, & grandemente ampliate da Leonico Goldioni.*] Venice: Ghirardo, & Iseppo Imberti, 1624.

Dürer, Albrecht. *Trachten-bilder … aus der Albertina* [text by M. Thausing]. Vienna: W. Braumüller, 1871.

Elyot, Sir Thomas. *The Book Named the Governor,* 1531. A facsimile. Menston: Scolar Press, 1970.

Fabri, Alessandro de. *Diversarum nationum ornatus.* Venice, 1593.

Feyerabend, Sigmund. *Kunst- und Lehrbüchlein.* Frankfurt: Feyerabend, 1578.

– *Wapen und Stammbuch darinnen der Keys. Maiest. Chur und Fürsten, Graffen, Freyherrn, deren vom Adel &c. Mit kunstreichen Figuren, durch den weitberühmpten Josten Amen gerissen, sampt iren Symbolis und mit Deutschen Reymen geziert.* Frankfurt am Main: Feyerabend, 1589.

Filiarchi, Cosimo. *Trattato della guerra, et dell'vnione de' principi christiani contra i Turchi, & gli altri infedeli.* Venice: Giolito di Ferrari, 1572.

Fonte, Moderata. *The Worth of Women: Wherein is Clearly Revealed their Nobility and their Superiority to Men.* Edited and translated by Virginia Cox. Chicago: University of Chicago Press, 1997.

Franco, Giacomo. *La città di Venetia con l'origine e governo di quella. Estratte dall'opere di G. N. Doglioni. Parte seconda.* Venice, 1610.

– *La città di Venetia con l'origine e governo di quella.* Venice, Antonio Turini, 1614.

– *Effiggie naturali dei maggior prencipi et piu valorosi capitani.* Venice: Giacomo Franco, 1596.

– *De excellentia et nobilitate delineationis libri duo.* Venice, 1611.

– *Habiti delle donne intagliate in rame nuovamente.* Venice: Giacomo Franco, 1610.

– *Habiti d'huomeni et donne venetiane con la processione della ser.ma Signoria et altri particolari cioè trionfi feste et ceremonie publiche della nobilissima città di Venetia.* Venice: Giacomo Franco, 1610.

Froís, Luís. *La première ambassade du Japon en Europe, 1582–1592. Première partie le traité du Père Frois.* Edited and annotated by J.A. Abranches Pinto, Yoshitomo Okamoto, and Henri Bernard. Tokyo: Sophia University, 1942.

Fuchs, Leonhard. *De historia stirpium commentarii insignes.* Basel, 1542.

Galle, Philippe. *Virorum doctorum de disciplinis benemerentium XLIIII imagines.* Antwerp, 1572.

Garzoni, Tommaso. *La piazza universale di tutte le professioni del mondo, nuovamente formata.* Venice: Roberto Meietti, 1599.

Giannotti, Donato. *Libro de la republica de Vinitiani.* Rome: Antonio Blado, 1542.

Gigliotti, Domenico, and Capriolo, Aliprando. *Ritratti di cento capitani illustri.* Rome, 1596.

Giovio, Paolo. *Gli elogi degli uomini illustri, letterati, artisti, uomini d'arme.* Edited by Renzo Meregazzi. Rome: Istituto poligrafico dello Stato, Libreria dello Stato, 1972.

– *Elogia veris clarorum virorum imaginibus apposita quae in Musaeo Ioviano Comi spectantur.* Venice: Tramezzini, 1546.

– *Elogia virorum bellica virtute.* Basel: P. Pernæ, 1575.

– *Elogia virorum bellica virtute illustrium veris imaginibus supposita quae apud Musaeum spectantur.* Florence: Torrentino, 1551.

– *Elogia virorum literis illustrium.* Basel, 1577.

– *Musei Ioviani imagines.* Basel: T. Müller, 1577.

– *Ritrattti degli uomini illustri.* Palermo: Sellerio editore, 1999.

Glen, Jean de. *Des habits, moeurs, ceremonies, facons de faire anciennes & modernes du monde, traicté non moins utile, que delectable, plein de bonnes & sainctes instructions.* Liege: Jean de Glen, 1601.

Gualtieri, Guido. *Relationi della venuta degli ambasciatori giaponesi a Roma sino alla partita di Lisbona.* Venice: Gioliti, 1586.

Guazzo, Stefano. *La civil conversazione.* Edited by Amedeo Quondam. Modena: F.C. Panini, 1993.

Guicciardini, Francesco. *Dialogue on the Government of Florence.* Translated by Alison Brown. Cambridge: Cambridge University Press, 1994.

– *The History of Italy.* Translated by Sidney Alexander. Princeton, NJ: Princeton University Press, 1984.

Gutierrez, Beniamino. *La prima ambascieria giapponese in Italia: Dall'ignorata cronaca di un diarista e cosmografo milanese della fine del XVI sec.* Milan: Perego, 1938.

Heylyn, Peter. *Microcosmus, or a Little Description of the Great World: A Treatise Historicall, Geographicall, Politicall, Theologicall.* Oxford: John Lichfield, and James Short, 1621.

Howell, James. *S.P.Q.V. A Survey of the Signorie of Venice, of her ... policy; and method of government; With a cohortation to All Christian Princes to resent her dangerous condition at present.* London, 1651.

Kafadar, Cemal. 'A Death in Venice (1575): Anatolian Muslim Merchants Trading in the Serenissima,' in Raiyyet Rüsûmu, ed., 'Essays Presented to Halil Inalcik on His Seventieth Birthday by His Colleagues and Students,' *Journal of Turkish Studies* 10 (1986): 198–202.

Loredano, Giovanni Francesco, the Elder. *La Turca; comedia.* Edited by S. Loredano. Venice: Libraria della Speranza, 1597.

Machiavelli. *Florentine Histories.* Translated by Laura F. Banfield and Harvey C. Mansfield, Jr. Princeton, New Jersey: Princeton University Press, 1990.

– *The Prince.* Translated by George Bull. Harmondsworth: Penguin, 1981.

Malipiero, Domenico. *Annali Veneti dell'anno 1457 al 1500.* 2 vols. Florence: Vieusseux, 1843–4.

Marcello, Pietro. *Vite de' prencipi di Vinegia.* Venice: P. Pietrasanta, 1557.

Marcucci, Giacomo Crulli di. *Vite et effigie di tutti li pontifici romani con le loro armi.* Rome: Antonio Tempesta, 1624.

Marinella, Lucrezia. *The Nobility and Excellence of Women and the Defects and Vices of Men.* Edited and translated by Anne Dunhill. Introduction by Letizia Panizza. Chicago: University of Chicago Press, 1999.

Menavino, Antonio. *Trattato de costumi et vita de Turchi.* Florence: Torrentino, 1548.

Michele, Agostino. *Oratione di Agostino Michele nella coronatione della Serenissima Prencipessa di Vinegia, Moresina Grimani.* Venice: Marco Claseri, 1597.

Molino, Antonio. *Manoli Blessi nella rotta dell'armata de Sultan Selin, ultimo re de Turchi.* Venice: G.B. Guerra, [1571].

Moryson, Fynes. *An Itinerary Containing His Ten Years of Travel.* London: J. Beale, 1617.

Müller, Theobald; Giovio, Paolo. *Musæi Joviani imagines artifice manu ad vivum expressæ.* Basel: Petri Pernae, 1577.

Münster, Sebastian. *Cosmographia universalis.* Basel: Henricus Petrus, 1550.

Nicolay, Nicolas de. *L'art de naviguer de maistre Pierre de Medine, Espaignol: etc.* Translated, augmented, and illustrated by Nicolas de Nicolay. Lyon: Guillaume Roville, 1554.

– *Les quatre premiers livres des navigations et pérégrinations orientales de N. de Nicolay ... Avec les figures au naturel tant d'hommes que de femmes slon la diversité des nations, et de leur port, maintien, et habitz.* Lyon: G. Roville, 1567.

Palazzi, Giovanni. *La virtu in giocco overo dame patritie di Venetia famose per nascita, per lettere, per armi, per costumi.* Venice: Giovanni Parè Libraro, 1681.

Panvinio, Onofrio. *XXVII pontificum maximorum.* Rome: Antoine Lafréry, 1568.

Paruta, Paolo. *Della perfettione della vita politica ... libri tre, etc.* Venice: D. Nicolini, 1579.

– *The History of Venice ... written originally in Italian ... likewise the wars of Cyprus.* Translated by Henry Earl of Monmouth. London: Printed for Abel Rober and Henry Herringman, 1658.

– *Opere politiche.* 2 vols. Edited by C. Monzani. Florence: F. Le Monnier, 1852.

Piave, G.M. 'Feste fatte in Venetia pella incoronatione della Serenissima Dogaressa Morosina Morosini Grimani.' In *Emporio Artistico-Letterario ossia raccolta di amene lettere, novità. II.* 1847.

Pinargenti, Simon. *Isole che son da Venetia.* Venice, 1563.

Porcacchi, Tommaso. *Le attioni d'Arrigo Terzo Re di Francia, et quarto di Polonia, descritte in dialogo, etc.* Venice: Giorgio Angelieri, 1574.

– *L'isole piu famose del mondo …intagliate da G. Porro etc..* Venice: Simon Galignani and Girolamo Porro, 1576.

Porta, Giovanni Battista della. *De ea naturalis physiognomioniae parte quae ad manuum lineas spectat libri duo.* Edited by Oreste Trabucco. Naples: Edizioni scientifiche Italiane, 2003.

– *Della fisonomia dell'uomo.* Parma: Ugo Guanda, 1988.

– *Della fisonomia dell'huomo, libri VI. tradotti dal Latino in volgare.* Naples: G.G. Carlino & C. Vitale, 1610.

– *De humana physiognomonia libri IIII.* Vico Equense: Iosephum Cacchium, 1586.

– *Phytognomonica octo libris contenta.* Naples: Horatium Salvianum, 1589.

– *De refractione, optices parte.* Naples: Jo. Jacobum Carlinum, & Antonium Pacem, 1593.

– *La turca comedia nuova.* Venice: Pietro Ciera, 1606.

Portello, Luigi dal. *Trattato de'costumi.* Venice, 1561.

Priuli, Girolamo. *I diarii.(1494–1512).* Edited by Arturo Segre. Bologna: Zanichelli, 1921–41.

Ptolemy, Claudius. *Geografia di Claudio Tolomeo.* Translated by Girolamo Ruscelli and amplified by Giuseppe Rosaccio. Venice: Heirs of Melchior Sessa, 1598.

Quicchelberg, Samuel. *Theatri amplissimi, complectentis rerum vniuersitatis singulas materias et imagines eximias.* Monaco: Adami Berg, 1565.

Ramusio, Giovanni Battista. *Primo volume & seconda edtione delle navigationi et viaggi.* Venice: Giunti, 1554.

Rasarius, Joannes Baptista. *J.B. Rasarii de victoria Christianorum ad Echinadas: Oratio.* Venice, 1571.

Rava, Agostino [Menon, pseud.]. *Vettuoria incontra el Turco.* Venice, 1571.

Reusner, Nicolas. *Icones sive imagines vivae, literis clarorum virorum, Italiae, Graeciae, Germaniae, Galliae, Angliae, Ungariae.* Basel: C. Valdkirch, 1589.

Ridolfi, Carlo. *Le maraviglie dell'arte overo le vite degl'illustri pittori veneti e dello stato.* Venice: Gio. Battista Sgava, 1648.

Rosaccio, Giuseppe. *Il microcosmo … nel quale si tratta brevemente dell'anima vegetabile, sensibile, & rationale. Dell'huomo sua complessione, & fisionomia. Delle infirmità, che nascono in tutte le parti del corpo, & loro cura.* Florence: Francesco Tosi. 1600.

– *Viaggio da Venetia, a Costantinopoli per mare, e per terra, & insieme quello di Terra Santa.* Venice: Giacomo Franco, 1598.

Rota, Giovanni. *Lettera nella quale si descrive l'ingresso nel Palazzo Ducale della serenis-

sima Morosina Morosini Grimani prencipessa di Vinetia. Venice: Gio. Ant. Rampazetto, 1597.

Sansovino, Francesco. *Annali Turcheschi: ovvero le vite de principi ed Signori della casa othomana.* Venice, 1571.

– *Gl'annali overo le vite de principi et signori della Casa Othomana, Turcheschi etc.* Venice, 1573.

– *Delle cose notabili che sono in Venetia libri due. etc.* Venice: Comin da Trino, 1561.

– [Anselmo Guisconi, pseud.]. *Dialogo di tutte le cose notabili che sono in Venetia.* 1556. Reprint. Venice: Tipografia Emiliana, 1861.

– *L'edificio del corpo humano.* Venice: Rizzo, 1550.

– *L'historia di Casa Orsina.* Venice: B. & F. Stagnini fratelli, 1565.

– *Historia universale dell'origine et imperio dé Turchi.* Venice: M. Bonelli, 1573.

– *Informatione della militia turchesca, & de gli habiti de soldati turchi.* Venice: Altobello Salicato, 1582.

– *Informatione … a soldati christiani et a tutti loro che sono su la potentissima armata della … signoria di Venetia.* Venice, 1570.

– *Lettera overo discorso sopra le predittioni fatte in diversi tempi da diverse persone.* Venice, 1570.

– *Della origine e fatti delle famiglie illustri d'Italia, libro primo, etc.* Venice, 1582.

– *Ritratto delle più nobili et famose città d'Italia, etc.* Venice, 1575.

– *Venetia città nobilissima e singolare* [Venice, 1581]. Bergamo: Leading Edizioni, 2002.

– and Giovanni Stringa. *Venetia città nobilissima e singolare.* Venice: Alto bello Salicato, 1604.

Santonino, Agostino. *Canzone nella publica letitia, per la felicissima vittoria navale ottenuta contra turchi, à i cuzzo ari.* Venice, 1572.

Sanuto, Marin. *I diarii di Marino Sanuto (MCCCCXCVI–MDXXXIII) dall' autografo Marciano ital. cl. VII cod. CDXIX–CDLXXVII.* Venice: F. Visentini, 1879–1903.

– *Itinerario di Marin Sanuto per la terraferma veneziana nell'anno 1483.* Edited by Rawdon Brown. Padua, 1847.

– *De origine, situ et magistratibus urbis venetae ovvero la citta di Venetia (1493–1530).* Edited by Angelo Caracciolo Arico. Milan: Cisalpino, La Goliardica, 1980.

Sarpi, Paolo. *Lettere ai protestanti.* 2 vols. Edited by D. Busnelli. I. Bari: G. Laterza & figli, 1931.

Savonarola, Girolamo. *Prediche del Rev. P.F. Hieronymo Sauonaruola* [*sic*] *… sopra alquanti salmi & sopra Aggeo Profeta fatte del mese di Novembre & Dicembre l'anno 1494.* Venice: Bernardino de Bindoni, 1544.

Scamozzi, Vincenzo. *Discorsi sopra le antichità di Roma.* Venice: Francesco Ziletti, 1582.

Serlio, Sebastiano. *Tutte l'opere d'architettura et prospetiva.* [1619]. Reprint, Ridgewood, NJ: The Gregg Press Incorporated, 1964.

Sluperius, Joannes. *Omnium fere gentium, nostraeq aetatis nationum habitus et effigies.* Antwerp: Ioanni Bellero, 1572.

Stella, Aldo., ed. *Nunziature di Venezia, 9.* Rome: Istituto Storico Italiano Per l'Età Moderna e Contemporanea, 1972.

Straub, Georg. *Trachten oder Stambuch.* Sanct. Gallen: Georg Straub, 1600.

Tiepolo, Giacomo. *Tre sorelle; corone di sonetti... sopra la felicissima vittoria navale.* Venice: Altobello Salicato, 1572.

Toscanella, Orazio. *Essortatione ... a i cristiani contra il turco.* Venice: Sigismondo Bordogna et Franc. Patriani, 1572.

Toscano, Rafaello. *Le feste et trionfi de li honorati mercanti della seta, con il superbo apparato fatto in Rialto nuovo per l'allegrezza della Vittoria, ottenuta contra Turchi.* Venice, 1571.

Tutio, Dario. *Ordine et modo tenuto nell'incoronatione della Serenissima Moresina Grimani Dogaressa Di Venetia.* Venice: Nicolò Peri Libraro, 1597.

Valignano, Alexandro. *Il cerimoniale per i missionari del Giappone.* Edited and introduction by Josef Franz Schütte. Rome: Edizioni di Storia e Letteratura, 1946.

– 'Les instructions du Père Valignano pour l'ambassade japonaise en Europe.' Edited by J.A. Abranches, J.A. Pinto, and Henri Bernard. *Monumenta Nipponica* 6 (1943): 391-403.

Valignano, Alessandro. *Sumario de las cosas de Japón.* Edited by J.L. Alvarez-Taladriz. Tokyo: Sophia University, 1954.

Vasari, Giorgio. *Der Literarische Nachlass Giorgio Vasaris herausgegeben und mit Kritischen Apparate verschen von Karl Frey.* 3 vols. Munich: G. Muller, 1823–.

– *Le opere di Giorgio Vasari con nuove annotazioni e commenti di Gaetano Milanesi.* Florence: Le lettere, 1998.

Vecellio, Cesare. *De gli habiti antichi, et moderni di diverse parti del mondo libri due, fatti da C. V. e con discorsi da lui dichiarati.* Venice: Damian Zenaro, 1590.

– *Habiti antichi et moderni di tutto il mondo; di nuova accresciuti di multe figure. Vestitus antiquorum, recentiorumque totius orbis, per S. Gratilianum Latine declarati.* Venice: Gio. Bernardo Sessa, 1598.

Venice, Legislative Bodies. *Relazioni degli ambasciatori veneti, Relazioni dagli Stati Ottomani.* Vol. III. Florence: 1840–55.

Vico, Enea. *Diversarum gentium aetatis habitus.* Venice, 1558.

– *Reliquae Augustarum imagines a Plotina ad Saloninam.* Venice: Giacomo Franco, 1601.

– *Vetustissimae Tabulae Aeneae Hierglyphicis* [1559]. Venice: Giacomo Franco, 1600.

Vives, Juan Luis. *De institutione feminae Christianae.* In *Selected Works of J.L. Vives.* Edited by C. Fantazzi and C. Matheeussen. Translated by C. Fantazzi. Leiden: E.J. Brill, 1987. Vol. I, Liber Primus, 1996; Vol. II, Liber Secundus & Liber Tertius, 1998.

Waldseemüller, Martin. *The Cosmographiae Introductio of Martin Waldseemüller in Facsimile.* Edited by Charles George Herbermann. New York: United States Catholic Historical Society, 1907.

Weiditz, Christopher. *Authentic Everyday Dress of the Renaissance.* Reprint of *Das Trachtenbuch des Christoph Weiditz von seinen Reisen nach Spanien (1529), und den Niederlanden (1531/32).* Edited by Dr. Theodor Hampe. Berlin: Verlag von Walter de Gruyter & Co., 1927. New York: Dover Publications, 1994.

Weigel, Hans and Amman, Jost. *Habitus praecipuorum populorum, tam virorum quam foeminarum singulari arte depicti. Trachtenbuch: darin fast allerley und der fürnembsten Nationen ... Kleidungen ... abgerissen sein.* Nuremberg: Hans Weigel, 1577.

Voisin, Lancelot du. *Les trois mondes.* Paris: L'Olivier de Pierre L'Huillier, 1582.

Zangrius, Jean-Baptiste(?). *Album amicorum, habitus mulierum omniu nationu Europae tum tabulis ac scutis vacuis in aes incisis adornatum, ut quisque et sÿmbola et insignia sua gentilitia in iis depingi commode curare possit.* Leuven: Ioannem Baptis. Tam Zangrium, 1599.

Zen, Nicolò. *Dell'origine d'Barbari.* Venice: Plinio Pietrasanta, 1557.

– *Dell'origine di Venetia.* Venice: Francesco Marcolini, 1558.

Secondary Sources

Adler, Kathleen, and Marcia Pointon, eds. *The Body Imaged: The Human Form and Visual Culture since the Renaissance.* Cambridge: Cambridge University Press, 1993.

Agnew, Jean-Christophe. *Worlds Apart: The Market and the Theater in Anglo-American Thought, 1550–1750.* Cambridge: Cambridge University Press, 1986.

Akerman, James, and David Buisseret. *Monarchs, Ministers and Maps: A Cartographic Exhibit at the Newberry Library on the Occasion of the Eighth Series of Kenneth Nebenzahl, Jr., Lectures in the History of Cartography.* Chicago: The Newberry Library, 1985.

Albéri, Eugenio. *Relazioni degli ambasciatori veneti al senato. Serie III: I Turchi.* 3 vols. Florence: Tipografia all'Insegna di Clio, 1840.

Allerston, Patricia. A. 'The Market in Second-Hand Clothes and Furnishings in Venice, c. 1500–1650.' PhD diss. European University Institute Florence, 1996.

 – 'Reconstructing the Second-Hand Clothes Trade in Sixteenth and Seven-teenth-Century Venice,' *Costume* 33 (1999).
 – 'Wedding Finery in Sixteenth Century Venice.' In *Marriage in Italy, 1300–1650*. Edited by Trevor Dean and K.J.P. Lowe, 25–40. Cambridge: Cambridge University Press, 1998.
Almagià, Roberto. 'La cartographia dell'Italia nel Cinquecento, con un saggio sulla cartografia del Piemonte II.' *Rivista, G.I.* 22 (1915): 1–26.
 – *Monumenta Italiae Cartographica. Riproduzioni di carte generale e regionali d'Italia dal secolo XIV al XVII*. Florence: Istituto Geografico Militare, 1929.
 – 'Cristoforo Sorte e i primi rilievi topografici della Venezia Tridentina,' *Rivista G.I.* 37 (1930): 117–22.
 – 'On the Cartographic Work of Francesco Rosselli,' *Imago Mundi* 8 (1951): 27–34.
Althusser, Louis. 'Ideology and Ideological State Apparatuses.' In *Cultural Theory and Popular Culture: A Reader*. Edited by Jon Storey, 153–64. Athens: University of Georgia Press, 1998.
Ambrosini, Federica. '"Descrittioni del mondo" nelle case Venete dei secoli XVI e XVII.' *Archivio Veneto* (1981): 67–79.
Ammerman, A.J., M. De Min, R. Housley, and C.E. McClennen. 'More on the Origins of Venice.' *Antiquity* 69 (1995): 501–10.
Angeleri, Carlo. *Bibliografia delle stampe popolari a carattere profano dei secoli XVI e XVII conservate nella Biblioteca Nazionale di Firenze*. Florence: Sansoni, 1953.
Anzieu, Didier. *The Skin Ego*. Translated by Chris Turner. New Haven: Yale University Press, 1989.
Appadurai, Arjun. *Modernity at Large: Cultural Dimensions of Globalization*. Minneapolis: University of Minnesota Press, 1996.
 – ed. *The Social Life of Things: Commodities in Cultural Perspective*. Cambridge, UK: Cambridge University Press, 1986.
Armstrong, Lilian. 'Benedetto Bordon, *Miniator*, and Cartography in Early Sixteenth-Century Venice.' *Imago Mundi* 48 (1996): 65–92.
Arrigoni, Paolo, and Achille, Bertarelli. *Le stampe storiche conservate nella raccolta del Castello Sforzesco. Catalogo Descrittivo*. Milan: Popolo d'Italia, 1932.
Ascarelli, Fernanda. *La tipografia cinquecentina italiana*. Florence: Sansoni Antiquariato, 1953.
Ascarelli, Fernanda, and Marco Menato. *La tipografia del'500 in Italia*. Florence: L.S. Olschki, 1989.
Atasoy, Nurhan 'The Birth of Costume Books and the Generci Mehmed Album.' In *Fenerci Mehmed, Osmanli kiyafetleri: Fenerci Mehmed Albümü*, 22–3. Istanbul: Vehbi Koç Vakfi, 1986.

Austin, John Langshaw. *How to Do Things with Words.* Oxford: Clarendon Press, 1975.

Bagrow, Leo (Lev Seminovich Bagrov). *Giovanni Andreas di Vavassore. A Venetian Cartographer of the 16th Century. A Descriptive List of His Maps.* Jenkintown: George H. Beans Library, 1939.

– *History of Cartography.* Revised and enlarged by R.A. Skelton. Translated by D.L. Paisey. London: 1964.

– *Matheo Pagano. A Venetian Cartographer of the 16th Century.* Jenkintown: George H. Beans Library, 1940.

Bakhtin, Mikhail. *Rabelais and His World.* Bloomington: Indiana University Press, 1984.

Barbieri, Franco, and Guido Beltramini, eds. *Vincenzo Scamozzi.* Venice: Marsilio, 2003.

Barkan, Leonard. *Nature's Work of Art: The Human Body as Image of the World.* New Haven: Yale University Press, 1975.

Barkey, Karen. *Bandits and Bureaucrats: The Ottoman Route to State Centralization.* Ithaca: Cornell University Press, 1994.

Barnes, Susan. 'The *Uomini Illustri,* Humanist Culture and the Development of a Portrait Tradition in Early Seventeenth-Century Italy.' In *Cultural Differentiation and Cultural Identity in the Visual Arts.* Edited by Susan Barnes and Walter Melion. Studies in the History of Art 27, 81–92. Washington: National Gallery of Art, 1989.

Barthes, Roland. *The Fashion System.* London: Cape, 1983.

Bartsch, Adam von. *The Illustrated Bartsch.* New York: Abaris Books, 1978–.

Barzaghi, Antonio. *Donne o cortigiane? La prostituzione a Venezia, documenti di costume dal XVI al XVIII secolo.* Verona: Bertani Editore, 1980.

Bataillon, Marcel. 'Mythe et connaissance de la Turquie en Occident au milieu du XVIe siècle.' In *Venezia e l'Oriente fra tardo Medioevo e Rinascimento.* Edited by Agostino Pertusi, 452–3, 457–69. Florence: Sansoni, 1966.

Bates, E.S. *Touring in 1600: A Study in the Development of Travel as a Means of Education.* Boston: Houghton Mifflin, 1911.

Baxandall, Michael. *Painting and Experience in Fifteenth-Century Italy: A Primer in the Social History of Pictorial Style.* Oxford: Clarendon Press, 1972.

Becker, Carl. *Jobst Amman, Zeichner und Formschneider, Kupferätzer und Stecher ...* etc. Leipzig: R. Weigel, 1854.

Bellavitis, Giorgio, and Giandomenico Romanelli. *Venezia.* Rome: Edizione Laterza, 1985.

Belkin, Kristin Lohse. *Corpus Rubenianum Ludwig Burchard. Part XXIV. The Costume Book.* Antwerp: Arcade, 1980.

Bellini, Paolo. 'Stampatori e mercanti di stampe in Italia nei secoli XVI e XVII.' *I Quaderni del Conoscitore di Stampe* 26 (1975): 19–45.

Belting, Hans. *Likeness and Presence: A History of the Image before the Era of Art.* Translated by Edmund Jephcott. Chicago: University of Chicago Press, 1994.

Belyea, Barbara. 'Images of Power: Derrida/Foucault/Harley.' *Cartographica* 29, no. 2 (Summer 1992): 1–9.

Benjamin, Walter. *Illuminations. Essays and Reflections.* Edited by Hannah Arendt. New York: Schocken Books, 1968.

– 'The Work of Art in the Age of Mechanical Reproduction,' 217-251. *Essays and Reflections.* Edited by Hannah Arendt. New York: Schocken Books, 1968.

Benzoni, Gino, ed. *Il Mediterraneo nella seconda metà del '500 alla luce di Lepanto.* Florence: L. S. Olschki, 1974.

– ed. *I dogi.* Milan: Electa Editrice, 1982.

Berchet, Guglielmo. 'Documenti,' *Archivio Veneto* 13 (1876).

– 'Documenti del saggio storico sulle antiche ambasciate Giapponesi in Italia.' *Archivio Veneto* 14 (1877): 150–203.

– *Le antiche ambasciate Giapponesi in Italia.* Venice: Marco Visentini, 1877.

Beringuer, Luigi, and Floriana Colao, eds. *Crimine, giustiza e società veneta in età moderna.* Milan: 1989.

Berlin. Miscellaneous Institutions Staatliche Museen. *Katalog der Lipperheideschen Kostümbibliothek.* Revised by Eva Nienholdt and Gretel Wagner-Neumann. 2 vols. Berlin: Verlag Gebr. Mann, 1965.

Bertarelli, Achille. *L'imagerie populaire italienne.* Paris: Éditions Duchartre & Van Buggenhoudt, 1929.

Bettini, Sergio. *Venezia.* Novara: Istituto geografico De Agostini, 1953.

– *Venezia: Nascita di una città.* Milan: Electa, 1978.

Bevilacqua, Eugenio. 'Geografi e Cosmografi,' in *Storia della cultura Veneta: Dal primo quattrocento al Concilio di Trento,* II: *355–74.* Vicenza: Neri Pozza, 1980.

Bhabha, Homi K. *The Location of Culture.* London: Routledge, 1994.

Biadene, Susanna. 'Il saggio di cartografia della regione Veneta.' *Bollettino Musei Veneziani d'Arte e di Storia* 25 (1980): 38–51.

– ed. *Carte da navigar: Portolani e carte nautiche del Museo Correr 1318–1732.* Venice: Marsilio, 1990.

Bistort Giulio. *Il magistrato alle pompe nella repubblica di Venezia; studio storico.* Venice: a spese della Società, 1912.

Boerio, Giuseppe. *Dizionario del dialetto veneziano.* Venice, 1829.

Boholm, Åsa. 'The Coronation of Female Death: The Dogaressas of Venice.' *Man* 27 (1992): 91–104.

– *The Doge of Venice: The Symbolism of State Power in the Renaissance.* Gothenburg: The Institute for Advanced Studies in Social Anthropology, 1990.

Bolzoni, Lina. *The Gallery of Memory: Literary and Iconographic Models in the Age of the Printing Press.* Translated by Jeremy Parzen. Toronto: University of Toronto Press, 2001.

Bonaffe, Edmond. *Voyages et voyageurs de la Renaissance.* Geneva: Slatkine, 1970.

Bonino, Guido Davico. *La commedia italiana del cinquecento e altre note su letteratura e teatro.* Turin: Tirrenia Stampatori, 1989.

Bonner, Mitchell. *Italian Civic Pageantry in the High Renaissance. A Descriptive Bibliography of Triumphal Entries and Selected Other Festivals for State Occasions.* Florence: Leo S. Olschki Editore, 1979.

Bonora, Elena. *Ricerche su Francesco Sansovino: imprenditore, librario e letterato.* Venice: Istituto veneto di scienze, lettere ed arti, 1994.

Boscaro, Adriana. 'Giapponesi a Venezia nel 1585.' In *Venezia e l'Oriente.* Edited by Lionello Lanciotti, 409–29 ff. Florence: L.S. Olschki, 1987.

– *Sixteenth Century European Printed Works on the first Japanese Mission to Europe. A Descriptive Bibliography.* Leiden: E.J. Brill, 1973.

– 'La visita a Venezia della prima ambasceria giapponese in Europa.' *Il Giappone, anno V.* Rome: 1965.

Bottari, Giovanni Gaetano. *Raccolta di lettere sulla pittura, scultura ed architettura scritte da' più celebri personaggi dei secoli XV, XVI e XVII.* 8 vols. Milan: Giovanni Silvestri, 1822–5.

Bouwsma, William. *Venice and the Defense of Republican Liberty: Renaissance Values in the Age of the Counter Reformation.* Berkeley: University of California Press, 1968.

Boxer, C.R. *The Christian Century in Japan, 1549–1650.* Berkeley: University of California Press, 1951.

Branca, Vittore, ed. *Rinascimento europeo e rinascimento veneziano.* Florence: Sansoni, 1967.

Bratti, R. *La pianta prospettica di Venezia dell'anno 1500.* Venice: Zanetti, 1827.

Braudel, Fernand. 'Bilan d'une bataille.' In *Il Mediterraneo nella seconda metà del '500 alla luce di Lepanto.* Edited by Gino Benzoni, 109–20. Florence: Olschki, 1974.

– *Civilization and Capitalism, 15th and 18th Century,* vol. 3: *The Perspective of the World.* Translated by Siân Reynolds. New York: Harper and Row, 1979.

– *The Mediterranean and the Mediterranean World in the Age of Philip II.* 2 vols. Translated by Siân Reynolds. New York: Harper and Row, 1972.

Braunstein, P., and C. Klapisch-Zuber. 'Florence et Venise: Les rituels publiques à l'époque de la Renaissance.' *Annales: Economies, Sociétés, Civilisations* 38, no. 5 (1983): 1110–24.

Braunstein, Philippe, and Robert Delort. *Venise. Portrait historique d'une cité.* Paris: Éditions du Seuil, 1971.

Bremmer, Jan, and Herman Roodenburg. *A Cultural History of Gesture from Antiquity to the Present Day.* Cambridge, UK: Polity Press, 1991.

Broc, Numa. *La géographie de la Renaissance 1420–1620.* Paris: Éditions du C.T.H.S., 1986.

Brown, H.F., ed. *Calendar of State Papers and Manuscripts Relating to English Affairs Existing in the Archives and Collections of Venice*, vol. 10: *1603–1607*. London: Stationary Office, 1864.

– *The Venetian Printing Press: An Historical Study.* London: J.C. Nimmo, 1891.

Brown, Judith. 'Courtiers and Christians: The First Japanese Emissaries to Europe.' *Renaissance Quarterly* 47 no. 4 (Winter 1994): 872–906.

Brown, Patricia Fortini. 'Behind the Walls: The Material Culture of Venetian Elites.' In *Venice Reconsidered: The History and Civilization of an Italian City-State 1297–1797*. Edited by John Martin and Dennis Romano, 295–338. Baltimore: Johns Hopkins University Press, 2000.

– 'Measured Friendship, Calculated Pomp: The Ceremonial Welcomes of the Venetian Republic.' In *All the World's a Stage … Art and Pageantry in the Renaissance and Baroque. Part 1*. Edited by Barbara Wisch and Susan Scott Munshower. University Park: Department of Art History, The Pennsylvania State University, 1990.

– *Venetian Narrative Painting in the Age of Carpaccio*. New Haven: Yale University Press, 1988.

– *Venice and Antiquity: The Venetian Sense of the Past*. New Haven: Yale University Press, 1996.

Brown, Rawdon. *Notice of, and Extracts from The Report presented to the Doge and Senate of Venice, by Sebastian Venier, Captain General of the fleet of the Republic a Lepanto, on his return from service, On 29th of December, 1572*. Translated by Mr Rawdon Brown.

Brulez, Wilfrid. *Marchands Flamands à Venise I (1568–1605)*. Brussels: Universa, 1965.

Brusatin, Manlio. 'Theatrum Mundi Novissimi.' In *Aldo Rossi: Teatro del mondo*, 145–8. Venice: Cluva Libreria Editrice, 1982.

Bryson, Norman. *Vision and Painting: The Logic of the Gaze*. New Haven: Yale University Press, 1983.

– *Visual Theory: Painting and Interpretation*. Cambridge, UK: Polity Press, 1991.

Buisseret, David, ed. *Monarchs, Ministers, and Maps: The Emergence of Cartography as a Tool of Government in Early Modern Europe*. Chicago: University of Chicago Press, 1992.

Burckhardt, Jacob. *The Civilization of the Renaissance in Italy: An Essay*. London: Phaidon Press, 1960.

Burke, Peter. *The Historical Anthropology of Early Modern Italy: Essays on Perception and Communication*. Cambridge: Cambridge University Press, 1987.

Bury, Michael. *The Print in Italy, 1550–1620*. London: The British Museum Press, 2001.

Butler, Judith. *Gender Trouble: Feminism and the Subversion of Identity*. New York: Routledge, 1990.

– 'Performative Acts and Gender Constitution: An Essay in Phenomenology and Feminist Theory,' *Performing Feminisms: Feminist Critical Theory and Theatre.* Edited by Sue-Ellen Case, 270–82. Baltimore: The Johns Hopkins University Press, 1990.

– *Subjects of Desire: Hegelian Reflections in Twentieth-Century France.* New York: Columbia University Press, 1987.

Calabi, Donatella. 'Images of a City "in the Middle" of Salt Water.' In *An Atlas of Venice: The Form of the City on 1:1000 Scale Photomap and Line Map.* Edited by Edoardo Salzano, 11–24. Princeton: Princeton Architectural Press, 1990.

Campbell, Tony. 'Portolan Charts from the Late Thirteenth Century to 1500.' In *The History of Cartography.* Edited by J.B. Harley and David Woodward, 371–461. Chicago: University of Chicago Press, 1987–.

Cappi Bentivegna, Ferruccia. *Abbigliamento e costume nella pittura italiana. Rinascimento.* Rome: Carlo Bestetti, Edizioni d'Arte, 1962.

Caraci, Giuseppe. 'Avanzi di una preziosa raccolta di carte geografiche.' *La Bibliofilia* 29, no. 5–6 (August–September 1927): 178–92.

Caroli, Flavio. *L'arte dalla psicologia alla psicanalisi: Teoria artistica e richerche sul profondo dal XV al XX secolo.* Bologna: Pàtron editore, 1984.

– *Storia della fisiognomica: Arte e psicologia da Leonardo a Freud.* Milan: Leonardo, 1995.

Casini, Matteo. '"Dux habet formam regis": Morte e intronizzazione del principe a Venezia e Firenze nel cinquecento.' *Annali della Fondazione Luigi Einaudi* 27 (1993): 273–353.

– *I gesti del principe: La festa politica a Firenze e Venezia in età rinascimentale.* Venice: Marsilio, 1996.

– '*Triumphi* in Venice in the Long Renaissance.' *Italian History and Culture* (1995): 23–41.

Cassini, Giocondo. *Piante e vedute prospettiche di Venezia (1479–1855).* Venice: La Stamperia di Venezia Editrice, 1982.

Cassirer, Ernst. *The Individual and the Cosmos in Renaissance Philosophy.* Translated with an introduction by Mario Domandi. Oxford: Basil Blackwell, 1963.

Cessi, Roberto. *La repubblica di Venezia e il problema Adriatico.* Naples: Edizioni Scientifiche Italiane, 1953.

– *Storia della repubblica di Venezia.* 2 vols. Milan: Giuseppe Principato, 1944–6.

– *Venezia Ducale.* Venice: Deputazione di Storia Patria, 1963.

Chabod, F. 'Alcune questioni di terminologia: Stato Nazione, patria nel linguaggio del Cinquecento.' In *Scritti sul Rinascimento*, 625–61. Turin: Einaudi, 1967.

Chambers, D.S. *The Imperial Age of Venice 1380–1580.* London: Thames and Hudson, 1970.

Chambers, David, and Brian Pullan, with Jennifer Fletcher. *Venice: A Documentary History, 1450–1630.* Oxford: Blackwell, 1992.

Chambers, David, Cecil H. Clough, and Michael E. Mallett, eds. *War, Culture, and Society in Renaissance Venice: Essays in Honour of John Hale.* London: Hambledon Press, 1993.

Chartier, Roger. *Cultural History: Between Practices and Representations.* Translated by Lydia G. Cochrane. Ithaca, NY: Cornell University Press, 1988.

— *The Order of Books: Readers, Authors and Libraries in Europe between the Fourteenth and Eighteenth Centuries.* Translated by Lydia G. Cochrane. Stanford, CA.: Stanford University Press, 1994.

— ed. *The Culture of Print: Power and the Uses of Print in Early Modern Europe.* Translated by Lydia Cochrane. Cambridge: Polity Press, 1989.

Chojnacka, Monica. *Working Women of Early Modern Venice.* Baltimore: Johns Hopkins University Press, 2001.

Chojnacki, Stanley. 'Marriage, Legislation and Patrician Society in Fifteenth-Century Venice.' In *Law, Custom, and the Social Fabric in Medieval Europe; Essays in Honor of Bryce Lyon.* Edited by Bernard S. Bachrach and David Nicholas, 163–84. Kalamazoo, MI: Medieval Institute Publications, 1990.

— 'Marriage Regulation in Venice, 1429–1535.' In Chojnacki, *Women and Men in Renaissance Venice: Twelve Essays on Patrician Society,* 53–75. Baltimore: Johns Hopkins University Press, 2000.

— 'Subaltern Patriarchs: Patrician Bachelors in Renaissance Venice.' In *Medieval Masculinities:Regarding Men in the Middle Ages.* Edited by Clare Lees, 73–90. Minneapolis: University of Minnesota Press, 1994.

— *Women and Men in Renaissance Venice: Twelve Essays on Patrician Society.* Baltimore: Johns Hopkins University Press, 2000.

Cicogna, Emmanuele. *Delle inscrizioni Veneziane raccolte ed illustrate.* 6 vols. Venice: Giuseppe Picotti, 1824–53.

Cicogna, Emmanuele Antonio. *Corpus delle iscrizioni di Venezia e delle isole della laguna veneta, ovvero Riepilogo sia delle Iscrizioni edite ... che di quelle inedite ...* Work compiled by Piero Pazzi with Sara Bergamasco. Venezia: Biblioteca orafa di Sant'Antonio abate, 2001.

Cicognara, Leopoldo. *Catalogo ragionato dei libri d'arte e d'antichità posseduti dal Conte Cicognara.* Pisa: Niccolò Capurro, 1821.

Clough, Cecil. 'Italian Renaissance Portraiture and Printed Portrait-Books.' In *The Italian Book: Studies Presented to Dennis E. Rhodes.* Edited by Dennis E. Rhodes and Denis V. Reidy, 183–223. London: British Library, 1993.

Clubb, Louise George. *Giambattista della Porta, Dramatist.* Princeton, NJ: Princeton University Press, 1965.

Cocke, Richard. *Veronese's Drawings: A Catalogue Raisonnée.* London: Sotheby, 1984.

Coco, Carla, and Flora Manzonetto. *Baili veneziani alla sublime porta: storia e caratteristiche dell'ambasciata veneta a Costantinopoli.* Venice: Stamperia di Venezia, 1985.

Colas, René. *Bibliographie générale du costume et de la mode.* Paris: Librairie René Colas, 1933.

Colla, Angelo. 'Tipografi, editori e libri a Padova, Treviso, Vicenza, Verona, Trento.' In *La stampa degli incunaboli nel Veneto.* Vicenza: Neri Pozza Editore, 1984.

Concina, Ennio. *A History of Venetian Architecture.* Cambridge: Cambridge University Press, 1998.

Conley, Tom. *The Self-Made Map: Cartographic Writing in Early Modern France.* Minneapolis: University of Minnesota Press, 1996.

Cortelazzo, Manlio, ed. *Arti e mestieri tradizionali.* Milan: Amilcare Pizzi Editore, 1989.

Cosgrove, Denis. 'The Myth and the Stones of Venice: An Historical Geography of a Symbolic Landscape.' *Journal of Historical Geography* 8, no. 2 (1982): 145–69.

– *The Palladian Landscape: Geographical Change and Its Cultural Representations in Sixteenth-Century Italy.* University Park: The Pennsylvania State University Press, 1993.

Cox, Virginia. 'The Single Self: Feminist Thought and the Marriage Market in Early Modern Venice.' *Renaissance Quarterly* 48, no. 3 (Autumn 1995): 513–81.

Cozzi, Gaetano. *Ambiente veneziano, ambiente veneto: Saggi su politica, società, cultura nella repubblica di Venezia in età moderna.* Venice: Marsilio, 1997.

– *Il Doge Nicolò Contarini. Ricerche sul patriziato veneziano agli inizi del Seicento.* Venice: Istituto per la collaborazione culturale, 1958.

– 'Domenico Morosini e il *De bene instituta re publica,*' *Studi Veneziani* 12 (1970): 405–58.

Cozzi, Gaetano, Michael Knapton, and Giovanni Scarabello. *La repubblica di Venetia nell'età moderna. Dalla guerra di Chioggia al 1517.* Turin: UTET, 1986.

Crary, Jonathan. *Techniques of the Observer: On Vision and Modernity in the Nineteenth Century.* Cambridge, MA: MIT Press, 1990.

Cristofari, Maria. 'Editori vicentini del XV e XVI secolo.' In *Vicenza Illustrata.* Edited by Neri Pozza, 179–88. Vicenza: Neri Pozza Editore, 1976.

Crouzet-Pavan, Elizabeth. 'Immaginaire et politique: Venise et la mort à la fin du Moyen Age.' *Mélanges de l'École Française de Rome. Moyen Age, Temps modernes* 93, no. 2 (1981): 467–93.

– 'Sopra acque salse': Espaces, pouvoir et société à Venise à la fin du Moyen-Âge.* 2 vols. Rome: École Française de Rome, 1992.

– 'Venice and Torcello: History and Oblivion.' *Renaissance Studies* 8, no. 4 (1994): 416–27.

Cruciani, Fabrizio. 'Gli allestimenti scenici di Baldassare Peruzzi.' *Bollettino del Centro Internazionale di Studi di Architettura Andrea Palladio* (1974): 155–72.

Damisch, Hubert. *The Origin of Perspective.* Translated by John Goodman. Cambridge, MA: The MIT Press, 1994.

Da Mosto, Andrea. *I dogi di Venezia nella vita pubblica e privata.* Florence: Aldo Mantello, 1977.

Davanzo Poli, Doretta. *Le cortigiane di Venezia dal Trecento al Settecento: catalogo della mostra: Venezia, Casinò municipale Ca' Vendramin Calergi, 2 febbraio–16 aprile 1990.* Milan: Berenice, 1990.

Davis, Fred. *Fashion, Culture, and Identity.* Chicago: University of Chicago Press, 1992.

Davis, James C. *The Decline of the Venetian Nobility as a Ruling Class.* Baltimore: The Johns Hopkins Press, 1962.

– *A Venetian Family and Its Fortune, 1500–1900: The Donà and Conservation of Their Wealth.* Philadelphia: American Philosophical Society, 1975.

Davis, Natalie Zemon. *Fiction in the Archives: Pardon Tales and Their Tellers in Sixteenth-Century France.* Stanford: Stanford University Press, 1987.

– *The Gift in Sixteenth-Century France.* Madison: University of Wisconsin Press, 2000.

– *The Return of Martin Guerre.* Cambridge, MA: Harvard University Press, 1983.

– *Society and Culture in Early Modern France.* Stanford: Stanford University Press, 1991.

Davis, Robert C. *The War of the Fists: Popular Culture and Public Violence.* New York: Oxford University Press, 1994.

Davis, Whitney. *Replications: Archaeology, Art History, Psychoanalysis.* University Park: The Pennsylvania State University Press, 1996.

– 'The Subject in/of Art History.' *Art Bulletin,* 76 (December 1994): 570–75.

– '"Virtually Straight." Review of *The Origin of Perspective* by Hubert Damisch.' *Art History* 19 (September 1996): 434–44.

Dazzi, Manlio. *Feste e costumi di Venezia.* Zanetti, 1937.

de'Barbari, Jacopo, Giandomenico Romanelli, and Susanna Biadene. *A volo d'uccello, Jacopo de'Barbari e le rappresentazioni di città nell'Europa del Rinascimento.* Venice, Mestre: Arsenale Editrice, 1999.

De Certeau, Michel. 'The Gaze: Nicholas of Cusa,' *Diacritics* 17 (Fall 1987): 2–38.

– *The Practice of Everyday Life.* Translated by Steven Rendall. Berkeley: University of California Press, 1988.

– *The Writing of History.* Translated by Tom Conley. New York: Columbia University Press, 1988.

Defert, D. 'Un genre ethnographique profane au XVIe: les livres d'habits (essai d'ethno-iconographie).' In *Histoires de l'anthropologie (16e–19e siècles). Colloque la pratique de l'anthropologie aujourd'hui.* Edited by Britta Rupp-Eisenreich, 25–42. Paris: Klincksieck, 1984.

Deleuze, Gilles, and Felix Guattari. *A Thousand Plateaus. Capitalism and Shizophrenia.* Translated by Brian Massumi. Minneapolis: University of Minnesota Press, 1988.

Denaro, Furio de. *Domenico Tempesti e i discorsi sopra l'intaglio ed ogni sorte d'intagliare in rame da lui provate e osservate dai più grand'huomini di tale professione.* Florence: Studio per Edizioni Scelte, 1994.

Deny, Jean. 'Les pseudo-prophéties concernant les Turcs au XVIe siècle.' *Revue des études islamiques* 10 (1936): 201–20.

Derrida, Jacques. *Edmund Husserl's Origin of Geometry: An Introduction.* Translated by John P. Leavey. Stonybrook, NY: Nicolas Hays, 1978.

– *The Truth in Painting.* Translated by Geoff Bennington and Ian McLeod. Chicago: University of Chicago Press, 1987.

Didi-Huberman, Georges. 'Ressemblance mythifiée et ressemblance oubliée chez Vasari: La legende du portrait "Sur le Vif,"' *Mélanges de l'école française de Rome, Italie et Méditerranée* 106, no. 2 (1994): 383–432.

Dizionario enciclopedico Bolaffi dei pittori e degli incisori italiani dal 'XI al XX secolo XI. 11 vols. Turin: Gilio Bolaffi Editore, 1976.

Doege, Heinrich. 'Die Trachtenbücher des 16. Jahrhunderts.' *Beiträge zur Bücherkunde und Philologie.* Edited by August Wilmanns, 429–44. Leipzig: Otto Harrassowitz, 1903.

Dürer, Albrecht. *Trachten-bilder ... aus der Albertina.* [Text by M. Thausing.] Vienna: W. Braumüller, 1871.

Dursteler, Eric. 'Identity and Coexistence in the Early Modern Mediterranean: The Venetian Nation in Constantinople.' PhD diss., Brown University, 2000.

Dwyer, Eugene. 'André Thevet and Fulvio Orsini: The Beginnings of the Modern Tradition of Classical Portrait Iconography in France,' *Art Bulletin* 75 (1993): 467–80

– 'Marco Mantova Benevides e i rittratti di giureconsulti illustri,' *Bollettino D'Arte* 76 (November/December 1990): 59–71.

Early Venetian Printing Illustrated. Venice: Ongania, 1895.

Eisenstein, Elizabeth, L. *The Printing Revolution in Early Modern Europe.* Cambridge: Cambridge University Press, 1983.

Elias, Norbert. *The Civilizing Process. The History of Manners and State Formation and Civilization.* Translated by Edmund Jephcott. Oxford: Blackwell, 1996.

– *The Court Society.* Translated by Edmund Jephcott. Oxford: Basil Blackwell, 1983.

Elkins, James. *The Poetics of Perspective.* Ithaca, NY: Cornell University Press, 1994.

Emison, Patricia. 'Prolegomenon to the Study of Italian Renaissance Prints.' *Word and Image* 11, no. 1 (January–March 1995): 1–15.

Empson, William. *The Structure of Complex Words.* London: Penguin. 1995.

Enenkel, Karl, Betsy de Jong-Crane, and Peter Liebregts, eds. *Modelling the Individual: Biography and Portrait in the Renaissance.* Atlanta: Rodopi, 1998.

Essling, Victor Masséna. *Les livres à figures vénitiens de la fin du XVe siécle et du commmencement du XVIe: Études sur l'art de la gravure sur bois à Venise.* Florence: L.S. Olschki; Paris: H. Leclerc, 1907–14 [1915]. Reprinted, Mansfield: Maurizio Martino, 1994.

Fahy, Conor. 'The Venetian Ptolemy of 1548.' In *The Italian Book.* Edited by Denis V. Reidy, 89–116. London: British Library, 1993.

Falchetta, Piero. 'La misura dipinta: Rilettura tecnica e semantica della veduta di Venezia di Jacopo de' Barbari.' *Ateneo Veneto* 29, anno academico 179 (1991): 273–305.

Fanelli, Giovanni. *Firenze.* Rome: Laterza, 1980.

Fantelli, P.L. 'L'ingresso di Henrico III a Venezia di Andrea Vicentino.' *Quaderni della Soprintendenza ai Beni Artistici e Storici di Venezia* 8 (1979): 95–9.

Fasana, Enrico, and Giuseppe Sorge. *Civiltà indiana ed impatto Europeo nei Secoli XVI–XVIII: L'apporto dei viaggiatori e missionari italiani.* Milan: Jaca Book, 1988.

Fasoli, G. 'Liturgia e ceremoniale ducale.' In *Venezia e il Levante fino al secolo XV.* Vol. 1. Edited by Augustino Pertusi, 261–95. Florence: L.S. Olschki, 1973.

Fasolo, U., and N. Vianello, eds. *Unità e diffusione della civiltà veneta. Relazioni e communicazioni del convegno degli scrittori veneti, Gorizia Ottobre, 1974.* Associazione Degli Scrittori Veneti, 1975.

Favaro, Elena. *L'arte dei pittori in Venezia e i suoi statuti.* Florence: L.S. Olschki, 1975.

Fenlon, Iain, 'Lepanto: The Arts of Celebration in Renaissance Venice.' In *Proceedings of the British Academy* 73 (1988): 201–36.

Finlay, Robert. *Politics in Renaissance Venice.* New Brunswick, NJ: Rutgers University Press, 1980.

Fletcher, Angus. *Allegory: The Theory of a Symbolic Mode.* Ithaca, NY: Cornell University Press, 1964.

Fletcher, Jennifer. 'Fine Art and Festivity in Renaissance Venice: The Artist's Part.' In *Sight and Insight: on Art and Culture in Honour of E.H. Gombrich at 85.* Edited by John Onians, 128–51. London: Phaidon, 1994.

Flugel, J.C. *The Psychology of Clothes.* London: The Hogarth Press and the Institute of Psycho-Analysis, 1971.

Foucault, Michel. *The Order of Things. An Archaeology of the Human Sciences.* New York: Vintage Books, 1994.

Franzoi, Umberto. *Storia e leggenda del Palazzo Ducale di Venezia.* Venice: Storti, 1982.

Freud, S. *The Basic Writings of Sigmund Freud.* Translated and edited by A.A. Brill. New York: Modern Library, 1938.

Frigo, Daniela. 'Dal caos all'ordine: sulla questione del "prender moglie" nella trattatistica del sedicesimo secolo,' *Nel cerchio della luna: figure di donna in alcuni testi del XVI secolo.* Edited by Virginia Baradel and Marina Zancan, 57–93. Venice: Marsilio, 1983.

Fulin, Roberto. 'Documenti per servire alla storia della tipografia veneziana.' *Archivio veneto* 23 (1882): 84–219.

Gabinetto disegni e stampe degli Uffizi. [Marucci, Luisa]. *L'incisione Bolognese nel secolo XVII.* Florence: L.S. Olschki, 1953.

Gallo, Rodolfo. 'Le mappe geografiche del Palazzo Ducale di Venezia.' *Archivio Veneto* 33 (1943): 47–54.

Gent, Lucy, and Nigel Llewellyn, eds. *Renaissance Bodies: The Human Figure in English Culture 1540–1660.* London: Reaktion Books, 1990.

Ghering van Ierlant, M.A. *Mode in Prent (1550–1914).* The Hague: Nederlands Kostuummuseum, 1988.

Gilbert, Felix. 'The Date of the Composition of Contarini's and Giannotti's Books on Venice.' *Studies in the Renaissance* 14 (1967): 172–84.

– 'Religion and Politics in the Thought of Gasparo Contarini.' In *Action and Conviction in Early Modern Europe.* Edited by Theodore K Rabb and Jerrold E. Seigel. Princeton, NJ: Princeton University Press, 1969.

Gilmore, Myron. 'Myth and Reality in Venetian Political Theory.' In *Renaissance Venice.* Edited by John Hale, 431–44. London: Faber and Faber, 1974.

Giomo, Giuseppe. 'Le spese del nobil uomo Marino Grimani nella sua elezione a doge di Venezia,' *Archivio veneto* 33 (1887).

Giurgea, Adrian. 'Theatre of the Flesh: The Carnival of Venice and the Theatre of the World.' PhD diss., University of California, Los Angeles, 1987.

Gleason, Elisabeth. *Gasparo Contarini: Venice, Rome, and Reform.* Berkeley: University of California Press, 1993.

– 'Reading between the Lines of Gasparo Contarini's Treatise on the Venetian State.' In *Culture, Society and Religion in Early Modern Europe. Essays by the Students and Colleagues of William J. Bouwsma.* Edited by Ellery Schalk. *Historical Reflections* 15, no. 1 (Spring 1988).

Göllner, Carl. *Turcica die europäischen Türkendrucke des XVI. Jahrhunderts.* Bucharest: Editura Academiei Republicii Socialiste România, 1961.

Gombrich, Ernst. 'Celebrations in Venice of the Holy League and the Victory of Lepanto.' In *Studies in Renaissance and Baroque Art Presented to Anthony Blunt.* London: Phaidon, 1967.

Greenblatt, Stephen. 'Psychoanalysis and Renaissance Culture.' In *Literary*

Theory/Renaissance Texts. Edited by David Quint and Patricia Parker, 210–24. Baltimore: Johns Hopkins University Press, 1986.

– *Renaissance Self-Fashioning from More to Shakespeare.* Chicago: University of Chicago Press, 1980.

Grego, Mario. 'Viaggiatori inglesi nel Veneto.' In *Voyageurs Étrangers a Venezia: Actes du Congres de l'Ateneo Veneto.* Geneva: Slatkine, 1981.

Grendler, Paul F. *Culture and Censorship in Late Renaissance Italy and France.* London: Variorum Reprints, 1981.

– 'Form and Function in Italian Renaissance Popular Books.' *Renaissance Quarterly* 46, no. 3 (Autumn, 1993): 451–85.

– 'Il libro popolare nel cinquecento.' In *La stampa in Italia nel cinquecento. Atti del Convegno Roma, 17–21 Ottobre 1989.* Edited by Marco Santoro, 211–36. Rome: Bulzoni Editore, 1992.

Grieco, Sara F. Matthews. 'Georgette de Montenay: A Different Voice in Sixteenth-Century Emblematics.' *Renaissance Quarterly* 47, no. 4 (Winter 1994): 798–803.

Grosz, Elizabeth. 'The Body of Signification.' In *Abjection, Melancholia and Love: The Work of Julia Kristeva.* Edited by John Fletcher and Andrew Benjamin, 80–103. London: Routledge, 1990.

Grubb, James S. 'Memory and Identity: Why Venetians Didn't Keep *ricordanze,*' *Renaissance Studies* 8, no. 4 (1994): 375–87.

– 'When Myths Lose Power: Four Decades of Venetian Historiography.' *The Journal of Modern History,* 58, no. 1 (March 1986): 43–94.

Gunji, Yasunori. *Dall'isola del Giapan: La prima ambasceria giapponese in Occidente.* Milan: Edizioni Unicopli, 1985.

Hale, J.R. *Artists and Warfare in the Renaissance.* New Haven: Yale University Press, 1990.

– *The Civilization of Europe in the Renaissance.* New York: Touchstone, 1994.

– *England and the Italian Renaissance: The Growth of Interest in Its History and Art.* London: Faber and Faber, 1954.

– 'Printing and Military Culture of Renaissance Venice.' *Medievalia et Humanistica. Studies in Medieval and Renaissance Culture. Transformation and Continuity,* n.s., 8 (1977): 21–62.

– *War and Society in Renaissance Europe, 1450–1600.* Leicester: Leicester University Press, 1985.

– ed. *Renaissance Venice.* London: Faber and Faber, 1973.

Harley, J.B. 'Silences and Secrecy: The Hidden Agenda of Cartography in Early Modern Europe.' *Imago Mundi* 40 (1988): 57–76.

Harley, J.B., and David Woodward, eds. *The History of Cartography.* Chicago: University of Chicago Press, 1987–.

Harvey, David. *The Condition of Postmodernity: An Enquiry into the Origins of Cultural Change.* Oxford: Basil Blackwell, 1989.

Harvey, P.D.A. *The History of Topographical Maps. Symbols, Pictures and Surveys.* London: Thames and Hudson, 1980.

Haskell, Francis. *History and Its Images: Art and the Interpretation of the Past.* New Haven: Yale University Press, 1993.

Head, Randolph C. 'Religious Boundaries and the Inquisition in Venice: Trials of Jews and Judaizers, 1548–1580.' *Journal of Medieval and Renaissance Studies* 20, no. 2 (1990): 175–204.

Helgerson, Richard. *Forms of Nationhood: The Elizabethan Writing of England.* Chicago: University of Chicago Press, 1992.

Heller, Thomas C., Morton Sosna, and David E. Wellbery, eds. *Reconstructing Individualism. Autonomy, Individuality, and the Self in Western Thought.* Stanford: Stanford University Press, 1986.

Hiler, Hilaire, and Meyer. *Bibliography of Costume. A Dictionary Catalog of about Eight Thousand Books and Periodicals.* Edited by Helen Grant Cushing. New York: The H.W. Wilson Co. 1939.

Hillman, David, and Carla,Mazzio, eds. *The Body in Parts: Fantasies of Corporeality in Early Modern Europe.* New York: Routledge, 1997.

Hirsch, Eric Donald. *The Aims of Interpretation.* Chicago: University of Chicago Press, 1976.

Hochmann, Michel. 'Le mécénat de Marin Grimani. Tintoret, Palma le Jeune, Jacopo Bassano, Giulio del Moro et le décor du palais Grimani; Véronèse et Vittoria à San Giuseppe.' *Revue de l'Art* 95 (1992): 41–51.

Hope, Charles, and Jane Martineau, eds. *The Genius of Venice 1500–1600.* London: Royal Academy of Arts, in association with Weidenfeld and Nicolson, 1983.

Howard, Deborah. *The Architectural History of Venice.* New York: Holmes and Meier, 1981.

– 'Venice as a Dolphin: Further investigations into Jacopo de'Barbari's View.' *Artibus et historiae* 35 (1997): 101–11.

Hughes, Diane Owen. 'Distinguishing Signs: Ear-Rings, Jews and Franciscan Rhetoric in the Italian Renaissance City.' *Past & Present* 112 (August 1986): 3–59.

– 'Representing the Family: Portraits and Purposes in Early Modern Italy.' *Journal of Interdisciplinary History* 17, no. 1 (Summer 1986): 7–38.

– 'Sumptuary Law and Social Relations in Renaissance Italy.' In *Disputes and Settlements. Law and Human Relations in the West.* Edited by John Bossy, 69–99. Cambridge: Cambridge University Press, 1983.

Hunt, Alan. *Governance of the Consuming Passions: A History of Sumptuary Law.* New York, 1996.

Hurlburt, Holly. *Dogaresse of Venice, 1200–1500: Wives and Icons.* Houndmills, Basingstoke, Hampshire/New York: Palgrave, 2004.

Huse, Norbert, and Wolfgang Wolters. *The Art of Renaissance Venice: Architecture, Sculpture, and Painting, 1460–1590.* Chicago: University of Chicago Press, 1990.

Inalcik, Halil. *The Ottoman Empire. The Classical Age 1300–1600.* Translated by Norman Itzkowitz and Colin Ember. New York: Praeger Publishers, 1973.

Inalcik, Halil, and Cemal Kafadar. *Süleymân the Second and His Time.* Istanbul: The Isis Press, 1993.

Inalcik, Halil, and Donald Quataert, eds. *An Economic and Social History of the Ottoman Empire, 1400–1914.* Cambridge: Cambridge University Press, 1994.

Ivins, Williams M. *Prints and Visual Communication.* Cambridge, MA: The MIT Press, 1992.

Jackson, Peter. *Maps of Meaning: An Introduction to Cultural Geography.* London: Unwin Hyman, 1989.

Jacquot, Jean. *Les fêtes de la renaissance.* Paris: Éditions du Centre National de la Recherche scientifique, 1956–60.

Jameson, Fredric. *The Political Unconscious: Narrative as a Socially Symbolic Act.* Ithaca, NY: Cornell University Press, 1981.

Jammer, Max. *Concepts of Space: The History of Theories of Space in Physics.* New York: Dover Publications, 1993.

Jardine, Lisa, and Jerry Brotton. *Global Interests: Renaissance Art between East and West.* Ithaca, NY: Cornell University Press, 2000.

Jirousek, Charlotte. 'More than Oriental Splendor: European and Ottoman Headgear, 1380–1580,' *Dress* 22 (1995): 25.

Johnson, Barbara. *In the Wake of Deconstruction.* Cambridge, MA: Blackwell, 1994.

Jones, Ann Rosalind, and Peter Stallybrass. *Renaissance Clothing and the Materials of Memory.* Cambridge UK: Cambridge University Press, 2000.

Jones, Eldred. *Othello's Countrymen: The African in English Renaissance Drama.* London: Oxford University Press, 1965.

Jordan, Winthrop, *White Over Black: American Attitudes toward the Negro, 1550–1812.* Baltimore: Penguin Books, 1968.

Junkerman, Anne Christine. '*Bellissima Donna*: An Interdisciplinary Study of Venetian Sensuous Half-Length Images of the Early Sixteenth Century.' PhD diss., University of California at Berkeley, 1988.

Kanceff, Emanuele, and Gaudenzio Boccazzi. *Viaggiatori stranieri a Venezia.* Atti del Congresso dell'Ateneo Veneto. Geneva: Slatkine, 1981.

Kant, Immanuel. *The Critique of Judgement.* Translated by James Creed Meredith. Oxford: Clarendon Press, 1952.

Kaplan, Paul. 'Veronese and the Inquisition: The Geopolitical Context.' In

Suspended License: Essays in the History of Censorship and the Visual Arts. Edited by Elizabeth Childs, 85–126. Seattle: University of Washington Press, 1997.

– 'Veronese's Images of Foreigners.' In *Nuovi studi su Paolo Veronese.* Edited by Massimo Gemin, 308–16. Venice: Arsenale, 1990.

Karrow, Robert W. *Mapmakers of the Sixteenth Century and Their Maps.* Chicago: Published for the Newberry Library by Speculum Orbis Press, 1993.

Kelso, Ruth. *Doctrine for the Lady of the Renaissance.* Urbana: University of Illinois Press, 1956.

King, Margaret L. 'Personal, Domestic, and Republican Values in the Moral Philosophy of Giovanni Caldiera.' *Renaissance Quarterly* 28 (1975): 535–74.

– *Venetian Humanism in an Age of Patrician Dominance.* Princeton, NJ: Princeton University Press, 1986.

Klapisch-Zuber, Christiane. *Women, Family, and Ritual in Renaissance Italy.* Chicago: University of Chicago Press, 1985.

Klinger, Linda Alice, 'The Portrait Collection of Paolo Giovio,' PhD diss., Princeton University, 1991.

Klinger, Linda, and Julian Raby. 'Barbarossa and Sinan: A Portrait of Two Ottoman Corsairs from the Collection of Paolo Giovio.' In *Arte veneziana e arte islamica: atti del Primo simposio internazionale sull'arte veneziana e l'arte islamica.* Edited by Ernst J. Grube and Stefano Carboni Stefano. Venice: L'Altra Riva, 1989.

Koerner, Joseph Leo. *The Moment of Self-Portraiture in German Renaissance Art.* Chicago: University of Chicago Press, 1996.

Kruft, Hanno-Walter. 'Ein Album mit Porträtzeichnungen. Ottavio Leonis.' *Storia dell'Arte* 4 (October–December 1969): 447–58.

Kuehn, Thomas. *Law, Family, and Woman: Toward a Legal Anthropology of Renaissance Italy.* Chicago: University of Chicago Press, 1991.

Kultzen Rolf, and Peter Eikemeier. *Venezianische Gemaelde des 15. und 16. Jahrhunderts.* Munich: Bayerische Staatsgemaeldesammlung, 1971.

Kunst, Hans-Joachim. *The African in European Art.* Bad Godesberg: Inter Nationes, 1967.

Kunt, I. Metin. *The Sultan's Servants: The Transformation of Ottoman Provincial Government, 1550–1650.* New York: Columbia University Press, 1983.

Küp, Karl. 'Some Early Costume Books.' In *Costume, Gothic & Renaissance.* Edited by Karl Kup and Muriel Frances Baldwin, 3–9. New York: The New York Public Library, 1937.

Kurz, O., and H. Kurz. 'The Turkish Dresses in the Costume-Book of Rubens.' *Nederlands Kunsthistorisch Jaarboek* 23 (1972): 275–90.

Labalme, Patricia H. 'Venetian Women on Women: Three Early Modern Feminists.' *Archivio Veneto* 117 (1981): 81–109.

Lacan, Jacques. *The Four Fundamental Concepts of Psycho-Analysis.* Edited by Jacques Alain Miller. Translated by Alan Sheridan. New York: W.W. Norton, 1981.
– 'The Mirror-Phase as Formative of the Function of the I.' In *Mapping Ideology.* Edited by Slavoj Žižek. London: Verso, 1995.
Landau, David, and Peter Parshall. *The Renaissance Print. 1470–1550.* New Haven, CT: Yale University Press, 1994.
Lane, Frederic C. *Venice: A Maritime Republic.* Baltimore: Johns Hopkins University Press, 1973.
Laplanche, Jean. *Life and Death in Psychoanalysis.* Baltimore: Johns Hopkins University Press, 1976.
Laqueur, Thomas. *Making Sex: Body and Gender from the Greeks to Freud.* Cambridge, MA: Harvard University Press, 1992.
Lawner, Lynne. *Lives of the Courtesans: Portraits of the Renaissance.* New York: Rizzoli, 1987.
Lefebvre, Henri. *The Production of Space.* Oxford: Basil Blackwell, 1984.
Le Goff, Jacques. *Time, Work, & Culture in the Middle Ages.* Translated by Arthur Goldhammer. Chicago: University of Chicago Press, 1986.
Lestringant, Frank. *Mapping the Renaissance World.* Berkeley: University of California Press, 1994.
Levenson, Jay A. 'Jacopo de'Barbari and the Northern Art of the Early Sixteenth Century,' PhD diss., New York University, 1978.
Locatelli, Tommasso. 'Feste spettacoli e costume di Venezia.' In *Venezia e le sue lagune,* vol. 2 (1847). Venice: Antonelli, 1847.
Lowry, Martin. *The World of Aldus Manutius. Business and Scholarship in Renaissance Venice.* Oxford: Basil Blackwell, 1979.
Macintyre, Alasdair. *After Virtue: A Study in Moral Theory.* Notre Dame, IN: University of Notre Dame Press, 1984.
– *A Short History of Ethics.* New York: Macmillan, 1978.
Mackenney, Richard. *Tradesmen and Traders: The World of the Guilds in Venice and Europe, c.1250–c.1650.* London: Croom Helm, 1987.
Maclean, Ian. *The Renaissance Notion of Woman.* Cambridge: Cambridge University Press, 1980.
Magli, Patrizia. *Il volto e l'anima: Fisiognomica e passioni.* Milan: Bompiani, 1995.
Mallett, Michael. *Mercenaries and Their Masters. Warfare in Renaissance Italy.* London: The Bodley Head, 1974.
– *The Military Organization of a Renaissance State: Venice, c. 1400–1617.* Cambridge: Cambridge University Press, 1984.
Mann, Nicholas, and Luke Syson, eds. *The Image of the Individual: Portraits in the Renaissance.* London: British Museum Press, 1998.

Marin, Louis. 'Notes on a Semiotic Approach to *Parade, Cortege,* and *Procession.*' In *Time Out of Time: Essays on the Festival,* 220–8. Albuquerque: University of New Mexico Press, 1987.

– *Portrait of the King.* Minneapolis: University of Minnesota Press, 1988.

– *Utopics: Spatial Play.* Translated by Robert A. Vollrath. Atlantic Highlands, NJ: Humanities Press, 1984.

Martin, John. 'The Imaginary Piazza: Tommaso Garzoni and the Late Italian Renaissance.' In *Portraits of Medieval and Renaissance Living: Essays in Memory of David Herlihy.* Edited by Samuel K. Cohn Jr and Steven A. Epstein, 439–54. Ann Arbor: University of Michigan, 1996.

– 'Inventing Sincerity, Refashioning Prudence: The Discovery of the Individual in Renaissance Europe.' *The American Historical Review* 102, no. 5 (December, 1997): 1308–42.

– 'Spiritual Journeys and the Fashioning of Religious Identity in Renaissance Venice.' *Renaissance Studies* 10, no. 3 (September 1996): 358–70.

– *Venice's Hidden Enemies: Italian Heretics in a Renaissance City.* Berkeley: University of California Press, 1993.

Martin, John, and Dennis Romano. *Venice Reconsidered: The History and Civilization of an Italian City-State 1297–1797.* Baltimore: Johns Hopkins University Press, 2000.

Martines, Lauro. *Power and Imagination.* New York: Alfred A. Knopf, 1979.

Mason Rinaldi, Stefania. *Palma il Giovane, l'opera completa.* Milano: Alfieri: Electa, 1984.

Massey, Lyle. 'Anamorphosis through Descartes or Perspective Gone Awry.' *Renaissance Quarterly* 50, no. 4 (Winter 1997): 1148–89.

Masson, Georgina. *Courtesans of the Italian Renaissance.* London: Secker and Warburg, 1975.

Matthew, L.C. 'The Painter's Presence: Signatures in Venetian Renaissance Pictures.' *The Art Bulletin* 80, no. 4 (December 1998): 616–48.

Mattozzi, Ivo. 'Mondo del libro e decadenza a Venezia (1570–1730).' *Quaderni Storici* 72, no. 3 (December 1989): 743–86.

Mazzariol, Giuseppe, and Terisio Pignatti. *La pianta prospettica di Venezia del 1500.* Venice: Cassa di risparmio di Venezia, 1962.

Mazzarotto, Biance Tamassia. *Le feste Veneziane: I giochi popolari, le cerimonie religiose e di governo.* Florence: Sansoni, 1961.

Melchior-Bonnet, Sabine. *The Mirror: A History.* New York: Routledge, 2001.

Menetto, L., and G. Zennaro, eds. *Storia del malcostume a Venezia nei secoli XVI–XVII.* Abano Terme: Piovan Editore, 1987.

Merkel, Ettore. 'Allegoria della vittoria di Lepanto.' In *Paolo Veronese restauri:*

[mostra] 1 guigno–30 settembre [1988], 67–75. Venice: Soprintendenza ai beni artistici e storici di Venezia, 1988.

Merleau-Ponty, Maurice. *The Primacy of Perception and Other Essays on Phenomenological Psychology, the Philosophy of Art, History and Politics.* Edited by James M. Edie. Evanston: Northwestern University Press, 1964.

I mestieri della moda a Venezia. Serenissima: The Arts of Fashion in Venice from the 13th to the 18th Century. Venice: Consorzio Maestri Calzaturieri del Brenta, 1995.

Michiel, Giustina Renier. *Origine delle feste veneziane.* Milan: Annali universali delle scienze e dell'industria, 1829.

Mitchell. *The Majesty of the State. Triumphal Progresses of Foreign Sovereigns in Renaissance Italy (1494–1600).* Florence: Leo Olschki Editore, 1986.

Moffit, John F. 'Ptolemy's *Chorographia* in the New World: Revelations from the *Relaciones geográficas de la Nueva España* of 1579–1581.' *Art History* 21, no. 3 (September 1998): 367–92.

Molinari, Cesare. 'Gli spettatori e lo spazio scenico nel teatro del cinquecento.' *Bollettino del Centro Internazionale di Studi di architettura Andrea Palladio* 16 (1974): 145–54.

Molmenti, Pompeo. *La dogaressa di Venezia.* Turin: Roux e Favale, 1884.

– *Sebastiano Veniero e la battaglia di Lepanto.* Florence: G. Barbèra, 1899.

– *Sebastiano Veniero dopo la battaglia di Lepanto.* Venice: Premiate Officine Grafiche di Carlo Ferrari, 1915.

– *La storia di Venezia nella vita privata dalle origini alla caduta della repubblica.* 3 vols. Trieste: Lint, 1973.

Moran, J.F. *The Japanese and the Jesuits: Alessandro Valignano in Sixteenth-Century Japan.* London: Routledge, 1993.

Moro, Giacomo. 'Insegne librarie e marche tipografiche in un registro veneziano del '500.' *La Bibliofilia* 1 (January–April 1989): 51–80.

Morolli, Gabriele, et al. *Le Procuratie Nuove in Piazza San Marco.* Rome: Editalia, 1994.

Morosini, Domenico. *De bene instituta republica.* Edited by Claudio Vita-Finzi. Milan: Guiffrè, 1969.

Morton, A.G. *History of Botanical Science: An Account of the Development of Botany from Ancient Times to the Present Day.* London: Academic Press, 1981.

Moschini, Giannantonio. *Dell'incisione in Venezia: memoria.* Venice: Zanetti, 1924.

Moss, Ann. *Printed Commonplace-Books and the Structuring of Renaissance Thought.* Oxford: Oxford University Press, 1996.

Mostra del costume in libri e stampe. 29 Gennaio–4 Febbraio 1959. Florence: L.S. Olschki, 1959.

Mueller, R.C. 'Charitable Institutions, the Jewish Community, and Venetian

Society. A Discussion of the Recent Volume by Brian Pullan.' *Studi Veneziani* 14 (1972): 38–78.

Muir, Edward. *Civic Ritual in Renaissance Venice.* Princeton, NJ: Princeton University Press, 1981.

– 'Images of Power: Art and Pageantry in Renaissance Venice.' *The American Historical Review* 84, no. 1 (February 1979): 16–52.

– 'The Ritual of Rulership in 16th-Century Venice: A Study in the Construction of Myth and Ideology. PhD dissertation, Rutgers University, 1975.

Muir, Edward, and Ron Weissman. 'Social and Symbolic Places in Renaissance Venice and Florence. In *The Power of Place: Bringing together Geographical and Sociological Imaginations.* Edited by John A. Agnew and James S. Duncan, 81–104. Boston: Unwin Hyman, 1989.

Muraro, Luisa. *Giambattista della Porta mago e scienziato: In appendice l'indice della taumatologia.* Milan: Feltrinelli, 1978.

Muzzarelli, Maria Giuseppina. *Gli inganni delle apparenze: Disciplina di vesti e ornamenti alla fine del Medioevo.* Turin: Scriptorium-Paravia, 1996.

Necipoğlu, Gülru. *Architecture, Ceremonial, and Power. The Topkapi Palace in the Fifteenth and Sixteenth Centuries.* Cambridge, MA: The MIT Press, 1991.

– 'Süleymân the Magnificent and the Representation of Power in the Context of Ottoman–Hapsburg–Papal Rivalry.' *Art Bulletin* 71, no. 3 (September 1989): 401–27.

Neuber, Wolfgang. 'The "Red Indian's" Body: The Physiognomy of the Indigenous American between Exoticism and Learned Culture in the Early Modern Period.' In *Modelling the Individual: Biography and Portrait in the Renaissance.* Edited by K. Enenkel et al., 93–107. Atlanta: Rodopi, 1998.

Newett, Mary Margaret, 'The Sumptuary Laws of Venice in the Fourteenth and Fifteenth Centuries.' In *Historical Essays First Published in 1902 in Commemoration of the Jubilee of the Owens College Manchester.* Edited by Thomas Frederick Tout and James Tait. Manchester, 1907.

Newton, Stella Mary. *The Dress of the Venetians. 1495–1525.* London: Scholar Press, 1988.

Nickson, M.A.E. *Early Autograph Albums in the British Museum.* London: British Museum, 1970.

Nolhac, Pier de, and Angelo Solerti. *Il viaggio in Italia di Enrico III Re di Francia e le feste a Venezia, Ferrara, Mantova e Turino.* Turin: L. Roux, 1890.

Nunn, Dr George E. *World Map of Francesco Rosselli.* Philadelphia: Privately printed, 1928.

Nuti, Lucia. 'The Perspective Plan in the Sixteenth Century: The Invention of a Representational Language.' *Art Bulletin* 76, no. 1 (1994): 105–28.

– *Ritratti di città: Visione e memoria tra Medioevo e Settecento.* Venice: Marsilio, 1996.

O'Dell, Ilse. 'Jost Amman and the Album Amicorum. Drawings after Prints in Autograph Albums.' *Print Quarterly* 9 (1992): 31–6.

– *Jost Ammans Buchschmuck-Holzschnitte Für Sigmund Feyerabend. Zur Technik der Verwendung von Bild-Holzstöcken in den Drucken von 1563–1599.* Wiesbaden: Otto Harrassowitz, 1993.

Olian, Jo Anne. 'Sixteenth-Century Costume Books.' *Costume Society of America* 3 (1977): 20–48.

Omodeo, Anna. *Mostra di stampe popolari Venete del '500.* Florence: L.S. Olschki Editore, 1965.

Ong, Walter. *Orality and Literacy: The Technologizing of the Word.* London: Routledge, 1995.

Origo, Iris. 'The Domestic Enemy: The Eastern Slaves in Tuscany in the Fourteenth and Fifteenth Centuries.' *Speculum* 30 (1955): 321–66.

Ortega, Steve. 'Ottoman Muslims in the Venetian Republic from 1573 to 1645: Contacts, Connections and Restrictions.' PhD diss., University of Manchester, 2001.

Ozzòla, Leandro. *Il vestiario italiano dal 1500 al 1550. Saggio di cronologia documentata.* Rome: Casa Editrice Fratelli Palombi, 1940.

Pagden, Anthony. *European Encounters with the New World: From Renaissance to Romanticism.* New Haven: Yale University Press, 1993.

Palumbo-Fossati, Isabella. 'L'interno della casa dell'artigianato e dell'artista nella Venezia del cinquecento,' *Studi Veneziani* 8 (1984): 109–53.

Panofsky, Erwin. *Perspective as Symbolic Form.* Translated by Christopher Wood. New York: Zone Books, 1991.

Parks, George B. 'The Decline and Fall of the English Renaissance Admiration of Italy.' *Huntington Library Quarterly* 31 (1967): 341–57.

– *The English Traveller to Italy.* Rome: Edizioni di Storia e Letteratura, 1954.

Parshall, Peter W. '*Imago contrafacta:* Images and Facts in the Northern Renaissance.' *Art History* 16, no. 4 (1993): 554–79.

Pasero, Carlo. 'Giacomo Franco, editore, incisore e calcografo nei secoli XVI e XVII.' *La Bibliofilia* 37, no. 8–10 (August–October 1935): 332–56.

Pastorello, Ester. *Bibliografia storico-analitica dell'arte della stampa in Venezia.* Venice, 1933.

– *Tipografi, editori, librai a Venezia nel secolo XVI.* Florence: L.S. Olschki, 1924.

Pavoni, Rosanna. 'Paolo Giovio, et son Musée de Portraits à propos d'une exposition,' *Gazette des Beaux-Arts* (March 1985): 109–16.

Pelc, Milan. *Illustrium imagines: Das Porträtbuch der Renaissance.* Leiden: Brill, 2002.

Perocco, G., and A. Salvador, eds. *Civiltà di Venezia,* vol. 2: *Il Rinascimento.* Venice: Stamperia di Venezia, 1976.

Pertusi, Agostino, ed. *Venezia e l'orient fra tardo medioevo e rinascimento.* In *Civiltà europea e civiltà veneziana: Aspettei e problemi 4.* Venice: Sansoni, 1966.

Petrioli, Anna Maria. 'Stampe populari venete del cinquecento agli Uffizi.' *Antichità Viva* 4, no. 2 (1965): 62–71.

Piaget, Jean. *Structuralism.* Translated and edited by Chaninah Maschler. New York: Basic Books, 1970.

Pignatti, Terisio. 'La pianta di Venezia di Jacopo de'Barbari.' *Bolletino dei Musei Civici Veneziani* 9, 1–2 (1964): 9–49.

– *Venice.* New York: Holt, Rinehart and Winston, 1971.

– *Veronese.* 2 vols. Venice: Alfieri, 1976.

– ed. *Le scuole di Venezia.* Milan: Gruppo Editoriale, Electa, 1981.

Pignatti, Terisio, and Filippo Pedrocco. *Veronese.* 2 vols. Milan: Electa, 1995.

– *Veronese: Catalogo completo dei dipinti.* Florence: Cantini, 1991.

Piloni, Fabio. 'Nicolò Nelli. Contributi per un catologo.' *Grafica d'arte. Rivista di storia dell'incisione antica e moderna e storia del disengo* 31 (July–September 1997): 7–14.

Pilot, A. 'L'elezione del doge Marino Grimani e una canzone inedita,' *Pagine istriane.* Anno II, fasc. 2, 1904.

Pincus, Debra. 'Geografia e politica nel Battistero di San Marco: la cupola degli Apostoli.' In *San Marco: Aspetti storici e agiografici,* 459–73 ff. Venice: Marsilio, 1996.

– 'Venice and the Two Romes: Byzantium and Rome as a Double Heritage in Venetian Cultural Politics.' *Artibus et Historiae* 13, no. 26 (1991): 101–14.

Pisetzky, Rosita Levi. *Il costume e la moda nella società italiana.* Turin: Giulio Einaudi, 1978.

– 'Moda e costume.' In *Storia d'Italia. Volume quinto. I documenti,* 939–79. Turin: Giulio Einaudi, 1973.

Pocock, J.G.A. *The Machiavellian Moment: Florentine Political Thought and the Atlantic Republican Tradition.* Princeton, NJ: Princeton University Press, 1975.

Podro, Michael. *The Critical Historians of Art.* New Haven: Yale University Press, 1991.

Pollak, Martha. *Military Architecture, Cartography and the Representation of the Early Modern European City. A Checklist of Treatises on Fortification in The Newberry Library.* Chicago: The Newberry Library, 1991.

Pozza, Neri, ed. *La stampa degli incunaboli nel Veneto.* Vicenza: Neri Pozza Editore, 1984.

– ed. *Tiziano e Venezia: Convegno Internazionale di Studi, Venezia, 1976.* Vicenza: Neri Pozza, 1980.

Pozzi, G. 'Occhi Bassi.' In *Thematologie des Kleinen = Petits thèmes littéraires.* Edited by Edgar Marsch and Giovanni Pozzi, 162–205. Fribourg: Editions Universitaires, 1986.

Preto, Paolo. *Venezia e i Turchi*. Florence: G.C. Sansoni, 1975.

Preziosi, Donald. *Rethinking Art History.* New Haven: Yale University Press, 1989.

Pullan, Brian. 'The Inquisition and the Jews of Venice: The Case of Gaspare Ribeiro, 1580–81.' *Bulletin of the John Rylands University Library of Manchester* 62, no. 1 (1979): 207–31.

– *The Jews of Europe and the Inquisition of Venice, 1550–1670.* Oxford: Blackwell, 1983.

– 'Natura e carattere delle Scuole.' In *Le scuole di Venezia*. Edited by Terisio Pignatti, 9–26. Milan: Gruppo Editoriale, Electa, 1981.

– *Rich and Poor in Renaissance Venice: The Social Institutions of a Catholic State, to 1620.* Oxford: Basil Blackwell, 1971.

– '"A Ship with Two Rudders": "Righetto Marrano" and the Inquisition in Venice,' *Historical Journal* 20, no. 1 (1977): 25–58.

– ed. *Crisis and Change in the Venetian Economy in the Sixteenth and Seventeenth Centuries.* London: Methuen, 1968.

Puppi, Lionello, ed. *Architettura e utopia nella Venezia del cinquecento: Mostra, Venezia, Palazzo Ducale, Luglio–Ottobre 1980.* Milan: Gruppo Editoriale Electa, 1980.

Quarti, Guido Antonio. *La battaglia di Lepanto nei canti popolari dell'epoca.* Milan: Istituto Editoriale Avio-Navale, 1930.

– 'La morte di Agostino Barbarigo nella battaglia di Lepanto.' *Crociata Anno IV* 15, no. 5 (September–October 1937): 169–77.

Queller, Donald. *The Venetian Patriciate: Reality versus Myth.* Urbana: University of Illinois Press, 1986.

Raby, Julian. *Venice, Dürer and the Oriental Mode.* Totowa, NJ: Islamic Art Publications, 1982.

Rampello Davide, ed. *700 anni di costume nel Veneto: Documenti di vita civile dal XII al XVIII secolo.* Treviso: 'La Tipografica,' 1976.

Randolph, Adrian W.B. 'Introduction: The Authority of Likeness,' and other essays in *Word & Image* 19, nos. 1 & 2 (January–June 2003), 1–5.

Ravid, Benjamin. 'Christian Travelers in the Ghetto of Venice: Some Preliminary Observations.' In *Between History and Literature: Studies in Honor of Isaac Barzilay.* Edited by Stanley Nash, 111–50. Bnei-Brak, 1997.

– 'From Yellow to Red: On the Distinguishing Head-Covering of the Jews of Venice.' *Jewish History* 6, no. 1–2 (1992): 179–210.

Redolfi, Maddalena ed. *Venezia e la difesa del Levante: da Lepanto a Candia 1570–1670.* Venice: Arsenale Editrice, 1986.

Reidy, Denis V., ed. *The Italian Book 1465–1800. Studies Presented to Dennis E. Rhodes on His 70th Birthday.* London: The British Library, 1993.

Reisser, Ulrich. *Physiognomik und Ausdruckstheorie der Renaissance. der Einfluss char-akterologischer Lehren auf Kunst und Kunsttheorie des 15. und 16. Jahrhunderts.* Munich: Scaneg, 1997.

Rendina, Claudio. *I dogi: Storia e segreti.* Rome: Newton Compton editori, 1984.

Renga de messer Thomado Mocenigo doxe alla Signoria. In *Bilanci generali della repubblica di Venezia. (Serie seconda.).* Venice, 1912.

Rhodes, Dennis E. *Silent Printers. Anonymous Printing at Venice in the Sixteenth Century.* London: The British Library, 1995.

Richardson, Brian. *Print Culture in Renaissance Italy: The Editor and the Vernacular Text, 1470–1600.* Cambridge: Cambridge University Press, 1994.

Rodler, Lucia. *I silenzi mimici del volto: Studi sulla tradizione fisiognomica italiana tra cinque e seicento.* Pisa: Ospadaletto, 1991.

Romanelli, Giandomenico, and Biadene Susanna. *Venezia piante e vedute: Catalogo del fondo cartografico a stampa.* Venice: Stamperia di Venezia Editrice for Museo Correr, 1982.

Romano, Dennis. 'Gender and the Urban Geography of Renaissance Venice,' *Journal of Social History* 23 (Winter 1989): 339–53.

– *Housecraft and Statecraft: Domestic Service in Renaissance Venice, 1400–1600.* Baltimore: Johns Hopkins University Press, 1996.

– *Patricians and Popolani: The Social Foundations of the Venetian Renaissance State.* Baltimore: Johns Hopkins University Press, 1987.

Rosand, David. *Myths of Venice: The Figuration of a State.* Chapel Hill, NC: University of North Carolina Press, 2001.

– *Painting in Sixteenth-Century Venice: Titian, Veronese, Tintoretto.* Rev. [and updated] ed. Cambridge: Cambridge University Press, 1997.

– '*Venezia figurata.*' In *Interpretazioni Veneziane. Studi di Storia dell'Arte in onore di Michelangelo Muraro.* Edited by David Rosand, 177–96. Venice: Arsenale, 1984.

Rose, Sonia V. '"The Great Moctezuma": A Literary Portrait in Sixteenth-Century Spanish American Historiography.' In *Modelling the Individual: Biography and Portrait in the Renaissance.* Edited by Karl Enenkel et al., 109–32. Atlanta: Rodopi, 1998.

Rosenheim, Max. 'The Album Amicorum.' *Archaeologia* 62: 251–308. Oxford: Society of Antiquaries of London, 1910.

Rosenthal, Margaret F. 'Fashion and Identity in the Venetian Republic: Foreign Travelers and Their Illustrated Costume Albums in the Late Sixteenth Century.' Paper presented at the conference 'Venice Reconsidered: Venetian History and Civilization, 1297–1797,' Syracuse University, Syracuse, NY, September 1997.

– *The Honest Courtesan: Veronica Franco. Citizen and Writer in Sixteenth-Century Venice.* Chicago: University of Chicago Press, 1992.

Rossi, Paola. *Jacopo Tintoretto: I ritratti.* Milan: Electa, 1974.

Ruggiero, Guido. *Boundaries of Eros: Sex Crime and Sexuality in Renaissance Venice.* New York: Oxford University Press, 1985.

Sahlins, Peter. *Boundaries: The Making of France and Spain in the Pyrenees.* Berkeley: University of California Press, 1989.

San Juan, Rose Marie. *Rome: A City out of Print.* Minneapolis: University of Minnesota Press, 2001.

Santillana, Giorgio de. *Reflections on Men and Ideas.* Cambridge MA: The MIT Press, 1968.

Saxl, F. 'Costumes and Festivals of Milanese Society under Spanish Rule.' *Proceedings of the British Academy,* 400–56 ff. London: Oxford University Press, 1937.

Schatzki, Theodore R., and Wolfgang Natter, eds. *The Social and Political Body.* New York: The Guilford Press, 1996.

Scheller, Robert. *Exemplum: Model-Book Drawings and the Practice of Artistic Transmission in the Middle Ages (ca. 900–ca. 1470).* Translated by Michael Hoyle. Amsterdam: Amsterdam University Press, 1995.

Scheller, R.W. *A Survey of Medieval Model Books.* Haarlem: De Erven F. Bohn N.V., 1963.

Schilder, Paul. *The Image and Appearance of the Human Body: Studies in the Constructive Energies of the Psyche.* New York: International Universities Press [1950].

Schulz, Juergen. *La cartografia tra scienza e arte: Carte e cartografi nel Rinascimento italiano.* Modena: Franco Cosimo Panini, 1990.

– 'Cristoforo Sorte and the Ducal Palace of Venice.' *Kunsthistorischen Institutes in Florenz* 10, no. 3 (1961–2): 193–208.

– 'Jacopo de'Barbari's View of Venice: Map Making, City Views, and Moralized Geography before the Year 1500.' *Art Bulletin* 60 (1978): 425–74.

– 'New Maps and Landscape Drawings by Cristoforo Sorte.' *Kunsthistorischen Institutes in Florenz* 20, no. 1 (1976): 107–26.

– 'The Printed Plans and Panoramic Views of Venice (1486–1797).' *Saggi e memorie di storia dell'arte* 7 (1970).

– 'Urbanism in Medieval Venice.' In *City States in Classical Antiquity and Medieval Italy.* Edited by Anthony Molho, Kurt Raaflaub, and Julia Emlen, 419–66. Ann Arbor: University of Michigan Press, 1991.

Schütte, Josef Franz, *Valignano's Mission Principles for Japan,* vol. 1, parts 1 and 2. St Louis: Institute of Jesuit Sources, 1980–5.

Scott, James. *Weapons of the Weak: Everyday Forms of Peasant Resistance.* New Haven: Yale University Press, 1985.

Sebastian, Peter. 'Ottoman Government Officials and Their Relations with the

Republic of Venice in the Early Sixteenth Century.' In *Studies in Ottoman History in Honour of Professor V.L. Ménage*. Edited by Colin Heywood and Colin Imber. Istanbul: Isis Press, 1994.

Seccareccia, Stefania. 'Gaspare Osello. Contributi per un catalogo.' *Grafica d'arte. Rivista di storia dell'incisione antica e moderna e storia del disegno* 27 (July–September 1996).

Segarizzi, Arnaldo. *Bibliografia delle stampe populari italiane. Marciana*. Bergamo: Istituto italiano d'arte grafiche, 1913.

Sella, Domenico. 'Crisis and Transformation in Venetian Trade.' In *Crisis and Change in the Venetian Economy in the Sixteenth and Seventeenth Centuries*. Edited by Brian Pullan, 88–105. London: Methuen, 1968.

Senechal, P. 'Sadeler, Justus. Print Publisher and Art Dealer in Early Seicento Venice.' *Print Quarterly* 7 (1990): 22–35.

Shiff, Jonathan. *Venetian State Theater and the Games of Siena. 1595–1605. The Grimani Banquet Plays*. Lewiston: The Edwin Mellen Press, 1993.

Shirley, Rodney. *The Mapping of the World. Early Printed World Maps 1472–1700*. London: The Holland Press, 1983.

Silverman, Kaja. *Male Subjectivity at the Margins*. New York: Routledge, 1992.

– *The Threshold of the Visible World*. New York: Routledge, 1996.

Simhart, Max. 'Stampe popolari.' *La Bibliofilia* 35, no. 4 (1933): 129–49.

Simons, Pat. 'Women in Frames: The Gaze, the Eye, the Profile in Renaissance Portraiture.' *History Workshop: A Journal of Socialist and Feminist Historians* 25 (Spring 1988): 4–30.

Sinding-Larsen, Staale. 'The Changes in the Iconography and Composition of Veronese's Allegory of the Battle of Lepanto in the Doge's Palace.' *Journal of the Warburg and Courtauld Institutes* 19 (1956): 298–302.

– *Christ in the Council Hall: Studies in the Religious Iconography of the Venetian Republic*. With a contribution by A. Kuhn. Acta ad archaeologiam et artium historiam pertinentia (Institutum Romanum Norvegiae) no. 5. Rome: L'Erma di Bretschneider, 1974.

Skinner, Quentin. *The Foundations of Modern Political Thought*, vol. 1: *The Renaissance*. Cambridge: Cambridge University Press, 1990.

Sman, Gert Jan van der. 'Print Publishing in Venice in the Second Half of the Sixteenth Century' *Print Quarterly*, 16 (2000): 235–47.

Smith, Logan. *The Life and Letters of Sir Henry Wotton*. Oxford: Clarendon Press, 1907.

Smith, Robert. 'In Search of Carpaccio's African Gondolier,' *Italian Studies, An Annual Review* 34 (1979): 45–59.

Sorge, Giuseppe. *Il Cristianesimo in Giappone e il de missione*. Bologna: Cooperativa Libraria Universitaria Editrice Bologna, 1988.

– *Il Cristianesimo in Giappone e la seconda ambasceria Nipponica in Europa.* Bologna: Cooperativa Libraria Universitaria Editrice, 1991.

Sperling, Jutta. *Convents and the Body Politic in Late Renaissance Venice.* Chicago: University of Chicago Press, 1999.

Spike, John T. 'Naturalism. Ottavio Leoni's Portraits "alla macchia."' In *Baroque Portraiture in Italy*, 12–19. Sarasota: The John and Mable Ringling Museum of Art, 1984.

Spitzer, Leo. 'Notes on the Empirical and Poetic "I" in Medieval Authors.' *Traditio* 4 (1946): 414–22.

Staley, Edgcumbe. *The Dogaressas of Venice: The Wives of the Doges.* London: T. Werner Laurie, n.d. [but 1910].

Stallybrass, Peter. 'Worn Worlds: Clothes and Identity on the Renaissance Stage.' In *Subject and Object.* Edited by Margreta De Grazia, Maureen Quilligan, and Peter Stallybrass, 289–320. Cambridge: Cambridge University Press, 1996.

Stallybrass, Peter, and Allon White. *The Politics and Poetics of Transgression.* London: Methuen, 1986.

Stewart, Susan. *On Longing: Narratives of the Miniature, the Gigantic, the Souvenir, the Collection.* Baltimore: John Hopkins University Press, 1984.

Storia della cultura veneta. Dal primo quattrocento al Concilio di Trento. 3 vols. Vicenza: Neri Pozza, 1980.

Strong, Roy. *Art and Power: Renaissance Festivals 1450–1650.* Woodbridge: The Boydell Press, 1984.

Swan, Claudia. '*Ad vivum, near het leven,* from the Life: Defining a Mode of Representation,' *Word & Image* 11, no. 4 (October–December 1995): 353–72.

Tafuri, Manfredo, ed. '*Renovato Urbis': Venezia nell'età di Andrea Gritti (1523–1538).* Rome: Officina Edizioni, 1984.

– *Venice and the Renaissance.* Cambridge: The MIT Press, 1989.

Tassini, Giuseppe. *Feste, spettacoli, divertimenti e piacere degli antichi Veneziani.* Venice: Libr. Fil. Editrice, 1961.

Tenenti, Alberto. *Piracy and the Decline of Venice: 1580–1615.* Translated by J. and B. Pullan. Berkeley: University of California Press, 1967.

Teza, E. *La fisiognomia. Trattatello in Francese antico colla versione Italiana.* Bologna: Gaetano Romagnoli, 1864.

– *Vocabulario nuovo con il quale da se stessi, si può benissimo imparare diversi linguaggi, cioè, italiano e greco, italiano e turco, et italiano e todesco, E di nuovo con somma diligentia, ricoretto.* Venice: Pietro Donato, 1580.

Tondro, Maximilian. 'Memory and Tradition: The Ephmeral Architecture of the Dogaresse of Venice in 1557 and 1597.' PhD diss., University of Cambridge, 2001.

Trebbi, Giuseppe. 'La società veneziana.' *Storia di Venezia*, vol. 6: *Dal Rinascimento al Barocco*. Edited by Gaetano Cozzi and Paolo Prode, 129–213. Rome, 1994.

Trexler, Richard, ed. *Persons in Groups: Social Behavior as Identity Formation in Medieval and Renaissance Europe. Papers of the Sixteenth Annual Conference of the Center for Medieval and Early Renaissance Studies*. Binghamton, NY: Medieval and Renaissance Texts and Studies, 1985.

Ulvioni, P. 'Stampatori e librai a Venezia nel seicento.' *Archivio Veneto* 144 (1977): 93–124.

Urban, Lina. 'Apparati scenografica nelle feste veneziane cinquecentesche.' *Arte Veneta* 23 (1969): 145–55.

– 'La festa della sensa nelle arti e nell'iconografia.' *Studi Veneziani* 10 (1968): 291–353.

– 'Feste ufficiali e trattenimenti privati.' *Storia della cultura Veneta. Il seicento.* Vicenza: Neri Pozza Editore, 1983.

– 'I ludi mariani ossia la festa delle Marie.' In *Processioni e feste dogali: 'Venetia est mundus,'* 29–50. Vicenza: Neri Pozza, 1998.

– *Processioni e feste dogali: 'Venetia est mundus.'* Vicenza: Neri Pozza, 1998.

– 'Teatri e "Teatri del Mondo" nella Venezia del cinquecento.' *Arte Veneta* 20 (1966): 137–46.

Venezia e i Turchi: Scontri e confronti di due civiltà. Milan: Electa, 1985.

Ventura, Angelo. 'Le trasformazioni economici nel Veneto tra quattro e ottocento,' *Bollettino del Centro Internazionale di Studi di Architettura Andrea Palladio* 18 (1976): 127–42.

Viallon, Marie F. *Venise et la Porte Ottomane (1453–1566).* Paris: Economica, 1995.

Verheyen, Egon. 'The Triumphal Arch on the Lido: On the Reliability of Eye-witness Accounts.' In *The Verbal and the Visual.* Edited by Karl-Ludwig Selig and Elizabeth Sears, 213–23. New York: Italica Press, 1990.

Vitali, Achille. *La moda a Venezia attraverso i secoli. Lessico ragionato.* Venice: Filippi Editore, 1992.

Warner, Marina. *Monuments and Maidens: The Allegory of the Female Form.* New York: Atheneum, 1985.

Wheatcroft, Andrew. *The Ottomans.* London: Viking, 1993.

White, Hayden, ed. *Tropics of Discourse: Essays in Cultural Representation.* Edited by Hayden White, 121–34. Baltimore: Johns Hopkins University Press, 1978.

Wolters, Wolfgang. 'Le architetture erette al Lido per l'ingresso di Enrico III a Venezia nel 1574.' *Bollettino del Centro Internazionale di Studi di Architettura Andrea Palladio* 21 (1979): 273–89.

– *Storia e politica nei dipinti di Palazzo Ducale. Aspetti dell'autocelebrazione della repubblica di Venezia nel cinquecento.* Venice: Arsenale, 1987.

Wood, Christopher. 'Review of *The Origin of Perspective* by Hubert Damisch.' *The Art Bulletin* 77 (December 1995): 677–82.

Woodward, David. *Art and Cartography: Six Historical Essays.* Chicago: University of Chicago Press, 1987.

– *Maps as Prints in the Italian Renaissance: Makers, Distributors and Consumers. The Panizzi Lectures, 1995.* London: The British Library, 1996.

– *The Maps and Prints of Paolo Forlani: A Descriptive Bibliography.* Chicago: The Newberry Library, 1990.

Wootton, David. *Paolo Sarpi: Between Renaissance and Enlightenment.* Cambridge: Cambridge University Press, 1983.

Zagorin, Perez. *Ways of Lying: Dissimulation, Persecution, and Conformity in Early Modern Europe.* Cambridge, MA: Harvard University Press, 1990.

Zimmerman, Susan, and Ronald F.E. Weissman, eds. *Urban Life in the Renaissance.* Newark, NJ: University of Delaware Press, 1989.

Zimmerman, T.C. Price. *Paolo Giovio: The Historian and the Crisis of Sixteenth-Century Italy.* Princeton, NJ: Princeton University Press, 1995.

Žižek, Slavoj. *Enjoy Your Symptom: Jacques Lacan in Hollywood and Out.* New York: Routledge, 1992.

– *The Invisible Remainder: An Essay On Schelling and Related Matters.* London: Verso: 1996.

– *The Sublime Object of Ideology.* Lincoln, NE: University of Nebraska Press, 1989.

– ed. *Mapping Ideology.* London: Verso, 1994.

Zorattini, P.C. Ioly, ed. *Processo del S Uffizio di Venezia contro Ebrei e Giudaizzanti (1548–1560), Storia dell'Ebraismo in Italia, Studi e Testi II, Sezione Veneta I.* Florence: L.S. Olschki, 1980.

Zorzi, Alvise. *Venice, 697–1797: City, Republic, Empire.* London: Sidwick and Jackson, 1983.

Zorzi, Ludovico. 'Costumi e scene italiani: il codice Bottacin di Padova.' In *Storia d'Italia*, vol. 2: *Dalla caduta dell'Impero romano al secolo XVIII*, n.p. but between 1466 and 1467. Turin: Giulio Einaudi, 1974.

– *Il teatro e la città: Saggi sulla scena italiana.* Turin: Giulio Einaudi, 1977.

Zorzi, Marino. 'Stampa, illustrazione libraria e le origini dell'incisione figurative a Venezia.' In *La Pittura nel Veneto. Il Quattrocento*, vol. 2: 686–702. Milan: Electa, 1990.

Index

Studies in Book and Print Culture

General Editor: Leslie Howsam